PREVENTIVE LAW and PROBLEM SOLVING:
Lawyering for the Future

To Dr. Richard Atkinson –

Thank you for your contributions
to the CWSL Board of Trustees!

Best wishes,

PREVENTIVE LAW and PROBLEM SOLVING:
Lawyering for the Future

Thomas D. Barton

VANDEPLAS PUBLISHING

UNITED STATES OF AMERICA

Preventive law and problem solving: lawyering for the future

Barton, Thomas D.

Published by:

Vandeplas Publishing - June 2009

801 International Parkway, 5th Floor
Lake Mary, FL. 32746
USA

www.vandeplaspublishing.com

ISBN: 978-1-60042-076-4

Dedications

The author wishes to express heartfelt gratitude to many persons, without whose help this book would not have been possible:

- to the Brown Family–Louis and Hermione, and their son Harold–for their immense generosity of ideas, support, and patience;

- to Edward A. Dauer, whose brilliance has challenged and educated, and whose kindness has both touched and inspired many;

- to Dean Steven R. Smith of the California Western School of Law, for his leadership, vision, and constant encouragement;

- to Janet W. Weinstein, for her excellent editing and many insights;

- to my wonderful other colleagues at California Western School of Law–Janet Bowermaster, Jamie Cooper, Janeen Kerper, Linda Morton, and Katharine Rosenberry to name a few--who created and developed its creative problem solving mission and with whom it has been my privilege to work most closely on these issues;

- to Helena Haapio, who champions Proactive Law in Europe and beyond, and who continues to broaden my horizons about what lawyers can achieve;

- to those who have so competently authored and graciously permitted me to use formal chapters or parts of chapters for this book: James P. Groton, Helena Haapio, Robert G. Knaier, Janeen Kerper, Jack Maypole, Linda Morton, Samantha Morton, Amy D. Ronner, Rana Sampson, Douglas N. Turner, Michael J. Weaver, and Janet Weinstein. Parts of several works by Edward A. Dauer and Louis M. Brown are also used with the generous consents of Dauer and Harold A. Brown.

- to Jonathan Cohen, Susan Daicoff, David Wexler, Bruce Winick, and the many other fine scholars in Therapeutic Jurisprudence and Alternative Dispute Resolution whose work I have admired, and without whose ideas, encouragement, and values my thoughts would never have been possible;

- to David Fleming for his mentorship long ago;

- and above all to my wife Sharon L. Foster, for everything she is, always.

PREVENTIVE LAW and PROBLEM SOLVING:
Lawyering for the Future©

By Thomas D. Barton

TABLE OF CONTENTS

INTRODUCTION TO PARTS ONE AND TWO

The Functions of Law and Changing Conceptions of How Those Functions May Be Achieved 1

A. The Dilemma of Romance 1

    1. Sexually Segregated Dormitories: Separation and Power 2

    2. Coed Dormitories: Understanding, Integration, and Accommodation . 3

B. Human Engagement: The Fundamental Human Dilemma and How It is Addressed 4

    1. Non-legal Alternatives 5

    2. Western Individualism and Law 5

    3. Rights and Social Mobility 6

    4. Liberal Democracy and the Industrial Revolution 7

    5. The Emergence of the U/I/A Paradigm in Western Legal Systems 8

C. The Format of this Book: Bridging The Past and the Future 9

PART ONE: PREVENTIVE LAW AND PROACTIVE LAW 13

CHAPTER I
PROBLEM-SOLVING SYSTEMS: The Integration of Problems, Rules, Procedures, Skills, Ethics, Culture, and Philosophical Concepts 15

A. Problem-Solving Systems: How They Change 19

B. Taking Seriously the Legal "System" 21

C. The Current Paradigm of Western Legal Systems: "R/S/P" 23

D. Summing Up 25

CHAPTER II

PROBLEM-SOLVING SYSTEMS: The Influence of Context 27
How Context Matters 28
    1. A Sample Problem: A Hungry Person Sees a Bit of Food 28
    2. Lessons for Shifting Procedures to Match Contextual Demands 30

CHAPTER III

PROBLEM-SOLVING SYSTEMS: An Introduction to Procedures 33
  A. Flipping a Coin: Random But Not Arbitrary 33
    1. The Problem of First Positions 33
    2. The Procedure: Flipping a Coin 33
    3. The Problem Itself 34
    4. Skills 34
    5. Ethics 34
    6. Cultural Influence 34
    7. Truth and Knowledge 35
  B. Legal Procedures and Legal Systems 35
    1. Problems and Procedures 35
    2. Skills and Procedures 38
    3. Ethics and Procedures 39
    4. Culture, Problems, and Procedures 40
    5. Learning in a Law Office 41

CHAPTER IV

AT THE BOUNDARY OF CHANGES: Lawyers Thinking Preventively and Proactively 45
  A. Where We Start 45
  B. Where We Want to End: The Goals of Preventive Law 49

CHAPTER V

PREVENTIVE LAW: The Dauer Matrix 55
Private Problem: The Seashore Neighbors Example 55

CHAPTER VI

PREVENTIVE LAW: Applying and Defining the Method 67
  A. A Three-Way Problem 67
  B. Refining the Method: Five Steps to Preventive Lawyering 70
    *1. Understand Problems as Troublesome Relationships Between People
       and Their Environments* 71

      2. *Identify the Various Elements in the System That are Leading to a Particular Problem* 71

      3. *Understand the Dynamics Among the Problem Holders and Their Social and Non-social Environments that Create the Problem* 72

      4. *Describe What Gives Each Element of this Problem Dynamic Its Peculiar Importance.* 73

      5. *Imagine Various Interventions By Which the Problem Dynamic Could Be Broken or Slowed.* 73

  C. *The Preventive Approach Applied: Another Example* 74

CHAPTER VII (James P. Groton)

  PREVENTIVE PRACTICES: Lessons from the Construction Industry . . . 79

  Problem Prevention Tools 80

  Problem Solving Tools 84

  Dispute Control Tools 85

  "Real Time" Resolution Tools 85

  Reasons for Using Prevention Provisions in Business Agreements 89

CHAPTER VIII (Helena Haapio)

  PROACTIVE LAW: Cross-Border Contracting 93

  INVISIBLE TERMS & CREATIVE SILENCE 93

    QUICK QUIZ: True or False? 94

    Statement 1: It usually costs less to avoid getting into trouble than to pay for getting out of trouble. 95

    Statement 2: "Reports shall be submitted bimonthly" means that reports shall be submitted twice a month. 95

    Statement 3: The absence of a warranty means that the supplier is not liable for defects 96

    Statement 4: The expiration of a warranty means that the supplier is no longer liable for defects 97

    Statement 5: If the goods fail, the buyer suffers a loss as a consequence, and the warranty/contract is silent, the buyer is not entitled to compensation for its loss 98

    Statement 6: If the goods fail, the buyer suffers a loss as a consequence, and the contract is silent, the buyer is entitled to compensation for its loss, including loss of profit 98

    Statement 7: If the goods fail, the buyer suffers a loss as a consequence, and the warranty/contract is silent, the law will determine what the buyer is entitled to 99

    Statement 8: In international dealings, between businesses located in

different countries, the law of the buyer's country is applied to the supplier-buyer relationship 100

Statement 9: No international sales law exists 101

Statement 10: The shorter and simpler the contract, the better . . . 102

Statement 11: Contracts can prevent problems and communication failures 102

Going forward: Action Plan 105

CHAPTER IX

THE "ETHICS" OBSTACLE: Advocacy/Adversarial Rules of Professional Responsibility 107

CHAPTER X

THE "PROBLEM" OBSTACLE (Part I): Limitations of Labels and Imagination 115

A. *Introduction: The Difference Between Quick-Fix Solutions and Preventive Thinking* 115

B. *The Elements of Preventive Thinking* 118

    1. *Finding a Better Metaphor* 118

    2. *Seeing Problems as Systems* 120

    3. *Expanding the Problem Context to Identify Elements of a Problem Dynamic* 120

    4. *How Preventive Thinking Leads to Better Solutions* 121

C. *The Relative Difficulty of Preventive Thinking* 124

    1. *Not All Problem Elements May Be Under Central Control* 125

    2. *Preventive Solutions May Be Relatively Slow and Invisible* 125

    3. *Metaphors by Which We Understand Problems* 126

    4. *An Instrumental Mentality?* 128

CHAPTER XI (Janeen Kerper)

THE "PROBLEM" OBSTACLE (Part II): Asking Better Questions and Building Better Frames 131

A. *Asking Questions of Clients and Witnesses* 131

B. *Building Better Frames* 135

    1. *Framing Problems by Information and Beliefs* 136

    2. *Framing Problems by Procedures* 138

    3. *Framing Problems by Traditional Solutions* 138

    4. *Conclusion: How Can Framing Be Done Better?* 140

C. *Asking Fuller Questions* 140

CHAPTER XII

THE "TRUTH" OBSTACLE: Legal Truth and the Dilemmas of Post-Enlightenment Thought 143
I. A COMMON HERITAGE: FOUR IDEAS OF THE ENLIGHTENMENT THAT INFLUENCE WESTERN LEGAL SYSTEMS 145
    A. The Individuation of Investigation 146
    B. Reliability Through The Detachment of Mind and Nature 150
    C. Segmentation and Validity 151
    D. Abstraction and Instrumentalism 153
II. CHALLENGES TO ENLIGHTENMENT THOUGHT 155
    A. Romanticism 156
    B. Relativism 156
    C. Post-Enlightenment Thought and Culture 158
III. THE DILEMMAS OF POST-ENLIGHTENMENT THOUGHT 159
    A. Cultural and Constitutive Dilemmas in the Law 160
    B. Cultural and Constitutive Dilemmas in Science 162
IV. CONCLUSION 163

CHAPTER XIII

THE CULTURAL OBSTACLE: Understanding the Inertia of Expectations and Self-interest 165
A. Who May Speak Within the System to Voice the Problem, Set Criteria for Its Resolution, or Suggest Solutions? 165
B. What Counts as a Legitimate Argument? 166
C. What are the Taboos? 166
D. What Constitutes Success, and What Failure? 166
E. What Are Our Fears? 168
F. Understanding and Counseling in the Face of Risk? 169

A NOTE IN TRANSITION TO PART II 177

END OF PART ONE 181

PART TWO:
PROBLEM SOLVING AND THERAPEUTIC JURISPRUDENCE 183

CHAPTER XIV
A REVIEW OF THE EMERGENCE OF THE U/I/A PARADIGM AND OVERVIEW OF PART TWO 185
A. Problems with Rationality 186

B. *Problems with Separation* 187

C. *Problems with Power* 189

D. *Fitting Problem Solving and Therapeutic Jurisprudence into the U/I/A*
    Paradigm 190

CHAPTER XV
THE "WHAT" OF PROBLEM-SOLVING: Purpose, Meaning, Values, and Goals 193

A. *Introduction: The Nature of Problems* 193

B. *Problems Explain Procedures; Procedures Do Not Define Problems* 194

C. *Fitting Procedures to Problems* 195

    1. *Why Law Needs Its Own Problem-solving Analysis* 195

    2. *Mechanical Problems* 196

    3. *"Market Exchange" Problems* 198

    4. *Technical Problems and Expert Advice* 200

    5. *Legal Problems* 202

D. *Describing Problem-Solving in a Legal Context* 204

CHAPTER XVI
THE "WHAT" OF PROBLEM-SOLVING: The Fit and Misfit of Problems and Procedures 205

A. *The Problem Context of "Simplex" v. "Multiplex" Human Relationships:*
    Can the Procedure Safely Ignore the Past or Future? 206

B. *An "Interactive" Problem: Can It Fit with R/S/P Procedures that Assume*
    "Simple" Variables? 207

C. *Problems for Which Decisional Criteria are Unknown or Disputed, Clashing*
    with R/S/P Assumptions of Knowable Rules 212

D. *Public versus Private Problems* 214

E. *Whether Private Resolution of the Problem is Feasible or Infeasible* . . . 216

F. *"Predictive" and "Planning" Problems that Clash with R/S/P Assumptions of*
    Judging Past Events 217

    1. *Predictive Problems* 219

    2. *Planning Problems* 223

CHAPTER XVII
THE "WHAT" OF PROBLEM-SOLVING: Tools and Techniques of Problem Solving 227

A. *Expanding the Pie* 227

B. *Exchanging Concessions* 228

C. *"Cost-Cutting" and "Bridging"* 229

    D. *Using Promises Rather than Threats* 230
    E. *Example: Facilitating a Solution to a Community Problem* 230
        1. Bringing Stakeholders to the Table 232
        2. Listening and Communicating 232
        3. Understanding Conflict by Understanding Interests 233
        4. Collaborating and Finding Solutions of Mutual Gain 233
        5. Developing Insight, Creativity, and Judgment 234
        6. Shaping a Culture 235
        7. Designing Systems to Prevent Problems 235

CHAPTER XVIII
THE "WHAT" OF THERAPEUTIC JURISPRUDENCE: Introduction in the Context of Problem Solving 237
Therapeutic Jurisprudence, Preventive Law, and Creative Problem Solving: An Essay on Harnessing Emotion and Human Connection 237
    Bringing the Accommodation Style to the Legal System 239
    1. Caveats and Prospects for the Accommodation Style 239
    2. Finding the Appropriate Access Point for Emotion and Relationship in the Legal System 242

CHAPTER XIX
"WHY NOW, and WHY LIKE THIS?" 251
    A. *The Pervasiveness of the Law in Everyday Culture* 252
        1. The Substantive Doctrines of the Law 252
        2. Procedures for Preventing and Addressing Legal Problems 253
        3. The Trend: A Higher Proportion of Troublesome Problems 254
    B. *Changing Criteria of Truth* 255
    C. *The Movement From an Industrial to Information Age Economy* 256
        1. Industrial Age Economics, Organization, and Distribution 257
        2. Industrial Era Legal Systems 259
        3. Information Age Economics, Organization, and Distribution 259
        4. Information Age Legal Systems 264
    D. *The Cultural Importance of the U/I/A Paradigm* 265
        1. Background and Overview 265
        2. The Problem Defined 266
        3. The Tension of Preservation and Unfairness 269
        4. Opening Up Legal Truth 275
        5. Provide Moral Leadership 277
    E. *Conclusion* 277

CHAPTER XX (Janet Weinstein, Linda Morton, and Amy D. Ronner)
THE "HOW" OF U/I/A: Creativity, Insight, and Counseling 279
  A. *Creative Thinking* 280
      CREATIVE THINKING IN LEGAL PROBLEM SOLVING 280
  B. *Confession and Insight* 285
      DOSTOYEVSKY AND THE THERAPEUTIC JURISPRUDENCE
        CONFESSION 285

CHAPTER XXI (Michael J. Weaver and Robert G. Knaier)
THE "HOW" OF U/I/A: In-House Counsel 289
  I. Common Sense and Sound Business Practices 290
  II. Specific Areas of Concern 291
    Employment Disputes 291
    Americans with Disabilities Act 293
    Securities Issues 295
  III. Consider a Settlement 299

CHAPTER XXII
THE "HOW" OF U/I/A: The Judiciary and Public Defenders 301
  A. *Judging* 301
  B. *Public Defenders* 306
  C. *The Rule of Law* 308

CHAPTER XXIII (Rana Sampson)
THE "HOW" OF U/I/A: The Example of Domestic Violence 311
  A. *Problem-Solving Police Officers* 311
  B. *Family Lawyers* 317

CHAPTER XXIV
THE "HOW" OF U/I/A: Contractual Relations 321
  A. *Why Has Contracting Failed to Realize its Full Potential?* 322
    1. Relational rather than Discrete Bilateral Contracts 323
    2. Strategic Alliances 324
    3. Accommodative Behaviors When Trouble Arises 324
  B. *Case Study: When is a Relational/Alliance Contract Advisable?* 325
  C. *Relational Contract Provisions* 327

CHAPTER XXV (Douglas N. Turner)
THE "HOW" OF U/I/A: The Meaning and Building of Trust 331
  A. *What Is Trust?* 331

    B. *Trust – Some Definitions* 332
    C. *What Happens When Trust is Present?* 333
    D. *What is Trust Made of?* 334
    E. *The "Bank Account" of Trust* 334
    F. *Integrity* 336
    G. *Accountability* 336
    H. *Tell It Like It Is* 338
    I. *Treat Others As You Want To Be Treated* 338
    J. *Be Authentic* 339
    K. *When Things Go Wrong…Step up* 340
    L. *Loyalty* 341
    M. *Do What You Say You'll Do* 341
    N. *Listen* 342
    O. *Raise Your Bar* 342

**CHAPTER XXVI (Samantha Morton, Thomas D. Barton, and Jack Maypole)
COLLABORATION: A Reprise on Preventive Law in the Context of
Preventive Medicine** 343
I. INTRODUCTION 343
II. PREVENTIVE LAW AS A CONCEPT 345
    A. *A Brief History* 345
    B. *The Elements and Methods of Preventive Law* 346
III.   ANTECEDENTS IN PREVENTIVE MEDICINE 347
**IV. PREVENTIVE LAW AND LEGAL SERVICES DELIVERY TO LOW-
      INCOME CLIENTS** 350
    A. *Legal Services Delivery to the Poor Historically* 350
    B. *Medical-Legal Partnership | Boston at Boston Medical Center:*
         Preventive Law and Preventive Medicine in Action 352
    C. *Training and Education of Health Care Workers* 353
    D. *Legal Assistance to Patients* 355
    E. *Systemic Advocacy* 357
    F. *Research and Evaluation* 358
    G. *Replication and Professional Integration* 358
V.   EXPANDING THE INTEGRATION OF PREVENTIVE LAW . . . 360
VI.   CONCLUDING RECOMMENDATIONS 363

PREVENTIVE LAW and PROBLEM SOLVING:
Lawyering for the Future

By Thomas D. Barton©

INTRODUCTION TO PARTS ONE AND TWO

The Functions of Law and Changing Conceptions of How Those Functions May Be Achieved

A. *The Dilemma of Romance*

In some parts of the world, unmarried men and women do not freely mingle. They are kept apart except in public places, or when they can be chaperoned. In these cultures, romantic attraction is deemed so powerful, and the dangers of unsupervised encounters so uncontrollable, that single men and women are not permitted to be alone as a couple. To breach this practice is shameful, reflecting the presumption that illicit relations must surely follow when temptation is unconstrained by physical separation or the watchful eye of an older relative or chaperone.

In these places, orderly premarital relationships are managed through physical separation. To accomplish this requires rules to be elaborated that limit the interaction of eligible unmarrieds, under a broad variety of circumstances. These rules must be backed up by cultural practices and moral judgments that are strong enough to ensure their effectiveness.

And yet, of course, people must get together. This is the dilemma of romance. The same attractions and activities that are perceived as immoral or deeply threatening to authority and social stability are also the lifeblood of future generations. Mates must somehow be selected. Hence, young people may be permitted to interact in groups; or community rituals may be devised for determining partners; or close relatives may arrange marriages without consultation of the betrothed.

When facing any dilemma, choosing between one or the other of its competing goals is

1

not really an option. Both aspects of the dilemma must be accommodated, even while their coexistence generates friction. In coping with the dilemma of romance, we cannot choose separation or access. We must practice both simultaneously, acknowledging and somehow managing the risks we know will follow.

The dilemma of romance is real. For all the beauty of loving individuals finding one another, there is the danger of one person sexually or relationally exploiting another. For all the social stability brought by long term committed relationships, the wildness of unconstrained emotion remains. The same conditions of human interaction that spark romance also carry the threat of exploitation and disruption. Human intimacy must be fostered, but so must self-protection of the individuals and their surrounding communities.

> **Human intimacy must be fostered, but so must self-protection of the individuals and their surrounding communities.**

1. Sexually Segregated Dormitories: Separation and Power

Lest we dismiss this as the province of exotic societies, we should bear in mind that little more than a generation ago college dormitories across America and Europe were routinely segregated sexually. Many residence halls maintained rigidly enforced curfews and visitation rules, permitting contact only under tightly controlled conditions. The residence hall rules reflected what is universal. In every human society, norms of propriety or formal laws evolve that regulate access of persons to one another, and ritualize the stages by which intimate relations unfold and are recognized.

Segregated residence halls operated through basic rules of physical separation, punctuated by carefully prescribed exceptions. They made sense in their own way. The rules were rational, and even attempted to be reasonable. But they required significant applications of power or authority to maintain. Breach of the rules could mean expulsion from the living quarters, or even expulsion from the university.

Eventually, the system fell. The culture outside the dormitories changed so significantly that sexual segregation no longer seemed feasible, or desirable. Given the growing resistance, the power to keep the system in place no longer seemed adequate or worth the cost. Colleges that held out too long with the old system risked being viewed as unprogressive or out of touch, losing out in admissions to schools that had adopted a coed system. Eventually, the general practice changed, with some schools maintaining a choice of segregated dorms as a cultural throwback. A system based on rules, separation, and power was largely abandoned, replaced by a completely different paradigm in which the students self-regulate issues of intimacy according to evolving norms of respect, stronger interpersonal communication, and mutual consent.

In many ways, the story of how dormitory life evolved is the story of this book about the evolution of law and lawyering. Institutional rules, enforced by separation and power, describe how legal systems throughout the West responded to many problems set before them over the past two hundred years. A new paradigm for addressing legal problems is visible in many places, surfacing in diverse ways, and for a broad variety of human issues.

The purposes of this book are first, to help understand where legal systems have been–the methods they have used to confront problems and regulate human purposes. Second, it seeks to articulate why and how legal systems (and the cultures in which they are embedded) are moving past old formalities. Finally, it offers examples of settings in which the new paradigm is already being employed. The book is offered as an aid toward understanding law at its highest level of functioning. Toward that end it may speak to those about to begin the study of law as well as those who teach it. But the book also seeks to inspire innovation among the judges and lawyers who create and practice legal procedures.

Before moving to more traditionally legal matters, however, let us build out more fully our analogy to the dilemma of romance. Dilemmas are defined by their contending, antagonistic ends. They can be managed in various ways, some more successful than others. Which of its horns shall be privileged, and which suppressed? By what means, and under what circumstances? Every decision about a social dilemma reflects an outlook on the nature of humans or their relationships. Further, every response builds or reinforces cultural attitudes or beliefs about the problem being addressed.

The dilemma of romance is a case in point. We can readily see a range of options by which it has been managed. Human separation enforced through power is not the sole or inevitable way to confront the dilemma of romance. Formal education has not stopped in those universities that maintain coed dormitories, and almost certainly self-understanding has grown as greater license has been granted to young people to make their more of their own decisions about intimacy. In place of rules and power we now find a deeper understanding and thoughtfulness than many would have imagined possible.

2. Coed Dormitories: Understanding, Integration, and Accommodation

New ways to address the dilemma of romance were discovered on college campuses. When the change was made toward integrated dormitories, stronger protections against unwanted or exploitative relations were needed–no one is doubting that the dilemma is real. But those protections were found largely informally, through changed attitudes and peer pressure. The different physical environment enabled different ways for people to relate to one another. Coed dorms evolve a different sort of community. Spontaneous ordering capabilities were trusted, and imposed rules could be relaxed.

Almost certainly, behaviors in coed dorms are probably sometimes more disruptive than in segregated dorms. But ironically, *less* power is needed to manage the dilemma. Dormitory life moved from a system based on control, rules, separation and power to one based on understanding, integration, and ability of individuals to accommodate themselves to one another.

3

But that raises other issues. Why, in another place or time, was the practice different? Why did it change? Or why in another place has it *not* changed with the discovery of different options? The practices surrounding human relations, especially intimate relations, are often deeply embedded

> Dormitory life moved from a system of rules, separation, and power ("R/S/P") to one based on understanding, integration, and accommodation ("U/I/A").

in a culture. But to acknowledge the variance of culture should not paralyze all efforts at analysis or assessment. Greater understanding, choice, and change are always possible.

Perhaps those who manage the dilemma of romance by a rigid segregation of the sexes are gripped in their imaginations by scenes of unbalanced, licentious abandon when young people are left to themselves. Perhaps they have never seen examples of less formal, more spontaneous ways by which sexual exploitation or social disruption can be socially managed. Perhaps managing sexual relations somehow secures power for those in authority. Or perhaps the culture in which segregation practices hold are fragile, settings in which a change of one basic element threatens destruction of too many others. In such circumstances people are gripped by fears that an entire cultural edifice may fall. As a consequence people can become deeply conservative against change. We cannot know with certainty why sexual segregation persists, nor for how long it will continue. All we know for certain is that alternatives exist for coping with the dilemma of romance, all with different consequences for traditions and for individual human development.

And so it is with law. In this book I identify some of the dilemmas surrounding legal systems, both among the external thorny social issues law is charged with managing and the dilemmas internal to its own procedures and identity. I also describe some of the unfolding changes in both mentality and method, the new paradigm I assert is being built within the legal profession. Along the way I stop to ask, why now and not before? Why here, at this place and this problem, and not yet otherwise?

Perhaps most importantly, I try to imagine what further changes may be ahead. The arrangements we make about problems define us, for better or worse. Our procedures for problem solving inevitably express beliefs about trust, empowerment, rationality, and responsibility. Every problem is an opportunity for moral reflection and human growth. Every procedure that is devised is an opportunity to announce, as a culture, what is valued. In the interaction of problems and procedures, we measure our integrity as well as our creativity.

B. *Human Engagement: The Fundamental Human Dilemma and How It is Addressed*

Western legal systems now face difficult choices that are analogous to those of University dormitory administrators thirty years ago. The dilemma of romantic interaction is one sub-species of a more fundamental dilemma, that of human engagement. ***The fundamental dilemma is this: on the one hand, we all need one another.*** We cannot live outside of social communities. At some level, we must trust one another. No community can endure without a basic level of dependence on the good will and reliability of others. On the other hand, however, we are all potentially dangerous. We all threaten the well-being of one another through violence or exploitation. ***We must simultaneously facilitate human interaction, and yet also protect ourselves from that very interaction.***

Each branch of the dilemma of social order was famously articulated in Western history. John Locke advocated facilitating human interaction through advancing trade. He saw the legitimate domain of the state as securing that interaction. Thomas Hobbes, in contrast, stressed self-protection. The state, represented in his vision as the Biblical sea monster Leviathan, was a necessary evil to which we offered some share of our individual freedom in exchange for governmental protection against the prospects of a life which was "nasty, brutish, and short."

Each of their visions legitimates one of the two functions, human interaction and self-protection, that must be discharged in any social community. The two functions are clearly in tension–that is what makes it a dilemma, rather than just a choice. The closer the ties among people and the more far flung the network of interaction, the more vulnerable people are to domination. Those who would exploit others have more and easier opportunities to do so, as connections multiply and thicken. The eternal quest is to find some mechanism that achieves a balance, or at least co-existence, between the two essential functions.

1. Non-legal Alternatives

Not every society uses law as the means or device for coping with the fundamental dilemma. Societies without formal, developed legal institutions resort to a broad and ingenious variety of social and cultural practices. Even where law is present, these other practices supplement law's role in discharging both functions simultaneously. "Honor," for example, is a common alternative device. It can be used in many close-knit, face-to-face societies or among hierarchical, aristocratic groups. People both get together but control those interactions by powerful cultural beliefs and peer pressure about social position, dignity, and saving face. Another common device is "social harmony." In utopian or deeply religious communities, the fundamental dilemma is addressed by seeking uniformity of deeply held beliefs, through common values and prescribed behaviors.

2. Western Individualism and Law

For most of Western history, resolving the dilemma was thought to be possible only by structuring the community as a whole according to some sort of overriding principle or belief system. This community solution could be construction of a Platonic hierarchy in which each person occupies and acknowledges an appropriate position; or creation of a set of interlocking feudal obligations; or by forging and safeguarding the like-mindedness of shared religious beliefs or ideology; or by collectivizing the ownership of the means of production; or, sadly often, through capitulation to the total power of monarchs or military. A great deal of historical misery may be laid at the feet of such community-conformity organizing concepts.

But the concept of order and how it may be achieved shifted dramatically in the Enlightenment[1] era, begun in the mid-18th Century through the writings of Immanuel Kant and Adam Smith. They conceived order to be attainable not by conformity to community-wide structures of beliefs, but by essentially its *opposite*: by equipping every *individual* with the means of protection from others and the privileges of interaction with them. By granting every individual the means of self-protecting and self-enablement (at least in theory), society could function *in the aggregate* in an orderly way even if the particular cultural beliefs or behaviors were unpredictable.

Pushing aside communities as the ordering device in favoring of equipping individuals to perform that function required a stronger role for law and the courts, as the protectors of liberties. Western societies came to employ a particular style of law as a significant means of addressing the fundamental human dilemma, and thereby assuring social order.

Through the law, people could simultaneously be put together, and yet be protected one from another. Contract law, for example, can be imagined as a miniature model for how the law in general manages this. Human interaction is advanced where people choose to enter transactions with one another. In classic Contracts theory, the boundaries of the relationship between the parties is limited to the four corners of the document they have created. The parties stay "at arms' length." By observing certain formalities and structures, the parties gain legal rights against one another, and become burdened by reciprocal duties. If trouble arises, the parties can rely on legal rules and the power of the state for protection: the state will enforce and protect the relationship created in the contract.

3. Rights and Social Mobility

By giving every individual mobility and basic civil rights–the ability to forge and break social connections of his or her choosing, the power to form relationships and governments but then escape or end them-- people are accorded significant protection from the oppression and excesses of political and economic power. This was revolutionary thought that eventually swept

---

[1] The Enlightenment, sometimes also called "Modernism," built on the earlier Renaissance shift in focus from church authority and religious truth to human-centered inquiry. By the 18th Century, secular values of rationality and objectivity dominated philosophical discourse. Political and moral values of individualism and formal equality paired with scientific theory to form the collection of ideas commonly known as the Enlightenment. The terms "post-Modernist" or "post-Enlightenment" refer to newly emerging values about truth and power that question prevailing Enlightenment assumptions about rationality and individualism.

away the old order throughout Europe and the New World. But in the process, notice what happened to binding social ties. Ascribed social relationships–status roles unchangeable from birth--came to be seen as challenges to personal freedom and to the social order that emerged the free movement of individuals. In the mid-19th century Sir Henry Maine famously described this social evolution as societies moving from "status" in the old order to "contract" in the new order.

Law supplies a primary means of effecting this movement from status to contract. Through it, Western law also strongly shapes an image of humanity. The law enables interactions by equipping discrete individuals with strong legal rights. Individuals are then seen as free to make whatever connections they may choose with other individuals--connections that are presumed to be mutually beneficial. The connections need not be permanent. An individual's identity, at least for legal purposes, is provisional–always subject to possible re-making. If another individual threatens the bodily integrity or legal identify of another, defensive legal rights are triggered. The law will safeguard the theoretical independence and potential social mobility of every individual. In the idea of strong individual rights, the law found a way of managing the dilemma of human interaction without forced conformity. People are safe to initiate contacts with strangers, because the law will safeguard the benefits agreed to between the parties, even while protecting them against exploitation. Social and economic progress is achieved by this atomization of individuals who connect and disconnect again and again from other individuals.

4. Liberal Democracy and the Industrial Revolution

The strong individualism used by the law also thrived because of its consistency with the flourishing during that same era of democracy, market capitalism and the Industrial Revolution. Individualist legal identities helped markets to emerge and function that addressed a broad range of life goals: where one lives, what one studies, the profession one enters, virtually all everyday needs. Maine and his status-to-contract evolution was consistent with the Darwinian model that so gripped social imagination beginning in the second half of the 19th Century. Social refinement and progress were seen to result from constantly churning recombinations and decouplings. The more successful encounters survived and copied, and failed experiments were discarded. The scientific method, and the technology it produced to fuel Industrial Era successes, all reinforced the growth of the legal system practiced throughout the 20th Century.

The methods that came to prevail in the West were roughly akin to that used in sexually segregated dormitories. The default understanding of the law was that individuals were disconnected, separated from one another–just as the default rule in the

> Darwinism, the growth of democracy, and successes of technology in the Industrial Revolution shaped our legal system.

dormitories was that the sexes were separate. In both the law and in dormitory life, however, temporary or provisional connections could be made under specified conditions and rules. In the dormitories, visiting hours and supervised group interactions were permitted. In the law, relationships like master/servant, landlord/tenant, bailor/bailee, guardian/ward were recognized and came with pre-packaged rights and duties. Contract law permitted flexible, enforceable connections with the consent of each party but certain formalities had to be observed. Connections were permitted cautiously, in other words, packaged with rules that were backed by the power of the state. As we shall see later, analysis of these relationships and rules followed a precise, but narrow, kind of rationality.

5. *The Emergence of the U/I/A Paradigm in Western Legal Systems*

In both the segregated dormitory and traditional legal method, the dilemmas were managed by favoring protection, and being careful about human interaction. In each, a paradigm was employed that I term "R/S/P: Rationality/Separation/Power." These represent the primary tools by which problems were institutionally addressed, whether by college officials or the legal profession. When, in response to cultural pressure, dormitories largely abandoned sexual segregation, they needed new methods by which to manage the ever-present dilemma of romance.

The dormitories shifted their mentality and method from the paradigm of "R/S/P" to that of "U/I/A": Understanding/Integration/Accommodation. "Rationality," or at least a rarefied form of it, gives way to a broader "Understanding." "Separation," in the sense of isolating people from the objects of their concern, coalesces into "Integration," conscious designs that seek strong connections and personal relationships. Finally, hierarchically controlled "Power" opens out to personal and cultural "Accommodation." The assumption of unlimited power to effect judgments and remedies will soften, to be replaced by greater reliance on the ability of people to make mutual adjustments one to another. From "R/S/P" to "U/I/A:" in law and social order as well as in particular problem solving and prevention, that is the progression described and celebrated in this book.

Broad cultural changes are pressuring a change from the law's traditional reliance on the R/S/P tools for managing problems, be they large or small, internal or external. The most visible sign of the U/I/A paradigm is the exploding use of alternative dispute resolution (ADR) methods. But beneath these procedures is a shift in how human beings and their social relationships are understood and trusted. Connection, rather than separation, is the default approach of the U/I/A to understanding and preventing problems. Consent and accommodation, rather than power, are the default methods of addressing problems that do arise.

We may be at a historical watershed in which a new approach to the fundamental dilemma of human engagement can be imagined–one in which freedom of thought can be accorded to individuals even while thicker connections are promoted. The

> The R/S/P paradigm seeks to preserve and protect individuals by giving them the means to escape. The U/I/A alternative paradigm seeks to *strengthen* self-protection *by putting people together,* in settings that promote strong personal communication and healthy relationships.

U/I/A paradigm seeks to facilitate strong chosen social relationships as a method for legal problem prevention and resolution. In this vision, the law need not necessarily set people as adversaries for their disputes. In many (although not all) instances, the law can contribute toward order and self-protection even while it facilitates human interaction by promoting communications and connected relationships. As we shall see later, the law must tread cautiously, taking care not to impair the escape from social role-typing and oppression that still be needed in many places and for many minority persons. Relying on relationships carries dangers, as we shall explore. But candid, thoughtful communication and committed relationships offer potential strengths upon which the law could sometimes draw. Sometimes, in other words, ***putting people closer together actually lends them greater self-protection.***

Keeping people apart through power and conflict does not always lead to the thoughtful and responsible resolution of their problems, or the safeguarding of their interests. Connection coupled with trust and mutual regard–a willingness to accommodate to one another's needs or goals--can sometimes work as well or better. Instead of enveloping people in isolating cocoons of rights, the law can instead work like a suspension bridge. A suspension bridge facilitates movement and connection, even as it is anchored strongly at each end. Its multiple strands of cables permit an endless variety of vehicles to pass from one end to another. Law as a suspension bridge rather than isolating cocoons seeks to connects people through the entwined strands of self interest, emotion, morality, loyalty, and trust. Those aspects of life seem "non-legal" to those who are strongly trained in traditional legal methods, but they comprise part of the systemic contexts, environments and experience in which human problems actually arise.

C. The Format of this Book: Bridging The Past and the Future

This book reflects work for several years on two lines of research: (1) understanding the intellectual history underpinning modern adjudication; and (2) Preventive Law, Problem-solving, and Therapeutic Jurisprudence--the future of both the legal profession and legal system. For a long time, these were quite separate in my mind. Professor Susan Daicoff, who coined the phrase and describes the "Comprehensive Law Movement,"[2] encouraged me to think about how these two topics connect. I am much indebted to her insight and urging. This book is an attempt to follow her recommendation.

The bridge between the two topics–understanding the heritage of traditional legal structures and thinking about new possibilities--is a recognition of the fundamental dilemma of human engagement. Our inherited legal system can be understood as a response to this dilemma following the collapse of feudalism and the rise of Renaissance and Enlightenment ideas. But with globalization of both cultural and commercial activities, our philosophical and legal responses to the human dilemma are shifting. Emerging from that shift is the U/I/A paradigm,

---

[2] Susan Daicoff, *Law as a Healing Profession: The "Comprehensive Law Movement,"* 6 PEPPERDINE DISPUTE RESOLUTION LAW JOURNAL 1 (2006).

which shall be described over the course of this book.

U/I/A methods are not likely to supplant traditional R/S/P structures, or at least not soon. The R/S/P paradigm is not likely to be overthrown, and for good reasons. For some problems, resolution through the public, state-enforced, norm-pronouncing judgments of R/S/P is highly desirable. The law can sometimes act successfully as a moral beacon, dragging a reluctant culture along with it.[3] Furthermore, sometimes the people embroiled in a controversy are too belligerent or unscrupulous to recognize interests beyond their own. But U/I/A methods are destined to become increasingly important as a supplement to mentality and procedures that have dominated the legal problem solving over the past two centuries.

Several new approaches to law and lawyering reflect the emerging U/I/A paradigm: **Preventive Law, Proactive Law, Problem-Solving, and Therapeutic Jurisprudence.** The goals of the book are to help readers understand:

(1) *what* these new approaches are;

(2) *why* they exist;

(3) *how* the approaches can be practiced successfully; and

(4) *when* one of the U/I/A approaches may be likely to work better than the traditional R/S/P lawyering.

Different readers will focus more strongly on one or the other of these topics. The text is arranged for students and the general reader, offering an overview of all four topics. At various spots, the reader will be alerted to further readings that reach more deeply into a topic introduced in the main text. The hope is that every reader will learn more about the "why" as well as the "how" of the U/I/A approaches.

Hearing client stories too narrowly, and labeling their problems too quickly as legal, discourage lawyers from imagining that their professional methods could be re-conceived as part of a more complex, more helpful system that could avert problems from arising, and that could help clients better achieve their personal, business, or organizational goals. ***Undoing this neglect of the contexts or environments in which problems arise is the particular focus of the Preventive Law and Proactive Law approaches toward law and lawyering.***

The Preventive Law approach was conceived and developed by Louis M. Brown in the 1950's. Brown was a leading practitioner and academic who authored books, manuals, articles and columns explaining the preventive outlook and applying it to a variety of substantive legal fields as well as legal ethics. Collaborating with Edward A. Dauer, the pair produced the

---

[3] *See* Owen Fiss, *Against Settlement,* 93 YALE LAW JOURNAL 1073 (1984).

textbook PLANNING BY LAWYERS: MATERIALS ON A NON-ADVERSARIAL LEGAL PROCESS in 1978, and co-founded the PREVENTIVE LAW REPORTER journal published from 1982 until 2004. They also began the National Center for Preventive Law, today found at *www.preventivelawyer.org* and housed at the California Western School of Law, an institution that also works toward developing the concepts and skills of legal Problem-Solving. As a set of ideas, Problem Solving picks up where Preventive Law leaves off. If, despite the best efforts of a preventively-oriented lawyer, a legal risk has erupted in damages or potential liability, then the Problem Solving lawyer works toward resolutions that are effective, efficient, and mindful of the personal well-being of all concerned.

The historical concepts of Preventive Law, developed by Brown and Dauer, are seminal. When coupled with ideas about legal Problem-Solving and law itself, what emerges is a powerful integration of ethics, skills, concepts, and human regard. This book aims to explain that approach, explore both its ethics and efficacy, and suggest the skills and mentalities by which it may be adopted and advanced.

The "proactive" approach to legal problems and client counseling is the distinctive contribution of Helena Haapio and others in the Nordic region. It invaluably builds on the preventive focus of Brown and Dauer, stressing the positive contributions to a client's goals that a lawyer should always be looking for. The mentality of proactivity, like that of prevention, stands in contrast to the traditional image of the lawyer as merely reacting to legal defects in a client's arrangements. The proactive lawyer will think of him or herself as a potentially active contributor to a client's legitimate aims and activities. The author is greatly indebted to the work of Haapio and others in the Nordic group. Valuable links appear at the website http://www.lexpert.com.

New skills and an expanded professional understanding flow from the Preventive and Proactive approaches. Since they are so closely related, the approaches are addressed together in **Part One** of this work.

Traditional legal thinking also tends to neglect consideration for the psychological or relational well-being of the people who operate or use those procedures. To maintain the neutrality and universal rationality of legal process itself, the people behind the disputes are often consigned to a rather deep background. They are abstracted impersonally as "rights-holders." This neglect stems from the nature of legal rules and the tools by which their application is investigated.

Both the legal system and legal professionals could do better. Ideally, every encounter that a lawyer, client or judge has with the legal system should be an opportunity for moral growth, personal satisfaction, and stronger personal relationships. The legal system should model mutual respect among every user and professional. It should value consensual human relationships, personal accountability, and decentralized decision-making. Undoing the relative neglect of these human needs and psychology is the focus of the Therapeutic Jurisprudence[4] approach toward law and lawyering, addressed in **Part Two** of this work along with stronger attention to Problem-Solving.

Finally, throughout both Parts One and Two I hope that the depth of understanding sought will contribute to greater professional satisfaction–by beginning students of the law as well seasoned practitioners. By reflecting on the choice of approaches, each reader is invited to examine the values most important to him or her as a lawyer, and as a person. The study of law has never been more exciting, nor its practice so open to a fulfilling life of helping prevent and resolve problems.

---

[4] The Therapeutic Jurisprudence movement was founded by David B. Wexler and Bruce J. Winick, and is dedicated to furthering the psychological well-being of those who encounter the legal system. Professors Wexler and Winick worked originally in the context of mental health law and criminal justice, but their approach and philosophy has now been taken up by judges and lawyers in many countries and subject areas. *See, e.g.,* their works LAW IN A THERAPEUTIC KEY: DEVELOPMENTS IN THERAPEUTIC JURISPRUDENCE (1996); COURTS IN A THERAPEUTIC KEY: THERAPEUTIC JURISPRUDENCE AND THE COURTS (2003). Their website is www.therapeuticjurisprudence.org.

PART ONE

PREVENTIVE LAW

AND PROACTIVE LAW

PART ONE: PREVENTIVE LAW AND PROACTIVE LAW

CHAPTER I
PROBLEM-SOLVING SYSTEMS: The Integration of Problems, Rules, Procedures, Skills, Ethics, Culture, and Philosophical Concepts

As a teenager in rural Iowa, my father ventured out daily with his older brother to hunt food for the family. They fished in a nearby river, although the catch was never much. Armed with shotguns, the two boys sought rabbit, quail, and even squirrel to supply meat for dinner. To supplement the family income, they set traps for muscrat whose skins they would sell to make ladies' winter coats. This was during the Great Depression, and the human problem of finding food was immediate and persistent.

In Western developed societies, this hunter-gather subsistence economy has largely vanished over the past two generations. In our far richer urban and suburban society, the food supply has become far more abundant and secure. We could say that the human problem of "finding food" has morphed into "paying for meals" and for many, "limiting weight gain." We could stop there, perhaps noticing the division of labor and higher productivity that has caused this human problem to change so fundamentally over the past century. We could comment sociologically about a world that takes adequate daily calorie intake for granted. We could reflect on the public health implications, both good and bad, of a society that had largely overcome food scarcity.

Those connections would be important, and could prompt some interdisciplinary insight into how people's behaviors and personal relationships change under conditions of abundance. But we could also use the evolution of this human problem to understand better the connections between human problems and the procedures, skills, ethics, and culture that grow up to address those problems. We could even use the recent history of food production and distribution to reflect on underlying philosophical concepts: how humans think of themselves; how truth is to be sought; and the criteria constituting truth. If we dig deeply enough on any significant human problem, we will always find connections to procedures, skills, ethics, culture, and philosophy. That is because humans relate to the challenges of their physical environment not just through technology, but also through ideas and belief systems, and social structures of both cooperation and compulsion.

In understanding law and legal systems, therefore, we are inevitably drawn to questions about the human problems being addressed, by what methods, and through what ideas and values. Having then created these cognitive and social structures for coping with human problems, those structures begin to frame how we identify and react to human problems. Our perceptions, ideas, values, and structures also influence one another. ***Law cannot be fully understood except as part of a larger system of problems, procedures, skills, ethics, culture, and ideas about ourselves and what is true in the world.***

Putting flesh on the skeleton of this argument, as the *problem* of human sustenance has changed over the past century, the *procedures* for obtaining food have altered radically. Putting food on the table no longer entails hunting, but rather shopping. New social structures (like grocery stores) must develop to address the problem's new shape and the revised procedures for addressing the problem. As those procedures have changed, so also have the *skills* required for food gathering. For most people, hunting, fishing, and trapping are no longer practiced. Good aim with a shotgun is supplanted by dexterity in steering a shopping cart. The use of hunting skills has changed contexts, from a life necessity to mere hobby or sport.

With this change in context for employing hunting skills, the *ethics* of using those skills have also been redrawn. For many people, hunting animals and wearing their furs have become morally repugnant, perhaps for the very reason that those practices are no longer necessary for human survival. That moral assessment about hunting reflects a deeper *cultural* shift in how humans view nature. In hunter-gatherer worlds, nature is a resource to be exploited, but simultaneously is challenging and perhaps life-threatening. Notions of controlling, managing or even protecting nature are almost unimaginable to someone in a hunter-gatherer society. Humans simply do not possess that level of power. Actions taken toward animals seem intuitively justified, even a form of self-defense.

> To become a better problem solver:
>
> (1) Try to understand how the *problem* and traditional *procedure* for its resolution are related.
> (2) Then understand how *skills* and *ethics* are related to those procedures.
> (3) Then understand how *cultural attitudes* and *beliefs about truth and knowledge* affect not just the procedures and their use, but how we perceive and define the problem in the first place.

The earlier world of Ernest Hemingway and Jack London has slowly succumbed to that of John Updike. In modern life, people's basic needs are met not through personal, heroic encounters with a foreboding or tempestuous natural environment, but rather through long chains of dependency on strangers and institutions. Cultural activities associated with rural life, once celebrated, become marginalized and perhaps even ridiculed as provincial and old-fashioned. People begin to define themselves in different ways. Matters once taken to be eternal, unquestioned truths are gradually opened to skepticism and scrutiny.

In sum, since my father's time the entire system for human sustenance has evolved a new paradigm. Every part of the system changes together: what we regard as the problem, the procedures for addressing it, the skills needed to perform those procedures, the ethics regulating those skills and ensuring the smooth functioning of the procedures, cultural values concerning obtaining and consuming food, and certain philosophical concepts about truth and ourselves as humans. Each part of the system influences every other part in richly complex ways. No one element exclusively drives the system.

Although they may develop at different rates, each part must co-evolve. No element can fall too far behind the others if the system is to continue to function well. Imagine, for example, bringing a shotgun into a supermarket. Skill with a shotgun is paired with a procedure that addresses an outmoded version of the problem. Exercise of the outmoded skill becomes worse than ineffective: It could be threatening, even illegal. Every element of the system must adjust to change.

> Every part of a problem solving system influences every other part in richly complex ways.

Legal systems work in the same way. They too address problems in a system comprised of the problem itself, using procedures that are designed to address the problem and that are operated by professionals using particular skills and a code of ethics. The system is embedded in a broader non-legal culture, one part of which is particular beliefs about truth and the nature of human beings. The system also generates an internal sub-culture, a set of attitudes, understandings, and behaviors among legal professionals. A diagram of the legal system appears overleaf as Figure 1, representing a simplified version of the interactions among problems, procedures, skills, ethics, culture, and philosophical concepts. A few structural aspects of problems, *i.e.*, qualities of problems apart from actual content, are also shown.

To understand law, one must understand how each element of the legal system influences the other elements. To be a skilled and ethical legal professional of the 21st Century, one must understand what the legal system has been, and how it is evolving. The movement toward ADR–the *procedures*– is the most visible aspect of the emergence of a new paradigm in legal systems. The *skills* for operating within these new legal procedures must be mastered. We may expect, however, that new *ethical issues* will accompany their use. We may expect the internal *culture* among lawyers to change, generating different criteria of professionalism and personal satisfaction. We also can look for the reasons why a new paradigm seems to be forming. Have the *problems* being submitted for resolution changed? Has the surrounding culture changed, making traditional legal views seem old-fashioned? Have *ideas about truth and human nature* shifted?

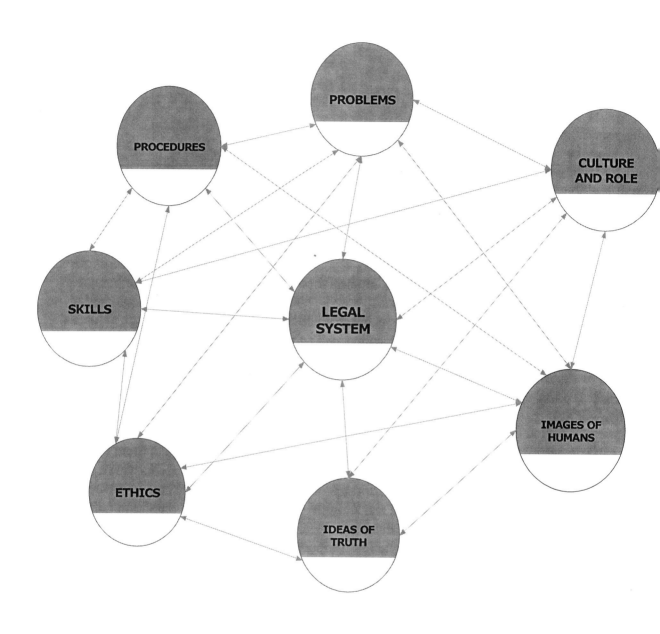

Figure 1: Elements of the Legal System and Their Interactions

A. *Problem-Solving Systems: How They Change*

The elements of a problem-solving system do not necessarily change at the same rates. Culture, and ideas about truth and knowledge, probably move more slowly than the other aspects of the system. The elements are distinct, but they also are all connected and mutually influencing. A change in technology from outside the system may broaden the capabilities of some skill that operates within the system. Or a change in the availability of outside resources may alter the efficiencies within the system. Or experience in dealing with particular problems may lead to a refinement in the system's procedures. As elements shift in response to one another, those changes will prompt yet other effects. The system is constantly seeking a balance among all the elements that will enable the system to continue its function of addressing a particular set of problems.

Suppose, for example, that we are back in the hunter-gatherer world of my father, but a sudden and dramatic change occurs in the *procedures* for addressing his problem of human sustenance. Suppose that a new technology became available to my father, perhaps a fishing net that could substantially increase his daily catch in the local river. The other elements in the system would all be forced to adjust to this change in procedure:

- The new procedure would immediately require new *skills*, and devalue old skills. Fishing with a line and hook, which requires finesse and patience, becomes displaced by finding good methods for dispersing and then dragging in the nets.

- An *ethical* debate would likely be sparked about the morality of using the new nets. Traditionalists may resist the invention, perhaps because at least initially they are unskilled in its use and fearful that they will be left behind technologically. Or they may view the nets as threatening authority structures that are based on the old ways. Or they may see use of the nets as somehow false, or wicked in a way that may be difficult for outsiders to understand.

  In this regard, I personally recall my grandparents, who began farming prior to mechanization, disparaging the use of tractors rather than a team of horses. They would say of people in the younger generation, "He will do anything a farmer does, so long as it is on the back of a tractor." The implication was that at some level of identity or legitimacy, the new mechanized procedures were disrupting what it meant to be a farmer. The instinct among those trained in the old ways was fear and resistance. Gradually, though, the culture changed to accommodate the more efficient technology. Ethical sensibilities tend to follow, with pockets of persistent dissent.

- Eventually, a significant change in *procedures* will reverberate to change the problem, or create new ones. Consider the example of the substitution of tractors for horses:

Dependency on tractors means that farmers have higher cash needs. A horse can be sustained from a variety of foodstuffs that are directly available on the farm itself. A tractor, however, requires gasoline that must be purchased, and ongoing maintenance that a farmer may not be able to supply personally. The farmer must therefore sustain a stronger cash flow. The seasonal nature of a farmer's income no longer fits with the regular purchasing needs. The farmer must therefore build a surplus, or must build credit relationships with local merchants, or diversify production to include a constant income producer like eggs or dairy products.

It may be rare that a problem-solving system is jolted into change by something new in the *ethics* element, but it certainly could happen. If a conscience-shocking world event occurs, like genocide, people in a variety of professions may begin to think differently about their everyday ethical principles. That elevated ethical sensitivity will prompt changes in what are regarded as legitimate procedures among that profession. That in turn will require at least subtle changes in skills or their application. What is deemed to be a suitable problem to be handled by that profession may be expanded or contracted, or the significance of certain problems will change within the profession.

Perhaps the most common impetus for system change is where some new problem, one with unusual attributes, is presented for resolution within an evolved system. The standard procedures will not easily accommodate the new problem, because the system has evolved particular procedures that respond well to the sorts of problems traditionally addressed. The round holes that the procedure has evolved, in other words, will not fit well with a new problem that possesses square edges. Nonetheless, the system may be required to cope with the new problem. This happens commonly in the legal system, because law is the default institution for resolving problems, and for a very good reason. If matters cannot be resolved by the individuals with the problem, and if the legal system turns away the problem, then the individual problem-holders will resort to self-help. This will be disorderly at best, violent at worst.

> As we struggle to fit new problems into our traditional legal problem solving system, the system itself is changed.

So instead, we expect our legal system to be flexible and accommodating in taking on problems for which its procedures are not necessarily well designed.[1] In coping with the mismatch, the legal system may file off the square contours of the problem to fit within the round holes of its procedures, perhaps by resorting to the creation of a legal fiction.[2] Alternatively, the

---

[1] Thomas D. Barton, *Justiciability: A Theory of Judicial Problem-Solving*, 24 BOSTON COLLEGE LAW REVIEW 505 (1983).

[2] Id.

law can begin to modify its procedures, at least in this subject area, by becoming more square-edged to fit the shape of the problem.[3] Somehow, a fit will be found unless the problem is pronounced "non-justiciable" and exiled from the legal system. Regardless whether the fit is achieved by changing the substantive features of the problem, or changing the structures of the procedures, all of the other elements of the legal system–ethics, skills, truth, and culture–will be affected.

My father's story also reflects larger points, all of which will be developed in this book. *We, meaning those learning and practicing the law, are in the position of my father. We have inherited an approach to lawyering that is adapted to problems that are set within a certain historical, social, technological, and intellectual environment. Our methods have worked well, but they may become less satisfactory as life changes around us.* Here is a synopsis:

B. Taking Seriously the Legal "System"

Human problems are always addressed within an existing integrative system comprised of several interconnected components or elements: rules, procedures, skills, ethics, culture, and philosophical concepts. Each component is separate, but each is connected to every other element in multiple, mutually influencing ways. A system moves organically, not mechanically. Like the flow of an amoeba, its trajectory eludes complete prediction.

A real system produces emergent properties that no one part could possibly achieve, like the human consciousness that emerges from the mutually interacting parts of our bodies. Taking the "legal system" seriously means exploring the broader set of components that interact toward resolving human problems. The approach pays immediate rewards for law students and practitioners alike. It reveals our **relativ**e neglect of aspects of the system beyond procedures and rules.

1. Respecting the Contexts, or Environments, in Which Problems Arise

Traditional legal thinking **neglects** the differing contexts or environments surrounding a problem. Such neglect often results in less helpful and durable decisions about the problem, and in greater unintended spill-over effects.

Neglecting the environment of a problem also virtually forecloses the possibility of taking steps to preventing the problem from arising, or helping turn an incipient problem into progress toward a client's ultimate goals. And yet most problems first appear as risks that can be contained or eliminated by a small, early intervention that may make positive contributions as well as eliminate risks.

---

[3] Id.

Even when this lack of attention to prevention is explicitly pointed out to legal professionals, however, they may fail to respond. This resistance could have many possible sources. It may be that lawyers are fearful of an approach where they lack of skills, and therefore are concerned about competence, ethical violations, and malpractice. Or the resistance could reflect a different ethical concern, based on deviating from the traditional "zealous advocate" image of being a responsible lawyer. Or the resistance may stem from a largely misguided concern that working to prevent problems will endanger the livelihood of lawyers. Most of all, however, the resistance to a preventive outlook on client problems may be the result of the very strong training that lawyers receive in a particular way of thinking.

Preventive thinking requires legal professionals to approach risks and problems with a completely different set of mentalities from their training. And therefore preventive thinking seems foreign, frightening, false, or all three. Here are several dimensions along which traditional legal thinking can be contrasted with preventive thinking (and with the other new approaches to lawyering that will be explored in Part Two of these materials, Problem Solving and Therapeutic Jurisprudence):

a. *Past versus Future:* Traditional legal thought is oriented to the past. The approaches of Preventive Law, Proactive Law, Problem-Solving, and Therapeutic Jurisprudence are oriented toward the present or future.

b. *Secrecy versus communication:* Traditional legal thought assumes that mutual gains unfold by each party acting independently to maximize his or her self-interest. Lack of information about the other party's goals or interests is not deemed necessarily for individual gain or the resolution of a problem. By contrast, the new approaches urge early and frequent communication between the parties–even parties whose interests would naturally seem antagonistic--throughout their dealings.

c. *Separation versus connection:* Traditional legal thought imagines people as radically disconnected individuals. The new mentality imagines people as connected in relationships.

d. *Binary, zero sum outcomes versus graduated, mutual benefits:* Traditional legal thought typically comes to winner-take-all solutions. The new approaches seek outcomes in which both parties benefit along a spectrum of self-identified preferences.

e. *Rules versus risks:* Traditional legal thought is conceptually rooted almost exclusively in legal rules. Although it does not ignore legal rules, the new thinking undertakes risk assessment and strives for its reduction. It also does not assume that solutions to problems are necessarily rooted in the law.

f. *Transactions versus Systems:* Traditional legal thought tends to encapsulate separate contracts into discrete transactions. The new thinking looks for patterns among contacts or events, and for the broader contexts in which single contacts or events operate.

        g. Narrow procedural methods versus multiple means for problem resolution: Traditional legal thought presumes the use of formal state-based judgments adjudicative mechanisms to resolve legal disputes. The new thinking affirmatively attempts to create a variety of alternative procedures or methods.

C. The Current Paradigm of Western Legal Systems: "R/S/P"

        As introduced above, **the identifiable paradigm that has prevailed in Western legal systems over the past three hundred years is what I call "R/S/P," standing for "rationality/separation/power."** This triad comprise the basic tools typically employed by our legal system in addressing human problems. A particular (and narrow) form of *rationality* is brought to bear investigating the facts and merits of a problem; the people who are parties to a dispute are often *separated* in some way from one another, or from the objects of their controversy; and coercive state *power* is employed to engineer some remedy. In civil matters, this power usually takes the form of a transfer of financial assets from one party to another. In criminal matters, it is often the separation of the convicted person from society, through imprisonment.

        The R/S/P paradigm evolved with the economic needs, social capabilities, and philosophical assumptions of the Industrial Revolution and Enlightenment. As the Industrial Revolution is slowly eclipsed by the Information Age, and as Enlightenment philosophical values are pushed aside by post-Modernist ideas, Western legal systems are in a period of significant turbulence. But the turbulence is necessarily destructive. On the contrary, our legal system may be on the verge of breakthroughs in greater accessibility, respect for human relationships, and flexible, helpful methods for preventing and solving problems. As Western culture moves into a "post-Enlightenment" or "post-Modernist" era, accompanied by economic changes brought about by Information Age technology, the traditional R/S/P legal paradigm faces two dilemmas. How the legal system responds to these two dilemmas will define the cultural role and impact of the law for the 21st Century.

        The "cultural" dilemma is the extent to which the traditional legal system will alter its working assumptions and methods to conform with emerging post-Enlightenment culture. Some of these new cultural understandings clash with fundamental traditional legal values. Will the law remain in step with evolving cultural norms? If it does not, law will relinquish at least some part of the central role it has come to play in modern society. The "constitutive" dilemma asks, however, how far the law *can* change its methods and still be identifiable as law--still fulfill the functions for which law was created.

        The upheaval in legal systems has several possible sources, which will be explored in greater depth in later chapters. The reverberations are intensifying, with consequences that are not fully visible. For now, we may at least note the following about how each of the elements or components of the system are changing, leaving for later their fuller explanation:

•   The nature of *problems* being presented to the legal system for resolution is diversifying. The law–both its explicit regulatory rules and its mentality--is pervading aspects of life that in the past were off limits.[4] Further, many of those new problems share features that are especially challenging for legal resolution using traditional methods.

•   New legal *procedures* are quickly proliferating, reflecting the explosion of interest in the ADR and prevention mechanisms. These are only the most visible manifestation, however, of a shift in every element in Western legal systems.

•   New *skills* for legal professionals are being identified that are better suited to the new problems and procedures.

•   *Ethical* rules of Professional Responsibility, once centered around the prevailing adversarial procedures of litigation, are developing to provide safeguards and promote the counselor role of lawyers in addition to the advocate role.

•   *Culturally,* Western societies are moving away from their traditional reliance on power and the separation of people to resolve problems, and instead are stressing consent and human connection.

•   Various *philosophical concepts* about truth and the nature of human beings are shifting. This element is the least visible among those comprising the legal system, and also the most difficult to understand.

This final element of the system is the least visible, and probably most difficult to understand. In part, this is because assumptions about knowledge and truth are very deeply embedded in a culture, and prompt little reflection. Many of us, for

> "Truth" does not look the same from problem to problem. Ask: "what must I learn to feel satisfied about this problem, and how stable must that knowledge be?"

example, imagine truth to be an on/off switch: either something is true or it is not. Actually, though, we investigate different problems and assess the truth of solutions with a broad variety of unspoken assumptions, based on the particular problem that confronts us. Wrestling with theological problems, for example, will generate proposed answers or resolutions that have quite different truth qualities from engineering problems. The resolution of problems in the relationship between a parent and child will have yet different truth qualities. Expectations about rigor, reliability, universality, timelessness or other variables differ about what we regard as "truth" in a given context.

---

[4] *See generally* Lawrence M. Friedman, TOTAL JUSTICE (1985).

D. Summing Up

To summarize, this book brings an unusual perspective to understanding law and practicing as a legal professional. It looks at the evolving relationships among six deeply connected concepts:

(1) legal *problems*;

(2) the *procedures and legal rules*[5] that have been devised over the years to prevent or resolve those problems;

(3) the *skills* of the professionals who use those procedures;

(4) the *ethical concerns* that accompany those attitudes and skills;

(5) *cultural attitudes*, beliefs, and values; and

(6) *philosophical ideas* about knowledge, truth and the nature of human beings.

Each of these six elements--problems, procedures, skills, professional ethics, culture, and philosophical concepts--influences the content and limitations of the others. Understanding and being effective within the legal system requires examining all six topics as elements in an integrated system that has evolved to cope with human problems. The R/S/P paradigm that describes the prevailing interaction and co-evolution of the six elements sets people apart as detached, rational individuals, and isolates their problems from their surrounding relational, historical, civic, and physical environment.

This book imagines approaches to lawyering that add back what the R/S/P paradigm tends to exclude:

> What will be the future of our legal system if it fails to adapt to cultural change?

- *the surrounding context, or environment, in which the problem arises;*

- *qualities of the problems themselves that suggest new ways of thinking about their resolution; and*

---

[5] Although legal rules are an obvious component of legal systems, from this point forward I collapse that element into "procedures." These two elements are strongly linked, and I wish to avoid too much attention to the content of particular legal rules. Conceptually, this book attempts to describe frameworks and methods that operate apart from the rules of traditional areas of law like Contract, Tort, Property, etc.

- *stronger concerns for the relational, emotional, and psychological well-being of the people involved in legal problem solving.*

Taken together, these broader approaches to understanding law and its functioning describe the emerging paradigm of Understanding/Integration/Accommodation (U/I/A) that may usefully supplement traditional methods for addressing legal problems.

CHAPTER II
PROBLEM-SOLVING SYSTEMS: The Influence of Context

"The legal system" may be a familiar phrase, but thinking systemically about law is not so familiar. This is so even among lawyers, but probably not surprising. Western culture does not emphasize connecting concepts and discovering their relationships. Instead, Western thought tends to find distinctions among things or ideas, then classify them. Westerners tend to be

> Lawyers are traditionally trained as *taxonomists,* encouraged to find distinctions and make classifications. Preventive Law and the other U/I/A approaches ask lawyers to think as *ecologists,* looking for connections and relationships.

"taxonomists" rather than "ecologists," and the training of lawyers to operate within traditional legal methods is a good example. The U/I/A approaches ask lawyers to think like ecologists, which is largely against their training.

Suppose two scientists walk into a pristine wilderness. One is a botanist, who works to understand plant life through first *classifying* each plant separately, and *analyzing the distinctions.* That is taxonomy, and it is how lawyers are trained. Lawyers tend to understand problems by hearing facts, and then identifying in which box of legal rules the facts best fit. Sometimes, legal arguments proceed by contesting in which legal rule box best applies to the problem. Almost always, legal argument is about determining whether the operative facts–like a plant that has been plucked from its larger environment–satisfy the criteria of particular legal rules. This is akin to the taxonomist determining whether a given plant specimen does, or does not, fit appropriately within a given classification.

But suppose the other scientist is an ecologist. This person will not be concerned with finding differences and making classifications. The ecologist will instead look for *connections and relationships* among the elements in the complex system that comprises this particular ecological niche. The ecologist will look at climate and rainfall; at the organic composition and structure of the soil; and at how their interaction supports both plant and animal life, which in turn support one another at many different levels. The goal is to understand the system as a whole–how each element of the environment has co-evolved with the other elements, and how a change to any one part will prompt changes to all other parts. The point is to ask and understand how this plant came to exist in this environment; what sustains it; and what would threaten its persistence.

Preventive Law is ecological. It looks at the contexts or environments in which problems arise, explores different perspectives from which the problem may be viewed, and tries to uncover and understand the connections among people and things that seems to set a problem in motion. That is essential because the very same substantive problem could arise in very different contexts, which may demand resolution by different methods. And these differing methods will be viewed differently by different stakeholders in a problem, each of whom may have quite a different perspectives on the problem. The larger point, like that of the ecologist, is to discover how this problem came to exist; what sustains the problem; and finally, how might I best intervene to resolve the problem and yet enable my client to thrive?

How Context Matters

Preventive Law focuses, contrary to traditional legal thinking, on the entire context in which a "legal" problem arises. The reasons for paying attention to context are: (1) the context of a problem should influence the tools we use to address a problem; and (b) if we do not pay attention to the context of a problem, somehow altering the larger environment that generated the problem in the first place, the problem is likely to recur even after we have rectified its initial damage.

1. A Sample Problem: A Hungry Person Sees a Bit of Food

To start thinking more seriously about the contexts in which problems arise, think again about food. Suppose the problem is a hungry person who says: *"I see a bit of food in front of me that I would like to eat."* That problem could arise in various contexts, each of which will create different demands on the procedures that are invoked to resolve the problem.

a. First Context: A Family Dinner Table

Suppose first that the problem arises around a typical family dinner table. One family member is hungry, and thinks *"I see a bit of food in front of me that I would like to eat."* In this simple context, the family (aided by cultural norms of etiquette) may have evolved an acceptable procedure: the hungry person may be entitled to grab a food item as a bowl is passed.

This seemingly simple response to the problem has several "structural" qualities, that can be described and that are related to the particular context (a family dinner table) in which the problem arises. As we begin to change the social contexts in which the problem arises, the structural qualities of the problem resolution will also change. For now, however, note that in this family setting:

- The resolution of the problem requires no elaborate preparation or satisfaction of preconditions. The problem holder may simply grab immediately for a solution.

> Different contexts can change the structural qualities of a problem.

- The information about what is available is easily accessible–*i.e.,* the hungry person can easily see the food and knows what it is.

- The hungry person need not negotiate with anyone else, nor need other parties participate in the problem resolution.

- The person deciding on the food item may freely use decisional criteria that are personal, *i.e.,* the person is not legislating a standard that others must follow.

- The resolution of the problem need not be transparent (i.e., it would be legitimate to put another muffin on one's plate even though everyone one else at the table is distracted in conversation, and not paying attention to the food grab).

- The conditions under which the problem is addressed are stable, rather than turbulent.

- Finally, spillover consequences of the allocation of the food may exist, but are likely minimal ("hey, who took the second drumstick?").

b. Second Context: A Open-Air Farmer's Market

Take again the same substantive problem, *"I see a bit of food in front of me that I would like to eat."* Change the context, however, to be that of shopping at an open-air farmers market. In this different context, the same substantive problem presents a somewhat different structure and, consequently, different demands on the procedures that can be used to resolve the problem. The dinner-table procedure of simply grabbing the food will not be legitimate. If one tries it, one will likely be arrested for shop-lifting. But that is only the most dramatic quality that has changed in the demands the problem makes on its resolution. The switch in context to the farmer's market also includes:

- Resolving the problem may have required at least the preparation in advance of a shopping list.

- The problem may need to be communicated and explored between problem holder and problem resolver. The shopper may need to know: is it organic? Fresh? How can it be prepared properly. Information may affect choices in the problem resolution, unlike at the family dinner table.

- The decider must also negotiate a solution with another person. Simply grabbing the food in this context constitutes shop-lifting. A consensual procedure for the transfer from one owner to another must be devised.

- Third parties may have to be consulted in resolving the problem (suppose family members are along at the market: "Are you home for dinner tonight so I can

29

prepare this fish while it is fresh?" "If I serve eggplant, will you eat it?").

- Resolution of the problem must be transparent, at least in the sense of securing the seller's awareness that the decider wishes to purchase the item.

- The background conditions of the problem may not be completely stable ("Was the truck hot in which these flowers were transported? Were they deprived of water?")

> c. Third Context: Back at the Family Table but the Hungry Person is Diabetic

Now imagine a third context of the same problem, *"I see a bit of food in front of me that I would like to eat."* Suppose we are back at the family dinner table but the decider is a brittle diabetic. The desired food item is chocolate cake with butter icing. Now the problem presents different demands on procedures for resolution because ***some of the various factors listed above may be contentious, and without a clear sense of the criteria to legitimize or stabilize them.***

Will another family member be entitled to intrude on the hungry person's decision? If so, by a verbal reminder to a diabetic, or instead by the more intrusive method of physically removing the cake from the diabetic's plate? Can the diabetic adequately prepare for the decision by taking a blood sugar reading just prior to the meal? If the diabetic eats the cake, what will be the consequences? Are they predictable or unstable? If a family member deprives the diabetic of this item, will the diabetic retaliate (dangerously) by raiding the refrigerator secretly in the middle of the night?

> 2. *Lessons for Shifting Procedures to Match Contextual Demands*

The examples illustrate how little attention in legal training to how the differing contexts in which the problem arises may affect the demands on procedures to resolve the problem. For now, the basic message for legal professionals is clear: Always learn as much as possible about the context in which a client's legal problem arises, and the perspective your client has on the problem. If the same legal problem arises among strangers who will never again interact, the demands on procedures to achieve a just and non-destructive resolution may be simpler than when the same legal problem arises between business associates, or among family members.

Once the context and perspectives of the problem are gathered, Preventive Law then attempts to understand the *connections* among elements that together form risks or opportunities. The thinking is always ecological, or systemic.

> Always learn as much as possible about the context in which a client's problem arises, and the perspective your client has on the problem.

Any problem that humans endeavor to address is embedded in a system that also contains the procedures invented by humans for addressing the problem. Different sorts of procedures may have been tried out for coping with a certain problem. The survivor of any such procedural trial and error is a part of the current system that we now tend to take for granted in addressing the problem. Those procedures, whatever they are, require certain skills for their successful operation. Accompanying the procedures and skills will be ethical rules for their appropriate and efficient use. The people using the system develop certain attitudes, beliefs, and norms within the system. An internal culture arises, in other words, although the system is always open to cultural influences from the larger social world. Finally, within a problem-solving system a certain style of truth will develop as appropriate for investigating and deciding the particular problem that is being addressed.

Virtually no one who works within various systems for resolving problems–neither lawyers, engineers, theologians, nor family therapists--tends to reflect much about either the separate components of their respective problem-solving system, or their functional interaction. The elements and their cooperative working of a problem solving system are largely taken for granted, just as we take for granted that our brains have evolved to integrate information received separately by our eyes, ears, nose, and skin.

In the next Chapter, we will focus not on the different contexts in which a problem may arise, but instead on the procedures that we tend traditionally to associate with certain problems. The adoption of a conventional procedure–and the limitations of that procedure's capabilities–affect our definition of the problem, our ethical sensitivities about the problem, and the truth style that we deem acceptable as a "resolution" of the problem.

CHAPTER III
PROBLEM-SOLVING SYSTEMS: An Introduction to Procedures

A. Flipping a Coin: Random But Not Arbitrary

Before embarking on the details of the preventive approach to lawyering let us solidify our understanding of problem-solving systems with another example from everyday life. This example once again highlights the strong relationships among the elements of the system, and especially how individual problems make particular demands on the procedures that must evolve to resolve those problems.

Evolved systems for problem solving often seem intuitive, a matter of common sense. We take for granted the relationships of the six elements of the system–problems, procedures, skills, ethics, truth and culture because, as suggested above, problems come to be defined in terms of the procedures that are traditionally used for resolving the problem. Further, the people who operate the procedures have learned the skills and observed the ethics needed for that procedure to be effective. They rarely need to reflect on alternatives. Finally, people develop instincts for what qualifies as information and truth about a given problem: information must be found, and truth must be shaped, to be consistent with the needs for operating the procedure and the formats of its resolutions. The following example shows an evolved system for problem-solving involving all six variables.

1. The Problem of First Positions

> The Coin Toss: Like all procedures, it is well-suited to resolving some, but not all, problems.

Consider the first thirty seconds of a typical sports event. A set of initial, related substantive problems present themselves: which person or team should first be on offense, and which on defense? Which person or team should have the wind or sun at their backs, or in their faces? Without a successful resolution of these problems, the game would be tainted by allegations of unfairness from the outset. I will clump the problems together as one, labeling it the "problem of first positions."

2. The Procedure: Flipping a Coin

Often, the procedure chosen is to flip a coin. We take for granted that this is a sensible way to begin a sporting event, and it is. But if we analyze this procedure as an interactive element within a system comprised of problem, procedure, skills, ethics, and even cultural and philosophical concepts, we will understand better why the humble coin toss has evolved as the procedure of choice to begin sporting events.

3. The Problem Itself

The coin-flip procedure is well suited to resolve the problem, for a number of reasons. First, the procedure produces two (and only two) clear alternative answers to any question put to it. The coin produces either "heads" or "tails," and nothing in between. But typically since the question posed concerns only two teams and which should go first, this primitive binary response of heads versus tails is all that is needed. In fact, if the procedure produced more alternative responses, or if responses were somehow contingent on other variables, the procedure would not fit well with the problem being addressed. The coin flip is also well suited to the problem because it is efficient: the procedure can be employed very quickly, very cheaply, and by virtually any person. This is important given the informality of many events that must be begun fairly.

4. Skills

A very limited skill set is demanded by the procedure of a coin toss. One need only make the coin spin so that when it stops, heads or tails appears randomly. Skills training for coin-tossers would consist only of that one capability. ***"Skills" for problem solving are functionally defined and measured by what is required to advance the particular procedure which we have selected to address the problem.***

5. Ethics

The ethics associated with a given procedure also derive from the procedure itself. Behaviors that would disrupt the smooth operation of the system are prohibited. Any behavior that deliberately attempts to influence or override the random nature of the coin toss would be unethical. Using a weighted coin that over-produces heads, for example, would be considered unethical. So also would be catching the coin and, stealing a quick glance at the outcome, turning it over somehow before revealing the outcome to others. The needed personal qualities apply not only to the umpires who flip the coin, but also to the team members who call the coin and observe its fall. Only designated team members are permitted to participate in the coin-toss. Appointed by a coach or elected by the team as team captains, the individuals chosen are honored for their abilities as well as trusted for their level-headedness in beginning the game smoothly.

6. Cultural Influences

We would not imagine using a coin toss to decide all sorts of other matters that demand different sorts of truth, or that require generation of information in non-random ways. We would not use a coin toss to choose between two candidates for President of the United States, or to determine liability between the plaintiff and defendant in a lawsuit. This is so even though a binary-structured truth like "the Republican wins," or "judgment for the defendant" could theoretically resolve the underlying problems in the sense that a clear winner is produced. Electing a President or determining legal liability are problems for which our culture demands a non-arbitrary style of truth. We want the decision to take into account human judgment.

7. Truth and Knowledge

Truth qualities and the nature of information produced by a coin toss stand deeply in the background of the design of the procedure. The problem of first positions in athletic events requires a black or white, either/or sort of truth; for this problem's outcome we cannot tolerate grey. But reaching that information must be done absolutely fairly, without human intervention or judgment. A simple random selection device that transparently produces a binary response suits the problem nicely.

We think we have good instincts about what sorts of procedures are appropriately used to resolve different sorts of problems. In fact, however, the appropriate matching of problems with procedures is not instinctive. It only seems so because successful problem solving systems are evolved procedures with the following qualities:

*   They satisfy our demands for truth and fairness in addressing the specific contours of that problem;

*   the skills required to operate the procedure competently are discernable and available; and

*   the ethical discharge of those skills can be enforced so that neither the efficacy nor the fairness of the procedure is compromised.

B. Legal Procedures and Legal Systems

We now can expand our thinking from the procedure of the coin toss to address the problem of first positions in sports, to that of the legal procedures that traditionally are employed to address legal problems. We rarely stop to consider the relationships among even those two the elements of our legal problem-solving system. The connections, however, are many and complex. Examining some of those connections takes an important first step toward broadening our understanding of the legal system.

1. Problems and Procedures

Procedures for addressing recurring human problems are yoked together. Problems drive the invention of procedures, but once designed, procedures shape how we

> Problems are deeply intertwined with the procedures for resolving them.

perceive problems. Said differently, nagging problems are the impetus for inventing procedures for resolving those problems. But the converse relationship also is strong: existing procedures come to shape our mental framing or categorization of problems.

Once we have a procedure available for resolving certain problems–be the procedure "the law," or "the market" or "politics," "therapy," or "technology"–the problems that are customarily addressed by that procedure tend to be shaped in our minds according to the inputs required to make that procedure work properly. This is a paradox of mental framing or categorization: the boxes in which we have learned to think offer us coherence and shortcuts, but at the same time those boxes constrain our imagination. ***Problem frames create structures through which we can see some parts of a problem without distraction, but those same structures then block our vision of other parts of the problem.***

As problems and procedures co-evolve, a tension builds between efficiency and imagination. If we process a problem according to the criteria by which the problem is traditionally resolved, we will gain reliability in our decision-making. That is, we will tend to resolve it the same way, again and again.

> Mistakenly, we often "frame" or understand problems by the procedures we traditionally use to resolve the problem

But are our solutions valid? Have we gotten it right? In assessing this we will have a strong tendency to compare the resolution of the instant problem against evolved, approved criteria for its resolution. Rarely will we stop to imagine whether altogether different criteria *should* be used to judge how well we have solved the problem. Even when we try to refine our decision-making on a given problem, we tend to imagine changes only in those criteria that will still fit easily within the procedures that we customarily use for addressing the problem.

For example, among lawyers a story involving two neighboring property owners with a border dispute or conflicting uses of property will likely be framed immediately as a "legal problem." As part of their training, lawyers have read cases involving similar problems, and how they were treated. They have learned the particular legal criteria by which such matters are judged. Even when lawyers consciously attempt to re-think the resolution of property squabbles, therefore, they will tend toward refining or reforming the legal rules. They will stay, in other words, within the criteria that are suitable for the procedures that have always been used to address what lawyers have come to understand as a "legal" problem. But what if the better way to resolve the problem involves aspects of the problem that legal rules tend to block from sight? What if the better way to address the neighbor problem is to simply to become more neighborly?

Here is how Louis M. Brown and Edward A. Dauer describe this processing of human problems as legal problems:

> People (and institutions) seldom have problems pre-labeled "legal."
> Even a matter which has crystalized into the receipt of a complaint and
> summons for, say, an unpaid obligation, comprises a large background" of
> persons and facts and a more immediate "figure" of legal proceedings. There
> is, even in such a common and minor matter: at least one broken-down

relationship between persons (debtor and creditor); a person (client) for whom a lawsuit is an extraordinary event (and the psychological perturbations which litigations' immanency generates); a financial disruption of greater or lesser degree; possibly, intra-family strains; social notoriety (either positive or negative) and accompanying anxiety, or the perception of community norms as they relate to enmeshment with the legal process–to name just a few. In a non-dispute matter the distinction between the "legal" and the "non-legal" is even more difficult to ascertain. Thus, in an estate plan there are a variety a hybrid issues: family structure; rewards and punishments; charitable propensities; protection of other persons; preservation of institutions created during life; expressions of affection; and so on and on.[1]

This book attempts to alert legal professionals that our procedures and special form of reasoning are not immune from psychological and institutional inertia. Does "thinking like a lawyer" presume that a particular procedure will be used in addressing legal problems?

> What does it mean to "think like a lawyer?" If lawyers used different procedures, would they think differently?

If we were to adopt different procedures for preventing or resolving legal problems, would not lawyers "think" differently? If we maintain an inflexible understanding of what legitimately can constitute legal reasoning, will we not unconsciously limit the invention or effectiveness of new procedures?

Legal professionals have learned well how to resolve an immense diversity of problems. We have built up a huge pile of legal rules, and developed appellate review procedures to ensure consistency in our decisions. No doubt we have gotten it right pretty often. As suggested in the Introduction, the evolution of legal systems is arguably one of the finest achievements of human history. But could we do better, at least regarding some problems?

Actually, a better question might be whether we could seriously imagine otherwise. Can we seriously believe that we have reached the end of procedural history, the best of all possible problem-solving worlds? Or do perhaps our evolved legal procedures and legal reasoning leave out aspects of risk, relationship, emotion, or environmental design that we should be considering? Could we better prevent some problems from happening? For those problems that do erupt, could legal professionals address them in ways that minimize their potential for recurrence? Can we imagine that encounters with lawyers and the legal system actually improve rather than strain the social relationships of our clients? Can we imagine that lawyers and their approaches to problems might serve as moral lessons for all who observe, rather than as fodder for jokes?

---

[1] Louis M. Brown and Edward A. Dauer, PLANNING BY LAWYERS: MATERIALS ON A NONADVERSARIAL LEGAL PROCESS 49 (1976) (hereafter PLANNING BY LAWYERS).

The preventive and problem solving approach to law and lawyering asks that we reconsider the system of procedures, skills, ethics, and mentality that we traditionally bring to human problems. *We should reconsider our approach for the sake of serving better our clients and profession. We should also reconsider our approach for our own sakes, so that we may build more satisfying professional lives. Finally, we should reconsider for the sake of the rule of law and sustaining it in the surrounding culture.*

As we build a prevention/problem solving framework for understanding and practicing law, we should keep in mind *seven Simple Truths*:

- 1. It is almost always better to *prevent* a problem than to fight it after it has arisen.

- 2. Lawyers are well-situated to *foresee* possible problems, and to suggest helpful interventions.

- 3. Honest, frequent, respectful two-way *communication* between lawyer and client is crucial.

- 4. Lawyers should always strive to *learn* as much as they can about a client's business, family, organization, or goals.

- 5. Reward and risk need not proceed in lockstep, with high reward attainable only through taking on high risk. Often the prospects for reward are enhanced by *lowering* risks.

- 6. When problems do arise, the *means* employed for addressing those problems matters deeply. *How* we attempt to solve problems goes far to constituting ourselves ethically.

- 7. Methods for resolving problems are *humanly invented*, and we have not reached the end of that human history.

2. Skills and Procedures

The relationship of problems to procedures is highly complex, but also helpful in understanding our legal procedures and legal mentality. The relationship of procedures to skills is far simpler, but only slightly less significant.

Human capabilities limit the design of procedures for addressing problems. However theoretically attractive, a procedure simply will not be designed for a problem if no one has the skill to implement the procedure, just as a musical composition that exceeds human technical abilities will be relegated to musical obscurity.

Once designed and implemented as feasible, however, procedures then prompt the refinement and democratization of human capabilities. More people will become more skillful at new procedures, if the procedures are effective. If a software engineer wants to create an innovative program, the computer demands that the engineer develop strong code-writing skills. If an attorney wants to be successful at litigation, legal procedures demand that the attorney must develop strong advocacy skills.

Building new preventive and problem-solving procedures must be practical. We should be mindful of what skills and sensibilities are within our grasp now, and what we may attain through training. And we should also beware: the behaviors that will be refined and practiced throughout our profession are shaped by the skills that our procedures reward. It does little good to urge that lawyers develop empathic skills toward their clients if the procedures for resolving legal problems ignore, or even punish, deeper connections between lawyer and client. We all want to be successful. Indeed, efforts toward that end for our clients are our professional responsibility. If our procedures reward contentiousness, then we will build debaters. If our procedures reward understanding and empathic communication, then we will build good listeners. On a day to day level, lawyers will behave as the skills of our legal procedures require. If we do not like the skills that legal procedures seem to force on us, then we should broaden the range of procedures. In building legal systems, let us adopt procedures that are not only effective, but that will create better client relationships, stronger respect for legal methods, and more satisfying careers.

3. Ethics and Procedures

Even professional ethics partake of this double-edged relationship with procedures. ***Ethics limit the design of our procedures. Once procedures are designed, however, those procedures then shape ethics.*** For example, morality clearly limits what procedures are deemed acceptable to use toward resolving a given sort of problem. We would not adopt the procedure of executing all burglars, even if we became convinced that the measure would drive prospective burglars into daylight hours so that they could be more easily detected. The measure is morally objectionable even though it could move us toward a worthy goal.

Conversely, though, we often define our professional ethics by the behaviors that will make our adopted procedures effective or ineffective. Behaviors that would disrupt the smooth operation of a procedure are likely to be declared professionally irresponsible. That makes sense: if society has invested in setting up a given procedure, especially one that is so rigorous that it can only be accessed or operated by professionally trained people, then we will not tolerate behaviors that compromise that very system. If we have constructed a procedure based on the testimony of people who have been sworn to tell the truth, then we will not tolerate a professional who promotes perjury when clients are placed on the witness stand.

4. Culture, Problems, and Procedures

Recall Simple Truth #6: "the **means** employed for addressing those problems matters deeply. **How** we attempt to solve problems goes far to constituting ourselves ethically." Our choice of procedures affects how we conceive problems, the skills or behaviors we use to address problems, and what we declare as professionally ethical and unethical. Those choices are influenced by the culture we have inherited, but that culture is evolving constantly.

Consider, for example, a hypothetical problem developed at New York University. A parent has learned from outside sources that a gifted teacher being considered for promotion to assistant principal at the child's school is prone to seizures. As an assistant principal, the teacher would be responsible for the students' welfare on field trips and inter-school events. Although the teacher takes anti-seizure medications, these carry their own side effects. The parent worries: if she alerts other parents and school officials about the teacher's illness, will the parent open herself to tort liability? If the school acts on the information by denying the promotion, will the school be violating the Americans with Disabilities Act?

Traditional legal procedures could be engaged to work through these relationships, but at what costs? Win or lose, would a sincere and talented teacher be humiliated? Would the parent be forced to withdraw the child? Would the school have spent thousands on litigation costs that could have been spent on enrichment activities for the students? Will the students take away a message about how power is summoned in our society to address risks that may be negligible, raised by people who are afraid of labels they do not understand?

A better approach may be to inform everyone at the school, teachers and students alike, about the nature of this illness and the course that a seizure would likely take. A substantial number of people could then be trained in how to respond if the assistant principle should happen to experience a seizure.[2] Acting preventively would very likely avert any negative consequences of a seizure, no matter when it may occur. Perhaps more importantly, educating the students (and their teachers and parents) about this illness would help shape a culture toward connecting supportively with the principal rather than limiting or excluding someone who carries an unusual personal quality.

It would be presumptuous to imagine that we can stand apart from the values and attitudes with which we were raised, and are every day surrounded. And yet the choices that we make about our procedures will also affect how others think, feel, and behave–both inside and outside the legal realm. As it runs alongside culture, the law can influence the direction that culture takes, if not precisely the style with which it moves. The choices facing our profession

---

[2] *See generally* Martha Minow, MAKING ALL THE DIFFERENCE: INCLUSION, EXCLUSION, AND AMERICAN LAW (1990).

and each person who practices within it are thus both sobering and exhilarating.

5. *Learning in a Law Office*

The six elements of addressing human problems–problems, procedures, skills, ethics, truth and culture--evolve together, as a system. That may account for our lack of reflection about their interaction. We take their many relationships for granted as a sort of natural category, an integrated whole that need not be disentangled.

The thesis of this book, however, is that taking apart these six elements and their various relationships will deepen our understanding of the legal system. Hopefully, it will also improve our effectiveness as legal professionals, advance our appreciation of both the genius and the limitations of legal problem-solving, and lead to a more thoughtful, reflective, respectful, and satisfying practice.

As considered in Chapter II, much stress will be laid on considering the differing contexts in which matters arise. In studying Preventive/Proactive Law, the context will often be within a lawyer's office. The simple picture of a conversation between lawyer and client, perhaps before any problem or dispute, before any adversary appears--that is the context in which many legal decisions are made, and much preventive action taken. By studying the law office context, we can gain many insights, not only about relationships between lawyer and client, but about important aspects of the legal system. Here is how Brown and Dauer explain the legal functions discharged within a law office, and how those functions differ institutionally from other sources of law:

> [T]he law office (by which we mean the solo lawyer as well as the large law firm) may usefully be regarded as the law's fourth significant institution, the other three being the judiciary, the legislature, and the executive (and its administrative agencies). The law office bears certain interesting characteristics which make it similar to the other three, and certain others which make it dissimilar. Yet when viewed from another perspective, the law office also shares certain relevant features with numerous *non*-legal institutions (and individuals).

> Consider, for example, two functions which law offices serve ... . One is the giving of advice concerning present or proposed courses of action. The other is the rendering (often the implementation) of decisions concerning some person's ... affairs.

> Law offices give advice constantly, and on a broad range of matters. ... [T]he bulk of all law practice involves advising clients. Other legal institutions serve this advising function as well, but in significantly different ways.

Legislatures, for example, do so only in a highly attenuated sense of the word–all public laws with sanctions attached have some educational function, but the range of possible "client" behaviors addressed is extraordinarily small, and the function is virtually never personalized to any one individual's set of goals and opportunities. Courts do advise on occasion–the declaratory judgment, for example, is a form of judicial advising. However, the range of possibilities is quite narrow–first because the substantive limits on declaratory relief severely constrain the sorts of questions which can be entertained; secondly because the court's decision is typically "yes" or "no." The court will not *sua sponte* raise and advise with respect to alternative courses of future action not expressly presented by the supplicant. ...

Administrative agencies vary considerably in their advising function: the Federal Trade Commission, the Federal Reserve Board and others often publish "compliance manuals" designed to advise individuals and businesses on the methods of satisfying some statute or agency rule. And, on occasion, agencies such as the Internal Revenue Service will offer a rough equivalent to declaratory interlocutory judgments. In both cases, however, the subject matter is narrowly constrained, the advice is either impersonal or is of the yes-no variety, and–as with courts–access is often procedurally difficult and sometimes geographically more remote than is the case with the law office.

The lawyer differs in significant ways from these other legal institutions. His advice potentially extends to any matter of concern to [the] client; ... considerations may include alternatives never theretofore imagined by the client and may expose areas of consultation which the client did not have in mind. And, while there are economic and sometimes geographic constraints on the offering of the lawyer's advice, these are normally less of a barrier than is the case with the other legal institutions. Figures are not available to show how many lawyer-client consultations take place in a given time period; it seems intuitively sound to suggest that they compare favorably in number with the direct contacts of people with courts, many executive agencies, and legislative institutions. Moreover, while the "macrojustice" lawsuit may affect large numbers of people, ... the greatest run of decisions by courts and agencies have but an attenuated effect on most private individuals' affairs. The law office, on the other hand, impacts on its clients directly, frequently, and significantly.

Advice comes from many quarters–from family, friends, business associates, ministers, real estate brokers, insurance agents, and so on. With respect to a wide variety of matters the lawyer is only one of innumerable sources of advice and counseling. Nevertheless, there are two points to be observed. One is that, for some portion of the range of all possible matters, the law office is the only legally permissible source of professional advice.

Second, and perhaps more important, is the fact that lawyer's decisions *are qualitatively* different from those made by many of those other sources.

Legislatures, courts and agencies all make decisions. Within the limits of appeals and judicial review, their decisions are binding on the individual. Pragmatically, they are most often "obeyed"–social suasion and the threat of sanction both tend to instigate conformity. Lawyers' decisions share in this obedience to a considerable degree–the lawyer's conclusions that some matter should be handled in this-and-such a way is typically observed, probably more so than would be that of the friend or family member. The lawyer is seen, with respect to a broad range of matters, as "authoritative" in the sense that [her] decisions are predicated upon The Law, and that [she] is society's only legally sanctioned source for such decision-making.

This view of the lawyer, then, leads to the following hypothesis: The law office is unlike other legal institutions (courts, legislatures, and agencies) in that its advice and decision functions are more generally available and are often more widely used; it is virtually unlimited in counseling scope and possibility, not "binary" or "yes-no" but rather expansive and potentially thorough; and for a relatively wide range of matters the law office is the only "authoritative"source of professional guidance and decision. But, unlike other non-legal sources (friends, family, etc.) obedience to a law office's advice or decision is relatively high; indeed, it is in this respect more like a legally authoritative source than is any other type of "advisor." Therefore, the decisions a lawyer makes for (and about!) [the] client are frequent, binding, and wide-ranging in scope. They have potentially enormous (future) impacts on important aspects of the client's affairs. And, once made, lawyers' decisions are hard to undo. The decision to omit an attorney's fee provision in a contract, for example, as a practical matter is about as binding as the decision of any court–there is no "appeal" from such a lawyer's decision. An irrevocable trust, once established, cannot normally be revoked: Rights fixed or lost in the present determine the future, often irrevocably and without right of appeal.

What, then, is at stake in lawyer-client counseling? And what is the empirical importance of the law office as a social institution? ... One more question: The decisions which emerge from the lawyer-client consultation–from the lawyer's advice and the lawyer's or the client's act–are often marked by finality. To whom is this attributable–the lawyer? Or the client? Who decides to make the trust irrevocable?[3]

---

[3] PLANNING BY LAWYERS, *supra* note 1, at 49–52 (citations omitted).

CHAPTER IV
AT THE BOUNDARY OF CHANGES: Lawyers Thinking Preventively and Proactively

A. Where We Start

Consider a hypothetical:[1] Miller owns a parcel of land, on one half of which Miller owns and operates an "outdoor living" business. The other half of Miller's property is a vacant lot. Periodically, Miller stores shipping crates and packing materials on the vacant lot. On the other side of that vacant lot is Jones, who is a metal sculptor. For many years, Jones has stored wire, scrap metal, and flat steel mounting plates on the vacant lot owned by Miller. These two uses of the lot easily co-existed: the land was large enough to accommodate the storage of both Miller's packing and shipping materials and Jones's metals supplies. In this hypothetical, Jones may or may not have asked permission from Miller to use Miller's land; certainly nothing is in writing between the two parties. Although Jones's metal is clearly visible to Miller, Miller has never charged Jones any rent or storage fees. Jones has never offered to help with the upkeep or taxes on the property.

Miller's business has now expanded, and Miller needs a larger building. Miller is looking to build on the vacant lot, which would displace Jones's metals storage space. Each of the parties now consults his or her respective lawyer. If you were the attorney for either party, how would you approach this problem?

This hypothetical illustrates a centuries-old recurring type of human problem, the sort of problem which shaped our law as a problem solving system. Again and again in the agricultural economy in

> Using traditional legal procedures, legal rules have a binary quality, producing one winner.

which the law developed, neighboring landowners had disputes over conflicting uses of land.

Common law rules evolved to speak unequivocally in favor of one party or the other. The law framed the problem as a boundary dispute between Miller and Jones. Miller, as the title owner of the vacant lot, had unfettered control over the possession and use of the land, entitling Miller to oust Jones as a trespasser. The rule was simple, and easily proven by documents describing the boundaries of Miller's lot. If Jones were obstreperous, the sheriff could be dispatched to enforce Jones's ejectment. On the other hand, Jones could satisfy the elements of adverse possession, then Jones would be awarded title to the land or easement for Jones's

---

[1] This example is based on problems created at William and Mary College of Law as part of their award-winning course integrating professional ethics with legal skills training. The generosity of Prof. James Moliterno in sharing content from the course he developed is greatly appreciated.

historic access and use of the land.

Such simple, clear property rules with binary outcomes have much to recommend them, especially in an agrarian economy characterized by relatively low literacy rates. The information costs are low for such rules in that they are easily spread by word of mouth. Further, these rules permit only a narrow range of what is considered relevant evidence. Hence discovery costs are also low.

Procedures for applying such laws can also be simple and fast. Land is the economic lifeblood of the agrarian economy, so no one is benefitted by acreage lying unused while a protracted legal proceeding determined ownership. Finally, clarity makes corrective negotiations available. Even if Jones's utility for the land were higher than Miller's, a judgment in favor of Miller could facilitate the start of negotiations between Miller and Jones for the sale or easement of the property.

What role would the attorneys play in this system? An attorney meeting Miller or Jones for the first time would be concerned to uncover such facts as the land boundaries; any possible consent by Miller to Jones's use; the length of time of Jones's use; the degree of its openness and exclusivity; and any possible break in Jones's possession or use. The attorneys' conversations with their respective clients would focus on how the facts map onto the legal elements of license and adverse possession. Each attorney would envision the courtroom, with the judge delivering that binary declaration of rights between the parties. By design of those legal procedures, not much would be open for conversation. The court would proceed rationally, however narrowly defined. With the sheriff lurking in the background, the court would employ power instrumentally to a prescribed end of vindicating the legal rules. The end result would be to take these parties whose interests were seen as intersecting ominously, and separate them crisply.

Employing the R/S/P paradigm–the tools of rationality, power, and separation--social order is safeguarded against the otherwise possible violent self-help by Miller or Jones. No place would be reserved in the system for a conversation about the needs of the broader community; nor, between these two individuals, for conversations about charity, mercy, empathy, grace, dignity, or even respect. The court would not care about their future personal relationship. The court would not imagine empowering the disputants to collaborate toward something mutually beneficial. Instrumental power, narrow rationality, and a prudent separation of people: the R/S/P paradigm contains the primary tools of our traditional legal heritage.

So can we perhaps forgive our attorneys who, in representing Jones and Miller historically, would confine their imaginations and their client conversations to questions that fill out the attorney's respective courtroom arguments about trespass and adverse possession?

Yes and no. Yes, in that gathering facts from their clients that are pertinent to applicable legal rules is both an essential skill and a professional responsibility of our legal system. Clients must always be protected, and sometimes the only way to do that is through summoning the court-directed power of the state. In narrowing their gaze to parallel that of the judge, they would be representing their clients in a fail-safe way.

But gathering those legally-essential facts is not mutually exclusive with potentially doing far more, both preventively and proactively. So in that sense we must answer "no," the attorneys should be held to a higher standard of practice.

First, if either attorney had a stronger relationship with his or her client, the problem could have been easily averted. If Miller, having noticed that Jones was using Miller's property, had communicated with Miller's attorney for even a brief conversation, that attorney would have drawn up a rental or license agreement–even for a nominal consideration–that would have foreclosed any later argument about adverse possession. Reciprocally, if Jones were aware of Miller's ownership of the land Jones was using, a low cost permanent easement might have been arranged.

Here is the irony: ***by behaving only in the fail-safe mode of client representation that mimics how a courtroom would treat this problem, the attorney will not develop a relationship with the client that permits the client to benefit from law-office treatment of the problem.*** If the attorney sees the client merely as a vehicle for filling out the facts of a legal argument, the lawyer is not acting as a counselor. The lawyer is not inviting the sort of relationship that will prompt the client to communicate with the lawyer in advance of a problem erupting. And thus the lawyer is not able to practice, nor the client to benefit from, Preventive Law.

Counseling clients differs from interviewing them.[2] It requires learning as much as possible about them as people, as participants in business ventures, family or estate matters, or even as criminally accused persons. ***A client should leave an attorney's office feeling heard, with a sense that the attorney cares about the client's well-being and personal relationships, and that the attorney can be helpful.*** And all the more helpful the more regularly the client has a conversation with the attorney, because that is how the attorney can work with the client to identify and address risks before they become real problems.

> If the attorney sees the client merely as a vehicle for filling out the facts of a legal argument, the lawyer is not acting as a counselor.

It is almost always better to prevent a problem than to fight it once it has arisen. This is the first of our seven Simple Truths introduced above, and one that virtually any client can understand if the attorney takes a moment to explain it. The attorney should also convince the client that the attorney is not simply trying to extract additional fees from the client. Quite the contrary. The attorney should be conveying to the client that ***regular conversations or "legal***

---

[2] Louis M. Brown, *Analyzing a Lawyer/Client Consultation*, 7th Annual Institute on Estate Planning, Univ. of Miami Law Center 9-2 (1973).

check-ups" are often the most effective and cheapest legal representation. The client is not always in a position to discern or measure the gravity of a possible legal risk. By periodic conversations with a client about all aspects of a client's life, incipient legal problems can be addressed quickly and efficiently. Often, making a small but early intervention will not only avoid future costs, but proactively help the client achieve the client's goals.

We could also fault the exclusive use of the fail-safe approach by the Jones and Miller attorneys if, faced with an actual problem, they do not explore more imaginative problem-solving possibilities:

- If the attorneys understand that the rationality employed in formal litigation is narrowly understood to wring out human emotion or sentiment, they could try expanding that rationality on their own.

- If the attorneys understand that the legal system routinely separates people by articulating rights and duties that the people have against one another, the attorneys could think about solutions to the problem that connect the claimants in shared interests, or at least in an accommodative settlement.

- If the attorneys understand that the power exercised by a court is a command-and-control to effectuate a particular state of affairs, the attorneys could consider trying to employ the power of cooperation or reciprocity, and seeing what the parties can make for themselves.

Once again, even after a problem has arisen, the nexus between attorneys and clients should not be solely that of legal rules and liability. The purpose of our legal system is not to vindicate legal rules. The purpose of our legal system is simultaneously to facilitate human interaction and self-protection. Attorneys can often accomplish both of those aims by good advice delivered from a law office. It does not always require the intervention of legal rules or the power of a court.

Consider again Jones and Miller. Their businesses could be complementary. Homeowners interested in outdoor environments are interested in the appearance of their homes. Such prospective customers are good for a metal sculptor, especially one that may be capable of fabricating large works that could be the design centerpiece of a patio or pool area. Sometimes fencing and artistic gates could use custom metal ornamentation, hinges, or handle grips. And artists often have strong design backgrounds. What better way to supplement the sculptor's art sales than to branch out into outdoor hardscape design that would expand what Miller has been able to offer customers? Could Jones and Miller jointly develop the vacant lot to suit both of their storage needs? Could they turn part of it into a public showcase displaying their design efforts, furniture, and art? Once the attorneys broaden their gaze beyond the fail-safe legal rules, alternative ways to address the problem arise that draw on the power of mutual interest and imagination.

If the attorneys understand the legal problem as taxonomists, limiting their interaction with Jones and Miller by framing their questions as part of a "trespass" case or an "adverse possession" case, then this human problem between Jones and Miller has been captured too strongly by the legal doctrines and procedures that were designed to resolve it. The input demanded by legal procedures—i.e., facts that map onto the elements of legal rules—will have pushed from anyone's imagination alternative possibilities for resolving it. In the chapters that follow, we will examine the phenomenon of framing issues and suggest ways to use framing to open rather than to close windows. We will also explore further the ideas of the U/I/A paradigm by opening up the legal understanding of rationality; by preventing and solving problems through connection rather than separation; and by understanding power as the ability to enlist the cooperation and contributions of others.

B. Where We Want to End: The Goals of Preventive Law

Here is how I once expressed the limitations of traditional "thinking like a lawyer." It first appeared as *Practicing Law Preventively and Proactively*, 23 EUROLAWYER 12 (2005):

> Traditional lawyering is often reactive and constrained. Frequently, a client comes to the lawyer only after some injury or loss has occurred. The lawyer selectively questions the client, looking for particular facts that the attorney then maps onto legal rules so as to assess liability. Aspects of the client's social relationships, emotional make-up, financial prospects, or organizational structure that do not contribute to proving or disproving these rules are not, legally speaking, relevant. And so they often remain unspoken.

> Unspoken and unresolved. The problem may not stay in the immediate legal boxes into which the attorney has attempted to stuff it. It may spill over into other aspects of the client's life or enterprise, and it may attack the client again. Practicing preventively means building a larger and more secure container--one that will constrain consequences that are both legal and non-legal, both immediate and likely for the future.

> Consider, for example, the problem of sexual harassment in the workplace. A purely legal approach to the problem would begin *only* when a complaint has been lodged or injury suffered—when, in other words, a legal rule is claimed to have been violated, leading to possible legal liability. The purely legal approach would assess the merits of the claim by investigating the facts, and then analyzing those facts against the elements of existing statutes and regulations. If the facts satisfy the legal criteria constituting harassment, then settlement negotiations may begin. Where legal or factual arguments may be raised to contest the claim, the lawyers may prepare for litigation. The purpose of the litigation would be to determine two issues only: blame or exoneration

under the rules; and the extent of compensation where liability is proven.

Issues of legal liability are frequently vital to a client's concerns. Preventive lawyers understand that well, and work as needed within those traditional frameworks. But they also do more. Just because the legal dimension is particularly serious does not mean that the non-legal aspects of a problem are somehow lessened. Indeed, as the severity of legal concerns rise for a client, it is likely that the severity of non-legal consequences will also rise. Non-legal issues may matter greatly to the client, since many of the problems that prompt people to consult lawyers are accompanied by personal stress or disruptions of personal or business relationships. Furthermore, these dimensions contribute significantly to the risk that the immediate problem, ***even if addressed satisfactorily from a legal standpoint,*** will recur in similar or disguised form.

In the example of sexual harassment, strong feelings may well exist on both sides of the controversy: shame, embarrassment, anger, guilt, or frustration. Furthermore, the conflict is set within an organization that may or may not promote awareness and understanding of this specific issue, or in general promote mutual respect among the employees. If the emotional, organizational, and cultural aspects of the immediate problem are not addressed through better everyday communication and stronger informal dispute resolution channels, then the problem will not go away. Contests over legal liability will continue, and meanwhile employee morale and productivity will suffer.

Practicing law preventively therefore means examining problems more broadly, in two ways: first, by expanding the context of the problem to include pertinent impacts on the client's social or business relationships, personal well-being, financial capabilities, or organizational efficacy. Second, practicing preventively means stretching the time dimensions in which the problem is considered. The attorney should explore with the client not only the immediate effects and legal blameworthiness of the problem, but also the *antecedents* to the problem. What caused it to occur?

In considering the underlying causes of problems, preventive/proactive lawyers think systemically. That is, they understand problems as the end result of what may be a long series of interactions within a system comprised of people (and their attendant ambitions, relationships, and patterns of communication) along with physical, technological, or economic opportunities and constraints. Understanding problems as starting within these complex systems of interactions will enable the attorney to assess the likelihood that the problem will recur, and take preventive measures.

Furthermore, the same expanded vision that can help lawyers prevent future legal harms may also open the attorney's imagination to a variety of possible non-legal interventions that can help clients achieve their objectives. This is so even where the lawyer is not expert in the particulars of the client's operations or relationships. Such proactive advice is neither unrealistic nor unprofessional. Lawyers are well trained to think clearly, objectively, analytically, and systemically. During years of practice, lawyers also accumulate a reservoir of experiences about human foibles and potential, and about complex financial and political environments. That combination of objective analytical thought and long-term observation of a variety of client settings places attorneys in a good position to offer helpful counsel on social, political, financial, organizational, and emotional issues.

Doing so may step beyond the formal role that is traditionally perceived for lawyers. It does not, however, step beyond the practical, informal role that lawyers have served for generations. Lawyers have long been valued for the strength of their judgment, character, and intellect as well as for their formal legal opinions. So long as the attorney does not overstep his or her training or experience, the more proactive role is not unprofessional. Indeed, it can make the lawyer's traditional legal work more effective by encouraging clients to consult attorneys earlier in the development of a problem or prospective transaction. The earlier the lawyer is consulted, the more legal alternatives or arrangements are typically available. And the more alternatives available, the broader the range of strategic planning that can make transactions more efficient and effective.

Skills for Practicing More Preventively and Proactively

The skills for practicing more preventively and proactively include: (1) communicating more broadly and frequently with clients to widen the context in which problems can be understood; (2) thinking systemically about how problems arise, so that problem antecedents can be comprehensively identified; and (3) devising interventions that will smooth existing frictions, create multiple channels of communication so that future friction is reduced, and assist in the quick, non-legal resolution of problems that do arise.

(1) Communicating Better with Clients

The preventive/proactive vision of lawyering challenges attorneys in two ways: first, to create closer relationships between themselves and their clients; and second, to think beyond the legal rules and legal solutions of their formal training. This second challenge toward stronger, broader, thinking cannot occur unless the first challenge–better communication with clients–is first achieved.

Growing numbers of lawyers find that they can move gradually toward a more preventive practice by learning more about their clients, and enlisting the help of their clients regarding factual matters. Because lawyers traditionally need to match the particulars of a client's situation with legal rules, lawyers often limit their communications with clients to pointed questions about factual issues that are directly pertinent to those rules. Becoming more preventive and proactive begins by lawyers learning more about the general backgrounds and goals of all their clients; and for business clients in particular, attorneys should become familiar with the client's products, operations, financing, and markets.

Going to visit the premises of business clients, for example, has many benefits. Looking around a factory or service operation may help identify legal risks that could be invisible to the client. Or it may reveal more efficient ways to comply with legal regulation, areas in which employee training should be stronger, or opportunities for better systems of communication within the organization. Furthermore, becoming better informed about the client and its operations will help the lawyer be more practical as well as imaginative in suggesting needed interventions.

Quite apart from how greater intimacy with a client's business will enhance lawyering, it will strengthen the lawyer/client relationship. Clients tend to think more highly of their lawyers when lawyers make an effort to become more familiar with the client. For the client, such efforts mirror what they regard as essential business practice: knowing an environment thoroughly–economically, geographically, or personally--before making business judgments that must be carried out in that environment. Furthermore, when a lawyer shows genuine interest in what the client does or cares about, the client may appreciate how the lawyer is respecting their individuality and demonstrating a willingness to work creatively on their behalf.

(2) Thinking Systemically About Problems and Their Solutions

Problems are best conceived as friction between human purpose and the environments or settings in which those purposes are pursued. Effective lawyering can help to eliminate that friction, no matter its source. But reconciling purpose with environment always starts by understanding both.

Human purposes are pursued in a broad variety of settings, typically from within a set of social relationships that are subject to physical, economic, or regulatory constraints. Each separate dimension of a client's environment–social, physical, financial, legal–may be the source of some friction or obstacle to achieving the client's purposes. Pathologies may stem from clumsy or hateful social interactions among individuals; or from awkward or even dangerous physical environments that people must navigate; or from shriveled communications within inflexible bureaucracies or hierarchic organizations.

If recurrences of a client's immediate problem are to be prevented, then something in those pathological patterns must be changed. The greater the depth of understanding of the multiple contributing causes of a problem, the greater the latitude for suggested interventions that may reverse existing frictions. Happily, however, the very complexity and systemic quality of most recurring problems is also their vulnerability. The more problematic links that can be identified, the more opportunities for intervention by lawyers who understand the dynamics of the system.

(3) Devising Interventions

Traditional legal solutions--stronger legal rights or better compliance with legal regulation–are often helpful interventions. This is particularly so where some aspect of a client's environment requires more regularity or structure. But lawyers can also advance client goals by, for example, identifying people within an organization who are working consciously or unconsciously at cross purposes. Or they can devise training sessions or videos for employees that will reduce behaviors that are chronically resulting in legal liability. Or they can construct workplace procedures for quickly receiving suggestions or hearing grievances. They may set up methods for the regular review of contracts, and insert clauses that will protect against loss. They may suggest incentive systems for executives, shop-floor workers, and even client customers to improve productivity or sales. Lawyers are constrained in their possible suggestions only by their imagination and knowledge. Expanding both will make practice more interesting, as well as rewarding.

Conclusion

Preventive Law broadens the relationship of law to human problems. To the preventive lawyer, problems represent more than questions about the demands or breach of legal rules. Preventive lawyers understand that legal problems often emerge from dysfunctional patterns of interactions–and that those patterns may not explicitly carry a "legal" label. Smoothing disruptive patterns can prevent problems from becoming chronic, and can also affirmatively help a client achieve the client's objectives.

Being effective at preventive/proactive lawyering requires greater familiarity with the client, by asking more and better questions of the client. Doing so, however, can strengthen one's lawyering, one's relationship with the client, and ultimately, one's sense of purpose as a lawyer.

CHAPTER V
PREVENTIVE LAW: The Dauer Matrix

Private Problem: The Seashore Neighbors Example

The drawing below is another example of a problem between adjoining land owners, one originally suggested and analyzed by Edward A. Dauer:

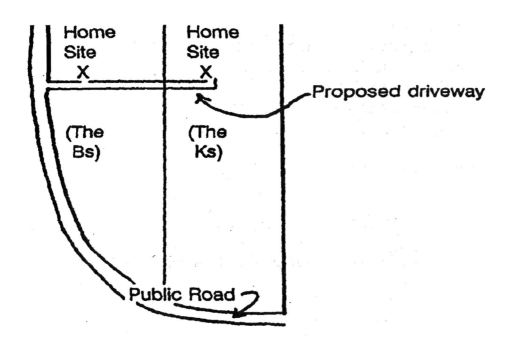

This diagram represents a dilemma for the "B's," a family owning the plot of ground and vacation home just to the west of ground owned by the "K's." The setting is a beautiful seashore, with the ocean stretching westerly from the public road. The K's now wish to build a house on their lot. The terrain is steep and rugged, with the only feasible building site for the K's at the spot as indicated on the map. The K's cannot practicably build a driveway from the public road that approaches their house from the south. But to approach their house from the west, as indicated above by the "proposed driveway" arrow, requires that the K's driveway cross land owned by the B's.

Suppose that the B's, wanting to cooperate and be good neighbors, are willing to accommodate this. Suppose further that you are the attorney for the B's, who have consulted you for advice. Analyzed purely as a "legal" problem, the solution is to create an easement in favor of the K's. Would you simply draft up an agreement for an easement, after agreeing on a one-time payment by the K's for an easement that runs with the land? Would this constitute competent legal representation of the B's? Would your professional responsibility be discharged? Would you have imagined and addressed the risks to B? Would you have solved the problem well?

If we think of the responsibilities of a lawyer to be confined solely to analysis of legal rules, conceivably the answer to the first two questions is "yes." But the answers to the final two questions are clearly "no," as explored below. Therefore perhaps we should rethink exactly what constitutes lawyer competence, and the role of a lawyer in counseling a client.

Here are at least some of the risks to the B's:

- What if much of the B's purpose of having a vacation home is a quiet respite from an otherwise hectic, demanding, jostling work environment?

- What if the K's purpose of having a vacation home is to invite all their friends to frequent, well-lubricated, late-night parties?

- What if the K's own a motor home that could accommodate a 12-piece rock band on tour, the weight of which would prematurely degrade the driveway as it comes and goes? And suppose this vehicle must be parked permanently at the site, potentially blocking the B's view to the southeast.

- Or what if the K's decide to run a bed & breakfast with the six spare bedrooms they have built into their house?

Transferring a permanent easement to the K's is legally proper, but potentially most unwise for the B's. In the long run, noise from shouting people and honking vehicles leaving late at night could ruin the quiet enjoyment of B's vacation stays. Vehicles parking along the shared driveway could even block the B's access at times to their own home. If you begin to think "Well, we could address those problems with a nuisance action," you are not really preventing the problem: you are simply planning how to win a lawsuit that could end up making the problem worse.[1]

For Dauer, foreseeing and addressing potential risks entail considering the ***direct***

---

[1] James Frierson, *Pre-Action Advice May Not Be Preventive Law Advice,* http://preventivelawyer.org/main/default.asp?pid=essays/frierson.htm (hereafter *Pre-action Advice).*

parties (here the B's and K's); but also imagining ***third parties*** and their later involvement (visitors at K's residence; possible trespassers; future grantees of the K's); and any possible ***government regulation or other involvement*** (building and zoning codes; police or judicial intervention). As to each of these distinct sets of human players, measures can be taken at varying stages of the progression from the problem from initial risk, to immunizing against possible damage, to dealing with an injury if such does occur.

- At the initial ***planning*** stage, for example, we could imagine risks associated with the direct parties; the third parties; or the government. Still in the planning stage, we could imagine various structures and methods that might prevent any of those identified risks from erupting into full problems.

- In the event a problem does arise, for each of the groupings of people we could think about ***addressing the problem*** quickly through early warning systems. The hope would be to unearth information that could suggest quick responses to prevent contentious escalation of the problem.

- If that cannot be avoided, then each of the three groupings–direct parties, third parties, or government bodies--can play a foreseeable role in ***resolving the dispute***.

- Finally, ***feedback and follow-up*** measures can help to prevent a recurrence of the problem and foreclose unintended consequences of the solutions adopted.

Dauer's systematic analysis (which I am calling the "Dauer Matrix)" can be expanded yet further to think about steps that may be taken not only among human players, but also on the physical environment in which the problem arises. Represented visually, we create a matrix in which the four domains of "Direct Parties;" "Third Parties;" Government Regulation or Facilitation;" and "Physical Environment" appear on the X axis. Along the Y axis we create the various stages of planning, addressing the problem, resolving a dispute, and feedback/follow-up. The matrix looks like this (see overleaf):

DAUER MATRIX

	Direct Parties	Third Parties	Government Regulation or Facilitation	Physical Environment
1a. Planning: Imagine the risks				
1b. Planning: Imagine various structures and methods to prevent problems from arising				
2. Addressing Problems: Use early warning systems and resulting information to prevent problems from escalating into "disputes"				
3. Dispute Resolution: Take steps to resolve disputes fairly and efficiently, using a succession of methods				
4a. Feedback and Follow-up: Anticipate and foreclose adverse spill-over effects of the resolution itself;				
4b. Feedback and Follow-up: Feed back the nature of the problem and dispute to Step 1, the Planning process				

Through a combination of information supplied by the client, additional attorney research, and imagination, the attorney counseling the B's could begin to fill in the boxes above. The point is to expand systematically the contexts in which the problem, and its attendant risks, are understood. At each stage in the unfolding of a problem, a variety of imaginative possible interventions begin to suggest themselves once the full system is described.

To address client issues in this comprehensive way obviously requires the attorney to think well beyond legal rules. The attorney must gather information from the client about lifestyle, values, and personal relationships with the K's. The attorney must also begin to imagine non-legal sources of risk and solutions. *Failure to supply non-legal solutions would not violate rules of legal ethics. But failure to supply these non-legal interventions would also fail to serve the client as fully as possible.*

Recall Simple Truth #2: that owing to their training in analytical reasoning and broad experience with a variety of human problems, lawyers are well-situated to foresee possible problems and suggest helpful interventions–legal and non-legal. One achieves this through Simple Truths #3 and #4: Honest, frequent, respectful two-way communication between lawyer and client is crucial; and lawyers should always strive to learn as much as they can about a client's business, family, organization, or goals.

In this example, consider the first row of "1A. Planning: Imagine the Risks." One could imagine risks to the B's from the K's through noise; the blocking of access; visual blight from vehicles; overuse of the driveway, especially at night; or a gradual estrangement between the B's and the K's. Risks from third parties include noise and litter from visitors, but also concerns from other neighbors, and new personal relationships that may have to be formed with any successor in interest to the K's. As to risks from the government, these would include any potential violations of building or zoning codes from installing this shared driveway. Finally, the risks to or from the physical environment from building this extended driveway include visual blight from vehicles; possible water drainage problems and ensuing erosion; a possible need for snow removal in the winter; the need for good lighting to ensure safety; and the expense of ongoing upkeep to the driveway, which is made worse by heavy vehicle use.

The resulting chart appears so far as follows (see overleaf):

	Direct Parties	Third Parties	Government Regulation or Facilitation	Physical Environment
1a. Planning: Imagine the risks	noise; estrangement; over-use, especially at night; blocking access of other party	noise from visitors; trespassers; concern of other neighbors; possible new owners upon transfer of land	building codes	visual blight; poor lighting; poor soil; poor drainage; snow removal; need for upkeep

The risks are significant. However, each of the columns represents a potential source of *addressing* the risk as well as creating the risk. This is a happy irony of prevention: the more complex the problem, the more possible points of intervention exist to prevent the problem.

In this example, if the B's were to interact with the K's in certain ways, many of the foreseeable risks could be averted. Perhaps most importantly, the B's could simply attempt to maintain ongoing social interaction and communication with the K's. Strong mutual respect and regard will often prompt mutual accommodation by parties, even to significant injuries that might otherwise lead to blame and lawsuits. Further, the B's and K's could create a clear contract setting out a variety of rights and duties regarding usage of the common driveway (including noise levels and numbers of guests), upkeep expenses, and possible transfer of rights if the B's or the K's were to sell their properties to others.

Third parties are also a source of possible preventive action. For example, signs could be posted at the mouth of the driveway indicating that the driveway is shared and asking for politeness and quiet in their use of the driveway plus respect for the B's continued need for access to their own home and garage. More inventively, the driveway could be made a toll road for visitors. That would discourage overuse and contribute to upkeep costs. It risks unintended consequences, however: if people have paid for the use of the road they may be less respectful or polite in how they use it. As to the government, here contract and easement laws (and their state enforcement) could be useful prevention tools. Finally, thoughtful physical design of the driveway could help considerably in preventing certain problems. The driveway could be located optimally to prevent overcrowding and visual blight. A visual hedge or other landscaping could also help preserve B's views. A turnaround could be supplied for safety so that drivers need not back out of a long, steep drive. Motion sensing lights could illuminate the driveway as needed.

Now our "Planning" rows would be completed:

	Direct Parties	Third Parties	Government Regulation or Facilitation	Physical Environment
1a. Planning: Imagine the risks	noise; estrangement; over-use, especially at night; blocking access of other party	noise from visitors; trespassers; concern of other neighbors; possible new owners upon transfer of land	building codes	visual blight; poor lighting; poor soil; poor drainage; snow removal; need for upkeep
1b. Planning: Imagine various structures and methods to prevent problems from arising	ongoing social interaction and communication; contract setting out rights and duties about costs, usage, transfer of property	signage indicating shared driveway, asking for quiet and no blocking; possible toll road for visitors	contract, easement enforcement	location of driveway; sturdiness; visual hedge; turnaround for vehicles; motion sensing lights

If a problem arises notwithstanding our best planning, then quick action may prevent the problem from escalating into a "dispute." The key is to prompt early communications among the parties affected, and to attempt to make those discussions positive and useful. Between the B's and K's, the contract could require advance notification of any special noise from guests or construction work. Conceivably, the scheduling of parties or noisy driveway maintenance work could be arranged to occur at times that the B's will not be at their home. Another early warning requirement could be about either party's intention to escalate the resolution method of a problem into the legal system.

Third parties, government or private, could be used to address quickly certain sorts of problems. A private security firm could be hired to patrol regularly the driveway and vicinity. Public police could also shine lights onto the driveway as part of their typical neighborhood patrol pattern. Even the physical environment could be altered if needed to respond to particular problems. Speed bumps could be installed to slow down drivers; surveillance cameras could be used to deter noisy, drunken party-leavers. The "addressing the problem" row thus looks like this:

	Direct Parties	Third Parties	Government Regulation or Facilitation	Physical Environment
2. Addressing Problems: Use early warning systems and resulting information to prevent problems from escalating into "disputes"	advance notification requirements for parties or construction work that could create special noise or damage; advance notification requirement prior to invoking escalating dispute resolution methods	regular communication with other neighbors about usage, noise; private security patrols	regular police patrols in neighborhood	speed bumps; surveillance cameras

If problems do escalate into real disputes, then further steps could be triggered that were planned in advance. The contract between the B's and K's could mandate a succession of non-litigation dispute resolution methods: good faith conferring clauses; mediation if negotiation is unavailing; or arbitration if mediation fails. The help of third parties can be anticipated as mediators or arbitrators, but ahead of that the contract could nominate a mutually respected person to be consulted for advice in the event of a dispute: a person whose wise counsel could be taken seriously and hopefully head off escalation. Last resort would be to the government, in the form of police or the judiciary.

In resolving disputes, we should keep in mind our humanity. Recall Simple Truth #6: That when problems do arise, the **means** employed for addressing those problems matter deeply. *How* we attempt to solve problems goes far to constituting ourselves ethically. We should also strive for innovation and pragmatism: we should try to find something that works. Simple Truth #7: Methods for resolving problems are humanly invented, and we have not reached the end of that human history. Hence our table for disputes that must be resolved:

	Direct Parties	Third Parties	Government Regulation or Facilitation	Physical Environment
3. Dispute Resolution: Take steps to resolve disputes fairly and efficiently, using a succession of methods	Contract provisions calling for succession of non-litigation dispute resolution methods	possible disinterested advice-givers; mediators; increasing authoritativeness of third party intervention	possible police or judicial intervention	

Finally, where problems actually arise and are resolved, we should do our best to learn from them. This is important so that we can change our attitudes, relationships, behaviors or environments so that problems will not recur. Learning from our problems or mistakes requires that we think about the antecedents for the problem; take accountability for them; and get information about what went wrong.

We should also be aware that the problems may actually be the unintended consequences of a prior effort to prevent a problem. For example, guests at the K's could be offended by surveillance cameras, or admonitions about noise, or almost certainly by being charged a toll fee for visiting a friend's house. Passively aggressive countermeasures in retaliation could be taken in a variety of ways. These would provide expensive lessons for us. A better approach would be to encourage feedback that could be used to make simple adjustments or accommodations, and hence make previous efforts more effective and less intrusive. We would fill out our final two rows as follows:

	Direct Parties	Third Parties	Government Regulation or Facilitation	Physical Environment
4a. Feedback and Follow-up: Anticipate and foreclose adverse spill-over effects of the resolution itself	assess effect of addressing a problem on future cordiality of communication between parties	guests may be offended by signage, speed bumps, turn-around requirements surveillance, noise regulation, tolls	police will adjust attitudes about future interventions based on legitimacy of previous calls	possible deterioration of driveway owing to conscious avoidance of the problem
4b. Feedback and Follow-up: Feed back the nature of the problem and dispute to Step 1, the Planning process	gauge usage patterns re volume, time of day to adjust license fees and maintenance fees; assess effectiveness of various methods for regular communication and dispute resolution	adjust treatment of guest use of driveway		adjust physical arrangements, plantings, lighting, drainage, maintenance schedule

Putting it all together, the Dauer Matrix expands the context and methods for preventing and resolving issues between the B's and K,'s and becomes this (see overleaf):

DAUER MATRIX: The Problem of B's and K's

	Direct Parties	Third Parties	Government Regulation or Facilitation	Physical Environment
1a. Planning: Imagine the risks	noise; estrangement; over-use, especially at night; blocking access of other party	noise from visitors; trespassers; concern of other neighbors; possible new owners upon transfer of land	building codes	visual blight; poor lighting; poor soil; poor drainage; snow removal; need for upkeep
1b. Planning: Imagine various structures and methods to prevent problems from arising	ongoing social interaction and communication; contract setting out rights and duties about costs, usage, transfer of property	signage indicating shared driveway, asking for quiet and no blocking; possible toll road for visitors	contract, easement enforcement;	location of driveway; sturdiness; visual hedge; turnaround for vehicles; motion sensing lights
2. Addressing Problems: Use early warning systems and resulting information to prevent problems from escalating into "disputes"	advance notification requirements for parties or construction work that could create special noise or damage; advance notification requirement prior to invoking escalating dispute resolution methods	regular communication with other neighbors about usage, noise	regular police patrols in neighborhood	speed bumps; surveillance cameras

3. Dispute Resolution: Take steps to resolve disputes fairly and efficiently, using a succession of methods	Contract provisions calling for succession of non-litigation dispute resolution methods	possible disinterested advice-givers; mediators; increasing authoritativeness of third party intervention	possible police or judicial intervention	
4a. Feedback and Follow-up: Anticipate and foreclose adverse spill-over effects of the resolution itself	assess effect of addressing a problem on future cordiality of communication between parties	guests may be offended by signage, speed bumps, turn-around requirements surveillance, noise regulation, tolls	police will adjust attitudes about future interventions based on legitimacy of previous calls	possible deterioration of driveway owing to conscious avoidance of the problem
4b. Feedback and Follow-up: Feed back the nature of the problem and dispute to Step 1, the Planning process	gauge usage patterns re volume, time of day to adjust license fees, maintenance fees; assess effectiveness of various methods for regular communication and dispute resolution	adjust treatment of guest use of driveway		adjust physical arrangements of plantings, lighting, drainage, maintenance schedule

CHAPTER VI
PREVENTIVE LAW: Applying and Defining the Method

A. A Three-Way Problem

The Dauer matrix can be readily adapted to risks and problems where three parties are directly involved. The example below[1] has three main characters: two competing medical groups (Advanced Medical Procedures or "AMP" versus Skilled Surgical Associates or "SSP") plus a talented, technologically innovative cardiologist ("Cartwright").

Here are the hypothetical facts: Cartwright recently came to AMP and is enjoying a quickly growing reputation in the community and among possible referring primary care physicians. This is valuable to AMP. Employment of a widely-recognized doctor is especially important to a medical group beyond the actual work done by that individual. Patients may be attracted to the group's other medical specialists through the name recognition of the "celebrity" physician.

The number of both self-referred and physician-referred new patients has been steadily growing at AMP since Cartwright arrived. The original hiring of Cartwright by AMP was informal, an employment at will. Following Cartwright's success over the first few months of work, AMP sends a letter to Cartwright offering a one-year formal contract plus an option to renew. Cartwright and AMP officers discuss the letter orally, but no clear written acceptance is given by Cartwright.

Meanwhile, the principles at SSP covet the services and reputation of Cartwright, and make private overtures to Cartwright in an attempt to lure Cartwright away from AMP. Promises are made to Cartwright for career-enhancing opportunities: more funds for assistants and equipment; a chance to teach at a local medical school where SSP physicians have good contacts; and the possibility of working on especially interesting cases that SSP can access through affiliations with out-of-state medical groups. Cartwright jumps ship from AMP, and moves to SSP. As a result, AMP's new patient intake falls, with a resultant drop in insurance and medicare/medicaid revenue. The two medical groups are now seemingly poised for a lawsuit involving contract law and tortious interference with an employment relationship, as well as difficult possible intervention claims by AMP patients who were once Dr. Cartwright's patients, but no longer able to be seen by Cartwright.

---

[1] This problem is once again adapted from problems developed at the William and Mary College of Law.

Fitting these facts into the Dauer Matrix, the two competing medical groups could be termed the "Direct Parties," with Cartwright deemed a "Third Party." Patients could also be brought into this "Third Party"column. The "environment" consists of the complex contemporary system of health care delivery and reimbursement. The environment also includes, however, patients and the revenue streams they represent.

Suppose we position ourselves at a time *before* Cartwright has moved to the competitor SSP. This re-positioning from the stated facts is important for preventive work. ***Attorneys can only be fully effective when, in Lou Brown's terms, the facts are still "hot," or capable of being shaped. Once facts have become "cold," i.e. the risk has erupted into damages or full dispute, less flexibility is available.*** That is why lawyers should so strongly encourage their clients to meet with them periodically, so that lawyers can learn of risks at a time when the legal or factual environment is easily open to calculated interventions.

At the time that AMP first begins to appreciate the value of Cartwright, steps could readily have been taken through contract and other incentives to ensure that Cartwright would never be interested in speaking with a competing medical group. But even after that easy opportunity is no longer available, i.e. after AMP first begins to learn of SSP's interest in Cartwright, some preventive measures can be secured by renegotiating the contract or otherwise making Cartwright's position at AMP more attractive. Similarly, as soon as the SSP principals begin to think about hiring Cartwright, honesty and open negotiations with the AMP can result in an accommodation that will avert a lawsuit based on tortious interference.

Both medical groups and Cartwright face legal and business-related risks. These can be listed in the Dauer matrix. One conventional preventive intervention would be an agreed-upon settlement among all three parties for cash payments that would allocate Cartwright's services so as to best suit the interests of all concerned. Clearly the strength of the parties' respective legal rights would influence their bargaining positions.

Other possibilities exist, however, especially if one re-frames the problem so that Cartwright is not imagined to be an indivisible asset that is mutually exclusive between the two medical groups. A joint venture between AMP and SSP could be imagined in which Cartwright becomes a shared asset, locally available to patients of both groups. Further, just as innovative surgeons are no longer purely local in influence, so also are they becoming less constrained geographically. Robotic surgical procedures controlled by computer make talented physicians potentially available around the world. What if the joint venture between the two medical groups enabled Cartwright to project surgical techniques remotely where Cartwright's particular skills would not otherwise be available? The start-up expenses and increased risks of distance surgery could be more than either medical group might want to shoulder on its own. Together, however, the venture could be more feasible. It is conceivable, therefore, that a win-win can be envisaged. The incomes and reputations of both medical groups *and* Cartwright could possibly be made better off by sharing Cartwright's technological interests in distance surgery. If well structure this could be done without affecting the competing local practices of either medical group.

One might respond that whatever the collaborative potential of the two stations sharing the talent of Cartwright, if either could control Cartwright exclusively the revenues would be even greater. This is an empirical question that cannot be answered on the facts we have available. Certainly, however, the opportunity costs of foregoing exclusive control over Cartwright's services must be compared with the possible gains of the distance surgery consortium; by the potential litigation costs required to establish definitively the legal rights and duties of the three parties; and by the possibility that Cartwright's energy, medical judgment, and willingness to stay at *either* AMP or SSP could suffer from the distraction and accompanying rancor of ongoing lawsuits.

For this problem, therefore, the two planning rows of the Dauer Matrix could appear as follows:

	Direct Parties	Third Parties	Government Regulation or Facilitation	Physical Environment
1a. **Planning:** Imagine the risks	To Employer AMP: Loss of a valuable employee; loss of patients; loss of revenue and perhaps other AMP physicians. To Competitor SSP: Lawsuit for tortious interference with contract	To Cartwright: breach of contract liability by a move to competitor SSP; possible opportunity costs to career by staying at AMP. To existing Cartwright patients at AMP: loss of access to Cartwright	Contract law; Tort Law	Hospital privileges system and insurance groupings preventing free movement of patients and physicians

1b. **Planning:** Imagine various structures and methods to prevent problems from arising	1. Contractual settlement clarifying and buying out rights. 2. With Cartwright, both medical groups participating in distance surgery innovation	1. Expanded access by patients to potentially life-saving distance surgery. 2. Existing AMP Cartwright patients may be grandfathered through consensual agreements between AMP and SPP	Contract law; physician licensing laws and insurance implications of distance surgery	Technical ability to perform robotic surgery

B. Refining the Method: Five Steps to Preventive Lawyering

The approach underlying the creation of a Dauer Matrix can be summarized as follows: first, consider the various stakeholders in a problem, including any government interest and the physical environment. Second, gather information that would be useful to any of those parties or concerns at different stages in the life-history of a problem. Third, equipped with that information you will be well positioned to suggest interventions that will avoid the problem altogether, or fashion a creative, win-win solution to a problem that may arise.

The following pages elaborate on this insight, offering a step-by-step analysis.[2] It is certainly not the exclusive way to achieve more preventive solutions, but thinking about these steps and the theory on which they are based may be a useful beginning toward the gradual development of more and better principles for achieving preventive solutions. Dealing effectively with the antecedents and emergence of needs, rather than the needs themselves, requires taking the following steps.

---

[2] The five-step method for thinking preventively that appears in the next pages is taken from Thomas D. Barton, *Preventive Law: A Methodology for Preventing Problems*, published in program book NEW VISTAS IN DISPUTE RESOLUTION, 2002 ABA Section of Dispute Resolution Annual Meeting.

1. Understand Problems as Troublesome Relationships Between People and Their Environments (Social, Physical, Biological, or Financial).

As I have written previously, at least for legal purposes 'problems' do not exist in a purely natural realm: they are *mismatches between environment and human purpose.*[3] Hence in thinking preventively, always look for the connections between people and their surroundings. It is in those interactions that problems arise, and in those interactions that problems may be prevented.

2. Identify the Various Elements in the System That are Leading to a Particular Problem:

a. This will always include a person or persons–the problem holders.

b. However, it will likely include a social environment--other people with whom the problem holders do, or do not, interact.

c. Finally, there will usually also be aspects of a non-social environment--issues about the physical world, or people's biological needs, or financial markets, etc.

This second step builds on the first. Understanding that problems are generated in the systemic interactions between people and their environments, try to find as many connections as possible. Systems are often more elaborate than first imagined, because the causal links are not necessarily mechanical. That is, problems often emerge from systems in which the various elements are influenced and buffered by many other elements. Problem dynamics typically represent risks–i.e., probabilities rather than certainties that the full-blown problem will arise. With luck, particular trigger points may be identified that virtually assure the visible emergence of problem symptoms. If so, intervention strategies can usefully focus on the trigger points. Absent those triggering devices, however, as much information as possible should be uncovered about as many elements as possible.

Look, therefore, for links between human problem holders and the people with whom they interact–the social environment. Then look further for links with non-social environments–the physical or financial or regulatory worlds. A physical disability, for example, may emerge as a problem when the disabled person

> By identifying trigger points, the attorney and client can consider how to prevent the problems that can arise from perceived risks.

---

[3] Thomas D. Barton, *Creative Problem Solving: Purpose, Meaning, and Values,* 34 CAL. W. L. REV. 273, 273 (1998) (hereafter *Creative Problem Solving*).

attempts to interact with the physical environment: steps that cannot be climbed, street crossing lights that cannot be seen. Alternatively, the problem may emerge as discrimination by the social environment toward the person who looks or acts differently from others.

Thinking about all three dimensions–the particular human problem holder, the social environment, and the physical environment–opens up the possibilities for intervention points:

- The problem holder could be equipped with devices that serve as a functional substitute for some missing capability.

- The physical environment can be re-designed so that problems of inaccessibility never emerge: curbs can be designed for easy wheel-chair use, for example, and crossing lights can emit sound when street crossings are permitted.

- Alternatively, the social environment can be encouraged through both laws and sensitivity-enhancement measures to accept persons fully who suffer from some disability. The goal of all these interventions would be pragmatic–to rearrange the connections between disabled person, physical environment, and culture such that the disability becomes irrelevant.

- A final sort of possible intervention would be more psychological: to embolden the problem holder to venture further into activities previously thought impossible. Through setting an example, the courage of some can be preventive for others in the future.

3. Understand the Dynamics Among the Problem Holders and Their Social and Non-social Environments that Create the Problem

Once the various elements and connections of a pathological system are identified, the next two steps seek to understand *what keeps the system moving*. That is, what fuels the system to produce the visible problem on a recurrent basis? Not all problems are recurring, of course, or closely linked to similar problems that crop up as a result of the effort to resolve the first problem. Some problems are simple in structure, and will therefore succumb to quick-fix thinking. But to prevent those problems from recurring as a whole or in slightly different form, we must understand why it is that the antecedents to the system do not exhaust themselves.

Imagine, for example, tensions between some franchisers and their franchisees that in some instances may lead to the demise of the franchise. The franchisees have made substantial capital investments in obtaining the right to distribute goods or services of the franchiser. They do so because of the name recognition and method of distribution built up by the franchiser. Investment fees paid to the franchiser represent a return on the franchiser's initial entrepreneurial risk and marketing skill. Each new franchise added, however, has the potential to dilute the worth of all existing franchises. So also, even more dramatically, does all off-franchise marketing like direct online sales by the franchiser or distribution through grocery store chains or discount mega-stores. Even as overall sales expand, therefore, the franchisees may paradoxically realize less and less return until a tipping point is reached and the franchise system collapses of its own weight. This specific pathological dynamic involves franchisers and franchisees, but the same relationship exists between the buying practices of the public and the financial imperatives experienced by most public-held companies.

Incentives built into each element of the pathology that constantly fuel the system. The franchisees indirectly depend on the general name recognition and product reputation that flows from widespread market presence and design uniformity, but each individual franchisee benefits far more from its particular exclusivity of distribution in a given geographic area. Franchisees clearly want that geographic exclusivity to be as broad as possible. The incentives for the franchiser are reversed: Once branding is established, profit margins are enhanced and shareholder demands are satisfied through direct franchiser marketing or through mass marketing in grocery store chains, mega-stores, or online. Franchisers are also pressured by the limited consumer willingness to seek out full inventory speciality shops rather than select limited inventory from a more convenient marketing channel. On the other hand, such direct sales may compromise the reputation for personal service among consumers that franchisees may supply, and also the general cachet that comes from exclusive distribution.

4. Describe What Gives Each Element of this Problem Dynamic Its Peculiar Importance.

This step begins to approach the problem dynamic strategically. Given the elements of the system and the incentives or reinforcers that fuel its persistence, where is the system most vulnerable? *Why* is each element reinforced by the actions of other elements? By identifying susceptibilities, interventions may be made more effective.

5. Imagine Various Interventions By Which the Problem Dynamic Could Be Broken or Slowed.

Using Steps 3 and 4 to understanding the system incentives and pressures for franchisers, franchisees, integrated or online merchandisers, and the buying public reveals a dangerous dynamic for franchise operations. The system seems destined to collapse, at least among certain retail franchises. The analysis also suggests, however, various points of possible intervention that would enable the franchisees and non-franchise sellers not only to coexist, but possibly to benefit from one another. The purpose of Step 5 is to identify each of those possible points of intervention, and design a change that could be effective. For example, selected merchandise could be kept available exclusively for franchisees; special public promotional efforts could direct consumers to franchisees; newer, more fashionable goods could be distributed first to franchisees; off-franchise merchandisers could be required to recommend or promote local franchisees for merchandise that is unavailable through the integrated sellers; or consumer buyers could earn credits from off-franchise sellers that are redeemable only at franchise outlets, with the credits reimbursed to the franchisees from the franchiser.

C. The Preventive Approach Applied: Another Example

Suppose the problem (one that we shall also revisit in a later Chapter) is that too many transactions of a large business enterprise ("LBE") are creating legal problems. The particulars of the liability or rule violation may change, but the fact of liability is a recurrent problem.

Step 1 of thinking preventively would result in the problem being articulated more generally, and with a longer time frame in mind. Problems should be understood as troublesome relationships between people and their environments. Here, the problem would be understood as "recurring legal liability" of LBE toward outsiders, who could be customers, competitors, or the government.

Step 2 requires identification of the various elements of the problem dynamic. Here, the problem holder can be imagined as the in-house corporate counsel for the company--the person most directly responsible for legal matters. The social environment for the problem is the non-legal employees of the company, including managers and top executives. The non-social environment would be the service or good that is delivered to outsiders, and a set of legal rules that are sporadically but frequently breached, resulting in potential liability for LBE.

Step 3 of thinking preventively would attempt to understand the dynamics among the problem elements–how do they interact and what keeps fueling a pathological pattern? Here, goods or services are being produced or distributed under conditions that create liability risks. For that to happen regularly, the service performers or manufacturing workers must chronically be acting in impermissible ways. The managers who should be expected to understand and correct those behaviors are not doing so. Top executives are not creating an environment for their managers that makes reducing risk from liability a priority. Corporate counsel is being called in too late on issues, at a quick-fix stage rather than a preventive stage.

The pathology may be fueled by: (a) ongoing ignorance by the actual service providers or manufacturing workers about the lack of quality of what they are delivering, or about how their product violates legal rules; (b) the managers may have incentives that are arranged to reward short-term successes like the revenues generated by shoddy goods and services, and a bureaucratic company structure that allows them to avoid accountability for the eventual consequences of worker errors or use of inferior materials; c) the top executives may also be influenced by short term balance sheet demands of shareholders, compounded by accounting rules that make legal liability look like extraordinary events rather than the result of everyday practices within the company; and (d) corporate counsel may be acting in ways that discourage managers from contacting the attorney earlier, during the planning stages of projects when preventive action could be taken more easily.

Step 4 would attempt to assess what gives each element in this pathology its particular importance, and determine which part of the pattern could be most susceptible to intervention. Various profiles could emerge in a multi-level pathology like the suffering by this enterprise of too much legal liability. Upon investigation, it could be that identifiable component suppliers to LBE are unreliable with their delivery schedules, or supply parts with a high failure rate. Time pressures within LBE, however, may force use of these components without appropriate testing and rejection. It could be instead that LBE producers or service providers simply do not know the legal requirements or how to comply with them.

Managers may spend most of their time generating revenues or on recruiting workers, with insufficient attention to quality control. Or the managers may have insufficient experience with the actual production or service delivery to identify various quality assurance procedures that could be instituted. It could be that the top executives are too heavily recruited from the financial side rather than the production side, so that they, like their managers, are not sufficiently proactive in initiating production improvements.

Finally, it may be that trust between the corporate counsel and managers has deteriorated. In meetings with managers or executives, it could be that corporate counsel has too often raised potential legal problems that have caused LBE to pull back from transactions that could have been career advancing for managers or financially rewarding for the top executives. Or, the corporate counsel could be viewed as carrying ideas from managers to top executives in such a way that managers are not sufficiently credited for their initiative or creativity. For these or other reasons, the decision-makers within LBE may have come to regard early advice from the corporate counsel as more threatening than beneficial to their individual interests.

Which of these possible elements of the problem dynamic could be most susceptible to intervention and change?

- Some require dealing with outsiders (the inferior component supplier);

- Some require dealing with many people on an ongoing basis (the workers who may not understand how it is that what they produce violates legal rules);

- Some may suggest restructuring lines of authority and accountability (so that managers cannot externalize the consequences of their quality control omissions);

- Some suggest bringing in consultants (for the top executives who lack experience to assess production inadequacies); and

- Some require people to change the ways they communicate and interact within the company (e.g., the corporate counsel).

Any of these may be the most feasible single step for a given company: it is an empirical matter that should be carefully investigated. No intervention is necessarily mutually exclusive with any others. Indeed, a company-wide legal liability awareness and reduction campaign with initiatives taken at each level is most likely to have the fastest and most durable impact.

Step 5 would be to imagine all the possible ways that the problem dynamic could be broken or slowed through conscious intervention. The careful and sometimes difficult investigation required by preventive thinking into multiple elements pays off in the end with a far broader repertoire of possible ameliorative measures. None of these may be a "solution" in the easy sense of eliminating the problem entirely. For problems of complexity, however, single effort measures that are by themselves completely effective solutions are usually a fantasy of quick-fix thinking. Furthermore, by generating possible solutions well, taking appropriate measures to implement them sensitively and durably, and setting up a process for ongoing monitoring of the success of the interventions, side benefits may be achieved for the interacting elements that once were pathological.

For a problem like that faced by LBE, interventions could be initiated at any of the identified levels. Involving people with generating solutions at their own level not only tends to generate many

> "Quick fixes" generally do not work to resolve complex problems.

more ideas, but also can smooth the implementation of any measure. Furthermore, by directly involving each human element of the problem dynamic in fashioning interventions, directly relevant expertise is brought into the process. No one knows his or her job better than those who actually do it. Being given a role in designing solutions may also shift attitudes away from denial of the problem to a far more productive engagement with its solution. Rearranging incentives at each stage toward the long term use of the interventions, rather than punishments for past behaviors, also helps to ensure durability of the new measures.

CHAPTER VII (James P. Groton)
PREVENTIVE PRACTICES: Lessons from the Construction Industry

Construction is a high-risk business with a high potential for adversarial problems. Every project involves a multitude of players, all with potentially conflicting interests, but whose mission is to plan, design and build a structure, on time and within budget. Once the building process has begun, the work can't be interrupted or delayed without serious consequences. "Time is money," so the construction industry places a premium on quick solutions to problems and the prevention of disputes to avoid not only the completion delays that disputes cause, but also their corrosive effects on the relationships of people and organizations needing to work together toward common goals.

James P. Groton, a retired Atlanta lawyer with decades of experience in the construction industry, has pioneered the use of dispute preventive techniques in that industry, and in retirement has been advocating using those techniques as a model for prevention of business disputes. The pages below reflect the lessons contained in a workshop he conducted in Beijing at the behest of Lexis/Nexis. He summarizes a variety of successful innovations that may be applied well beyond the construction industry (used with permission of James P. Groton):

DISPUTE PREVENTION IN THE CONSTRUCTION INDUSTRY

Remarks of James P. Groton

"If the only tool you have is a hammer, then every problem looks like a nail." Similarly, "If the only tool you have is a trial lawyer, then every problem looks like a lawsuit." Accordingly, in order to prevent lawsuits we need more and better tools.

There are literally dozens of techniques and practices that knowledgeable business people can use to prevent, minimize and eliminate the kinds of disputes that escalate into litigation, arbitration and even mediation. These techniques can be classified into four categories:

Dispute Anticipation and Problem Prevention Tools, implemented during the planning stages of a business relationship, which structure the relationship in ways that avoid many of the problems that can create disagreements between the participants.

Problem-Solving Tools, which create a business environment that is conducive to mutual collaboration in solving problems and avoiding adversarial attitudes, and use various negotiation processes to deal constructively with problems that arise.

Control Tools, which level the playing field, provide transparency, and create an environment that is conducive to "fixing the problem rather than the blame."

"Real Time" Resolution Tools, chiefly the highly successful *standing neutral* concept, which not only provide immediate expert, objective and prompt solutions to problems whenever necessary, but also because of their mere existence and ready availability they encourage the parties to mutually solve problem rather than seeking assistance from the neutral.

By carefully combining tools from the various categories listed above into systems which anticipate problems and control them so they don't escalate into adversarial disputes, knowledgeable construction industry owners, contractors and project managers have managed to deliver complex building projects without experiencing a single dispute that has risen to the level where it has to be resolved through litigation, arbitration, or even mediation.

Techniques such as these can also be used in many other business contexts. They are not difficult to understand. And they are easy to implement if (and this is a big "if") business leaders have the foresight and good sense to implement them.

Problem Prevention Tools

Competence. Competence and quality in performance, good customer relationships and the establishment of a relationship of trust, are of course fundamental ways to prevent relation problems.

Structure business relationships and transactions in ways that help to keep problems from arising. Some specific practices and techniques are:

Good, Open Communications. Keep lines of communication open at all times. The best business relationships are maintained through good communications between participants in the relationship or transaction, so that any incipient problems can be identified, brought out into the open, discussed, and solved, before they can become serious problems. Channels need to be developed to open up dialogue between all participants.

Realistic Allocation of Risks. One of the most powerful ways to prevent and control disputes between contracting parties is to rationally allocate risks by assigning each potential risk of the business relationship to the party who is best able to manage, control or insure against the particular risk. Conversely, unrealistic shifting of risks to a party who is not equipped to handle the risk can increase costs, sow the seeds of countless potential disputes, create distrust and resentment, and establish adversarial relationships that can interfere with the success of the business enterprise. Misallocated risks are breeding grounds for problems that can disrupt any business transaction and create disagreements that end up in conflict. Therefore, always use clear contracts that allocate risks among the parties in a sensible, equitable and good faith manner.

Unfortunately, this fundamental principle of good business management and dispute prevention is not widely recognized or understood.

In particular, lawyers involved in contract negotiations for their clients who seek zealously to obtain the "best possible deal" by shifting all possible risks to the other party can sometimes create problems of a far greater magnitude than any temporary benefit or satisfaction gained by "winning" the "battle" of the contract negotiations.

Realistic risk allocation promotes efficiency, lowers costs, and creates better relationships. The result in nearly all cases will be fewer disputes and a greater chance for success of the enterprise.

Good risk allocation is best accomplished at the deal-making stage by realistically identifying each potential risk of the enterprise, analyzing and assessing the risk, and determining which party is in the best position to manage, eliminate or control the risk, or insure against the risk. In many cases it will be obvious that certain risks logically should be assigned to a particular party. Other risks can possibly be handled equally well by either party, and some risks may be such that they cannot be effectively handled or even insured against by either party; the assignment of those risks will have to be dealt with through bargaining, and the result of that bargaining will likely be reflected in the economic terms of the deal. Even where there are uncontrollable risks, contract mechanisms can often be developed for sharing or minimizing that risk.

In a one-time short-term transaction between two parties who never expect to do business again with each other, it may not make a difference to anyone but the parties themselves if the party with superior bargaining power shifts risks to the other party that the other party can't control. However, in any business relationship of long duration or where there are repeated transactions, or where the success of the relationship has an impact on third parties, there are advantages to having a balanced relationship where neither party is exposed to inordinate risk, and where both parties profit.

In multiple-party relationships, realistic assignments of risk are particularly important to the maintenance of healthy relationships and control of costs. In the classic multi-party example of the construction process, an owner's use of superior bargaining power to shift risks unrealistically to another party typically creates a chain reaction of cost inflation, resentment, downstream risk-shifting, defensive and retaliatory tactics, and misunderstandings caused by different perceptions as to the enforceability of some risk-shifting provisions. The result is usually adversarial relationships, disputes and claims, which could have been avoided by intelligent sharing of risks.

Try to predict the likelihood of the enterprise to generate disputes, and take action to prevent the most likely disputes.   At the inception of any business relationship it is helpful to perform a joint analysis of the potential for disputes in the relationship, and use this analysis to eliminate potential problems and design systems that will be suited to resolve the kinds of problems that are likely to occur.

The Construction Industry Institute, as the result of a study into the causes of construction disputes and whether certain characteristics of construction projects are more likely than others to generate disputes, has developed a predictive tool (called the "Disputes Potential Index" or "DPI") that identifies the presence of dispute-prone characteristics on a project, evaluates them, and reports the results to project team members so they can take action to correct them before they actually generate problems. This predictive tool is in the form of a questionnaire whose answers can be fed into a computer program which processes the answers, analyzes them, and calculates two sets of numbers: First, an overall numerical rating which will indicate generally whether the project is likely to fall into the good, bad or average range with respect to overall potential for disputes. Next the program calculates an individual score for each of eight key project variables, to identify the particular areas of the project that have the greatest potential for breeding disputes. If the DPI is administered at the beginning of the project, the test results enable project leaders to take action in any weak areas to minimize the risk of project disputes. The DPI in effect is a "cholesterol test" of the health of a construction project.

Provide incentives to parties to encourage cooperation. Where a business is contracting with a number of different organizations which have diverse interests, and where the cooperation of these organizations with each other and with the business is important to the success of a transaction or business objective, it is often helpful to structure a system of incentives to encourage such cooperation. Well-conceived positive incentive programs can be an effective means of aligning the goals of all of the participants, can encourage superior performance, and discourage conflict. Such incentives can take many forms.

One example of such an incentive system is the establishment by the leader of the enterprise of a bonus pool which, upon attainment of specific goals, will be shared among all of the organizations with whom the leader contracts. Under such a system the bonus is payable only if all of these participants as a group meet the assigned goals; the bonus is paid either to every organization, or to none. This device provides a powerful incentive to the participants to work cooperatively with each other, and reduces conflicts which can occur in a common enterprise when every participant might otherwise be motivated solely by its limited perception of its own short-term interests, rather than the success of the enterprise as a whole. It encourages participants to subordinate their individual interests temporarily to the legitimate needs and success of the enterprise as a whole, for the ultimate benefit of all project participants.

On construction projects such "bonus pool" arrangements have been used successfully to convince subcontractors to work together cooperatively as a project team.

Establish a Partnering Relationship. Partnering is a team-building effort in which the parties establish cooperative working relationships through a mutually-developed, extra-contractual strategy of commitment and communication. It is typically an "aspirational," good faith process. However it can be contractually reinforced by a mutual commitment of fair dealing and good faith.

In any common business enterprise, if individual parties are left to their own devices in trying to achieve their own goals, they are likely to be guided primarily by narrow self-interest, which is likely at some point to conflict with the narrow self-interests of other participants. This conflict can be a breeding ground for disputes. In partnering the parties develop and share mutual goals to the extent possible. This creates community of purpose, and, more importantly, cooperative action that serves to minimize disputes. Sharing mutual goals encourages the formation of synergistic relationships, leveraging the whole process to the advantage of all. The focus should be on "fixing the problem," not "fixing the blame."

Partnering can be initiated on an <u>ad hoc</u> basis, or by language in the contract. It can be used for long-term relationships, or on a transaction-specific basis. "Long term" partnering is typically a mutual commitment between two business organizations who are in a long-term relationship or who engage in repeated transactions, for the purpose of achieving specific business objectives through a strategic alliance which maximizes the effectiveness of each participant's resources. The relationship is based upon trust, dedication to common goals, and understanding of each other's individual expectations and values. The expected benefits from such a relationship include improved efficiencies and cost effectiveness, increased opportunity for innovation, and continual improvement of quality products and services.

When used on a transaction-specific basis, partnering is usually instituted at the beginning of the relationship by holding a retreat among all personnel involved in the transaction who have leadership and management responsibilities, in which the participants, assisted by an independent facilitator, become acquainted with each other's objectives and expectations, recognize common aims, develop a teamwork approach, initiate open communications, and establish nonadversarial processes for resolving potential problems.

Partnering is now gaining increasing acceptance by groups of businesses or organizations that can benefit from teamwork with each other. One example would be partnering between entities that have been brought together as the result of a merger or acquisition. Another example:

When the members of the hospitality industry in a vacation destination wanted to have an assured, long-term dedicated source of financing for its marketing campaign to increase tourism, the proposal they wished to advance was a tax on hotel room occupancy. In order to gain passage of the tax by the legislature, five segments of the hospitality industry (hotels, airlines, ground transportation, attractions, and retail) were identified, and representatives of all of these segments (some 50 people) participated in partnering in order to develop a common group plan to design and promote the adoption of the tax, and develop a plan for how the tax proceeds would be spent. The group met weekly, under the guidance of a partnering facilitator. The result was the successful adoption and implementation of the plan.

Another example: A large company had several different divisions which were operating independently, unwilling to give up power, and behaving like a dysfunctional family. A partnering facilitator was brought in, the leaders and key employees in all of the divisions participated in partnering exercises, and the result was an alignment of interests between all divisions, for the overall good of the company.

Problem Solving Tools

<u>**Notice and Cure Agreements.**</u> A useful provision to include in any agreement is a requirement that each party who experiences a problem must immediately give notice to the other party and propose a good faith solution, in writing; and that the other party must reciprocate with a good faith written response.

<u>**Agreements that Encourage Rational Behavior.**</u> When drafting contracts that deal with future economic conditions, consider using devices such as "buy/sell" agreements, or "baseball" arbitration agreements, to encourage rational behavior.

<u>**In-House Problem Solving Tools:**</u> There are a number of steps which an organization can take to "keep the peace" within the organization and encourage good prevention practices (and it should be noted that the experience of in-house problem solving can make it easier for an organization to engage in external problem solving):

Appoint an Ombudsman to deal confidentially with employee and internal problems. An Ombudsman can clear up communication problems or misperceptions of an employee's relationships with the organization or fellow employees.

Charge the transaction costs of a dispute to the budget of the department that generated the dispute so that managers are being made aware of the true costs of the dispute.

Institute sensible document-preparation and retention policies that can be useful in case disputes occur or escalate. For example: Preserve evidence that you acted reasonably. If an employee writes a "bad memo," it is good preventive practice to write other memos that put the earlier memo in perspective, and correct the errors in the bad memo.

Consider and make preparations in advance as to how the organization would handle various possible crises.

Dispute Control Tools

Encourage the open sharing of basic information. Create a level playing field and provide transparency for all participants by establishing a common web site or other system for full sharing of important information about the business enterprise or transaction.

Negotiation and Step Negotiations. Negotiation is of course the time-honored method by which parties try to resolve disputes through discussions and mutual agreement. There are many different techniques of negotiation. The most successful negotiations are those in which the negotiators conduct their discussions on the basis of the respective interests of the parties, rather than the traditional approach of focusing on the positions of the parties. Negotiation is not only a free-standing dispute resolution technique, but it also can be a useful adjunct to every other dispute resolution technique.

A variant of negotiation is the "step negotiation" procedure, a multi-tiered process that can often be used to break a deadlock. If the individuals at the lowest level in each organization who are involved in the dispute are not able to resolve a problem at their level promptly, their immediate superiors, who are not as closely identified with the problem, are asked to confer and try to resolve the problem; if they fail the problem is then to be passed on to higher management in both organizations. Because of an intermediate manager's interest in keeping messy problems from bothering higher management, and in demonstrating to higher management the manager's ability to solve problems, there is a built-in incentive to resolve disputes before they ever have to go to the highest management level.

"Real Time" Resolution Tools

Use a Standing Neutral. One of the most innovative and promising developments in controlling disputes between parties who are involved in any type of long-term relationship (such as a joint venture or construction project) is the concept of having a highly qualified and respected pre-selected or "standing" neutral to serve as a dispute resolver throughout the course of the relationship. A single neutral or a board of three neutrals (designated variously as a "standing neutral," "mutual friend," "referee," "dispute resolver," or "dispute review board") is selected mutually by the parties early in the relationship; is briefed on the nature of the relationship; is furnished with the basic documents describing the relationship; routinely receives periodic progress reports as the relationship progresses; and is occasionally invited to meet with the parties simply to get a feel for the dynamics and progress of the relationship. The standing neutral is expected to be available on relatively short notice to make an expert recommendation to the parties to assist them in resolving any disputes that the parties are not able to resolve promptly themselves. It is important to the effective working of this process that the parties be mutually involved in the selection of the neutral, and that they have confidence in the integrity and expertise of the neutral. Typically the neutral's role, if called in to help resolve a dispute, is to render an impartial nonbinding decision (not a compromise proposal) on the dispute.

Although the standing neutral's decisions are typically not binding, experience has shown that on those relatively rare occasions where a dispute is referred to the neutral, the neutral's decisions have generally been accepted by both parties, without any attempt to seek relief from any other tribunal. This result is enhanced where there is a contract stipulation that in the event of any subsequent arbitration or litigation, the decisions of the standing neutral will be admissible in evidence. When used in accordance with the guidelines advocated by the Dispute Resolution Board Foundation and carried forward in the AAA Dispute Review Board Procedures, this technique has been remarkably successful; in practice, 95% of all disputes actually referred to a DRB are resolved without arbitration or litigation. Three critical elements are essential to the success of the standing neutral technique:

1. Early mutual selection and confidence in the neutral.

2. Continuous involvement by the neutral.

3. Prompt action on any submitted disputes.

The existence of a pre-selected neutral, already familiar with the business relationship between the parties and its progress, avoids many of the initial problems and delays that are involved in selecting and appointing neutrals after a controversy has arisen. The ready availability of the neutral, the speed with which he or she can render decisions, and particularly the fact that this neutral will hear every dispute which occurs during the history of the relationship, all provide powerful incentives to the parties to deal with each other and the neutral in a timely and frank manner, by discouraging game-playing, dilatory tactics, and the taking of extreme and insupportable positions. In practice, the nature of this process is such that the mere existence of the neutral always results in minimizing -- and often totally eliminating -- the number of disputes that have to be presented to the neutral. In effect the standing neutral serves not only as a standby dispute <u>resolution</u> technique but also as a remarkably successful dispute <u>prevention</u> device. Even though some expense is involved in the process of selecting, appointing, initially orienting, and periodically reporting to the neutral, the costs are relatively minimal, even when the neutral is called on to resolve disputes.

The standing neutral concept is particularly appropriate for any type of continuing business relationship where a premium is placed on mutual understanding and cooperation to achieve a common objective. Examples would be joint ventures, outsourcing contracts, long-term supply contracts, or any other type of long-term business relationship. The neutral, who could be a trusted experienced business person, or an independent accountant or attorney, would serve as a "standby" resource to assist in the resolution of disputes. The neutral should be initially informed of the purpose and nature of the business relationship, and kept up to date through routine progress reports or meetings with the parties, to be aware of the evolution of the relationship. If the parties should later have a problem that they cannot readily resolve by themselves, they can call in the neutral advisor, explain the problem, and ask the neutral advisor to furnish promptly a non-binding expert opinion as to how the problem should be resolved.

On those occasions where it becomes necessary to refer a dispute to the neutral, the neutral is typically asked to make a decision initially only as to "entitlement," leaving the question of "quantum" to negotiations between the parties based on the neutral's decision.

The evaluative but non-binding nature of the standing neutral, available if necessary to provide a "dose of reality" to the parties, encourages them to be more objective in their dealings with each other, while at the same time giving the parties an opportunity to construct their own solutions to problems, tends to strengthen the relationship between the parties and create trust and confidence between them.

There can be many variations of the standing neutral process. For example, in the case of a closely-held corporation where there might be deadlocks between equal owners, there are a couple of techniques that can be employed in drafting the corporate charter and by-laws that can avoid the paralysis of a deadlock by using one or more outside directors as standing neutrals:

1. One technique is for the stockholders who have evenly-divided interests to elect as a director a neutral outsider who is knowledgeable about the business and has a reputation for integrity. (An example of such a person could be the Dean of a local business school.) This outside director is paid a significant director's fee, is furnished the key management reports that are provided to other directors, and is expected to attend all board meetings, ask questions, participate in discussions, and get a good perspective on the affairs of the company. However, this outside director has a vote only in the case of a disagreement among the "inside" directors, in which case the outside director has the deciding vote.

2. Another technique where there are two stockholders with equal ownership, and a concern about possible deadlock, is to establish a five-person board of directors, two of whom represent the evenly-matched "insiders" and three of whom are highly-respected independent "outside" directors. They all function as a real board, and each director has a vote. The advantage of the arrangement is that in any case where the two inside directors disagree, it takes the votes of at least two of the three outside directors to carry the vote.

3. In a business where there are two stockholders with a great disparity in ownership interests, and a concern that the majority stockholder will ride roughshod over the minority stockholder to the detriment of the company, the by-laws could provide for a five-person board of directors, two of whom are appointed by the majority stockholder, one of whom is appointed by the minority stockholder, and two more highly-respected independent "outside" directors are appointed jointly by both stockholders together. Under this system, the majority needs the vote of only one independent director, while the minority needs the vote of both independent directors. But in a case where the majority is acting abusively, the independent directors are likely to perceive the potential for abuse, and both are likely to vote with the minority stockholder.

In all of these situations, because the independent outside director(s) can control the outcome, there is an incentive for all directors to exercise good judgment and act reasonably for the best interests of the company.

Standing Arbitrator. A variant of the standing neutral process, useful in a situation where it is important to achieve early decisions that are binding, is to give the neutral the power to render binding decisions, thus acting as an arbitrator.   Because this process shifts control of the dispute to the arbitrator, it has the disadvantage of taking away the ability of the parties to cooperatively work out their own mutual resolution of the dispute. Also, parties faced with the prospect of a binding decision are usually represented by lawyers, tending to add expense, cause delay, and escalate adversarial attitudes.

Standing Mediator. Another variant of the standing neutral process is the designation by the parties of a mediator at the commencement of the relationship to assist the parties in negotiations to resolve disputes. In the construction industry this technique is rarely used, probably because what the parties need when a problem arises is not a facilitator to encourage them to compromise every issue, but rather an objective expert who can administer the "dose of reality" that is more likely to give the parties a principled basis for resolving the dispute. Also, since parties involved in mediation are likely to seek the assistance of lawyers, this can add expense and cause delay.

Reasons for Using Prevention Provisions in Business Agreements

Every relationship carries with it the potential for disputes. Common experience has demonstrated that problems, difficulties, differences of opinion, disagreements and disputes can occur at any time, even in the best of families and businesses. Given this reality of the business world, the parties to a business relationship, at the time they enter into that relationship, should always address the subject of how they are going to handle any problems or disputes that may arise between them. At this point they have a unique opportunity to exercise rational control over any disagreements that may arise, by specifying that any disagreements be processed in ways that are likely to avoid litigation. There are many excellent reasons for taking advantage of this opportunity:

Disadvantages of Litigation. Resolution of a business problem through litigation:

1. Deprives business leaders of the opportunity to maintain control over their disputes.

2. Takes too long. It will take at least several months (and in some jurisdictions several years) to get a civil case to trial; appeals can lengthen the process by a year or more. This delay can create uncertainty in business planning, adversely affect cash flow, and have other disruptive effects on the business.

3. Is too expensive. We all know what it costs to bring even the simplest business dispute to trial, in lawyers' fees, time and energy of business executives, and costs of experts and consultants.

4. Lacks expertise. The resolution of business and technical disputes requires expertise and sophistication. It is difficult if not impossible to find a judge or jury with the qualifications to resolve such issues.

5. Is too public. Court filings and proceedings are matters of public record. They are valuable sources of information for business competitors, and, if they are juicy enough or it's a slow news day, they can be reported in the media, or featured on Court TV.

6. Is too uncertain. Litigation is a very blunt instrument. It is often very difficult to predict how a judge, jury or appellate court will ultimately resolve a case.

7. Is too disruptive of business relationships. The hostility engendered by litigation makes it difficult for business people to continue to carry on normal business relationships and activities with each other.

(Nearly all of these reasons apply also to most modern-day arbitrations, which have become more and more like court litigation.)

Disadvantages of postponing a decision about how to deal with disagreements until after a problem or dispute has arisen. Deferring consideration of how disputes will be dealt with reduces a party's options. Once a dispute has developed, it is often difficult to get the participants to agree on the time of day, let alone discuss rationally the optimum method for resolving the dispute. At this point the parties are likely to have different agendas and preferences as to how they would prefer to resolve the dispute. One party may want to emphasize the facts and equities, or sophisticated business realities; the other side may prefer to be in a court of law or before a local jury. One party may want a quick resolution; the other party may prefer delay. One party may want to avoid publicity; the other party might prefer public exposure of the controversy. Whenever the parties are unable to agree on the method of dispute resolution, the only remaining dispute resolution system, by default, will be litigation.

Advantages of agreeing early on a process for dealing promptly with problems. Agreeing at the very beginning of a relationship on a method for quick processing and resolution of any future problems or incipient disputes that may arise has the following advantages:

Responsible business managers are accustomed to controlling costs, quality and other aspects of their business relationships. Using private dispute prevention and resolution techniques gives these managers an opportunity to control disagreements and disputes as well. The beginning of the relationship, when there is an atmosphere of business-like cooperation, and before any disputes have arisen, is the time when the parties can most rationally discuss the optimum method for dealing with any disputes.

Including the subject of designing a dispute prevention and resolution process as an element in the negotiations leading to the establishment of the relationship helps to define an important aspect of the relationship. For example, if you learn that the other party does not want to agree to have an efficient dispute resolution system, this knowledge can affect how you negotiate other terms of the agreement (such as pricing) -- or whether you want to enter into the relationship at all. Agreeing early on a method for dealing with potential problems can lead to creative business-oriented results, be a cooperative and satisfying experience, and is likely to help preserve continuing business relationships.

Foreign business people often have a real fear of the U.S. legal system. Exhibiting a willingness during the negotiations to set up a rational, fair and prompt private dispute prevention and resolution system should have special relevance in an international transaction.

The existence and ready availability of a fair, efficient, trusted and quick method for processing problems and incipient disputes tends to discourage game-playing, posturing, and delaying tactics; may well encourage the parties to cooperate and deal realistically with each other; and may result in the parties resolving the problem by themselves, without having to resort to the dispute resolution procedure at all.

Overcoming Resistance to the Use of Dispute Resolution Mechanisms.
Despite the acceptance of mediation and arbitration as alternatives to litigation in many areas of American business, there is still some resistance to the newer and more sophisticated prevention techniques. However, knowledgeable business managers and counsel should recognize and overcome the kinds of attitudes that interfere with advance agreement on a dispute control and resolution system. Some of these problems are:

Not Wanting to Spoil the Euphoria.
Some people may fear that addressing the subject of dispute prevention and resolution during the early stages of a relationship is akin to suggesting to a happy engaged couple that they should enter into a pre-nuptial agreement. However, business should not be an emotional relationship; and ignoring the fact that problems and disputes can routinely occur even between the nicest people is simply a triumph of hope over reality.

Lawyers' Traditional Resistance to Change.
Given that the private dispute resolution movement is relatively young and the concept of dispute prevention is so new, many lawyers may have never before included dispute resolution or prevention as a subject in their negotiation agendas and checklists. Accordingly there is often a built-in resistance to any new idea, or to change of any kind. One argument for overcoming this resistance might be that the lawyer's first duty is to his or her client, and that the client should be made aware of the various forms of dispute prevention and resolution that can benefit the client and save the client money. Another might be to suggest to the lawyer that much of the impetus for preventing and resolving disputes comes from business people, and that lawyers would be well advised to keep up with their clients – otherwise the client may seek more enlightened counsel..

A Perception that Multi-level Dispute Resolution Slows Down the Process.
Some lawyers may feel that specifying more than one level of dispute resolution, such as step negotiations or a standing neutral or mediation before resorting to arbitration, imposes an unnecessary and delaying process that will retard the ultimate resolution of a dispute. However lawyers experienced in the dispute resolution field know that the earlier in the life of a problem or dispute the parties address the problem and deal with it, the more likely they are to resolve it amicably; but that every dispute prevention and resolution system should contain a final and binding "backstop" resolution method of some kind, such as arbitration.

A Perception By One Party That It Will Benefit From An Inefficient Method of Resolving Disputes. A party that thinks that it has -- or is seeking -- superior bargaining power may think that it will benefit by denying the other party an opportunity to have a dispute resolved promptly and efficiently. And if such an intended strategy is revealed during contract negotiations, the other party can try to negotiate offsetting terms in the deal to offset the risk that it may be deprived of ready recourse to a remedy and increased transaction costs of handling a dispute -- or it may refuse to enter into the business relationship at all.

Bottom Line: In short, there is no rational excuse for a responsible business not to include in its agreements a system for processing disagreements as promptly and efficiently as possible.

CHAPTER VIII (Helena Haapio)
PROACTIVE LAW: Cross-Border Contracting

Helena Haapio, of Lexpert Ltd, Helsinki, Finland, www.lexpert.com, is an International Contract Counsel and one of the founders of the Proactive Law movement in Europe. She specializes in all aspects of contracting–planning, coaching, drafting, implementation, and management. Her thoughts below reflect the depth of her expertise in both contracts and language and the opportunities they both offer for business success and problem prevention in international dealings.

INVISIBLE TERMS & CREATIVE SILENCE:
What You Don't See Can Help or Hurt You in Cross-Border Contracts©

By Helena Haapio[****]

This chapter concerns the "invisible terms" and "creative silence" of contracts: what they are; whether they are good or bad; and why early action regarding them is important. The goal is to promote contract literacy in cross-border dealings.

The visible, explicit terms of contracts are of course important, and one should always take the time to read them carefully. For contracts in which goods or services cross border, it is particularly important to pay attention to those *visible* terms.

Confusing or ambiguous meanings in the explicit terms of a contract present obvious legal risks. To compound those risks, too often we neglect the *invisible* terms that exist in business contracts: provisions that do not appear but nonetheless have an impact. Parties should recognize mandatory requirements that are implied into contracts, and understand the effects of silence in agreements. Doing so can prevent problems and unpleasant surprises. The potential impact of mismanaged legal risk is graphically presented in the chart below.[1]

[****]   Helena Haapio, International Contract Counsel, Lexpert Ltd., Helsinki, Finland, www.lexpert.com. This chapter is based on a presentation made by the author at the National Contract Management Association's (NCMA) World Congress, 2009, in Long Beach, California.

[1] Hanna Hasl-Kelchner, THE BUSINESS GUIDE TO LEGAL LITERACY–WHAT EVERY MANAGER SHOULD KNOW ABOUT THE LAW (2006).

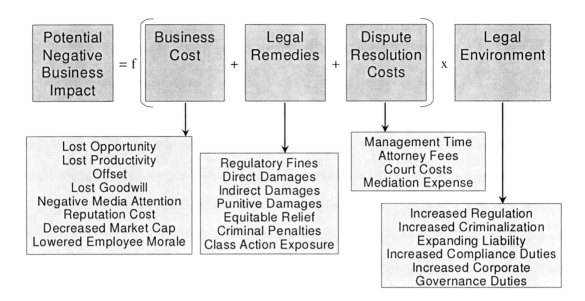

$$\text{Potential Negative Business Impact} = f(\text{Business Cost} + \text{Legal Remedies} + \text{Dispute Resolution Costs}) \times \text{Legal Environment}$$

Business Cost	Legal Remedies	Dispute Resolution Costs	Legal Environment
Lost Opportunity	Regulatory Fines	Management Time	Increased Regulation
Lost Productivity	Direct Damages	Attorney Fees	Increased Criminalization
Offset	Indirect Damages	Court Costs	Expanding Liability
Lost Goodwill	Punitive Damages	Mediation Expense	Increased Compliance Duties
Negative Media Attention	Equitable Relief		Increased Corporate
Reputation Cost	Criminal Penalties		Governance Duties
Decreased Market Cap	Class Action Exposure		
Lowered Employee Morale			

To demonstrate the importance of cross-border contract literacy in reducing business risk, try your hand at the questions posed in the Quick Quiz below:

QUICK QUIZ: True or False?

In international dealings, between businesses located in different countries ...

	T	F
1. It usually costs less to avoid getting into trouble than to pay for getting out of trouble	☐	☐
2. "Reports shall be submitted bimonthly" means that reports shall be submitted twice a month	☐	☐
3. The absence of a warranty means that the supplier is not liable for defects	☐	☐
4. The expiration of a warranty means that the supplier is no longer liable for defects	☐	☐
If the goods fail, the buyer suffers a loss as a consequence, and the warranty/contract is silent:		
5. ... the buyer is not entitled to compensation for its loss	☐	☐
6. ... the buyer is entitled to compensation for its loss, including loss of profit	☐	☐
7. ... the law will determine what the buyer is entitled to	☐	☐
8. The law of the buyer's country is applied to the supplier-buyer relationship	☐	☐
9. No international sales law exists	☐	☐
10. The shorter and simpler the contract, the better	☐	☐
11. Contracts can prevent problems and communication failures	☐	☐

Statement 1: It usually costs less to avoid getting into trouble than to pay for getting out of trouble.

      The first statement is clearly *true*. As Louis Brown wrote many years ago, "It usually costs less to avoid getting into trouble than to pay for getting out of trouble."[2] As is customary in the good old risk management process, we can begin by identifying problems, actual and potential, together with their causes. Once we know what, why, and how problems may arise, our findings become the basis for further analysis and treatment. With a little foresight, we can prevent problems before they arise.

      Preventive Law is much like preventive medicine. Preventive medicine works proactively, emphasizing healthy lifestyles, good nutrition, and regular checkups. So also, Preventive Law endeavors to minimize the risk of litigation, secure more certainty as to legal rights and duties, and help individuals and business improve their control over the factors that determine their "legal health." [3]

Statement 2: "Reports shall be submitted bimonthly" means that reports shall be submitted twice a month.

      This statement turns on the meaning of the word "bimonthly." But surely this is self-evident? As Ambrose Bierce once pointed out, "'Self-evident' means 'evident to oneself and to no one else.'"[4] That is particularly apt here, because the dictionary meaning of "bimonthly" is as follows:

      "Bimonthly:"

-     *adjective*

  1. Happening every two months.
  2. Happening twice a month: semimonthly

-     *adverb*

  1. Once every two months
  2. Twice a month: semi-monthly[5]

---

[2] Louis M. Brown, MANUAL OF PREVENTIVE LAW (1950).

[3] The Preventive Law movement has gained momentum in Europe, especially in the Nordic countries, where the philosophy is embodied in the Nordic School of Proactive Law (http://www.proactivelaw.org). In December 2008 the plenary session of the European Economic and Social Committee adopted an Opinion on the Proactive Law Approach (Ref. CESE 1905/2008). The author acted as Expert to the EESC in the preparation of this Opinion.

[4] Ambrose Bierce, THE SHORTER DEVIL'S DICTIONARY (1998).

[5] "Bimonthly," DICTIONARY.COM. THE AMERICAN HERITAGE DICTIONARY OF THE ENGLISH LANGUAGE (4th Ed., 2004) http://dictionary.reference.com/browse/bimonthly (Accessed: April 12, 2009).

Here is our first proactive, preventive suggestion for reducing legal risk: try to avoid ambiguity by spelling out what you really mean. Instead of "reports shall be submitted bimonthly," say, for instance, either "reports shall be submitted on the 1st and 15th of each month," or "reports shall be submitted on the first day of every second month."

Here is another example, familiar to lawyers: "No Warranty." Surely that has a clear meaning? Yes, but however clear, that meaning *is different* for different people, professions, and languages. Here are some alternative meanings of "no warranty:"

- goods (or software) are provided "as is;"

- seller assumes no responsibility for repairs; buyer will pay the costs for any repairs;

- no acceptance of liability;

- a statement somewhere to the effect that "no warranty express or implied is made;"

- the absence of a warranty: no such document or heading appears in the transaction documents.

Statement 3: The absence of a warranty means that the supplier is not liable for defects

In business-to-business dealings, does the absence of a warranty mean **no liability** for defects? This statement is *false*. In many countries and industries, the absence of a warranty means quite the opposite.

For example, in the Information Technology sector, it has been said that in 99% of the cases, the buyer would be far better off in the absence of the supplier's warranty. This is true in many other industries as well: business-to-business suppliers use warranties to **limit** their liability and the remedies available to buyers. In contrast, if you do not give or receive a warranty (or if you do not address something in your terms), the law will write your warranty for you. This is where the *invisible terms* enter the picture. The law can supply terms through mandatory rules; trade usage and established practices; and default rules that come in wherever uncontradicted. The entire contractual package looks a bit like this:

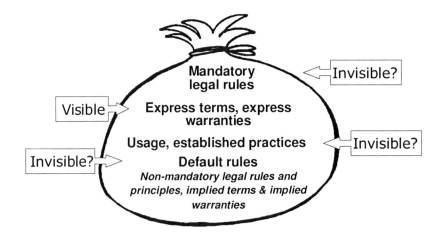

Statement 4: The expiration of a warranty means that the supplier is no longer liable for defects

Beware: All warranties are not created equal! The supplier's liability for defects *may* end at the end of the warranty period. It ends at that point when the warranty (or contract) says so. In business-to-business dealings, it is up to the parties to determine the duration of the supplier's liability. "The expiration of a warranty means that the supplier is no longer liable for defects" *may or may not* be true, depending on what the warranty says.

And if it is silent, what then? Whether you are the supplier or the buyer, you do not want to leave this question open, do you?

The expiration of a warranty does not automatically or necessarily cut off the supplier's liability. Yet many suppliers use contractual warranties to:

- specify (and shorten) their statutory liability or to limit their liability in other ways;

- set aside/disclaim implied warranties; and/or

- limit the remedies available to the buyer.

Yet not all suppliers do, as the following sample case will show. A Canadian Buyer had a contract with two gearbox suppliers. Both contracts included the following warranty clause:

> "Seller warrants that the goods shall be free from defects in design, material, workmanship, and title, ... If the equipment, or any part thereof, does not conform to these warranties and Buyer so notifies Seller within a reasonable time after its discovery, Seller shall thereupon promptly correct such nonconformity at its sole expense."

The warranty period was "twenty-four (24) months from the date of shipment, or twelve (12) months from the date of start-up, whichever occurs first." A design fault caused both suppliers' gearboxes to fail. The failures were discovered *after* the expiration of the warranty period. The Buyer claimed damages from both suppliers for the cost of repairing the gearboxes. They denied liability.

The Court stated that neither supplier was liable for breach of contractual warranty because that warranty had expired: the Buyer was out of time and could not rely on the contractual warranty provisions. However, despite the expiration of the *contractual* warranty, were there other grounds for liability?

The question of implied warranties remained. The Court found that the gearboxes were not reasonably fit for their purpose. Supplier 1 was liable for the failure because it was in breach of an *implied warranty*, namely the statutory warranty implied by the applicable Sale of Goods Act. Hence Supplier 1 had to pay the repair costs. These exceeded the original price of the gearboxes.

Supplier 2, however, had to pay nothing. But why? Why was Supplier 1 liable and Supplier 2 not? Because the applicable Sale of Goods Act, like many other similar Acts and Commercial Codes, provided that it was possible to contract out of the provisions of the Act. The warranty of Supplier 2 included one sentence more than that of Supplier 1. The sentence reads: *"The provisions of this paragraph represent the only warranty of the Seller and no other warranty or conditions, statutory or otherwise, shall be implied."*

The lesson here is that some warranties, like that of Supplier 1, are clearly defective and not fit for their purpose! Common examples of implied warranties that appear in various national or state laws include the implied warranty of fitness for a particular purpose, sometimes shorthanded to *warranty of fitness,* and the implied warranty of merchantability.

Goods must conform to contractual specifications and requirements. Sales laws contain obligations as to quality, conformity, and fitness. These add to the supplier's obligations, unless contractually excluded.

Keeping these implied provisions in mind, are your specifications, requirement and warranties clear and understood in the way intended? Do they work cross-border? What happens if the goods you sell or buy do not conform/meet the requirements? What if the defect/non-conformity causes considerable losses: loss of use, idle time during repair, loss of profit?

Statement 5: If the goods fail, the buyer suffers a loss as a consequence, and the warranty/contract is silent, the buyer is not entitled to compensation for its loss

Obviously, the answer will depend on the question **why:** why did the goods fail? Then there are questions related to the amount of the loss, the chain of events/causal chain/evidence, etc. Let us assume that the goods failed due to a reason for which the supplier is responsible (for example, supplier's faulty manufacture). Let us assume further that this is the sole cause of the buyer's loss, the amount of which is proven, true, and correct. If you are the supplier who breached the contract and you did not address the issue of compensation for a loss (i.e., damages) in your warranty or contract, where do you stand? The statements that follow will provide the answer.

Statement 6:   If the goods fail, the buyer suffers a loss as a consequence, and the contract is silent, the buyer is entitled to compensation for its loss, including loss of profit

Taking the facts assumed under Statement 5 as our starting point, if a failure of the goods, the reason for which is attributable to the supplier, causes a loss and the contract is silent:

- invisible terms (gap-filling laws; default rules) enter the picture;

- they may bring good news or bad; and

- they may contain pitfalls and traps for the unwary;

One common general principle of many gap-filling laws is the principle of full compensation: If you breach your contract, you have to compensate the other party for the loss it suffers due to the breach.

While the conditions and wordings in different countries' sales laws may differ, we will see later that Statement 6 can very well by *true*.

Yet the parties are free to opt out of default rules if they choose to. Remaining silent is an option, but often not a very wise one. Silence leaves room for invisible terms. In business-to-business contracts, you can work proactively and preventively and do any or all of the following:

- eliminate unintended, implied, or added promises;

- determine the existence and scope of your rights, responsibilities, and remedies;

- prevent the gap-filling laws from surprising you and your contracting partner;

- provide good-quality contracts and agreed remedies, where appropriate.

Statement 7: If the goods fail, the buyer suffers a loss as a consequence, and the warranty/contract is silent, the law will determine what the buyer is entitled to

True! If there is a gap in your terms, the law will determine what the buyer is entitled to. Again, the gap-filling laws and *invisible terms* enter the picture. Do those terms favor the buyer or the supplier? What is their legal and practical impact on your supply chain?

Invisible terms in Sales of Goods Acts and Commercial Codes allocate rights and obligations between parties in the absence of explicit terms dealing with those matters. These invisible terms may:

- write your warranty and contract for you;

- expose you (or your supplier/customer) to unexpected costs and liabilities;

- affect your notice and other requirements;

- interfere with and override your intention;

- fundamentally impact the existence and scope of your rights and obligations

- modify what you believed your rights and obligations were.

The diagram below[6] summarizes the express and invisible elements of a cross-border contract:

---

[6] This figure is adapted from Linda Mulcahy and John Tillotson, CONTRACT LAW IN PERSPECTIVE (2004).

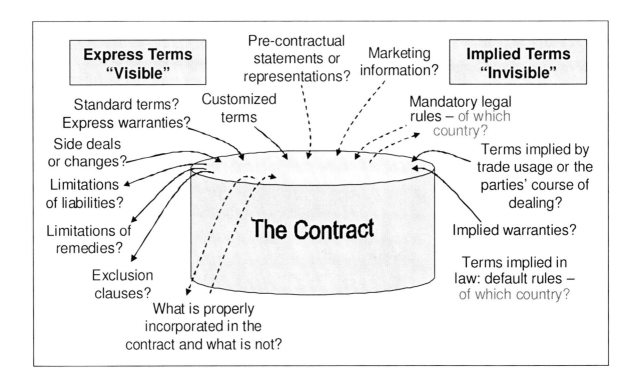

Statement 8: In international dealings, between businesses located in different countries, the law of the buyer's country is applied to the supplier-buyer relationship

Whose law applies, supplier's or buyer's? Once again, it depends. Here, it depends on:

- the parties' choice of law;

- but if no choice is made (*i.e.,* the contract is silent), then it depends on several matters, including:

  - the principles of conflict of laws;

  - the dispute resolution forum;

  - the place of business of the parties;

  - the parties' intent;

  - the scope and issues to be resolved.

In the absence of a choice of law clause in the contract, the strongest default rule is that it is ***not*** the Buyer's law, but the Supplier's law. In international dealings, you should never be silent on the choice of law! It is relevant to:

- the parties' rights, responsibilities and remedies;

- the balance of power and allocation of risks;

- the interpretation of words and concepts, such as "consequential loss," "Force Majeure," "warranty," "guarantee," and even "contract;"

- the duration of the parties' liability exposure; and

- if a dispute arises, the ability to:

    - foresee the parties' obligations and act accordingly;

    - predict the outcome and avoid unnecessary problems.

Statement 9: No international sales law exists

False! In international sales and purchases of goods, in many cases the CISG (Convention on Contracts for the International Sale of Goods[7]) applies automatically, by default (absent contrary agreement). The CISG is said to be the "international sales law" of more than 70 countries, accounting for more than three quarters of all world trade. Does the CISG apply to your international dealings? If it does, is it good news–or bad news? Are you aware of your rights, responsibilities, and remedies? Do you manage their impact?

Take our earlier example of a loss suffered by a buyer due to failed goods (or delayed delivery, for that matter): If the failure (or delay) was due to a breach of contract attributable to the supplier and the CISG applies, one needs to be aware of CISG Art 74:

> Damages for breach of contract by one party consist of a sum equal to the loss, **including loss of profit**, suffered by the other party as a consequence of the breach.   [emphasis added].

Some suppliers have learned the hard way that no mention needs to be made in the contract about damages for breach: they apply automatically, by default, unless contractually excluded–and that there is no maximum or monetary cap that would bear a relation to the purchase price for the supplier's liability, unless provided for in the contract.

Even if yours is not a CISG country, or if your contract terms exclude the CISG, in international

---

[7] The CISG is also known by various other names: the UN Convention; the Vienna Convention; the UNCITRAL Convention (United Nations Commission on International Trade Law); the International Commercial Code; and the International Sales Law. For a list of current CISG contracting states, texts of the CISG in various languages, cases, and other valuable information, see http://www.cisg.law.pace.edu.

sales and purchases of goods the CISG may still govern your contract. It may be, for example, that the other party' laws apply and make the CISG part of your contract by default; or your terms may not be part of the contract; or in a "battle of the forms" situation, the other party's 'last shot' may win–or the "knock-out" rule may be applied. Being aware of this possibility is crucial because risks can only be managed when they have been recognized. An unrecognized risk is an unmanaged risk.

Each contract party has its own views and concerns based on their own internal policies, experiences and attitudes to risk. When the parties have a clear view of the risks associated with the project and their significance, they can negotiate how best to allocate and manage the risks.

Statement 10: The shorter and simpler the contract, the better

True or False? Once again, it depends! As pointed out above, "silence" in contracts is not necessarily a good thing. In international dealings, problems are often encountered not because of what the contract says, but because of what it does *not* say. Gaps and silence can be risky, especially if you are a supplier who wants to balance risk with reward and avoid excessive, unlimited liability exposure.

A better approach is to improve your contract literacy and apply it proactively to all your future contracts. Contract literacy requires only two things: reading and understanding (1) what the contract says, and (2) what it does *not* say (but that still needs to be taken into account as invisible terms). An aliterate person is one who is capable of reading and writing, but who has little interest in doing so because of indifference or for other reasons. A literate person, in contrast, is well-informed, and educated. Contractual literacy is required of everybody involved in business dealings, not just the lawyers. A proactive, preventive lawyer can make a valuable contribution by helping clients become contractually literate so that they know how to use their contracts proactively for better business and problem prevention.

Statement 11: Contracts can prevent problems and communication failures

This final statement is *true!* Yes they can prevent problems, when they are fair, good-quality contracts, planned and used proactively. When the risks and opportunities have been recognized, contracts can actually be used:

- to guide and encourage desired performance;

- to clarify, allocate, manage, and pass on rights, responsibilities and remedies; and

- to prevent problems and communication failures.

Within organizations, it takes a team to create such terms. Contracts are often crucial to the success of business projects. And when those projects fail, it often comes down to poor communication, people not speaking the same language. As Mark Grossman, an experienced negotiator, put it:

> "Tech projects fail for many complex reasons. I've litigated those
> fiascos. One recurring theme is communication failure, which easily

occurs when you have techies, business people, bean counters, and lawyers in one room pretending to speak the same language.

Techies understand what they can build. Business people know what they want for their customers. Bean counters want it to be close to free, and the lawyers–what exactly is it that we do and why are we in the room anyway?"[8]

As proactive, preventive lawyers we can readily agree with Grossman's answer: "The lawyer is there to foster communication. You write a contract to prevent litigation." The contracting puzzle, in other words, begins to look like this:

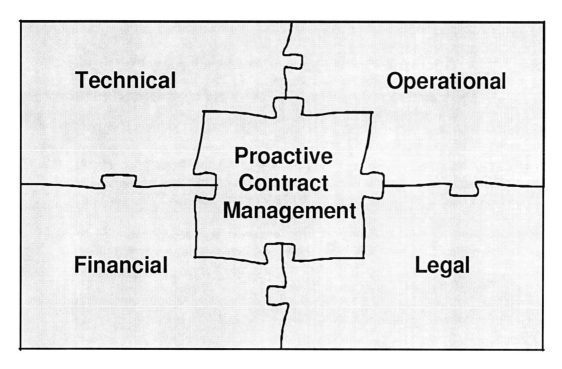

If problems arise, there is no magic to help either the lawyers or the other players in the puzzle. If the contract terms contain–or lack–provisions that we did not pay attention to, it is too late to change things. As Lou Brown once wrote, "When you 'sign on the *dotted* line,' *you obligate* yourself; before you sign, you have a freedom of choice not available later."[9] If our contract (or warranty) leaves room for *silence* or *invisible terms*, the outcome might not be what we or our counterpart expected. Negative surprises follow!

---

[8] Mark Grossman, *Contract Negotiation Crucial Before Website Development*, Miami Herald, Nov. 6, 2000.

[9] Louis M. Brown, How to Negotiate a Successful Contract (1955).

Everyone involved needs a true understanding of what the deal is and what cost and risk each has to carry (or pass on in the supply chain). Then we can synchronize our sell-side and buy-side contracts, warranties, and commitments. As either suppliers or buyers, we should strive for the following:

- recognize that the rights, responsibilities, requirements and remedies may differ from one jurisdiction to another;

- find out about the mandatory and default rules that apply;

- rather than relying on terms that are invisible to either party (or both), use our freedom of contract and:

    - define the terms of our relationship through explicit terms in the agreement;

    - choose expressly the desired rights, responsibilities, and remedies; and

    - make these and other important issues part of our negotiations and address them in our contracts.

What is customary in one industry, geographic area, or business may be risky and a reputational hazard in another. Warranties and contracts must be localized to mandatory laws. Finally, there is a limit to warranty/contract terms and reasonable demands even in business-to-business dealings. "Too favorable" terms may lead to lost protection. Using such terms is risky.

The pyramid figure overleaf–borrowed from preventive law, which in turn borrowed it from preventive medicine--prompts us to think along three basic domains of proactive contracting:

- first, prevent the cause from arising;

- second, prevent the cause from doing harm; and

- third, if harm occurs, limit the damage.

We can then apply those general domains and principles more particularly to the specifics of cross-border contracting.

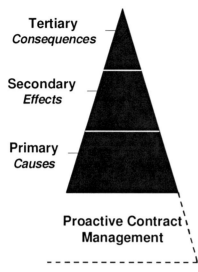

Being prepared for future events, both favourable and unfavourable
- securing prompt recovery
- limiting losses and expense
- promoting prompt resolution of disputes

Enhancing opportunities; minimising risk & friction
- providing instructions & clarity as to how to proceed
- open communication and good cooperation
- preventing problems from becoming disputes

Ensuring that objectives are achieved; maximising opportunities while minimising problems & threats
- recognising & aligning expectations -> identifying & resolving differences in interests early -> creating a common language -> shared meanings
- incentivising proper performance; making it easy to comply
- providing a solid foundation and framework for success
- keeping problems from arising; preventing negative surprises

Tertiary *Consequences*

Secondary *Effects*

Primary *Causes*

Proactive Contract Management

Going forward: Action Plan

For business, the contract is not the goal: its successful implementation is.[10] Contracts must translate into action and desired performance. Regardless of the skills of those who crafted the contracts, it is up to the delivery teams and the people in charge of performing the contracts to fully understand and successfully implement them. If someone in the supply chain encounters a negative surprise, everyone will suffer.

To provide a sound foundation for good business relationships and successful contract performance, with predictable outcomes and no negative surprises:

1. Have a fresh look at your cross-border business-to-business contracts and warranties: what they do and do not say;

2. Recognize silence/invisible terms and where they should not apply;

3. Localize your terms so that they comply with mandatory legal requirements, where applicable;

4. Redesign your inbound and outbound contracts and warranties (or convince those who "own" them to redesign them), if needed, and make sure they are clear and easy to understand for the people who are expected to implement them.

---

[10] *See* Danny Ertel, *Getting Past Yes: Negotiating As If Implementation Mattered,* HARVARD BUSINESS REVIEW, Nov., 2004; Danny Ertel & Mark Gordon, THE POINT OF THE DEAL: HOW TO NEGOTIATE WHEN YES IS NOT ENOUGH (2007).

With the help of *visible terms* containing a clear and fair allocation of tasks and costs, incentives for desired performance and clarity as to how to proceed, both suppliers and buyers can benefit: manage risks, reach savings, speed up performance and prevent unnecessary problems. You (or your contracting partner) may use *silence creatively*–but do you really want this to happen? Probably not, if you want to prevent unnecessary misunderstandings, claims, and disputes *and* if you want to promote successful business relationships.

CHAPTER IX
THE "ETHICS" OBSTACLE: Advocacy/Adversarial Rules of Professional Responsibility

The preventive/proactive approach offers the prospect for lawyers to keep their clients out of trouble and help them achieve their goals. Why, therefore, do so many lawyers seem resistant to expanding the contexts of problems, and gathering information accordingly? Why is the preventive approach not more widely taught or adopted? For decades, this question has beguiled those who have practiced preventively.

Once we understand the nature of evolved problem solving systems, at least we know where to look for answers: in each of the elements of the system. In other words, if traditional lawyering is supported by particular orientations to problems, litigation procedures, skills that are well trained to be successful in those procedures, rules of ethics that enable or protect those procedures, and a culture that comes to expect all of that together, *then each of those elements has evolved as a barrier to the development of a different approach.*

In the chapters that follow we will examine each of those elements, leaving aside for the moment the question of skills. We begin with the element of ethics.

Ironically, one basic obstacle to getting better information from clients is the influence of legal ethics. Louis M. Brown and Edward A. Dauer, founders and developers of Preventive Law, pose a hypothetical[1] based on the following provision of the California Civil Code:[2]

> If within a reasonable time after written or oral notice to the landlord ...of dilapidations rendering the premises untenable which the landlord ought to repair, the landlord neglects to do so, the tenant may repair the same himself where the cost of such repairs does not require an expenditure of more than one month' rent ... and deduct the expenses ... from the rent when due ... .

The intent of this provision, say Brown and Dauer, is "to prevent evictions for nonpayment of rent when the tenant makes such repairs."[3] Further, the provision furthers a public policy of keeping buildings in good condition. But suppose that after this provision is enacted, landlords begin inserting into their leases a waiver by tenant of these statutory rights to offset minor repairs. Not willing to see their housing reforms frustrated, the legislature responds by supplementing the statute by prohibiting tenant waivers. Although no criminal or civil

---

[1] Louis M. Brown and Edward A. Dauer, PLANNING BY LAWYERS: MATERIALS ON A NONADVERSARIAL LEGAL PROCESS 2,3 (1976) (hereafter PLANNING BY LAWYERS).

[2] Calif. Civ Code §1942 (2006).

[3] PLANNING BY LAWYERS, *supra* note 1, at 2.

penalties are stated, the legislature declares such waivers to be against public policy, and legally void.[4]

Now, say Brown and Dauer, suppose that a residential landlord is a new client at your law office. You draft up a proposed lease that, in accord with the clear intent of the law, omits any waiver of the tenant's statutory right to repair the premises.[5] Your client, however, insists that you insert such a waiver. When, however, you explain that such a clause would not be legally enforceable, the landlord responds that the tenants are unlikely to be aware of their rights.[6] Even if they were aware, the tenants are unlikely to take the risk of eviction if they were to withhold rent payments to cover repair costs: the tenants are unlikely to be able to afford to litigate the matter if challenged. What, ask Brown and Dauer, should you say to such a client?

First, of course, you will advise your client as to the risks of possible fraud or deceit liability, or of the injunctive relief that could be sought by the tenants even though the statute itself provides no remedy for violation of the prohibition against tenant waivers.[7] But suppose your client persists: the tenant is willing to bear those (probably remote) risks. What further do you say or do? As a practical matter, your decision is likely to be legally definitive. It will not likely be reviewed in a court of law. In a real sense, the law as it pertains to your client and your client's tenants is being made in your office.

What role or image of a lawyer will inform and guide your conversation with your landlord tenant?[8] Do you comply with the tenant's request? *Must* you do so, imagining the lawyer as champion of a client's needs, and loyal to a client's interests? *May* you do so, imagining the lawyer as embedded in an adversarial system of justice that defines truth as contingent on arguments actually presented to a legitimately empowered authority? Justice, loyalty and truth–do these basic values of the law and lawyering require you to act as an instrument of your clients' desires, even where those desires seem unscrupulous?

> Lawyers, in effect, make law when they counsel clients in the office setting.

Does it help to imagine yourself as an officer of the court, with a responsibility to the process of the legal system? But if so, what formal legal processes would be subverted by

---

[4] Id..

[5] Id.

[6] Id.

[7] Id. Brown and Dauer make the lawyer's choices harder by assuming that the lawyer would not be liable to the tenants.

[8] Id.

drafting the lease as the landlord demands? You are not lying to a legal officer. The law is effectively being applied and enforced (or not) in the privacy of your office, not in court, and by your decisions, not a judge's.

In litigation, attorneys are in a sense shielded from the full moral complexity of the issues presented. In playing out the role of the advocate for your client, within the boundaries of honesty you are free to present only one side of the arguments. Far more than the lawyers, it is the judge who faces the difficult legal and moral choices.

But in your office, in dealing with this landlord, no judge is or will likely be present to absolve you of those responsibilities. You may be able to withdraw from the representation of those whom you consider to be morally repugnant.[9] That may be both appropriate, and a powerful statement to the client of the strength of your personal objections. But withdrawal is the exceptional case, invoking a core of moral autonomy that a lawyer always retains in representing others. The escape valve of withdrawal suggests that the lawyer cannot continue the traditional role with a given client. It imagines lawyering as an on-off switch of advocacy and instrumentality of a client's desires. The issues are harder than that. As the authors have concluded, "This is a case in which the lawyer will be aiding the client in drafting a private law for numerous unrepresented others."[10]

By posing their hypothetical, Brown and Dauer are prompting us to imagine lawyering as broader and richer in its relationships with clients and the problems that they face. Advocacy is certainly not wrong. Sometimes it is the only alternative for protecting your client. But the lawyer as advocate should not so capture our imaginations that we are incapable of conceiving other roles for helping our clients and learning the new skills that would make those alternative roles effective.

"The roles of advisor and advocate must be carefully distinguished," say Louis M. Brown and Harold A. Brown in a jointly-authored article.[11] Historically, however, legal ethical codes have neglected the work of lawyers as advisors. In part, say the authors, this may be because

> [although] the advocate's effort is often of extreme public import, and
> occasionally political in nature, the advisor's effort is generally private and

---

[9] *See* ABA Model Rule 1.16, Declining or Terminating Representation (2002)

[10] Louis M. Brown and Edward A. Dauer, *Professional Responsibility in Nonadversarial Lawyering: A Review of the Model Rules,* 1982 AMERICAN BAR FOUNDATION RESEARCH JOURNAL 519, 530 (1982) (hereafter *Nonadversarial Lawyering)..*

[11] Louis M. Brown and Harold A. Brown, *What Counsels the Counselor? The Code of Professional Responsibility's Ethical Considerations–A Preventive Law Analysis,* 10 VALPARAISO LAW REVIEW 453, 454 (1976) (hereafter "Brown and Brown").

seemingly important only to the immediate parties. Frequently the advocate's most important decisions are designed to remain confidential. Because the Code of Professional Responsibility serves partly as a public relations device, it is only natural that the Code should focus on the more public, and more publicized, role of an attorney.[12]

The second explanation offered by Brown and Brown reflects the traditional integrated system of legal problems and procedures: "the advocate's role has been better defined by a well-delineated legal process. In contrast, the advisor performs many diverse functions for the client and generally is unconstrained by formal procedures. As a result, it is more difficult to state comprehensively the ethical considerations for an advisor."[13]

Helpfully, the authors elaborate the differing role of the advisor when counseling a client:

The advisor's role begins when a lawyer is contacted by a prospective client concerning a matter which the client perceives as "legal" or simply one with which an attorney might be helpful. In order to provide any assistance, the advisor must determine exactly what the client wants, since [her] real purpose in consulting a layer is likely to be more abstract than a desire to assert or defend a claim.[14]

In a footnote, the authors offer an easy example of this distinction: a parent who is dissatisfied with the behavior of a child. "An advocate," say Brown and Brown, "would be of little help, where there is no *case*. An advisor, on the other hand, may be of considerable assistance in helping the client use legal means to influence the child."[15] They continue in their explanation as follows:

The advisor's task in determining [her] client's purpose is made more difficult because a client may state [the] request for guidance in terms of a proposed solution to an unstated problem, or ... be somewhat secretive about the basic problem, or ... may not really know or be able to identify [the] basic purpose and goal. To take a simple example, a client may come to an attorney to ask whether ... gift tax [must be paid] on a gift ... to his child. Although this question seems simply stated and may have a definite answer, that answer may not respond adequately to the client's needs. To provide good advice, the lawyer must, among other things, determine the client's purpose in making the

_____

[12] Id., at 455 (citations omitted).

[13] Id., at 456 (citation omitted).

[14] Id., at 457.

[15] Id., at 458.

gift. The client may wish to provide for the child's education, to insure that the child enter or continue in the family business, or to use the gift as part of the parent's estate plan. The lawyer can assist the client in each of these possible goals by use of legal constructs–a will, a trust, certain provisions in the articles or by-laws of the family business–but only if the attorney knows the client's purpose.

Next, the lawyer must advise the client how best to effectuate his purpose. But determining the correct advice and course of action for the client is a process which requires cooperation between lawyer and client. The proper solution must be based on an accurate appraisal of the client's desires and abilities, coupled with the lawyer's ability to develop solutions and to coordinate the appropriate solution with the client's ultimate purpose.

From the attorney's perspective, the client seeking advice can be distinguished from the litigating client not only because the former is ordinarily a greater participant in the decision-making process, but also because the client is the actor; that is, the client is the one who will engage in the transaction or execute the contract. Consequently, any discussion of possible solutions must include the means of accomplishing those results. To do this, the lawyer must explain to the client in understandable terms the course and effect of each pertinent legal solution. When possible, the lawyer should also present non-legal solutions.[16]

These differences in role and client needs have significance for the ethical expectations of the lawyer:

When comparing the advisor's roles and duties with the advocate's several distinctions are immediately apparent. In the litigator's practice the client's goal is almost universally to "win the case." In the advisor's practice, the initial goal may not be explicitly stated. Secondly, because each planning solution is provisional and must be evaluated by both advisor and client, the amount of communication between advisor and client may be much greater than in the advocate's practice. In addition, since each participant has [her] own area of expertise, the communication must consist of an exchange of information. Finally, since the client is the actor, the number of decisions to be made by the attorney alone may be fewer and less significant than in the adversary situation. Thus, the advisor's task is to guide the client to structure the facts; that is, to act in such a manner that the result will be most beneficial. The emphasis is on planning the transaction before the legal effect is

_____

[16] Id., at 459-60.

rigidified.[17]

How are these differences treated in the ABA Model Rules of Professional Conduct? Rule 2.1, "Advisor," reads as follows: "In representing a client, a lawyer shall exercise independent professional judgment and render candid advice. In rendering advice, a lawyer may refer no only to law but to other considerations such as moral, economic, social and political factors, that may be relevant to the client's situation."

Also important is Comment [5] to Rule 2.1, which clarifies that the lawyer need not wait passively until a client asks about a problem. Where a lawyer, acting preventively, identifies a risk and wishes to alert a client to it, the lawyer may do so. The comment entitled "Offering Advice" reads in part: "A lawyer ordinarily has no duty to initiate investigation of a client's affairs or to give advice that the client has indicated is unwanted, but a lawyer may initiate advice to a client when doing so appears to be in the client's interest."[18]

Putting too much emphasis on the advocate role also can deter lawyers from being proactive. As "advocates," lawyers imagine themselves in a courtroom facing a judicial determination that will be based exclusively on the disinterested application of legal rules. Where that image become too salient, it becomes more difficult for lawyers to weigh client options realistically. A judge does not engage in cost-benefit analysis, but instead will hand down judgments that are binary: either the rules result in liability, or they do not. Traditional legal analysis is not probabilistic; it is instead a process of discerning distinctions and arguments that oscillate a conclusion back and forth between the two binary poles of "liability" or "no liability." Cost-benefit analysis, by contrast, directly embraces probabilities. Sometimes, that is what a client needs--advice about taking action in a world that is shaded with gray. For the lawyer to be fully effective in helping the client, the client must be given a sense of the *level* of legal risk and weigh it against the possible benefits of taking that risk. One difficulty, as suggested above, is the lack of formal training by lawyers in probability and statistics. Also, some risks may be impossible to quantify, such as harm to personal relationships, the stress of litigation, and feelings of hurt and loss.

Another intellectual obstacle facing lawyers who wish to advise clients more proactively is that traditional legal analysis does not include the "benefit" discussion, only the risk. The benefits of action often have little or nothing to do with the content of the legal rules: the benefits come from the larger context in which the legal rules become an issue. Learning to offer complete advice to a client therefore requires includes learning enough about the client's business or other circumstances to help the client think through those and weigh those benefits.

---

[17] Id., at 460.

[18] *See also Nonadversarial Lawyering, supra* note 10.

As developed in earlier chapters detailing the methods of Preventive Law, learning more about the broader contexts in which client problems arise is crucial. Without that knowledge and the attitude to engage a client in conversations that include such contextual information, the lawyer risks being limited to acting like either a "circuit breaker" or "damage control" expert.

When acting as "circuit breakers," lawyers focus so strongly on legal rules and the consequences of breaching those rules that consulting lawyers is like adding a circuit breaker to an electrical system. With any spike in electrical activity, the circuit breaker will shut down the system, making the appliance inoperable. Until, of course, the circuit breaker is reset. If we imagine that the client is consulting a lawyer about a transaction, for example, that would mean that the lawyer re-sets the system by inserting more and more cautionary language into a prospective contract. Then the appliance will operate again until another spike occurs (*i.e.* a risk is articulated to the lawyer), when the circuit breaker will trip yet again, necessitating yet more protective language in the contract. For clients, this process can at best make the contract less readable and raise transaction costs. At worst, each of the new protective provisions is a potential deal-breaker. The people on the other side of the transaction may resist a disclaimer or attempt to shift risks onto them. In reality the risk may be quite remote, perhaps too remote to be of concern on a cost-benefit basis. But that is not how a circuit breaker operates. Learning to think more probabilistically, and learning to consider benefits to the client as well as risks, will improve the lawyer's judgment and worth in the eyes of the client.

But would attorney ethical rules be violated by the intentional ignoring of a risk perceived by the lawyer, even where that risk may be remote? Ask the question from the other direction: Would it be unethical for lawyers to take extreme positions in contract negotiations that result in unnecessary friction, and that ultimately ruin a potentially "win-win," commercially reasonable contract for their clients? That is how many business clients would view the lawyer who clings to an exclusively circuit breaker role.

Consider a more specific example. Suppose Attorney A wishes to insert a liquidated damages clause into a prospective contract. This, of course, is a clause that specifies a formula in advance by which damages would be calculated in the event of a breach of the contract. Liquidated damages clause can be valuable both because they promote efficiency (by reducing the costs of litigation in the event of a breach), and also because the clauses can reduce risks. A party who is reluctant to make an agreement for fear of unpredictably high damages in the event of breach can sometimes make that risk manageable through the use of a liquidated damages clause. So suppose Attorney A proposes a reasonable liquidated damages clause, but Attorney B thinks that (unusual) punitive damages could be attainable in the event of a breach, damages that would be precluded by a liquidated damages clause.

Do professional ethics **compel** Attorney B to resist Attorney A's request for the liquidated damages clause? An attorney who thinks so would have to believe one or the other of two unsupportable propositions. The first proposition is that the attorney cannot take into account non-legal considerations in whether to resist the clause or not. Rather, so goes this proposition, attorneys are professionally constrained to work solely within their training, which is the law, and to advance the purely legal position which is best for the client.

I think this is unrealistic. What is legal and what is not legal are not so easily compartmentalized, especially when one is not in a courtroom. Would it be professionally irresponsible for the attorney to consider whether the long term advantages in business relationship between A and B might offset the possible advantage in damages in the event of a breach that goes to litigation? For the attorney to refuse to inquire of his or her client about that business reality on the *ethical* grounds that it is non-legal and therefore beyond the attorney's role is to make unrealistic categorizations about what is legal and what is not. "Zealous" representation should mean working hard to advance the clients interests, *and in the real world those interests are a combination of legal and non-legal considerations.*

Suppose it is actually the case that client B, all things considered, would be economically and reputationally better off by permitting party A to insert the liquidated damages clause. The deal would go through because A's risk aversion would be assuaged, and party A would consider party B to be a fair, reasonable business partner. But that would raise the second possible unsupportable ethical proposition, one that is almost comically ironic: could it be said that for Attorney B to permit A to insert the clause would be an act of *disloyalty* by Attorney B to his or her client? That is, by empathizing with Party A's concerns about risk Attorney B would be guilty of divided loyalty, an ethical breach?

Such a conclusion would be ironic, of course, because if Attorney B refuses to permit the clause, Attorney B's actions would thereby make his or her client worse off. Indeed, a refusal to permit the clause is arguably unethical on the ground of incompetence by Attorney B. "Competence" to the client is one of the cardinal ethical duties. Can ideas of loyalty interfere with the ethical responsibility of competence to a client? I think yes, if loyalty is taken unreflectively to mean that an attorney must fight to maximize his/her client's purely legal rights on every possible contestable legal issue. A better definition of loyalty–one that is more broadly consistent with ethics, competence, and the client's best interests, is for the lawyer to communicate well with the client about both legal and business issues and determine with the client how best to proceed.

CHAPTER X
THE "PROBLEM" OBSTACLE (Part I): Limitations of Labels and Imagination

Resistance to systemic thinking is not limited to lawyers. In our culture generally, "problems" are often processed and discussed as being the scarcity (or sometimes the surplus) of some single resource. And therefore the resolution of the problem is imagined to turn solely on the increased [or decreased] supply of that resource. I call this the "single need" fantasy, and it underpins many fruitless policy conversations. "If only there were more [or less] of *** in the world," this conversation says, "then the problem would be solved." The "***" here can be virtually anything: more oil, more money, or better access to health care. Or it can be the opposite: less traffic, less hatred, fewer greenhouse gases. If this single need were resolved, then the problem is imagined to go away. But it is largely a fantasy. Significant problems are rarely so simple.

We have all had those "single need" discussions, sometimes about personal problems and sometimes about national policy concerns. The conversations are doomed to be repeated, on the same topics, until we change the way we regard the underlying problem. By focusing simplistically on just one resource or need, these conversations fight systems thinking. In other words, *defining a problem in the unrealistically easy way of needing more or less of just one thing displaces trying to understand the problem as the systemic interaction of various elements.* Reducing the problem to just one dimension makes for easy conversation, but also makes actually resolving the problem far more elusive.

The reading below is taken, with small adaptations, from an article that first appeared in Volume 49 of SCANDINAVIAN LEGAL STUDIES, in 2006. In it, I confront some of the obstacles blocking widespread adoption of a helpful technique like the Dauer Matrix, and then offer one possible step-by-step approach to thinking preventively and proactively. I begin by considering an example raised in an earlier chapter, namely the Large Business Enterprise ("LBE") that is breaching too many of its contracts, thus resulting in significant and excessive legal liability fro the company. What is to be done?

THINKING PREVENTIVELY AND PROACTIVELY

A. Introduction: The Difference Between Quick-Fix Solutions and Preventive Thinking

... The particulars of the contract provisions being breached [by the LBE] may change from month to month, but what does not change is the fact of their ongoing, chronic liability. How might some executives and corporate counsel respond to this problem? They may seek settlements of their breaches on favorable terms, or they may fight the liability by resisting a lawsuit or government investigation. They may even change their standard contracts so as to limit their liability in the event of future breaches.

Such responses are certainly rational. They are probably also reasonable: immediate measures are needed to deal with a problem that has become visible. But none of these "quick-fix" relatively superficial responses to the symptoms of the problem are preventive, not even the change in contract language to apply to future breaches. Acting preventively is taking steps to prevent a problem from *occurring*, not planning how to win the next time a problem arises.[1]

The problem with quick-fix solutions like those taken by the executives and corporate counsel is not that they are wrong or unnecessary. The problem is that quick-fix steps stop short of a deeper, longer-term approach to problems that would likely serve the company very well. By rushing to fix an immediate, apparent problem *and then being satisfied and doing nothing more*, company leaders are missing the opportunity to restructure whatever within their business structure is causing them to breach their contracts again and again. In other words, quick-fix solutions are usually rational and may be reasonable, but they are not fully *responsible*. Being fully responsible would require additional pro-active measures to be taken. Being fully responsible requires thinking preventively, to identify ways that can reduce the number of contract breaches.

Ironically, the very reasonableness and rationality of taking immediate, quick-fix steps may interfere with our engaging in this deeper preventive thinking. When we act rationally and reasonably in response to problems it *feels* like we are being responsible. Furthermore, we often are pressed for time in reacting to problems. Taking *some* sort of quick action helps to quell our anxiety about the problem. Responding quickly to the symptoms of a problem therefore provides a temporary respite from the troublesome, risky symptoms of a problem. A behaviorist would explain that these temporary, superficial quick-fix solutions are negatively reinforced by their power to alleviate the immediate distress that accompanies a problem and thus make us feel better. But such feelings may deceive and ultimately betray us, because the quick-fix approach that these feelings prompt may well have deferred aversive consequences. Settling for nothing more than quick-fix solutions is like eating whenever we feel hungry. Frequent eating makes us feel better on an

---

[1] James Frierson, *Pre-Action Advice May Not Be Preventive Law Advice,* http://preventivelawyer.org/main/default.asp?pid=essays/frierson.htm (hereafter *Pre-action Advice).*

116

immediate basis, but in the long term we become less healthy.[2] Unless we address the *antecedents* of a problem and the dynamic by which the symptoms surface, we may be doomed to repeat the process again and again. Even emotionally, therefore, the quick-fix solution ultimately is unsatisfying: its ineffectiveness leads to frustration or despair.

Even worse, sometimes taking the superficial, quick-fix steps actually will make problems come back *more* strongly or *more* frequently than if we had done nothing. This will happen whenever the superficial, quick-fix solutions that we apply to an immediate need ends up *feeding* the antecedents of the problem. A quick-fix solution, in other words, can be counter-productive: it can sometimes reinforce one or more of the elements in a recurring, pathological interaction. Unless one is pro-active in uncovering the elements of this pathology and understanding how these elements interact to produce a visible problem, it is like stumbling through a darkened room, moving aside objects on the floor as we bump them. Moving aside any object is a quick fix toward moving toward the door and out of the room. Moving objects in the dark *without knowing what larger object may be tipped over by our actions* is not fully responsible. Attempting to navigate a physical environment without crucial information about what lies ahead or how our interventions are changing the environment is dangerous. It is reactive to an immediate need. What is really needed is to end the risky interaction of person and environment. We need to find some light or other way to reveal the objects in the room, even if that means we should stop and wait for one's eyes to adjust to the darkness; or retreat; or call for help.

We are drawn to superficial, quick-fix problem solving for the emotional reasons suggested above, but also because of ignorance about the alternatives. And we are ignorant about the alternatives because in general our culture understands "problems" through metaphors that are too simple, and that therefore suggest quick-fix solutions.

The metaphors commonly employed to understand or approach problems typically suggest a gap, or hole, or shortcoming. Fixing the problem, therefore, becomes merely a matter of supplying some resource to fill the hole or close the gap: the quick fix. Imagine, for example, that we were to use a pothole on an asphalt roadway as a metaphor of "problem." As we watch cars attempting to steer around the hole or being damaged by hitting it, our immediate, quick-fix impulse is to find something that will fill up the hole. This seems both rational and reasonable. If the problem is a hole produced by the absence of asphalt, then the obvious solution is to find some asphalt and

---

[2] B.F. Skinner, BEYOND FREEDOM AND DIGNITY 26-43 (1971).

shovel it into the hole. Applying a needed resource makes the hole go away and we feel better.

As those who have lived in cold climates know, however, potholes repaired in this way are likely to come back deeper or wider. The reason for this is that the collapse of the roadway surface is actually the result of a long interaction among elements of a system comprised of drivers, their vehicles, the qualities of the structural materials comprising the road, additives to the road that are applied to melt ice, and the weather. So long as these human and non-human elements continue to interact as they have been, the stresses on the roadway will continue. Potholes will continue to appear.

Indeed, merely shoveling more loose asphalt into the hole *may make things worse, like moving aside an unknown object in a darkened room.* Unless the repair material is properly compressed and sealed, even more water than before may seep into the road surface. As the water freezes and melts with winter weather, an *even larger* area of the roadway will be broken up and collapse under the weight of the traffic.

In sum, preventive thinking differs from superficial quick-fix solutions. This chapter will describe more fully what is meant by preventive thinking, stopping briefly to ponder why it is that so little theoretical attention has been paid to it. Then, the chapter suggests a step-by-step method to begin practicing more preventive thought.

B. The Elements of Preventive Thinking

1. Finding a Better Metaphor

The key difference between quick-fix solutions and preventive thinking is that quick-fix thinking is concerned with meeting needs, whereas preventive thinking focuses on the antecedents of needs and the processes by which needs emerge. Said differently, for quick-fix thinkers problems tend to be imagined as needs themselves, rather than as the processes by which needs are generated. Framing problems in this quick-fix way typically narrows the range of proposed solutions. A quick-fix thinker will attempt to supply new resources, thus eliminating the immediate need and therefore imagining that the problem itself is eliminated. Alternatively, a quick-fix thinker may attempt somehow to make the needs less relevant, thus bypassing the problem or imagining that the problem has been lessened in importance.

The beguiling appeal of quick-fix methods, however, mask their ineffectiveness. If problems are needs–shortfalls in resources–then naturally the solution is to supply or transcend the needed resources, *and nothing else.* That is how quick-fix thinking can feel so responsible and rational, and yet sometimes be so futile or counterproductive. Quick-fix thinking follows logically from how problems are understood. Hence, if the underlying premise about the nature of the problem is wrong or limited, then the logically derived solution will be equally flawed.

Here are a series of examples: statements of chronic problems, and how a quick-fix mentality would process these problems. In each instance, the problem will be understood through an invisible metaphor that suggests a hole, or gap, or shortcoming that can be filled or resolved through the addition of some resource. And therefore, *the problem understood through the metaphor can also be solved by the simple addition of some single, needed resource.* The quick-fix approach is always superficial because it never stops to consider *why the shortage arose.* The quick-fix approach is often ineffective because the antecedents of the shortage may still be in place. The quick-fix approach is sometimes even *counterproductive* because the resources that are supplied as an intended solution may actually feed the pathology by which the visible symptoms of the problem are produced.

For example, if poverty is understood merely as life necessities that are unavailable to a population (i.e. a shortcoming, hole or emptiness), then the quick-fix solution calls simply for food stamps and subsidized housing. If an energy crisis is simply understood as a lack of sufficient supplies of power, then the solutions call for more drilling or more power plants. If a troubled intimate relationship is understood as simply a lack of good fit between the two partners, then each person should just find a new partner. If sexual harassment in the workplace is simply the lack of conformity to required norms, then that disobedience should be extinguished through punishment or possible discharge. If a child custody dispute is about the limited resource of time for interacting with the child, then the solution is inherently a division of the child's time between the parents. If health care simply addresses illness, the health care delivery systems should devote its resources toward immediate, serious illnesses. All of the above solutions sound reasonable, *but only because each solution follows so logically from the needs-based, pothole metaphor that frames each problem.*

A better metaphor is needed for understanding the idea of having a problem. Problem solving would in the long run be more effective if problems were more often understood dynamically, as the result of a pathological interaction among various elements comprising a system. Once the underlying complexity and dynamics of a problem are uncovered, then various interventions can be imagined that may break the cycle of interaction. If the cycle can be broken, then the problem will not recur. The intervention may have nothing to do with supplying a resource or responding to a symptom. Yet so long as the pothole metaphor prevails, those helpful interventions will remain invisible, simply beyond our imagination.

2. Seeing Problems as Systems

Understanding problems dynamically requires seeing problems as a system of interacting elements, both human and non-human. A more dynamic view of poverty, for example, would be as the futile interactions of the problem holder (a poor person) within a social environment that fails to value what the person has to offer, either because of relatively limited skills of the poor person or because of relatively limited ways for generating wealth within a given physical/economic environment. This chain of pathological interaction could be broken at any of several points. The problem holder could be trained for new skills that could be more highly valued; environmental obstacles to the person being able to express existing skills (like child care requirements or transportation needs) could be removed; irrational social attitudes like racism or sexism that may prevent the social environment from recognizing or accepting existing skills of the problem holder could be eliminated through education or anti-discrimination laws; or wealth- generation opportunities could be diversified and barriers to entry could be reduced through even tiny loans [that] can enable the start-up of small scale enterprises.

3. Expanding the Problem Context to Identify Elements of a Problem Dynamic

Thinking preventively thus challenges us to conceptualize problems as the result of social interactions conducted within a broader physical or economic environment that constrains or rewards certain behavioral patterns. Each of the other examples introduced above can be re-framed as expressions of such a pathological dynamic. Take the "energy crisis" that recurrently plagues Western economies: the problem can be understood as individuals embedded in a sprawling social environment that requires almost constant human transportation across significant distances–obviously a primary generator of energy needs–and surrounded by various cultural practices and large-scale distribution patterns that are energy intensive and dependent rather than energy-conserving. Furthermore, just as a physical/economic environment may offer insufficient diversity of opportunity to poor persons, so also does an energy problem emerge in part from the failure to develop the technologies that would make diversification of energy sources (solar, wind, wave, etc) efficient.

Sometimes this preventive re-framing of problems into the interactions of people with one another in a given physical or economic environment, is especially difficult. For example, if a couple's relationship is troubled, thinking preventively requires trying to understand how the pathological interactions between the two persons could be generated and reinforced by their social and non-social environment.

Preventive thinking does not stop, in other words, simply with an analysis of the two individuals' personalities or with their immediate reactions to one another. Thinking preventively would require exploring their social context: What other persons are typically involved in the lives of the couple that may contribute to difficult interactions? Children? Employers? Parents-in-law? Neighbors? Can patterns be identified in which demands are seemingly made by such persons which outstrip the capabilities or coping skills of one or both individuals in the troubled relationship? More broadly, are the individuals burdened by heavy role-typing of expected behavior like the bread-winning husband or the subservient wife, social expectations that one or both persons cannot or do not wish to meet? Conversely, does the social culture offer diverse and helpful models for how people in an intimate relationship should act toward one another? Or does the culture instead offer up an exclusive diet of over-romantized or sexualized images of love and commitment?

Thinking preventively also requires expanding the problem context into the non-social environment: what are the typical sources of annoyance that may spark pathological interactions? Lack of money, noisy neighbors, insufficient time to devote to household tasks that create a more relaxing or ordered physical environment? Conversely, does the social or physical environment offer opportunities for building resilience to domestic annoyances? Are there opportunities for growth, optimism, inspiration, or a sense of accomplishment?

4. How Preventive Thinking Leads to Better Solutions

a. Expanding the options for interventions

Expanding the understanding of a problem into the broader, more dynamic interactions that characterize preventive thinking may make solutions seem far more elusive. How can one address at any practical level, for example, a culture that offers only narrow stereotypes of people's roles or interactions? How can any one person hope to diversify an economy or technological offerings? Yet one need not change all of the elements that comprise a pathological dynamic leading to the emergence of a need. *Because of the very complexity of the interactions, progress toward a solution can be made at any number of possible points of intervention.* One can address the immediate punishing behaviors of a couple toward one another; or attempt to remove some of the chronic sources of annoyance or disagreement; or help them seek out alternative models for how they regard themselves and their relationship; or help them build resilience in the face of future challenges.

Hence thinking preventively is not hopelessly idealized or unrealistic. On the contrary, it expands the possible positive steps that can help solve the problem. Preventive steps are not mutually exclusive: one sort of intervention that suggests a way to break the pathological chain does not normally exclude any other sort of intervention. Similarly, various steps can be taken simultaneously and the interventions can work at different speeds. Some interventions could have small, immediate effects, and others interventions could be a lifetime's work, but life altering. Further, preventive thinking does not preclude taking steps that may ameliorate an immediate need, although certainly one must be mindful not to add resources that feed the pathology and thus create future exaggerated needs. Understanding the elements of the pathology and their interaction will reduce the chances that adding immediately ameliorative resources will lead to the paradoxical long term consequences.

b. Investing others with finding a solution

Preventive thinking can also mean harnessing many minds toward a change. Rather than imagine that a problem is fixed by a one-time commitment of additional resources, preventive thinking could lead to creating a social *process* that will fuel itself toward a gradual elimination of the conditions that give rise to needs. Consider, for example, sexual harassment in the workplace. If a complaint is imagined as a need to correct the behaviors of a single offender, then the logical solution is punishment of that individual or possible removal from the workplace. The offender's replacement, however, may be just as bad. Or that offender's co-workers may react negatively to the discharge of the offender, and react in passive-aggressive ways that are hidden but even more offensive than the original behavior.

By looking beyond individual offenders and instead looking for the elements of a broader system that is pathologically generating the sexually offensive behaviors, interventions may be imagined that are pitched at creating a gradual process for building better communication, more empathy and sensitivity, and perhaps even incentives for positive rather than offensive behaviors. Awareness of the particular offensive behaviors, for example, can be furthered by setting up an anonymous suggestion, complaint, or inquiry box. Where appropriate, company responses or advice can be posted on a board next to the box. Or a variety of employees of both sexes, different ages, and different ranks within the company or institution can be trained to receive complaints or inquiries by both victims and potential offenders about appropriate standards. Those with questions or complaints could seek out a person whom they respect or with whom they feel comfortable. Private victim/offender reconciliation sessions can be instituted so that perspectives and emotional impacts of particular incidents can be communicated. The goal would be to move a culture from one that may currently be offensive, intimidating, or disrespectful into one of supportive accountability in which people understand origins, impacts and unacceptability of harassment. Such a move requires a process involving a large proportion of the employees rather than a rule-and-punishment based system.

c. Uncovering interests

The expansiveness of preventive thinking can also help to identify underlying interests that may be neglected in quick-fix thinking. In child custody cases, for example, quick-fix thinking may imagine the problem simply as the division of the "resource" of time with the child between the contending parents. In contrast, preventive thinking would attempt to imagine the interactions between child and each parent, between the parents themselves, among various people in any expanded or blended family, and others with whom the child may have significant contact like playmates, schoolteachers, sports coaches, and even doctors, orthodontists, etc.

Imagining these many different interactions–all elements in the social development of the child–helps shift the thinking about a child custody problem away from simply regarding the child as a resource to be allocated between two parents. Considering the child in that way may serve the immediate needs as perceived by the parents. However, it does not address many of the interests of the child in educational stability, friendships, extended family contacts, sports and play activity, and health care. The child is embedded in a larger system of contacts, some of which are rooted in or require particular sorts of physical environments. Attending to these elements both in isolation and as they may interact with one another will serve more of the child's interests, promoting a fuller and healthier upbringing. Conversely, if these various interests are real but not taken into account in the child custody arrangement, then future problems with the child's social development or among those people who care about the child are likely to increase.

d. Clarifying goals and methods

Finally, preventive thinking leads to better solutions than conventional quick-fix thinking because preventive thinking can stimulate richer, more imaginative reflection about the goals to be achieved in addressing a problem. For example, if one approaches public health care delivery (with its inevitable scarce resources) as simply a response to competing patient needs, then a logical solution is to triage among those needs, serving the most desperate but non-hopeless needs until resources run out.

In other words, attention will focus on the most acute needs and the procedures that could serve those needs. At some point the needs are so severe that they will not respond to the procedures available, and so the procedures are futile. But short of that, even heroic efforts may be devoted to saving those who are close to death.[3] This may be quick-fix thinking at its most dramatic.

The many ethical issues surrounding health care delivery are beyond the scope of this chapter. Suffice it to say, however, that although applying such heroic measures may feel courageous and life-affirming, if those sporadic episodes divert attention from the origins of disease and injury through the interactions between people and their social and physical environments, then much human suffering will not be prevented that might have been prevented through better nutrition and relatively easy public health measures. Thinking more fully about the origins of health needs in these systems of interaction would open up choices for goals and methods of public health care delivery.

———————————

The paragraphs above offer a window into additional obstacles facing the adoption of the Preventive approach to lawyering, again drawn from the article in SCANDINAVIAN STUDIES IN LAW:

C. The Relative Difficulty of Preventive Thinking

First, preventive thinking is more difficult than quick-fix thinking. It requires both a deeper investigation and a broader investigation. Not only must problems be situated in a context of elements that may be difficult to discern, but then the ways in which those elements interact with one another must be understood. Strong powers of imagination and access to particular information are required. Even when the elements and their pathological patterns are discovered, at least some of the interventions that suggest themselves for breaking those patterns may be very difficult or expensive. Broad cultural or environmental influences may undeniably contribute to the recurrence of a

———————————

[3] Guido Calabresi and Philip Bobbitt, TRAGIC CHOICES (1978).

problem, but making effective changes to those influences may be virtually impossible for any individual or group. A more feasible strategy may be to isolate or insulate the problem holder against those cultural or environmental factors, but even that could be expensive or lead to unintended secondary consequences.

1. Not All Problem Elements May Be Under Central Control

Second, it may turn out that this broadened context uncovers disparate elements that are beyond the reach or control of any single advisor or decision maker. Where this occurs, difficulties of coordination and resource contribution arise among the various persons who would be required for effective preventive action. Being effective preventively may require resolving issues of trust and free rider exploitation among problem solvers. In these instances, a process solution should be devised like that described for dealing with sexual harassment. Many people should be given the incentive and easy opportunity to contribute individually toward a general solution.

2. Preventive Solutions May Be Relatively Slow and Invisible

Third, preventive solutions are not always the "quick fix" that quick-fix thinking promotes. Especially where interventions target the more general cultural or environmental elements of a problem dynamic, breaking the links of the problem dynamic may take time.

Further, even a relatively fast-acting intervention could be almost invisible. The successes of preventive thinking are often measured by the *absence* of something: anger, waste, litigation, crime, drug abuse, mental or physical health problems. Even where these effects have been successfully lessened by a preventive intervention, it may be hard for some people to credit that the intervention is actually responsible for these positive changes. The intervention may not leave visible causal tracings for its effects, leading some to imagine that the problem somehow has fixed itself or that some person or persons in the problem pathology had suddenly been enlightened. It may be difficult to convince these observers that the original problem dynamic may have strongly and persistently reinforced the pre-existing patterns, so that a spontaneous moral revelation or intellectual epiphany by anyone in the system was highly unlikely.

This phenomenon of people failing to credit preventive interventions because effective results are merely the absence of new symptoms can be especially challenging to practicing lawyers whose clients must pay for their efforts. If preventive action will not be valued by a skeptical client, then the attorney will have an incentive to employ quick-fix thinking with its possibly more dramatic or visible results. Preventive lawyers must realize this phenomenon and take constant steps to apprize the client of what the lawyer understands as the problem dynamic and the affirmative steps taken to break the chain of pathology. A stronger client understanding of the lawyer's analysis and intervention strategy will help the client credit the preventive process for what it may have achieved, which is potentially high cost savings in the long run.

3. Metaphors by Which We Understand Problems

It may also be that the metaphors we commonly employ to understand problems do not promote preventive thinking. Metaphors are powerful tools by which we process and classify novel information that would otherwise be utterly confounding. Through metaphor we can draw a coherent picture in our minds of the data coming to our senses ,or of concepts that are otherwise too complex to process. Paradoxically, however, as soon as we are able to comprehend or cope with information through using a metaphor, that same metaphor has the potential either to capture and thus constrain our imagination, or even to corrupt our understanding concerning the problem.

Metaphor capture occurs when we become too heavily dependent on the metaphor, forgetting that it is merely a tool for understanding some phenomenon rather than the phenomenon itself. The danger is that the attributes of any single metaphor will suggest one particular logical solution. Any single solution may, however, not be adequate, not to mention that unless the metaphor is especially dynamic the solution suggested may be purely resource-based, which we recall is the scourge of quick-fix thinking. Using "pothole" metaphorically to picture and understand the nature of problems is a good example of a metaphor that will often be too crude to reach a preventive solution.

Metaphor "corruption" can occur because the use of metaphor involves understanding a novel phenomenon through its patterned similarities with some object or concept we already understand. The metaphor helps us see and understand facets of a problem that we could otherwise have overlooked. But that same helpfulness can be counterproductive if we may fail to discern the limitations of the similarities between the metaphor and the phenomenon we are really addressing. If that happens we may self-deceivingly attribute properties of the metaphor to the real problem. By not knowing when to drop the metaphor, our understanding of the phenomenon is not just incomplete, but becomes inaccurate. Hence once again we may be drawn to a possible solution that feels both rational and reasonable, but is actually flawed owing to the overuse of a metaphor for understanding the problem.

A historical example may be helpful, an example in which a metaphor was over-applied to the real problem, thus resulting in a solution that was counterproductive: Prior to our scientific understanding of infectious agents, disease was sometimes understood through the idea of "bad blood," which was akin to the spoiling of meat or lettuce. In the spoiling of food, something that normally is good is inexplicitly transformed into something bad. Regardless of the reason, however, when this transformation occurred the spoiled part would act as a polluting agent toward all that surrounded it. Spoiled meat or lettuce should therefore be cut away, removed from what remains healthy; otherwise everything would soon be bad.

When disease was understood through this metaphor, the organism's blood was likened to the role of the meat or lettuce. Under the metaphor, when the blood became inexplicitly bad it also became dangerous, polluting the organism and resulting in the illness that was manifesting various symptoms. Extending the metaphor further suggested a treatment for the disease that was often disastrous: leeches were applied to patients in an effort to remove the bad blood. The metaphor of spoilage had been taken too literally and completely. It captured physician's imaginations too strongly. Further, the metaphor actually corrupted understanding because physicians attributed too many attributes of the metaphor to the real problem. Drawing out the bad blood through leeching not only did nothing to cure the infection, but it actually weakened and ultimately killed many patients who otherwise would have survived their diseases through the normal operation of the human immune system. Acting through the metaphor, however, seemed both rational and reasonable.

In using any metaphor, therefore, two points are recommended. First, do not be satisfied with only one. Constantly attempt to understand how the problem is being framed or processed. Then consciously change the metaphor, perhaps by seeking advice from someone else for an alternative. Working with multiple metaphors will put sufficient skeptical distance between any one metaphor and the mind of the problem solver.

Second, try to find metaphors that are dynamic and interactive. For example, now that we understand better the systems quality of infectious disease better, infectious disease actually can work well as a general metaphor for understanding problems, or at least far better than the metaphor of a pothole. Infectious diseases inherently involve the interaction of an infected patient or problem-holder with a physical world pathogen (a bacterium or virus, which may thrive only in particular environments), through a human or animal carrier which is part of the patient's social or physical environment. Further, physicians and nurses–those attempting to treat or quarantine the pathogen--also become part of the patient's social environment. By thinking of problems in general through this more complex metaphor, various possible points of interaction between individuals and their social and non-social environments are prompted. Further, the possible intervention points that could break the pathological dynamic may become more visible.

4. An Instrumental Mentality?

A possible final factor that may impede the development of preventive thinking is a general instrumental mentality with which Westerners, perhaps especially Americans, approach life. Within Western formal legal institutions, issues of process in decision making are typically thoughtfully considered and carefully protected. Even so, its legal thought has been characterized as "instrumental rationality,"[4] converging relentlessly on a judgment. Outside of the formal legal system, within the popular culture, process concerns are far more limited. "Bottom line" thinking often prevails. That is, the results of an inquiry or problem solving effort are typically the major focus, rather than questions of how such result may have been achieved. This prevailing pragmatism may be both efficient and appropriate in countries comprised of disparate religious and ethnic traditions. Ideological or highly value-laden orientations to problem solving processes could be inflammatory or excluding, and therefore are not officially established.

Preventive thinking resists an instrumental mentality that leads to pressures, either internally or politically generated, to act quickly toward a problem by adopting crude quick-fix measures. In that sense it may be stylistically or superficially counter-cultural. Yet preventive thinking does not advance an ideology apart from seeking to relieve people of unnecessary pain or expense. Furthermore, preventive thinking is highly pragmatic. It may not always achieve quick or highly visible results, but it always seeks effective, efficient outcomes through imaginative interventions that disrupt a problem dynamic. Although requiring patience and careful, imaginative investigation, the ultimate goal of preventive thinking is human betterment, in real world terms.

. . .

[In conclusion], preventive thinking has many advantages over quick-fix thinking. It can address the most complex problems, and help people better

---

[4] Robert S. Summers, INSTRUMENTALISM AND AMERICAN LEGAL THEORY (1982).

understand their effects on other people as well as on the physical or financial environment. It can produce more comprehensive and durable solutions that are often cheaper than the results of quick-fix thinking. It does, however, require time, energy, and imagination. Sometimes, it also requires some convincing of clients and others who would prefer faster or more apparently visible results. By offering one set of steps that can generally be taken in preventive thinking, hopefully the preventive process will be made easier, its processes will be more boldly undertaken by lawyers and others, and more attention will be devoted to developing its principles.

THE "PROBLEM" OBSTACLE (Part II): Asking Better Questions and Building Better Frames

Becoming a more effective lawyer–preventive or otherwise--requires working strongly and imaginatively with the particular facts of each client. Prevention, like client counseling generally, does not work with a "one size fits all" mentality. At least initially, particular useful may be in the possession of a client or witness. Lawyers should therefore be well equipped for asking questions of others in a manner that is appropriate to the setting and source of information. Once the information is collected, however, the lawyer must learn to ask searching questions addressed to the lawyer's own imagination. The late Professor Janeen Kerper's insights on this skill are reprinted below, with permission.

A. Asking Questions of Clients and Witnesses

Problem Investigation and Client Needs Assessment
© Janeen Kerper

Basic Forms of Questions

The art of asking questions and gathering information is one of the most basic skills a lawyer can have. Different questions have different effects, and the skilled problem solver is acutely aware of how to ask questions to elicit the maximum of information, with a minimum of suggestion or contamination of the information by the questioner. Trial lawyers are especially conscious of the difference between leading and non-leading questions because leading questions are objectionable on direct examination, while the use of non-leading questions on cross-examination will often lead to a loss of control of the witness. The following provides a description of the most basic forms of questions and their effects and uses.

Open–ended questions: These questions invite the responder to talk. They begin with words or phrases like "what, where, when, why, how, please tell, please explain, describe," etc. Level 1 questions are especially useful to elicit information. They are the most desirable form of question on direct examination. Note that the most open-ended of all questions, and the one calculated to produce maximum information, is the one that begins with an **inviting imperative** such as "Tell me, describe, explain, share with me, etc."

Semi-closed questions: These questions usually begin with a verb such as "did you, have you, are you." Judges often rule that questions asked in this form are leading. These questions are particularly useful to focus an area of inquiry, to clarify an earlier statement, to follow up on the details of information that the responder has already presented in general form. For example if a witness has just given a general description of a robbery, you may want to follow up with level to questions like: "Did you see the robber's face? Was his clothing neat and clean or torn and dirty?, etc"

Closed questions: [These] are not really questions. They are statements with question tags. The responder is expected to answer merely yes or no. Examples: "Your name is Jack, isn't it?" "Bill Clinton is the President, right?" "You were born on the fourth of July, correct?" "Isn't it a fact that you missed class yesterday?" Level 3 questions elicit very little information and they tend to sound accusatory. They are very useful to control a witness on cross-examination.

Leading questions: Technically, a leading question is one that suggests the answer. [Open-ended] questions can be leading—e.g. "How blue was his jacket?" However, in actual practice judges seldom rule that [those] questions are leading. They frequently rule that [semi-closed] questions are leading. [Closed] questions are always leading.

Focusing questions: Clients being interviewed and witnesses on the stand sometimes tend to digress or ramble. One of the best ways to focus their attention on a particular topic or area is to ask a Level 1 question containing a modifier of place or time. *E.g.*, "What was it that *first* caught your attention?" "What were you doing at around *8:40 p.m.* that evening?" "What happened *after* the man stumbled *at the curb*? "Describe what happened *in the living room.*"

Non-judgmental questions: Often when they are asked questions concerning their opinions clients, witnesses or prospective jurors are concerned that they will be judged negatively for their thoughts. One way to reassure the responder that he/she will not be judged negatively is to preface the question with a range of opinions: *e.g.* "Some people feel very comfortable with people of other races; others feel strongly that the races should not mix. How do you feel on that issue?" ...

Looping questions: Looping questions are those which incorporate a piece of the responder's previous answer. Consider the following example:

Q1. "Why did you choose to go to law school?"

A: "I have always wanted to go to law school, ever since I was a kid. I loved to argue and my parents always told me I had a big mouth. I studied *debate in college* and I loved it!"

Q2. "What did you particularly like about *debate in college?*"

In this example, Q2 is the looping question because it incorporates a piece of the previous answer. The looping question is particularly valuable because it impresses the responder that they are truly being listened to, and provides the interchange with a sense of connectedness and continuity.

Reflective statements: Reflective statements are paraphrase the responder's statements and reflect back to them both the content of the statement itself as well as any accompanying unstated emotions implicit in the statement. Consider the following exchange between Joe and Jim:

"Hey Joe, how are you doing?"

"Not too well, Jim. I got my grades back, and I'm thinking of quitting law school"

"Wow, Joe! You're so disappointed with your grades, you're thinking of leaving? You must feel pretty sad about that."

Note that Jim hasn't really asked a question, he has simply reflected back both the content and the feeling implicit in Joe's statement. Reflective statements are at the heart of the skill known as "active listening." They are extremely useful to test and demonstrate understanding of what the responder has said. Surprisingly, even though they are not questions, reflective statements are also a very useful way to elicit information.

Being still: Closely related to the reflective statement is the art of silence. Very often the simple act of being quiet and saying nothing will encourage another to divulge more information. Negotiators are often very skilled at the use of silence, and find it very effective in negotiating with very aggressive, competitive people who often abhor silence and therefore will often give away more information than they initially intended to a negotiator who has mastered the art of silence.

Hypothetical questions: Hypothetical questions ask the listener to suppose or imagine something and to react to it. "Suppose we sued X and won a judgment against them, how would that make your life better? Hypothetical questions are very useful in helping clients think through their underlying interests and

133

what might be the impact of some of their decisions.

Ideal position questions: Ideal position questions press the interviewee to describe how he or she wishes it would be, *e.g.* "Picture yourself in your ideal occupation. What would you be doing? What would your day be like?"

Flawed position questions: Flawed position questions are the opposite of ideal position questions. They press to interviewee to speculate on the opposite of the desired state, *e.g.,* "Picture yourself in your worst nightmare of a job. What would you be doing? What would your day be like?" Flawed position questions are very helpful in getting interviewees to focus on things that may be wrong with their current situation, and in getting them to articulate what needs to be changed for them to solve their problems.

Interpretive or summarizing questions: Interpretive or summarizing questions tie together some of what you have been hearing and solicit further information from the respondent. *E.g.,* "You've told me about the water scarcity, the plumbing defects, and the heating and air-conditioning problems you are experiencing in your new home, are there any others? Which of these would you describe as most serious?"

Devil's advocate questions: Devil's advocate questions are designed to test the validity of underlying assumptions and to persuade a respondent to consider a position he or she might not have considered. *E,g.,* "Right or wrong, what do you think the other side will say about why they should win this lawsuit?"

Disconfirming questions: Disconfirming questions are closely related to devil's advocate questions. They are specifically designed to test the basis of assumptions and to verify that what you believe to be true is indeed true. Suppose for example that you have heard from several sources within a company that demand for a certain product is soaring. A disconfirming question might be: "Is it true there has been a recent slump in demand for this product?" Disconfirming questions are designed to counteract a common human failing known as "**confirmation bias**", i.e. our tendency to look for information that confirms our working hypothesis and to overlook or reject information that disconfirms it. To make sure we are on the right track in any investigation, we need to learn to ask disconfirming questions as well as confirming questions. Another form of disconfirming question is one that suggests an alternative hypothesis, *e.g.,* suppose you believe that some material missing from the company's plant might be stolen. A disconfirming question here might be: "How else could this inventory discrepancy be accounted for? Could there be an accounting error? Could waste be a problem?"

Reaction questions: Reaction questions provide the respondent with something specific to respond to. It might be a list, a graphic, a picture, a video or the like. *E.g.,* "I want you to listen to this audiotape of an exchange between your employee and myself, and tell me what you think of it."

Close-out questions: Close out questions are designed to make sure that you have covered all of the information available from a particular source about a particular topic. *E.g.,* "Do I have a complete picture this situation? "Is there anything else I should ask you about this?" Close out questions are very useful in investigations, negotiations and deposition settings. Sometimes they can be coupled with interpretative or summarizing questions to make sure that all the ground has been covered, *e.g.,* "You have told me about three conversations you had with your boss about the harassment you were suffering, one in October, one in November and one in December. Have you now told me all of the conversations you had with you boss on this topic?"

B. Building Better Frames

Metaphors and their less vivid cousins "frames" present a paradox. On the one hand, they give us intellectual footing where the ground is unfamiliar. They create an instant coherence for what we are examining, and thus enable us to ask questions about what may be missing. However, metaphors may be clung too longer than they should be, and they may even be misleading from the outset. Finally, they clearly are generated out of personal imaginations, experiences, and values. Generating multiple frames and metaphors will advance one's problem solving, but we should be aware of their possibility to lull us into a false sense of responsibility or detachment. Simply put, framing problems is both necessary and stifling.

Ed Dauer once communicated the following true story to me, which nicely illustrates both the power and the consequent dilemma of problem framing:

> Some years ago I had a friend named Jim, who had a wife named Jackie and a child named Laura, who had a cat. The cat got stuck in a tree. Jackie had a solution for that problem. She put sardines in the bottom of a large garbage pail, tied a rope to the handle, and tried to throw the rope over a branch above where the cat was. The theory was that the cat would be attracted by the sardines to jump into the pail, which could then be lowered on the rope to the ground.

> Jim also had an idea, rather different. He suggested that he get his shotgun, and shoot the cat out of the tree.

> I thought these were equally valid solutions, though to different

definitions of the problem. To Jackie, the problem was how to retrieve the cat from the tree. To Jim, the problem was how to rid the tree of the cat.

In fact, they did neither. After a day of not being able to throw the rope, Jackie gave up. Jim was disappointed that the cat came down by itself when it got hungry, rather than starving to death.

The diverging categories of Jackie and Jim show the power of framing: a particular frame can convey either that a given situation is not a problem at all, or may suggest particular processes for thinking about or deciding a matter, or may connote specific solutions. We inevitably do this sorting of problems, in order to make the problem more comprehensible or tractable. Ironically, however, the same classification process that makes problems more digestible also limits the imaginativeness and originality of their ultimate solution.

Almost as soon as a person has perceived a problem, the person begins framing the problem by sorting it along the following dimensions:

- *what one knows*

- *one's goals*

- *who one is.*

What One Knows

"What one knows" channels profoundly the likely outcome of a problem that one faces. Three dimensions of knowledge can be identified, all of which contribute to this channeling: (1) the *information and beliefs* one has about cause, magnitude, complexity, and context of the problem; (2) the repertoire of *processing* that one has available to apply to the information and decision making; and (3) the historical *solutions* that work as a model for solving the instant problem.

1. Framing Problems by Information and Beliefs

As with each of the other dimensions below, information and beliefs about a problem both advance and limit the solutions that are adopted. If *erroneous* information is collected, then obviously that could impede problem solution. Not so obviously, even if *accurate* information is collected, solutions may be impeded by the search for information.

This ironic result does not stem from the collected information itself. Rather, the *process* of obtaining information can be counterproductive toward reaching an optimal solution. This can occur for two reasons: first, the search for information may divert one from thinking harder about the problem and considering alternative possible solutions. Second, if accurate information is received and processed within an erroneous framework or metaphor, then the information may merely serve to strengthen misguided judgments. I amplify each of these possibilities in the paragraphs that follow.

Really creative problem solving is achieved by: (a) thinking seriously, questioningly, and flexibly about one's goals; (b) trying to understand any given problem within a systemic context in which actions inevitably ripple out and feed back; and © brainstorming various possible solutions, giving full rein to one's imagination. Were one to neglect those tools of problem solving, but instead simply to search for facts, one would likely come to a conventional, perhaps sub-optimal, solution. The lure of fact investigation is that to engage in it is almost unquestionably to act in a responsible, methodical, and empirically sound fashion toward the problem. Yet if done to the exclusion of other problem solving methods, fact investigation becomes an obstacle to creative solutions.

As a possible example of this shortcoming, imagine African governmental officials and environmentalists twenty five years ago facing the problem of the slaughter of elephants for their tusks. Suppose that again and again in response to the problem, these decision makers had done no more than attempt to discover information about the identities of the poachers. Searching for this information would certainly be both logical and responsible, if one frames the problem in terms of law enforcement.

The frame of a problem will *always* suggest a logical path to follow in gathering information toward problem solution. As a problem about criminality, gathering information about poacher identity would certainly help solve the problem framed: more poachers would be prosecuted. The decision makers would then label their efforts a success. Yet no matter how efficacious, they never would achieve more than the punishment of known offenders, plus an unknown deterrent effect on future poaching.

We now know, however, that framing the problem as purely one of criminality, which leads to factual investigation and subsequent prosecution, does not produce an optimal solution. We know that because historically those facing the problem actually went *beyond* framing the problem solely in terms of the apprehension and prosecution of the poachers, and that is what it took ultimately to address the problem better.

By thinking systemically, they were able to see that the relationship between villagers and poachers had become symbiotic: poor, hungry villagers ate the meat left behind by ivory-stealing poachers. To make real progress toward saving elephants, the officials needed to break the link between the poachers and the villagers. The officials finally did break apart this collaboration by enclosing portions of the elephants' range into a national park. Within this vast park, eco-tourism was supported through infrastructural developments. The result was that the decision makers created strong incentives for the villagers to preserve, rather than eat, the elephants. The villagers then were willing to assist in stopping poaching. Poaching declined, and the villagers were made better off through the multiplier effects of increased eco-tourism. Furthermore, non-endangered wildlife sharing the same habitat as elephants was made more plentiful due to the creation of the elephant reserves.

Stopping and thinking, rather than merely continuing to search for accurate information logically pertaining to the original framing of the problem, was the key to a broader, more creative solution to the elephant problem. At the "stop and think" point, one should consciously attempt to imagine how the evidence may actually *falsify* one's prevailing conceptions about the problem. By so imagining, one is forced to conceive an alternative framework for the problem.

2. *Framing Problems by Procedures*

Just as one can be deceived and trapped by an inaccurate frame or metaphor, really **creative solutions can be obstructed by framing a problem according to either a traditional method of processing a solution, or by the traditional solution itself.**

When, for example, we assume too readily that a given problem is a "legal problem," or an "economic problem," or a "moral problem," we are framing the problem in a way that preempts looking at the problem through a variety of alternative substantive and decisional assumptions. The same unnecessary self-limitation occurs where we too quickly assume that a problem is "personal"–and thus to be solved privately–or that it is "technical"–and thus to be solved mechanically, without reflection about higher purposes. Yet further, we may assume that a problem is "controversial," and thus to be solved in a particular authoritarian or democratic way, or that the result should be hidden from public view, or that the solution should be less ambitious so as to avoid giving offense or sparking opposition. The point is that when we affix these labels about appropriate process, we both identify to ourselves what we regard as the next logical step to take with the problem, and we also limit our opportunities to explore the problem in different ways.

3. *Framing Problems by Traditional Solutions*

Channeling one's definition and exploration of a problem by the traditional solution applied to it can be another way in which we both assist, and limit, our problem solving skills. We do this when we label a problem by its remedy. Where someone says, "Here's another zoning problem," they are forgetting that zoning is a particular solution to land use issues. By framing it as a "zoning" problem they are unconsciously foreclosing other possible ways of dealing with, or even thinking about, conflicting land use issues.

Considered more broadly, we frame problems by solutions each time we cite a rule regarding behavior and thereby consider the matter settled. Such invocation of a rule/solution may then move beyond simply framing a problem: using rules or traditional solutions may actually mask that a problem *exists*. When a parent watches a child struggle with eating peas, the parent may say, "Use your fork for eating peas, and use it in your right hand." In this example, the problem of how to eat peas has been framed by the rule/solution so completely that no one thinks of it as a real problem. "That's something we have already taken care of," the rule invoker is effectively saying. Clearly, however, more efficient ways of eating peas exist. Invoking taken-for-granted rules, although necessary for an ordered existence and unquestionably efficient, may for any given problem doom us to a sub-optimal solution. As fast as social and personal environments change, it is probably safe to say that at some point virtually every rule needs to be rethought.

The peas example is trivial, but it can stand for something far more important. Rules of decorum, taste, or hierarchy have for centuries masked or suppressed problems of social inequality and racial relations. *Some* rule/solutions, in other words, are insidious. They beguile us into passive inaction, or even active suppression of evidence that the rule is unjust.

One's Goals

One's goals influence one's framing of a problem and, thereby, the information one seeks about the problem and the consequent solutions to which one gravitates. This is clear from the anecdote about Laura's cat. Jim's goal was to eliminate the cat from his life. Hence the solution of shooting the cat out of the tree made sense to him. Indeed, the thought of it was quite agreeable to Jim. Jackie's goal, in contrast, was to save the cat from harm, and therefore she devised a plan to attempt to lure it. Each person framed a problem–either saving the cat or ridding the household of a nuisance–consistent with his or her goals. Assuming Jackie's framing of the problem, Jim's solution was monstrous. Given Jim's framing of the problem, Jackie's solution was wasteful and ineffective.

Jackie was probably lucky for having failed in her solution. If her solution had worked, the cat would likely have scampered back up the tree out of reach, having now been rewarded with a tasty fish treat for just that behavior. By driving her problem framing too strongly by her goal of getting the cat down without harm, Jackie neglected to imagine the unintended ripple effects of her solution. A better way of framing the problem, given Jackie's real goals, would perhaps be "how to discourage the cat from climbing the tree." Letting the cat climb down by itself, after the cat has effectively been punished for tree climbing by experiencing hunger, accomplishes Jackie's goal better than Jackie's own solution. Sometimes the best solution to a problem is to let the particular environment or behavior self-destroy from its own dynamic, rather than try to change things.

Who One Is

The influence of "who one is" on problem framing is also more or less self evident, although it is difficult to describe with any precision. One's identity--if by that one means one's loyalties, values, race, religion, memories, sources of pride and shame, biases, and fears--will figure toward how a problem is conceived. The problem of "law and order," for example, may well be framed differently by a minority person than a middle-aged white male. Different questions will be asked, different metaphors will be used, and information will be differently interpreted.

One's character–as distinct from one's goals–will also influence the identification and framing of problems. A person of strong character may regard behavior as problematic, perhaps even corrupt or repugnant, while a person of weaker character would accept that same behavior as inconsequential or as not worth some personal risk entailed by lodging an objection. Finally, one's sensitivity will also affect one's perception of problems. A relatively callous or obtuse person is obviously less likely to identify some pattern as problematic than a person who is more easily distressed, or who is more attuned to the feelings of others.

4. Conclusion: How Can Framing Be Done Better?

As suggested above, problems must always be framed. We cannot make sense of data in which we completely lack a frame for interpretation. Yet we need not frame a given problem *only one way.* Framing problems in multiple ways will naturally suggest alternative paths to investigate; alternative procedures for making decisions; and, finally, alternative solutions.

The first step toward developing better problem framing skills is simply realizing how strongly we get channeled in our problem solving by our search for information, our metaphors for interpreting that information, the traditional procedures and solutions by which the problem is typically discussed, and who we are.

The second step is to adopt habits of reflection that allow us to climb out of the channels and assess new possible directions. Three problem solving tools were mentioned above: (a) assessing goals flexibly, critically, and from various perspectives and levels of abstraction; (b) thinking systematically, trying to anticipate and appreciate the second and third order consequences to our actions; and c) brainstorming possible solutions with other people. Each of these tools requires imagination and self-skepticism; knowledge of, and respect for, the diversity of human background and values; and a willingness to admit limitations and mistake.

C. Asking Fuller Questions

Here is a little exercise to check your openness to those qualities.[1] Suppose I were to ask the question ***"Why do earthquakes happen?"*** Unless you are unusual, you are likely to respond in technical, causal terms referring to tectonic plates.

---

[1] This exercise builds on work done during the 1940's and 1950's by legal anthropologist Max Gluckman (*see* CUSTOM AND CONFLICT IN AFRICA (1955), and in the 1990's by moral philosopher Judith Sklar (*see* THE FACES OF INJUSTICE (1990)). In a different format, this exercise was first presented at the Spring, 2005 ABA-ADR Conference and is published on the website of the Subcommittee for Lawyers as Problem Solvers.

But we should note that when you respond in this way, the word "why" in the question has tacitly been changed to the word *"how."* In other words, you have generated an explanation in causal terms even where it is not called for explicitly. The question as posed is not necessarily technical at all, yet in our culture most people respond to natural events *only* in technical, causal terms. Other meanings for the word "why," in this context, are scarcely in our imagination.

Occasionally a person will respond to the original question with an explanation about God's will, or–even more rarely–in terms of "karma,"although that is more a relic of 1960's culture. An explanation based on religion or cosmic purpose represents a fundamentally different view of life. If someone expresses skepticism about this kind of response, the person articulating it could elaborate by saying, "Sure, I know technically what causes earthquakes, but knowing that does not answer the issues of 'why this place and not 100 miles north on the fault line? Why now and not next year? Why was my family affected, and not our next door neighbors?'"

As re-phrased, the difference in approach is at least more comprehensible. It is not necessarily even a minority view in our culture, but rather the view is being applied in an unusual context. People in our culture tend to reason either religiously or fatalistically to the particular questions about this place or that; my family versus another suffering the injury. The answers are either that the damage was random and the question is pointless ("karma"), or that the damage is the will of God and in a sense is thus imponderable.

At this point we can imagine that people from cultures quite different from our own would answer the original question "Why do earthquakes happen," quite differently than we do. People with less sophisticated understanding of natural causes may think about earthquakes in terms that are mythical or metaphorical. In the explanatory narratives that people offer, note how often moral lessons about community, or personal relationships, or the nature of evil are inserted. Imponderables, in other words, are turned into opportunities for moral education or civics lessons. Now that we have a more well-honed understanding of science and randomness in our culture, do we lose something in the way that we talk about problems?

That leads to a second question: ***"Who is responsible for earthquakes?"*** People in our culture are often slow to answer this question. This follows from the modal response to the first question in which the "how" question is technical and the "why" question is almost unanswerable.

When one starts to think in more detail about the ***damage*** caused by earthquakes, however, then suddenly human responsibility comes to mind, even to the lawyerly mind. Are the people responsible who designed or built buildings that were too flimsy? Is the government responsible for setting inadequate standards for those buildings? Is the water authority responsible for not providing emergency water supplies after the aqueducts broke from the shaking of the earth? Are the telephone and electricity companies responsible, for not burying their cables, as a result of which service was not available when most needed? Are the employers responsible who did not plan ahead with a building evacuation plan?

Attributing blame–*i.e.,* moving away from thinking about earthquakes as "misfortune" and moving instead to thinking of earthquakes as "injustice"[2]–requires different ways of thinking from the scientific, the fatalistic, the religious, or the mythical. It starts being deductive from certain overriding principles about standards of duty and care. We start to analogize from other life circumstances and duties to others–all part of the legal mentality. Thinking legally is not wrong–it is part of a legitimate repertoire of conceptualizations of a problem. It can be responsive to answer this second question about the responsibility for earthquakes.

Suppose we now start asking questions like ***"How may earthquakes be prevented?"*** If understood technically, the "problem" of earthquakes has no possible solution, since we cannot yet control or even affect those forces of nature. And yet if "earthquakes are understood through a different language system from the technical/scientific, it starts to have some possible solutions and even "preventions." If the problem of earthquakes is understood as the *damage* they cause from human omissions, then individuals and communities can be mobilized to prevent or at least soften the problem. Preventive/problem-solving mentalities may now be used: Organize a statement of the problem; brainstorm alternative points of intervention; then assess costs, side-effects, and effectiveness of solutions. But until we can re-frame the questions in different ways, we cannot even imagine earthquakes as a problem, much less bring the law or prevention strategies to bear.

Finally, let us ask a fourth question: ***"How may we console those who have suffered loss through earthquakes?"*** If we consider questions like how we approach people who have lost family members in earthquakes, or people who have been injured in some life-changing ways, or whether we should risk our own well-being to save others, then we may start to think about the answers in terms that are different from questions of justice, but also different from instrumental problem-solving.

Answering questions like this take us to issues about the value of belonging to others–either intimately or in communities. We begin to see how self-respect and integrity are tied to the fates of others. When we hear phrases like "turning problems into opportunities," it may entail thinking about loyalty and moral courage to gain a higher level of insight. Are such concepts foreign to lawyers? If so, are we satisfied with the level of counseling we are capable of offering to our clients? Are we satisfied with ourselves? In a wrongful death case, for example, the client is the deceased's estate. The family, however, will have suffered the loss. Asking after their welfare and inviting their memories of the deceased will give them an opportunity to share their grief. It would be not your burden, but rather a chance for your uplifting.

---

[2] Sklar, *supra* note 1.

CHAPTER XII
THE "TRUTH" OBSTACLE: Legal Truth and the Dilemmas of Post-Enlightenment Thought

Of all the various connections among elements comprising the legal system, ideas about "truth" may be most difficult to grasp. In part that is because we tend, unreflectively, to take for granted the criteria of truth that we apply to routine problems. And yet, as the essay below makes clear, what is satisfactory "truth" about legal questions may be quite different from what may be satisfactory about scientific questions. And those criteria for measuring scientific truth differ from how we instinctively measure truth about relationships, or about aesthetics, or about spiritual matters. Our culture gradually constructs varying standards about the truth, but those criteria operate at such a deep level that we rarely stop to think about whether the criteria are valid, are in need of reform, or how our criteria about truth influence the institutions or methods that we employ regarding various problems.

The essay below attempts to sketch some intellectual history about our criteria for "legal truth" by contrasting it with scientific inquiry. As Western culture moves beyond the Enlightenment philosophy that shaped the standards for both legal and scientific thought, the mutual influence between truth criteria, and the procedures by which we investigate problems becomes more clear. As discussed in earlier Chapters, the elements that comprise the legal system move together through their mutual interaction. Truth criteria may evolve more slowly, but their impact may be dramatic for ushering in the U/I/A paradigm.

The article below appeared originally in 13 SOCIAL EPISTEMOLOGY 99 (1999), published by Taylor and Francis (U.K.). The website of this British journal is found at http://www.informaworld.com. British spellings and various formatting have been changed to conform to the other Chapters in this book. The article is challenging, but largely because the social and cultural aspects of truth are so rarely explored. A careful reading of the article will offer rewards for understanding why legal procedures take their traditional shape, and how cultural changes pose challenges to the legal system.

LAW AND SCIENCE
IN THE ENLIGHTENMENT AND BEYOND
By Thomas D. Barton

What sort of truth should we demand of our law? Does it emulate the sort of truth we regard as scientific? Should it do so? To ask these three questions is to make three corresponding assumptions:

- First, that truth may take different shapes, possessing varying criteria of validity depending on the context in which it is to be used;

- second, that human actors have some choice in specifying the varying contours of truth; and

- third, that the truth we are currently getting from the law may be unsatisfactory.

Early in this century these three questions, together with the premises on which they rest, would have seemed flip–or even cynical–to both lawyer and scientist. Law and science had been joined at the epistemological hip from the early days of the Enlightenment, and neither relativism nor postmodernism had yet arrived to resist those shared assumptions. At century's end, the three questions may no longer seem novel, but they remain vastly important. They also are becoming increasingly urgent, as Enlightenment values and methods continue to be challenged by the growth of what may be termed the "Post-Enlightenment" movement.

In its quest for reason, autonomy, objectivity, precision, and control, Enlightenment thought adopted a strategy of divide and conquer. Enlightenment methods separated mind from nature, fact from value, beauty from utility, reason from belief, law from morality, morality from science, individuals from groups, identity from role, and law from science.[1] Across various cultural landscapes of the West, however, resistance seems to be mounting to both these separationist Enlightenment methods, and to the values they serve. Art, literature, ethics, religion, popular entertainment, even politics seem to be shaking off Enlightenment soil and moving to starkly different terrain. Expressed artistically, philosophically, or ideologically, the Post-Enlightenment movement can best be understood as an effort to reconnect aspects of life that had been disconnected in the Enlightenment quest for purity of knowledge. The goals are a fuller conception of self, and a more interactive conception of humans and environment.[2]

The methods employed to regain these connections are notable by their contrast to Enlightenment procedures and focus: feelings over reason; empathy over analysis; community over individuals; loyalty over self-determination;

---

[1] Thomas D. Barton, *Troublesome Connections: the Law and Post-Enlightenment Culture*, 47 EMORY LAW JOURNAL 163, 166-67 (1998).

[2] *See generally* Roberto M. Unger, 1976, LAW IN MODERN SOCIETY: TOWARD A CRITICISM OF SOCIAL THEORY (1976); Lawrence M. Tribe, *Technology Assessment and the Fourth Discontinuity: the Limits of Instrumental Rationality,* 46 SOUTHERN CALIFORNIA LAW REVIEW 617 (1973).

context over parsing; particulars over universals; concrete over abstract. How far should law or science travel along this Post-Enlightenment path? How far *can* they so journey without compromising either the qualities of truth that have constituted their distinctive outlooks, or the social functions that have justified their institutional power? Such questions define the dilemmas that may confront law and science in the next century. Although the strength of the Post-Enlightenment movement is difficult to gauge, the trends are strong enough to warrant speculation on the consequences of its possible prevalence.

Such conjecture is the primary purpose of this paper. In searching for firm footing, I first describe the influence of core Enlightenment concepts on the development of scientific and legal procedures. Next, I summarize the challenges to the Enlightenment heritage over the past two hundred years: first from romanticism, and then from relativism. Finally, I describe the dilemmas that would confront law and science, were Western culture to embrace more vigorously the Post-Enlightenment assumptions about knowledge, self, and the social and physical worlds.

I. A COMMON HERITAGE: FOUR IDEAS OF THE ENLIGHTENMENT THAT INFLUENCE WESTERN LEGAL SYSTEMS

Law and science share a common Enlightenment heritage about the criteria for knowing and judging phenomena. They agree, for example, on the relationship between mind and nature that makes knowledge possible; on how truth qualities of information are enhanced by rigorous formal testing; and about the legitimacy of using judgements instrumentally to further human purposes.[3] They share a common focus for their investigations, and shared understandings of how and why things change.

These commonalities of law and science–what is studied, how that study proceeds, the authority of judgement, and the uses made of such judgements–reflect their joint embrace of the general concepts by which Enlightenment thinkers wrested intellectual dominance from pre-modern authorities. Four of those Enlightenment ideas reveal the underpinnings of modern legal and scientific procedures: individuation, detachment, segmentation, and abstraction. "Individuation" focuses analytical attention on individuals and things rather than on communities or processes. "Detachment" seeks reliability of information by separating the subjective mind from the objective environment. "Segmentation" enhances the validity of information by parsing the objective environment from its historical and social context.

---

[3] Evelyn F. Keller, REFLECTIONS ON GENDER AND SCIENCE 18 (1985).

Finally, "abstraction" assists the quest for objectivity, and also permits information to be systematized.

These four general concepts will serve to organize this paper. First, a detailed look at each will highlight how thoroughly–and similarly--law and science embraced Enlightenment values. Then, in Part II, I revisit the four concepts to gauge the strength and significance of emerging Post-Enlightenment thought and culture.

A. The Individuation of Investigation

In Medieval Europe the natural order and the normative order were merged in theological and magical beliefs. Nature and society were foreordained by timeless laws set by the Maker, with glimpses of human understanding available only through revelation. Although much effort was expended in taxonomy,[4] those who sought to manipulate patterned existence–natural, social, or religious–could do so only through insights about *process*. Specifically, processes were invoked to transform some object or person into an alternative state.[5] Alchemists sought to understand and harness transformative and curative qualities of natural substances. Princes sought to become Gods. Wine became blood, and through that transformation sinners were purified into beings ready to receive the grace by which they could be yet further transformed after death.

In the pre-modern period, physical, social, and religious understandings thus turned more on comprehending the connections and relationships among things than upon understanding the components and functioning of the things themselves.[6] The prevailing pre-modern metaphor, the "great chain of being,"[7] suggested the inseparable links by which people and objects were connected. Few aspects of life could be conceived as wholly self-contained and disconnected, what I call "individuated." The links themselves were processes that could be invoked to achieve certain results, but their mechanisms could

---

[4] D. Oldroyd, D., 1986, THE ARCH OF KNOWLEDGE: AN INTRODUCTORY STUDY OF THE HISTORY OF THE PHILOSOPHY AND METHODOLOGY OF SCIENCE 32–35 (1986).

[5] Keller, *supra* note 3, at 43-56.

[6] *See,* for example, the related discussion of non-Western pre-scientific mentalities and the development of "systems of transformations," *in* Claude Levi-Strauss, THE SAVAGE MIND 75–79 (1966).

[7] *See generally* A. O. Lovejoy, *The Great Chain of Being* 59–66 (1936).

not be changed.[8] The arrangement of both the physical world and the social world was thus open to human discovery and operation, but not to human construction.

1. Things and Processes

The Enlightenment idea of individuation displaced the pre-modern mentality of transformation and connection by reversing pre-modern assumptions. First, the respective positions of things and processes were switched: things and individuals displaced process as the focus of analytical attention.[9] In the pre-modern period, objects and people were examined largely as evidence toward understanding processes. But in Enlightenment hands, processes (especially mathematics) became tools for understanding, rather than objects of study.[10] Processes were further extended by the development of better physical devices, useful in observation and manipulating conditions.[11] This shift in focus from processes to things and individuals reflected slow changes in social conditions and the general humanistic influence of the Renaissance.[12] More specifically, individualism had political roots in the liberal philosophy of John Locke,[13] and also a theological grounding in the religious protests of the Reformation.

---

[8] Lawrence M. Tribe, *The Curvature of Constitutional Space: What Lawyers Can Learn from Modern Physics.* 103 HARVARD LAW REVIEW 1, 4 (1989).

[9] Richard K. Sherwin, *Lawyering Theory: An Overview of What We Talk About When We Talk About Law,* 37 NEW YORK LAW SCHOOL LAW REVIEW 9, 28 (1992). John Veilleux, *The Scientific Model in Law,* 75 GEORGETOWN LAW JOURNAL 1967, 1971 (1987). Keller, *supra* note 3, at 19.

[10] *See* Joseph Needham, *Mathematics and Science in China and the West, in* B. Barnes (ed.), SOCIOLOGY OF SCIENCE 21-44 (1972).

[11] H. Brown, THE WISDOM OF SCIENCE: ITS RELEVANCE TO CULTURE AND RELIGION 7–14 (1986).

[12] Needham, *supra* note 10, at 41-42.

[13] John Marshall Mitnick, *From Neighbor-Witness to Judge of Proofs: the Transformation of the English Civil Juror,* 32 AMERICAN JOURNAL OF LEGAL HISTORY 201, 230, 231 (1988)

2. The Nature of Change

In contrast, it was scientific rather than social or religious thinking that reversed a second pre-modern assumption. This assumption concerned the nature of change itself, understood in the pre-modernist era as transformations wrought largely by human or divine agency.[14] Physical occurrences–blessings or misfortunes–were open to moral or religious explanations. The universe displayed patterns of immanent justness, reflective of relationships among people and the Deity. Changes in weather, droughts, death–all could find explanation in the health or decay of social and religious relationships.

The emergence of ideas of statistical probability[15] helped defeat these transformative, personalistic explanations of physical world dynamics. A mentality of transformation is one in which alternative states occur or not in absolutist ways, depending on whether the transformative power was successfully invoked. A probabilistic mentality, in contrast, is one in which alternative states are more or less likely to come about. That understanding, in turn, begins a shift away from personalistic assumptions about how and why the universe changes. Statistical explanations removed many events from explanations based in agency, and instead fostered explanations based on inexorable impersonal forces.[16] Matter could be investigated as part of "an autonomous universe, 'operating without intention or purpose or destiny in a purely mechanical or causal way.'"[17]

3. The Divergence of Natural and Normative Orders

This growing impersonality of cosmology led to yet another reversal of a basic pre-modern assumption: the fundamental unity of natural and normative worlds. Unsurprisingly, explaining events by reference to divine intervention and immanent justice declined faster in the physical world than in the social world. As a result, physical world rules began to be viewed as bearing different truth qualities than social world rules. In what Popper labels the emergence of "critical dualism," the realm of natural order thus became

---

[14] Lawrence Rosen, THE ANTHROPOLOGY OF JUSTICE: LAW AS CULTURE IN ISLAMIC SOCIETY 77 (1989).

[15] Id.

[16] Id.

[17] Keller, *supra* note 3, at 69 (*quoting* N. Elias, THE HISTORY OF MANNERS 256 (1978)).

conceptually distinct from the realm of normative order.[18]

"Nature" diverged from "convention" along the dimensions of human responsibility and truth qualities. The laws of nature remained "unalterable" and "beyond human control"[19] even while the focus of inquiry had shifted from agency to impersonal explanations. Normative laws, on the other hand, came to be seen as alterable. Concern for the collective relationship of humans to God gave way to concern for how human individuals could responsibly orient themselves to one another. Similarly, normative laws took on qualities of truth or falsity "only in a metaphorical sense."[20] A normative law that could not be broken failed of its purpose, which was to provide guidance for human discretion.[21] Normative order therefore was no longer described in term of invariant social structure, but rather reflected the aggregated decisions of autonomous individual wills. On account of those very capacities of rational self-determination, Kantian philosophy celebrated the inherent respect and dignity of human beings.[22]

Through a series of related ideas, therefore, the concept of individuation enabled Enlightened thought to escape pre-modernist assumptions. Ultimately, this individuation resulted in identifying the normative world as conceptually distinct from the natural world. The natural was atomistic and mechanical.[23] The normative was similarly atomistic, but also was contingent--ruled by autonomous individual wills, each responsible for moral choices.[24]

Yet *judging the exercise of such responsibility*, i.e., applying the

---

[18] Karl R. Popper, THE OPEN SOCIETY AND ITS ENEMIES, VOLUME 1: THE SPELL OF PLATO 57–61 (1966).

[19] Id., at 57.

[20] Id.

[21] Id.

[22] George P. Fletcher, LOYALTY: AN ESSAY ON THE MORALITY OF RELATIONSHIPS 13 (1993).

[23] Sandra Harding, THE SCIENCE QUESTION IN FEMINISM 225-227 (1986).

[24] Michael D. Weiss, 19 AMERICAN JOURNAL OF CRIMINAL LAW 71, 74-76 (1991); Thomas C. Grey, *Serpents and Doves: A Note on Kantian Legal Theory*, 87 COLUMBIA LAW REVIEW 580, 583 (1987).

normative laws to particular facts in the social world, continued to share the epistemological premises of science.[25] *How* knowledge was attained, in other words, remained similar in each realm. Each was guided by the further Enlightenment concepts of detachment, segmentation, and abstraction, concepts to which we now turn.

B. Reliability Through The Detachment of Mind and Nature

The second general Enlightenment tool was detachment, in which reason was conceived as wholly divorced from (and superior to) experience.[26] From that relationship of mind and nature, says Evelyn Keller, flow ideas of *how* one achieves knowledge.[27] The detachment of mind from matter in turn separated knowledge from belief, and action from intention.[28] Attaining valid knowledge required the pure reasoning of a mind that was autonomous from unreliable sensory information about the material world.[29] Knowledge, as opposed to mere speculation or belief, depended on constructing a set of objective, replicable procedures.[30] Only rigorous attention to such procedures could purify sensory information into a reliable form.[31]

In both law and science, procedures were designed to impart reliability of information in the following ways: through standardizing the information

---

[25] Catharine Pierce Wells, *Holmes on Legal Method: The Predictive Theory of Law as an Instance of Scientific Method,* 18 SOUTHERN ILLINOIS UNIVERSITY LAW JOURNAL 329, 343 (1994) (distinguishing between understanding law as predicting outcomes of cases, versus the process of judging, which should not attempt to comport to predictions).

[26] Scubert M. Ogden, *The Enlightenment is Not Over," in* KNOWLEDGE AND BELIEF IN AMERICAN: ENLIGHTENMENT TRADITIONS AND MODERN RELIGIOUS THOUGHT 322-323 (William M. Shea & Peter A. Huff, eds. 1995).

[27] Keller, *supra* note 3, at 18.

[28] J.B. Schneewind, *Autonomy, Obligation and Virtue: An Overview of Kant's Moral Philosophy*, in THE CAMBRIDGE COMPANION TO KANT 309-315 (Paul Guyer ed., 1992).

[29] Colin E. Gunton, ENLIGHTENMENT AND ALIENATION: AN ESSAY TOWARDS A TRINITARIAN THEOLOGY 5, 39 (1985). Norman Hampson, THE ENLIGHTENMENT 197 (1976).

[30] Sherwin, *supra* note 9, at 27.

[31] David M. Trubek, *The Handmaiden's Revenge: On Reading and Using the Newer Sociology of Civil Procedure*, 51 LAW AND CONTEMPORARY PROBLEMS 111, 114 (1988).

that was examinable in a given trial;[32] by prescribing how the information should be tested;[33] and by parsing the phenomenon being examined from potentially confounding background effects.[34] Both the scientific method and the formalism of legal procedures could be understood as methods for harnessing pure reason, so as to achieve universal knowledge in applying either the normative laws or the natural laws to particular phenomena under investigation.

Procedures in both law and science were virtually ritualized in an effort to advance the reliability of information, and also the legitimacy of human judging. Reliability in the law–treating like cases alike–was and is a fundamental philosophical value legitimating the authority of the system, as well as a standard for measuring progress in doctrinal refinement. So also, of course, reliability of information is a measure of the confidence with which a scientific explanation can be held, and a foundation for claiming authority through scientific explanation.

C. Segmentation and Validity

The method of both science and the common law, therefore, is to measure the world against principles and laws, using reason.[35] In designing both sets of investigatory tools, scientists and lawyers made use of the Enlightenment concept of segmentation.[36] Segmentation is the process of isolating particulars under scrutiny from their relational and historical contexts. So isolated, problems were seen to be more susceptible of reliable information, and ultimately more susceptible of human intervention and manipulation.[37]

---

[32] Mitnick, *supra* note 13, at 229–31.

[33] Id., at 231.

[34] *See* Peter A. Schouls, DESCARTES AND THE ENLIGHTENMENT 25 (1989); Tom Sorell, DESCARTES 2-3 (1987).

[35] Veilleux, *supra* note 9, at 1973.

[36] *See generally* Francis J. Mootz III, *Is the Rule of Law Possible in a Postmodern World?* 68 WASHINGTON LAW REVIEW 249, 253 (1993); Sherwin, *supra* note 9, at 27-28.

[37] Schneewind, *supra* note 28, at 310-318; Hampson, *supra* note 29, at 75-76.

1. Relational Isolation

Relational isolation was achieved in normative judging by segmenting human interaction into discrete episodes. Although a series of actions could be causally connected, they collectively would have no special status or privilege. The relationship *itself*, as something independent from the vignettes of behavior which constitute it, was largely ignored.

Denying ethical significance to human relationships themselves was inevitable, once the fundamental ideas of detachment had been accepted. Starting from the atomistic premise of a normative order governed by autonomous individual wills, relationships *had* to be subordinated. Ties of loyalty would only confound assessment of the exercise of pure reason upon which rested the understanding of human responsibility.[38] Hence Enlightenment moral reasoning separated "individuals from their particular social settings and attachments in an effort to ascertain which propositions would have appeal to persons solely in their capacity as rational agents."[39] Relational isolation in scientific judgement has a close analog, and is similarly prized. It is found in the familiar experimental technique of holding independent variables constant, so that the information about the behavior of the dependent variable can be more precisely determined.

2. Historical Isolation

The de-contextualization of phenomena under investigation did not stop with parsing the object of study from its immediate social or physical environment. Segmentation also extracted the object of study from its history. Concepts of time and causation were conceptually chopped into discrete, measured episodes that follow sequentially in impersonal, non-teleological ways. The linear view of time that emerged from such segmentation differed from premodern conceptions, which regarded time more cyclically.[40] Together with the new probabilistic view of causality, the changing conception of time permitted problems–in the social world as well as the physical world–to be viewed less fatalistically, and more instrumentally.

---

[38] Fletcher, *supra* note 22, at 12.

[39] Milton Regan, Jr., *Reason, Tradition, and Family Law: A Comment on Social Constructionism*, 79 VIRGINIA LAW REVIEW 1515, 1518 (1993).

[40] Carol J. Greenhouse, *Just in Time: Temporality and the Cultural Legitimation of Law* 98 YALE LAW JOURNAL 1631, 1631 (1989).

3. Instrumental Rationality

Segmented time and causation meant, first, that fewer references to earlier iterations of a problem or event were required for its understanding. Earlier instances of the phenomenon were recognized as having possible causative influence on the shape of a current event. The causative pattern *itself*, however, no longer had a foreordaining or cyclical quality. The treatment of history was thus analogous to the treatment of human relationships: interactional vignettes were understood to have causal significance for future behaviors, but were not seen as building a transcendent relationship with special moral qualities. Just as each new human behavior was ultimately the domain of a disconnected, responsible human will, so also future instances of real world events were deemed undetermined[41] as well as unknowable.[42]

Yet when time and causation are segmented, the treatment of problems and events can be more instrumental. A problem destined to recur is typically met with resignation and fatalism; a problem that *can* be transcended, on the other hand, is worth attempting to fix. Enlightenment concepts enabled instrumentalist attitudes in both law and science, attitudes which were further emboldened as both law and science developed a more abstract, systematic quality.[43]

D. Abstraction and Instrumentalism

The information gathered through scientific experimentation or legal judgements was gradually abstracted into generalizations and principles.[44] These higher order statements are intended to "posit explanations for seemingly disparate data."[45] Raising the level of abstraction at which a phenomenon could be understood did more, however, than simply create systematic principles. It also lent a higher sense of objectivity to the

---

[41] Karl R. Popper, The Open Society and its Enemies, Volume II: Hegel and Marx 84, 85 (1966).

[42] William N. Riley, *On the Telos of Man and Law: An Essay Concerning Morality and Positive Law*, 64 INDIANA LAW JOURNAL 965, 966 (1989).

[43] Wells, *supra* note 25, at 332-325.

[44] Id., at 336; Sherwin, *supra* note 9, at 29; Veilleux, *supra* note 9, at 1974.

[45] Wells, *supra* note 25, at 339.

investigation itself. To Michael Polanyi, however, these claims of objectivity were self-deceiving. The principles proved only a growing taste for abstract theory over sensory information.[46]

Furthermore, the abstracted principles could not themselves be *justifications* for outcomes.[47] According to renowned American judge Oliver Wendell Holmes, for example, legal judgements must be justified outside the system itself: by their fairness under the circumstances, and their consistency with the common law purposes of promoting stability and prosperity.[48]

Scientific judgements had a similar instrumentalist flavor among early Enlightenment thinkers like Francis Bacon,[49] who sought domination of nature through science as well as its understanding.[50] As J. M. Balkin put it, "[The Enlightenment] sought to master the world through science and remake the world according to the dictates of reason. It sought to understand and to recast society in rational and scientific terms."[51]

Abstracting and systematizing information thus was an attempt to create conceptual order, normative and natural. Kant understood this process as the mind imposing a framework on the world for understanding the information from the senses.[52] So ordered, reason and human will maintained their autonomy and priority over experience, values which were fully compatible with efforts toward social and technological engineering.[53]

---

[46] Michael Polanyi, PERSONAL KNOWLEDGE: TOWARDS A POST-CRITICAL PHILOSOPHY 4 (1962).

[47] Wells, *supra* note 25, at 340.

[48] Id., at 344.

[49] Mootz, *supra* note 36, at 265–271.

[50] Keller, *supra* note 3, at 37, 48, 64; Oldroyd, *supra* note 4, at 60.

[51] Jack M. Balkin, *What is a Postmodern Constitutionalism?* 90 MICHIGAN LAW REVIEW 1966, 1988 (1992); Lynn N. Henderson, L.N., *Legality and Empathy*, 85 MICHIGAN LAW REVIEW 1574, 1575-1576 (1987).

[52] Gunton, *supra* note 29, at 6, 23, 25, 45.

[53] Popper, *supra* note 41, at 84-85.

II. CHALLENGES TO ENLIGHTENMENT THOUGHT

As a consequence of Enlightenment ideas, modern law and science thus built a common vision of truth based in objectivity and reliability. Such truths were ensured by consistent application of rigorous procedures–the scientific method and common law pleading and practice. The rigid procedural standards that stood as gatekeepers to legitimated truth advanced the systemization of knowledge within the respective domains of science and law. That elaboration of abstracted legal and scientific principles, in turn, encouraged the instrumental use of the collected information.

Yet that same rigorous devotion to procedural regularity meant a lack of flexibility toward the criteria or legitimacy of truth, and neither Enlightenment rationalism nor its detached, reductivist methods have stood unchallenged. Over the past two centuries, three movements have offered alternative understandings of truth and how knowledge may be legitimately attained: romanticism, relativism, and a still-emerging "post-Enlightenment" thought. In the paragraphs below, the impacts of each will be briefly assessed.

Before proceeding to those particulars, however, it is worth noting that cultural shifts in epistemological assumptions are especially ominous to legal and scientific institutions. In other realms of life–artistic, economic, religious, or political–the respective structures for assessment and implementation of the core concepts–concepts like beauty, efficiency, devotion, or equality--are less rigid than those of law or science.

In art and music, for example, experimentation with the procedures by which the art form are produced is an acknowledged part of artistry itself. The process can partake intimately, in other words, with the progress of unfolding substantive ideas. Indeed, this may be one reason why art often anticipates cultural trends. Literature and religion are similar: the processes of interpretation and expression may change nearly as readily as the content of the works interpreted. Even politics can more easily accommodate changes of its own procedures for assessing truth and implementing policy than can law or science, although certainly changes of political structures are more difficult–and viewed as more significant–than mere changes in policy. In contrast, law and science in large part define the legitimacy of their judgements by how carefully their respective procedures are followed. The procedures must stand independent of the substantive issues, and must be used consistently from trial to trial. That separation of process and substance imparts a sense of objectivity to the judging, but also an inflexibility.

A. Romanticism

Romanticism opposes the idea that insight into truth must be achieved through human detachment from the object of study. Rather, in romantic thought human judgement is seen as open to personal insight–a "conjunction of one's self and ultimate truths."[54] Indeed, authenticity of judgement may turn on the quality of communication between self and object. Romanticism therefore views Enlightenment rationalism as creating a tension with spirit[55] or humanity.[56] Decontextualized, reductivist methods are said to leave out a sense of "feeling, heroics, ... or sacrifice."[57]

Romanticism is probably a more difficult challenge to the normative order than to the natural order, simply because an understanding of human motives and compassion is instinctively a part of making certain legal decisions.[58] The process of legal judging continues to struggle with ideas of romantic insight into attaining truth.[59] Still, the concept of individuation in both law and science--the focus of Enlightenment study on things and objects rather than process-- remains basically undisturbed by romanticism. As Richard K. Sherwin puts it, "the scientists and the romantics share one thing in common: they both believed that what they were thinking and talking about were the things themselves."[60] Similarly, romanticism did not seriously question the Enlightenment concepts of segmented causation and time. In both law and science, ideas about linearity and the autonomy of events easily endured the personalistic truth qualities of romanticism.

B. Relativism

Relativism is less deeply antithetical to Enlightenment epistemological assumptions than is romanticism. The basic premise of relativism has been assimilated more than resisted. Relativism generally challenges the idea that

---

[54] Rosen, *supra* note 14, at 71.

[55] Sherwin, *supra* note 9, at 28.

[56] Rosen, *supra* note 14, at 71-72.

[57] Sherwin, *supra* note 9, at 28.

[58] Rosen, *supra* note 14, at 72.

[59] Id.

[60] Sherwin, *supra* note 9, at 28.

truth can be abstracted free of the perspectives through which it was generated,[61] although in physics the concept takes on stronger meanings about the impossibility of isolating foreground phenomena from presumed "neutral" background conditions.[62]

Traditional conceptions of reliability and validity can survive relativism. A belief in objective reality can be maintained, even where the vision of truth is deemed limited to human perception, and even where perceptions are acknowledged to differ among individuals. Relativism is merely another obstacle–albeit a theoretically insurmountable obstacle--to *uncovering* objective truth. Furthermore, the effects of relativism may be reduced (and conversely our confidence in the validity of our hypotheses may be increased) by yet better fidelity to the accepted procedures of science or law. Through more careful, more imaginative application of those procedures, we may uncover and correct for human biases in making scientific or legal judgements. Relativism thus actually highlights the importance of the scientific method; its real impact has been substantive rather than procedural, revealing a universe of greater complexity and interactivity than previously understood.[63]

Relativism has similarly had little impact on the common law or its procedures for judging. The obvious differences in substantive legal rules across various societies– differences that never appear to impair the basic functioning of normative order within those societies--imparted a relativist skepticism to claims in legal philosophy about the existence of a Platonic natural law.

Furthermore, the power to create the common law has always been decentralized into local courtrooms. A certain level of variation in legal judgement was as a practical matter always expected in the common law. Two disparate judgements may each hold legitimacy, and some authority, in the common law system. Hence the relativistic idea that differences in judicial perspective theoretically limit the level of consistency of decisional outcomes could be easily folded into common law theory.

---

[61] *See generally* Bernard Williams, MORALITY: AN INTRODUCTION TO ETHICS 34-39 (1972).

[62] Tribe, *supra* note 8, at 19-20.

[63] Id., at 4.

C. Post-Enlightenment Thought and Culture

Post-Enlightenment thought and culture, in contrast, pose more serious challenges for the traditional procedures by which scientific and legal truth are attained and legitimated. Exploration of the sources of resistance to Enlightenment assumptions, and the many forms it takes, is beyond the parameters of this paper. Suffice it to say that in addition to objections to Enlightenment assumptions on epistemological grounds, Enlightenment values have also been variously opposed by those with political opposition to liberal institutions;[64] those with spiritual or communitarian perspectives,[65] and those seeking stronger group identity.[66]

The resulting Post-Enlightenment movement has two basic aspects. First, there is what many term "postmodernism," which is skeptical about the existence of an objective reality,[67] and substitutes a view of "reality as an undifferentiated whole in which we are situated as participants rather than as observers."[68] Second, spreading more broadly through the culture, the Post-Enlightenment movement embraces the idea that as we participate in constructing truth, we are more strongly tied to one another. It posits that we are connected to groups that shape our identities, and connected more durably to other individuals in relationships. Truth, in a sense, comes bundled with people, their histories, and their environmental conditions.

Put together, these two aspects of Post-Enlightenment thought raise an image of truth as constructed from within particular contexts. This image carries epistemological assumptions more like those that prevailed in the

---

[64] *See, for example*, Duncan Kennedy, SEXY DRESSING, ETC. (1993).

[65] *See, for example,* Milner S. Ball, THE PROMISE OF AMERICAN LAW: A THEORETICAL, HUMANISTIC VIEW OF LEGAL PROCESS (1981); Thomas L. Shaffer, *The Legal Ethics of Belonging,* 49 OHIO STATE LAW JOURNAL 703 (1988).

[66] *See, for example,* Katharine T. Bartlett, *Feminist Legal Methods*, 103 HARVARD LAW REVIEW 829(1990); Kimberle Williams Crenshaw, *Race, Reform and Retrenchment: Transformation and Legitimation in Antidiscrimination Law* 101 HARVARD LAW REVIEW 1331 (1988).

[67] Mootz, *supra* note 36, at 283; Hilary Lawson, *Stories about Stories, in* H. Lawson and L. Appignanesi (eds), DISMANTLING TRUTH: REALITY IN THE POST-MODERNIST WORLD p. xii (1989).

[68] Mootz, *supra* note 36, at 270.

premodern era. For example, the Enlightenment proceeds through detachment of reason and experience, but Post-Enlightened thought works toward empathic understanding. Enlightened law and science de-contextualize investigations to find transcendent patterns, yet Post-Enlightened thought explores context for uniqueness.[69] Linear time and segmented causality give way to holistic thinking.[70] The particular and concrete are often preferred to the general and abstract. Exaggerated to underscore the point, under Post-Enlightenment assumptions reliability becomes a matter of either coincidence, or the exercise of power. Validity is a transient, if not impossible, notion.

Yet Post-Enlightened thought and culture do not entail crude reversions to premodernist attitudes. That would be impossible, even if it were desired: the reversal of Enlightened assumptions takes place in the context of a highly technological, secularized world from which a turning back is difficult to imagine. In the concluding part of this essay, I will attempt to assess the likely impact that the shifting epistemological assumptions of the Post-Enlightenment would have on legal and scientific institutions, were the movement eventually to dominate Western culture.

III. THE DILEMMAS OF POST-ENLIGHTENMENT THOUGHT

Post-Enlightenment culture urges the law to develop a style which is more particularist, empathic, and fallabilistic, in which consistency of judgement would be far less important; to display greater sensitivity to how personal responsibility may be affected by issues of identity, loyalty, power and subordination; to acknowledge rights in groups as well as in individuals; and to seek remedies in which restoration of relationships is as important as vindication of rights.[71]

Post-Enlightenment thought makes equivalent demands on the procedure of the scientific method. To comport better with Post-Enlightenment understanding, scientific theory should acknowledge three things: the intrusiveness of observation,[72] the difficulties of understanding

---

[69] Peter C. Schanck, *Understanding Postmodern Thought and Its Implications for Statutory Interpretation*, 65 SOUTHERN CALIFORNIA LAW REVIEW 2505, 2573 (1992).

[70] Mootz, *supra* note 36, at 285.

[71] Barton, *supra* note 1, at 196.

[72] Tribe, *supra* note 8, at 5, 18-19.

phenomena in isolation of their dynamic background settings,[73] and the consequent reduced efficacy of instrumentalism.[74]

Collectively, these demands of Post-Enlightenment thought raise two distinct dilemmas for law and science. The first dilemma--what I call the "cultural" dilemma[75]–is whether lawyers and scientists *should* attempt to modify their procedures so as to comport with changing understandings about truth. The second dilemma–the "constitutive" dilemma–is whether it is *possible* for either law or science to so alter their procedures, or at least whether it is possible to do so without sacrificing altogether their distinct ways of understanding the normative or natural worlds.

In other words, suppose the culture were to demand utterly particularistic statements from its law or science. Is it clear that complying statements could continue to have any distinctive meaning as "legal" or "scientific?" Or do our understandings of law or science so inherently presuppose measurement against more abstracted standards, that under the radically fragmented, decentered assumptions of postmodernist thought "judgements" simply cannot be produced? If for either reason–by choice or by default–law and science remain wedded to Enlightenment truth notions while the broader culture embraces alternative assumptions, then the institutions of law and science will become by definition counter-cultural.

What would it mean for the affected institutions, and indeed for society generally, if the methods and understandings of law or science were to be relegated to a marginalized worldview? Would law or science be consigned to a cultural position equivalent to that suffered by the Church following the triumph of the Enlightenment?[76] That analogy may be logically attractive, but it quickly falls apart. A society simply does not have the option to make the law a matter of personal choice, in the same way that religion can be.

A. *Cultural and Constitutive Dilemmas in the Law*

The cultural dilemma is thus more ominous for the law than for

---

[73] Id.,at 19-20.

[74] Mootz, *supra* note 36, at 271, 289-90; Tribe, *supra* note 8, at 7.

[75] Barton, *supra* note 1, at 192–213.

[76] Id., at 164.

science. Unlike science, the very standards against which legitimacy of legal knowledge is measured depend on social acceptance. The law cannot point to real world occurrences to provide independent verification of its judgments. An unrepentant Enlightenment-based legal process would still be charged with the formal maintenance of the normative order. Yet if embedded in a thoroughgoingly Post-Enlightenment culture, the law could not count on popular comprehension of its reasoning, or respect for its decisional authority, or acceptance of the generalized application of its decrees. By default, law would require greater resort to power to implement its decisions. The law would be strongly pressured to conform its methods to popularly supported values, simply to avoid ineffectualness on the one hand, or oppression on the other.

Opposing those impulses to succumb to Post-Enlightenment values, however, is an important historical role played by the law: to assist people in separating themselves from others. Individuals often wish desperately to escape the role limitations placed on them by the people surrounding their upbringing.[77] Or they may seek freedom from demeaning or violent intimate relationships they have mistakenly taken on later in life.[78] Or they may seek relief from stereotyped judgments about them, made by people who do not know them at all. In each case, a person wishes to escape an unwanted aspect of social existence, and they often turn to the law to help them do so. They do not necessarily want the connections offered by the Post-Enlightenment, or at least not without the escape hatch provided by legal rights.[79]

Historically, the Enlightenment image of self-determining, autonomous individuals has been attractive to vast numbers of people. The opportunities of selfhood, however, have often required the assertion of individual rights through the legal process. Abstract ideas like the due process and equal protection of the laws has empowered individuals to resist unjust petty authorities, brutalizing spouses, exploiting employers, and invidious discriminators.[80]

---

[77] Lawrence M. Friedman, TOTAL JUSTICE 80-91(1985).

[78] Sally E. Merry, GETTING JUSTICE AND GETTING EVEN: LEGAL CONSCIOUSNESS AMONG WORKING-CLASS AMERICANS 181-182 (1990).

[79] Patricia J. Williams, *Alchemical Notes: Reconstructing Ideals from Deconstructed Rights,* 22 HARVARD CIVIL RIGHTS-CIVIL LIBERTIES LAW REVIEW 401, 414 (1987)

[80] Friedman, *supra* note 77, at 80-91.

An important cultural role of the law, in other words, has been to assist individuals to live and be judged *free* of the dense relational and group identity contexts in which others seek to embed them. So long as the surrounding culture accepts Enlightenment values, the law does not experience a conflict between the epistemological assumptions of its processes, and its substantive responsibility to protect individuals from unwanted relational or identity linkages. The law can play its protective, separationist role for individuals by observing its normal Enlightenment procedures. But what if a surrounding Post-Enlightenment culture were to reject the separationist methods inherent in ideals of autonomy and self-determination? Then the law would be forced to choose between popular acceptance of its methods, and protections for individuals wishing to escape a historical self.

Even if the clear answer to the cultural dilemma were that law should align its methods with Post-Enlightenment understandings, the constitutive dilemma would be forbidding: it not clear that the law *could* do so. Its rules of pleading are largely designed to limit the breadth of vision about individuals, focusing instead on their behavior. Its rules of evidence are largely designed to limit discussion to facts about discrete behaviors. Its substantive rules are largely intended to apply equally by geographical territory, not by social status or position. Its judges are steeped in the values of detached objectivity and following of precedent.

B. Cultural and Constitutive Dilemmas in Science

Both the cultural and the constitutive dilemmas are less serious for science than for law. First, even if the surrounding culture were to embrace epistemological assumptions that could not be absorbed within scientific practices, the authority of scientific truth would not likely be threatened. Scientific truth has never depended on popular acceptance for its legitimacy, especially not among deeply religious people left behind by the Enlightenment. Instead, science stands on the validity of its results: its ability to predict physical world events and to explain those events coherently. Science is thus in a better position to resist the cultural dilemma.

Science is also better placed to transcend the constitutive dilemma. The test of scientific epistemology will no doubt remain rooted in empirical verification. Scientists will experiment with the implications of post-Einsteinian understandings, altering their methods as well as their focus. If Post-Enlightenment assumptions are in fact superior to Enlightenment methods, then that superiority will eventually show up by enabling stronger explanations of the data. The increasing prevalence of densely connected ecological explanations to understand a variety of environmental questions, and of quantum mechanics to understand subatomic questions, are perhaps cases in point. If the emerging Post-Enlightenment assumptions have explanatory power, they will be used and science will adjust its procedures accordingly.

IV. CONCLUSION

Western thought has had relatively little need in the past three hundred years to reflect on the importance of the connection between a culture's epistemological assumptions, and its understanding of human beings and their social ordering. The natural order and the normative order were fundamentally compatibility in their assumptions underlying procedures for uncovering and evaluating information, in their orientation to the relationship of subject to object, and in their basic understanding of environmental stability and change. Most of us take for granted the resulting ground rules for rational discourse about the physical world, individual identity, and collective self-governance.

Those ground rules–built on Enlightenment ideas of individuation, detachment, segmentation, and abstraction–are being challenged by Post-Enlightenment discourse. At stake are the meanings of reality, causation, objectivity, responsibility, power, freedom, and justice by which we have come to know our world and ourselves. Although the outcome of this newest challenge is uncertain, perhaps this much can be ventured: the dialogue is healthy. Justice should never fully define truth. Emerging political and identity orientations are not worthy in themselves to redefine epistemological assumptions. But neither should truth fully define justice. Justice must respond to Post-Enlightenment questions, and unless it does so thoughtfully it will lose the popular support on which it depends. Truth will be watching, and will make its accommodations.

CHAPTER XIII
THE CULTURAL OBSTACLE: Understanding the Inertia of Expectations and Self-interest

"Culture" refers to a group, and the prevailing beliefs, attitudes, or values within it. Shared cultural values may attach to a small group of friends, those who operate within a legal system, those comprising a nation, or those comprising a nation. Uncovering the prevailing culture within a group can be useful in suggesting the points of likely irrationality, prejudice, and vulnerability. To uncover these beliefs within a problem-solving system, one can ask a series of questions.

A. Who May Speak Within the System to Voice the Problem, Set Criteria for Its Resolution, or Suggest Solutions?

In traditional legal culture, the formal answers to these questions disconnect from the practical answers. This separation of theory and reality can be revealed by breaking the questions into separate parts: first, who is *entitled* to speak; and second, who is *capable* of speaking. Legal rules and traditional legal processes articulate a vocabulary and way of speaking that is highly specialized and excluding. It takes years of studying to be able to summon legal power effectively. Theoretically, the legal system is open to full participation by problem-holders. At least rhetorically, the legal system emphasizes formal equality. In reality, legal processes are vastly less accessible than, say, tossing a coin.

Culturally, this translates into an exclusivity of the legal profession, which in turn sets up a barrier to reform. Lawyers are well paid for their abilities to harness the power of the state through law. A more easily accessed system–*i.e.,* making the system more open to those without specialized capabilities–can be seen as a threat to lawyers' livelihoods. This concern strikes more deeply than simply fewer hours being billed when the legal system moves toward negotiated or mediated solutions.

More than money is involved, however, in this issue of widening the voice of those who seek to be effective in legal problem solving. An ethical issue lies in wait. Broadening access to the legal system by broadening decisional criteria beyond legal rules begins to suggest that the resolution of legal problems, or some aspects of legal problems, may be handed to wise advisors rather than exclusively to those formally trained in the law. If the idea of a "legal problem" were expanded beyond legal rules, how do our ideas change about the (criminally enforced) rules that prohibit the unauthorized practice of law? Easy answers are not available. The gatekeeper function obviously protects the public from charlatans, but also protects the credentialed legal protection. We may remind ourselves about the interactive nature of problem-solving systems: If outside cultural values shift in favor of easier lay participation in resolving legal problems, an ethical debate would be sparked about the legitimacy and standards for authorizing legal representatives.

B. What Counts as a Legitimate Argument?

Within any problem-solving system, boundaries will be established as to the kind of argument or evidence that may be introduced. A certain style of truth prevails within a problem-solving system, defined largely by the inputs that will be taken seriously. In traditional legal culture, what counts as a legitimate argument is highly circumscribed by the rules of evidence. Only those matters that are both relevant and material to analyzing legal rules are ***permitted.***

The mechanisms for enforcing this are strong. In another topic to be developed more fully in the second half of these readings, our concepts of legal justice are tied to facts and legitimated authority. In contrast, those concepts are *separated* from many arguments based in nature, emotion, healthy social relationships, spiritual beliefs, and perhaps even human experience.

C. What are the Taboos?

In uncovering the culture of a problem-solving system, this is another provocative question to ask. Even if a system is generally open to fresh outside ideas, some topics are likely to be taboo–simply off-limits to critical analysis or shaking conventional wisdoms. These untouchable bedrock values of our legal system are, I believe, the ideas of formal equality before the law, and a vision of according freedom to individuals, rather than status.

D. What Constitutes Success, and What Failure?

Characteristically in traditional legal culture, but probably more broadly as well in our surrounding culture, success tends to be defined by victory, achieving some end by forcing another person to succumb to our assertion of rights. Success is seldom acknowledged when it is more subtle, such as when a person does not bend the environment to his/her desires, but rather reconciles oneself to the surrounding environment. "Making peace" with a problem, acknowledging its power, is frequently seen as failure. It need not be so, however. Consider the phrase in a different context, as where one makes one's peace with a terminal illness. That is not seen as failure, but rather a form of personal growth or deepening.

"Solving" a problem can occur in one or more of three different ways. The first two methods are not mutually exclusive.

- instrumentally, in which the environment is bent toward more compatibility with human purpose

- adaptively, in which human purpose is adjusted to fit better within environmental constraints

- through doing nothing, but acknowledging the enormity and intractability of the problem and understanding it as evidence of human limitation.

Lawyers tend strongly toward fashioning instrumental solutions. When people are given legal "rights," for example, that means that those individuals may assert their interests against the surrounding social, relational, or physical environment. The environment must bend in deference to the purposes of the rights-holder, *even where utilitarian principles would suggest that the individual interests should be subordinated to the good of the community.* That may be one reason why the process of asserting legal rights is often so antagonistic and contentious.

Legal rights are tools for bending the environment toward the interests of the rights holder, and sometimes it does not want to bend. If a client is denied access to some opportunity, lawyers will typically think of equipping the client with rights (as under Equal Protection concepts or the Americans with Disabilities Act) to pry open the environment. If the client has suffered a loss, the lawyer will typically assert client rights (like rights to be free from nonconsensual bodily intrusion or to be free of defamatory attacks on one's reputation), to force the environment to compensate the loss. In each of these instances, legal rights is a solution based on the (just) use power to reshape the environment.

Health professionals also typically think of instrumental solutions. Where a patient is ill, for example, that is a problem. The mismatch is between the individual's purpose of carrying on normal daily activity, and a physical environment (here the patient's body) which is somehow confining or debilitating. The physician uses drugs or surgical techniques to change the physical environment and restore the patient to normal activity.

Both health professionals and lawyers sometimes use the second devise of "adaptation." Where a patient has a chronic heart ailment that cannot be changed, the patient will be advised to alter his or her life style--to reduce activity levels or refrain from smoking, drinking, etc. Once again the problem is the mismatch between desired activities by the patient and the physical environment of the patient's body. In this example, however, the environment is considered non-malleable, because the heart condition cannot be cured. Therefore, what must change to "solve" the problem are the human "purposes." The person must learn healthier habits, and/or "slow down."

To take an example of "adaptive" solution in the law, consider a tax practitioner consulted by a client who wants to accomplish some business end without incurring tax liability. The lawyer could first try to fashion creative interpretive arguments about the meaning of the words in the Internal Revenue Code–this would be an "instrumental" solution, bending the regulatory environment to the client's purposes. At some point, however, such efforts reach a limit. The next lawyerly strategy may be to advise a change in the client's purposes. The business end may have to be accomplished more slowly, for example. Or other changes in the client's business will have to be made to accompany the end the client has in mind, if the client is to avoid taxation. Perhaps, for example, the business will have to open itself to an employee stock ownership plan. Here the lawyer is acknowledging the limited malleability in the regulatory environment, and is trying to work with the client's purposes to achieve a different sort of "solution."

With adaptive solutions, the professionals may have to work harder, and the client may not be as happy in the short term. Yet the adaptive solution also carries the possibilities of transforming side-effects that may in the long term be quite desirable. Perhaps the patient who is advised to slow down will spend more time with the patient's family, or will develop new hobbies that are rewarding. Or a new diet that is recommended will result in unanticipated long term health benefits apart from coping with the heart condition. The business client with the tax problem who is forced to shift purposes may find new efficiencies or better employee morale and productivity by reason of changing the business rather than bending the tax code.

As to the third sort of "solution," doing nothing but coming to understand better one's own limitations, many would not regard it as a solution at all. Indeed, many would regard it as failure. Perhaps it is both simultaneously. The important thing in such circumstances is what one can learn from having confronted and come to understand both the nature of the problem and ones own abilities.

Before leaving this section we may note two other criteria left out of measuring success in traditional legal culture, explicitly concerns of the Problem Solving and Therapeutic Jurisprudence approaches in Part Two: the psychological well-being of the individuals involved in the problem and the strength of their personal relationships. Every problem, and every encounter with the legal system, should be an opportunity for personal moral growth and stronger social relationships.

E. What Are Our Fears?

This final question reveals what, within a problem-solving system, sparks risk aversion. What inputs are exaggerated in importance because of a tendency within the system toward catastrophizing? The question also gets at what kinds of solutions are unacceptable. An example would be an irrational loss aversion that pushes ahead–even recklessly--on some process that risks a larger loss to avoid a sure, smaller loss.

The second half of this work will address this issue in a more general and historical way. To preview that, I speculate that Westerners in general, Americans in particular–are afraid of disorder, stagnation and domination. This explains much about what we will see in the second half of the readings: the law's historical privileging of securing order over facilitating human interaction, and why that order function is discharged as it is: by equipping individuals with rights and then giving them social and relational mobility. This creates order out of self-striving, and yet offers the possibility of escape from relationships that are subordinating or punishing.

On a more specific level, we may address this question about fears by exploring the idea of perception of risks within our culture. Doing so reveals that many of our attitudes are detached from empirical levels of threats. To be effective in serving clients, however, lawyers must be able to assess risks as objectively as possible, communicate those risks, and yet be aware that clients may be so influenced by the surrounding culture or by the clients' own goals that the lawyer' advice will be ignored. Perhaps even resented. Where lawyers realize that their advice is likely to be at odds with client attitudes (and lawyers should always know enough about their clients to predict that) then lawyers should strive to offer acknowledgment of the client beliefs or goals. Proactively, they should also strive to offer constructive alternatives. The section below attempts to understand better the idea of risk in our culture, so that lawyers will be able to counsel better in the face of it.

F. Understanding and Counseling in the Face of Risk?

Ed Dauer offers a powerful and entertaining example of the power of personal goals to override even the most obvious and serious risks.[1] It comes from his youth, when he worked after school in a costume jewelry factory. Manufacturing the jewelry entailed stamping sheets or coils of metal with thousands of pounds of pressure per square inch into the proper shape and design of cufflinks or bracelets.[2] As Dauer puts it, "the dies come down hard on the brass sheet with great speed. Any finger in the way is a lost cause."[3]

The factory operators were aware of the physical and legal risks, of course, and communicated these risks clearly to the employees. Dauer writes, "The factory I worked in had *rules* about this. People operating the presses could not wear loose clothing nor have long untied hair that might be caught in the machinery; they were disallowed–on penalty of being fired–from using any press that did not have a working guard screen in place; they were instructed repeatedly NOT to insert the brass sheet with one hand while operating the press with the other, lest the right hand not know what the left was doing and, in the lack of coordination, cut it off. Those were the rules."[4]

Being realists, however, the factory and maker of the presses tried to reduce the legal risk by changing the *facts.* The presses were designed with two large buttons, one on each side of the machine. The buttons were wired such that both of them had to be held down at the same

---

[1] The example appears in Edward A. Dauer, *The Role of Culture in Legal Risk Management,* 49 SCANDINAVIAN STUDIES IN LAW 93 (2006) (hereafter *Role of Culture).*

[2] Id., at 96.

[3] Id.

[4] Id.

time or the press would not stamp its die into the piece of brass. The point of that system was to force the operator to insert the brass sheet first, and then hold both buttons with both hands–thereby keeping both of them nicely out of the way–as a condition of having the tool come down and stamp out the [jewelry. It] would then be removed, a new piece of brass put in, both hands moved to the buttons, and so on. The two-button design was the fact [*–and a wise environmental intervention to disrupt a potential pathological pattern*].[5]

Yet having appropriate rules, and even designing the physical environment so as to minimize the risk, was insufficient. The goals of the workers were so powerfully felt that all efforts at prevention were thwarted. As Dauer puts it, "[t]he enemy was the shop's *culture*."[6] As he explains,

> Although the owners of the plant cared about safety, the environment they created was all about productivity. Jewelry manufacturing margins are slim, and labor is a major cost. A worker who produced more ... per hour was valued more than one who produced fewer. Bonuses and other perquisites conveyed that message. It did not take long for the workers to learn how to flout the rules and bypass the facts. With duct tape they permanently fastened one of the two buttons down, so they could use one hand to feed the brass sheets into the press while they operated the stamping with the other. They thought it would be faster. It was; but it was also riskier, and the risk of liability predictably followed.[7]

As Dauer generalizes, "This same kind of trumping, of rules and facts by culture, can be seen almost everywhere.[8]

Not always, however, are the disregarding of risks so conscious. Frequently, beliefs and attitudes about risks are buried so deeply within the surrounding culture that they are unquestioned–simply taken for granted. This can operate in either direction: the culture may imbue a risk with *less* significance than it merits (as in Dauer's jewelry factory example, which is dangerous), or far *more* (which is expensive as one over-invests in preventive efforts).

British sociologists Christopher Hood, Henry Rothstein, and Robert Baldwin have

---

[5] Id.

[6] Id., at 97.

[7] Id.

[8] Id.

revealingly investigated the link between culture and perceptions of risk.[9] Their insightful work presents a special challenge for Preventive Law, since one underlying premise of the preventive approach is that risks can be discovered, understood, measured, and minimized. If our perceptions of risk are, however, highly individualized or strongly affected by cultural values, then preventive measures may be inaccurate (in either direction).

Yet their investigations suggest that risk perceptions are indeed subject to strong cultural variation.[10] Writing in 1991, for example, one scholar noted that at the time in Canada, cyclamates were permitted but saccharin was banned. This was the exact *opposite* of the regulatory pattern at that time in the U.S., in which saccharin was permitted but cyclamates were banned.[11] The authors offer other examples:

> [A]fter a campsite tragedy in Spain in which 86 tourists died in a flash flood, a study revealed the extent of differences in campsite regulation across the EU countries. ... According to the study, campers in France would find their campsites tightly controlled, with extensive warning systems, and evacuation and contingency plans to deal with gas bottle explosions, avalanches, and floods. In contrast, campers in Greece or Ireland would experience minimal and relaxed regimes.

> Even neighboring states may take very different approaches to regulating risk. For instance, for a long time Germany had the most draconian system in Europe for checking the roadworthiness of cars, while France had none. Even now neighboring France and the Netherlands adopt sharply contrasting policies toward hemp products.

> Even more striking are variations in the ways risks and hazards are handled across policy domains in the same country. ... The result is a policy and intellectual 'archipelago' of risk domains isolated from one another, with very different policy stances across the various domains. For some hazards, governments adopt heavy-duty, anticipative, and intrusive regulatory arrangements ... . For other hazards, such as smoking, much lighter and more reactive approaches are adopted.

> The state in some cases sanctions what seem to be remarkably high levels of risk tolerance, as in the case of cancer risks from radon gas in the

---

[9] Christopher Hood, Henry Rothstein, and Robert Baldwin, THE GOVERNMENT OF RISK: UNDERSTANDING RISK REGULATION REGIMES (2001).

[10] Id., at 4–6.

[11] Id.

home ... . In other domains, however, as in the case of pesticide residue risks in drinking water, regulation encompasses extreme risk aversion.[12]

Further, who must bear the burden of risk management varies widely from risk to risk: "In a few cases, producers such as beef farmers have been partly or fully compensated for compliance with costly safety rules. But for most organizations or individuals subject to safety regulation, like restaurant operators, compliance has simply been required, without any compensation. In some domains of risk regulation–for instance, drinking water levels, distance vision requirement, or maximum permitted blood-alcohol levels for drivers–relatively formal and heavily quantified standards have been applied, while in others, like most aspects of driver fitness, standards are much vaguer and more general."[13]

The authors continue with yet other examples that illustrate a dissonance between objective levels of risk and the level of perception or regulation devoted to that risk: "[S]moking tends to be less heavily regulated than vehicles emissions although it is normally assumed to be a much bigger killer, and domestic accident risks are much more lightly regulated than occupational risks, even though the former claim ten times more lives a year than the latter in the U.K."[14]

Another anomaly in dealing with different risks is the level of empirical rigor with which the risk is approached: "Some risk domains are dominated by various forms of 'quantified risk assessment' culture, notably in nuclear power plant safety, in which risks are expressed in elaborate numbers but the costs and benefits of various forms of regulation or management are not. By contrast, other risks are handled by a culture of inter-agency bargaining–for example over who pays, how much and when over the EU Drinking Water Directive–or wholly qualitative 'seat of the pants' approaches to standard-setting, in cases such as the regulation of guns or activity holiday centres.[15]

Law professor Cass Sunstein voices frustration over the less than-rational approach within the culture toward certain risks.[16] For Sunstein, the generalized, slogan-like approach to various risks ignore crucial factual distinctions and result in unwise public policies. "Should

---

[12] Id

[13] Id

[14] Id.

[15] Id.

[16] Cass Sunstein, RISK AND REASON: SAFETY, LAW, AND THE ENVIRONMENT (2002).

pollution be 'prevented rather than 'cured,'" he asks.[17] "With respect to many problems, including illness, prevention does indeed seem best–cheapest and most effective. It is usually better to have a flu shot than to treat flu after the fact. For most people, a good diet and exercise, alongside a refusal to smoke, are a lot better than heart surgery and chemotherapy. Perhaps prevention should be the preferred approach in the domain of social risks."[18]

But prevention is not necessarily so wise in the domain of environmental risk, says Sunstein. "Often pollution prevention makes sense. The EPA was right to eliminate lead from gasoline; the government was also right to stop the use of CFC's which contribute to destruction of the ozone layer. But sometimes pollution prevention would be extremely unappealing, even ridiculous, simply because it is not worthwhile, all things considered."[19]

"Consider some examples," he writes. "The best way to prevent automobile pollution would be to stop relying on fossil fuels, now used by utility power plants. The best way to prevent the risks of genetically modified plants would be to ban the genetic modification of plants."[20] Yet, concludes Sunstein, we should not do any of those things. "

> Pollution prevention is not worthwhile as such; it is worthwhile when it is better, all things considered, than the alternatives. ... In many contexts ... risk prevention ... is literally paralyzing because no approach will actually 'prevent' pollution or risk. If the internal combustion engine is banned, substitutes will have to be introduced, and electric carts cause pollution of their own, above all because they currently require considerable energy. In fact the strongest argument for pollution prevention rests, at bottom, on cost-benefit balancing. What is not justified is to 'prevent' pollution without an inquiry into the consequences, good and bad, or prevention.[21]

Sunstein thus advocates use of an intelligent cost-benefit analysis approach to risk assessment and management. This is unquestionably true, and consistent with the preventive approach that we presented above. Having said that, however, can cost-benefit analysis really be as rational as Sunstein would hope for?

Lawrence Tribe has identified some limits of its operation, noting the doubtful underlying

---

[17] Id., at 100.

[18] Id.

[19] Id.

[20] Id.

[21] Id

premise that all policy options are capable of market measurement, and describing the "dwarfing of soft variables."[22] For cost-benefit analysis to be efficient, "users ... are under constant pressure to reduce the many dimensions of each problem to some common mesaure in terms of which 'objective' comparison seems possible–even when this means squeezing out 'soft' but crucial information merely because it seems difficult to quantify or otherwise render commensurate with the 'hard' data in the problem."[23]

Even more profoundly, says Tribe, *"entire problems tend to be reduced to terms that misstate their underlying structure and ignore the 'global' features that give them their total character."*[24] Tribe offers an example. Suppose that a dazzling light-show were developed that could provide intense entertainment to many people (Group "X"), but only by causing blindness among some other people (Group "Y").

> [T]he question might arise: should the members of Y have a "right" to the uninterrupted enjoyment of their eyesight, requiring the members of *X* to refrain from using the technology, and to compensate the members of *Y* if they do use it, ... or should the members of *X* instead be accorded a "right" to the pleasure this technology can bring, requiring the members of *Y* to suffer temporary blindness unless they have purchased in advance the forbearance of all the members of *X*?[25]

The legitimacy of such a hypothetical cost-benefit analysis overlooks, however, what Tribe calls a "structural complexity."[26] "[S]ome of the individuals in [both] X and Y would insist on a certain minimal quantity and quality of eyesight *as a matter of right* before they would voluntarily exchange any part of their opportunity to see for *any* quantity of any other good, and that our concepts of social justice would and should respect such insistence."[27] Measuring the costs and benefits by a single variable, *i.e.* wealth, is thus impossible, because "rights" must also be counted and they are essentially incalculable. And hence much of the purported objectivity or

---

[22] Lawrence H. Tribe, *Technology Assessment and the Fourth Discontinuity: The Limits of Instrumental Rationality,* 46 SOUTHERN CALIFORNIA LAW REVIEW 617, 627-29 (1973) (hereafter *Fourth Discontinuity)*; Lawrence H. Tribe, *Trial by Mathematics: Precision and Ritual in the Legal Process,* 84 HARVARD LAW REVIEW 1329, 1361-56, 1389-90 (1971).

[23] Tribe, *Fourth Discontinuity, supra* note 22, at 627.

[24] Id.

[25] Id., at 628.

[26] Id., at 629

[27] Id.

rationality for cost-benefit analysis is undermined. One way or another, there is no escaping culture, at least not fully. As Dauer says, "culture always wins."[28]

---

[28] Dauer, *Role of Culture, supra* note 1, at 98.

A NOTE IN TRANSITION TO PART II

The last two Chapters, dealing respectively with the legal system elements of truth and culture, are suitable transitions to Part II of this book.

Truth takes many forms, because we sculpt it into various shapes to satisfy our needs. The forms are dictated by criteria that we, as a society, unconsciously specify when we attempt to make sense out of the world, or manipulate the world to our purposes. Every inquiry has some point, every reflection is in response to some human emotional or intellectual need. We then demand that the form in which the answers appear satisfy those reasons for asking the questions. Whatever may be the substance of human inquiry, therefore, the responses will come to us in containers largely of our own making. These containers--the different ways, for example, that we package information about the physical world, or about human relationships, or spirituality, or beauty--make the information meaningful, both intellectually and emotionally. The shapes of these various containers suit the contexts of our inquiries; so naturally, we are hesitant to stray too far from our preconceptions of how various truths should look. Our conclusions fit us like the folds of an easy chair; comfortable, enveloping, conforming to the shapes we already are.

We thus regard truth in different ways, expressing it in different forms, depending on the subject and purpose of our inquiry. Sometimes truth can seem meaningful only if a proposition can be reliably replicated. At other times we treasure the uniqueness of an insight. Sometimes context matters, sometimes not. Sometimes truth must show us a goal, yet sometimes a focus on purpose seems to detract from the quality of truth. We summon the proper form almost unconsciously; matching forms to inquiries is a deeply ingrained cultural habit.

Paradoxically, however, the same forms that ease our comprehension come slowly to limit our understanding. Truth is contained by, as well as in, its vessels. Gradually our conceptions and imagination become captive to the packages we ourselves construct.

The law has not been immune to this human construction of truth: we have demanded that legal solutions look a certain way, satisfy various emotional, practical, and political criteria. Regardless of the particulars of each case, we have generally demanded that legal truth display strong authoritativeness, consistency, and independence. Only when law presents itself in this fashion do we tend to consider its judgments to be powerful, fair, and legitimate.

Ironically, the very strength we have demanded of our law may be becoming a weakness. The legal system has evolved a forceful and effective truth style, but one that is narrow, premised on cultural assumptions that may be outdated. The mix of problems presented to the legal system is changing swiftly due to changing technology, the expanding power of diverse subcultures, and the deterioration of traditional alternatives for resolving disputes. Hence the familiar container of legal truth may now need to become more flexible, so that we may expand its capacity. Without such a broadening of what is acceptable truth within the legal system, law risks a slow

177

detachment from both human context and higher purpose. And if that happens, we as a people will also be diminished.

Respect for truth may ironically be a primary intellectual hurdle to implementing changes to our legal system. Most of us feel a responsibility to "the truth," a sense that we are its servant, or at least its archivist. We believe that the truth is our heritage laboriously preserved through centuries in which it has been imperilled in various ways. We thus have a duty, we think, to uncover the truth neutrally--objectively and rationally--and with a careful sense of its fragility. As Richard Rorty points out, however, such feelings evidence the post-mortem grip of the "correspondence" theory of truth, *i.e.*, that truth is *exclusively* achieved when one has formed an accurate mental replica of reality. Although this notion has long been savaged by philosophers, the emotional hold of the theory continues to be powerful, perhaps (as we shall see in the article reprinted below) because we associate it closely with the scientific method, and that in turn with legitimacy.

The truth quest that emerges from adjudicatory procedures is to reconstruct in a courtroom a correspondence with historical events: human behaviors or understandings as they occurred at some previous time, the significance of which can be determined by their mapping onto legal rules. Legal judgments gain much of their legitimacy from the regularity of the procedures used to construct this correspondence between historical reality and the story that unfolds in court. The accuracy of those procedures is crucial because adjudication results in judgment: pronouncements of rights, liability, blame. Inside a courtroom, legal truth operates in a "rewind" mode. Preventive Law, Problem-Solving, and Therapeutic Jurisprudence, by contrast, tend to operate in a "fast forward" mode. These approaches are not so concerned with historical truth–what happened and whom to blame--as much as looking ahead for proactive ways to preempt problems, smooth fractious relationships, and find acceptable adjustments to that which cannot be changed.

Part Two of this book begins to look at alternative visions of truth--whether through the concepts of self-construction, or intimacy, belonging, or simple accommodation. We quickly, and appropriately, confront an intellectual barrier that warns against self-indulgence and the potential for chaos. Many people are troubled by any concept of truth that deviates from the correspondence theory. Some argue that these truth alternatives, especially when they question objectivity and consistency, undermine rationalism, a lynch-pin of Western culture. Others fear that alternative truth-styles will destroy meaning itself. "Without objectivity an untamed irrationalism will sweep all our civilized values from under us. We will be loose in a world without constraint, a world without guiding principles ... ."[1] We cannot ignore these real concerns. And yet, as we shall see below, the pressures to expand our ideas of truth may be inexorable.

---

[1]   Hilary Lawson, *Stories About Stories,* in Hilary Lawson and Lisa Appignanesi, DISMANTLING TRUTH: REALITY IN THE POST-MODERNIST WORLD xiii (1989).

Defining truth differently may, of course, change our concepts of social and ethical responsibility. If we accept the philosophical point that there are stronger connections than we have thought between subject and object, that we and the truth are mutually shaping, then we will view our responsibility to the truth--and to justice--differently. Our responsibility will not be passive, to be called out only in the event of a disturbance. Rather, we will see that truth is everyone's responsibility, not the exclusive province of those anointed by role or specialized knowledge.

Part One has addressed Preventive Law and Proactive Law. These approaches operate largely at the functional level, trying to repair or strengthen environments to relieve demands on the system by reducing problems. The Problem-Solving and Therapeutic Jurisprudence approaches to which we will now turn assume that the system has been engaged, that a problem has indeed arisen. They attempt to imagine making the system more effective by become more resilient or flexible through new ways of thinking, new structures or procedures for addressing problems, and different values within the legal profession.

In particular, we shall see that *the Problem Solving approach promotes respect for consensual relationships; decentralized decision-making inclusion; and participation by problem-holders in the resolution of their own problems.* Therapeutic Jurisprudence, not inconsistently with Problem Solving, asks us to add a new lens for assessing success and failure: the idea of psychological health as measured by happiness, social adjustment, the health or strength of personal relationships, and a sense of self-esteem and dignity. It also constitutes a theory of morality, judging what is right in the legal system according to how well that feature promotes (or inhibits) human well being. But it also retains some traditional Enlightenment values about choice and accountability. *Therapeutic Jurisprudence promotes new tools, methods, or skills that: (1) Accord people choice, wherever possible, about their life interests; (2) assure that people are given sufficient information to make choices meaningful; (3) make people accountable for their choices; but (4) are supportive in that accountability–helping people face and overcome obstacles to self-determination like substance abuse, or dependency.*

Both Problem-Solving and Therapeutic Jurisprudence will address the rationality and separation aspects of R/S/P, but both will work more explicitly with the aspect of R/S/P that did not arise much in the discussion about Preventive Law: the use of power in remedying problems.

"Power" may be the most imagination-stifling corner of how law is framed in Western societies. Legal systems in developed nations take for granted that state authority and enforcement will back up their statutes and court rulings. The judiciary, police, sheriffs, marshals, jails, prisons–occasionally even the army, as in enforcing school integration U.S. Supreme Court decisions in the 1950's–all serve to implement legal resolutions. Much of legal pronouncements are what J .L. Austin calls "performative statements," which are utterances that "do not 'describe' or 'report' anything, are not 'true or false,' and the *uttering of the sentence* is, is a part of, the doing of an action."[2] Examples would include statements by judges like "Defendant is hereby guilty as charged," or "liable to the plaintiff in the amount of ...." Lawyers in their offices, however, also frequently make place statements into documents: "This organization shall be called 'ABC, Inc. ...;" or "X hereby promises to paint Y's house in exchange for ...." Even lay persons can make such statements: "I take this man to be my wedded husband."[3]

What makes such words inherently a part of taking action in the world–the words themselves constituting acts of legal significance--is that *governmental power is summoned by those words*, so long as they are spoken in a given context or with authority that is bestowed by the state. The machinery of the state is in the background, supporting the significance and enforcing the words. Power flows downward from the idea of the rule of law itself, through the judges down to the lawyers and finally their clients, the petitioners of the system. Lawyers attempt to summon the powers of the law through argument, but it is a specialized vocabulary. The higher one climbs in the hierarchy of the various courts, the more concentrated the power, but the more remote from the facts of human problems and the people themselves. The quest is justice between the parties, seen as the accurate pronouncement of personal responsibilities: rights, liability, and blame.

What if no such state power existed? What if governmental authority were suddenly removed from legal pronouncements? How dramatically would the effectiveness of the legal system be undermined? Would the law still be capable of solving problems? What would be left of legal methods if we were to re-frame our vision of the law to leave out state power?

The exercise may seem fanciful at first, but consider the plight of psychologists. People come to therapists with a broad variety of individual and relational problems. The therapists will announce solutions, but never does the psychologist have the power of the state to back up those pronouncements. Instead, the psychologist must use the behaviors, cognitions, emotions, and relationships of the people who have the problem. The psychologist can never order a solution. But solutions are frequently found.

In their formal traditional procedures for addressing problems, Western legal systems do not rely much on the tools employed by psychologists. In some matters it may not even occur to lawyers to do so, because the legal system has such vast power at its disposal. If a client has a legal right, then a lawyer will imagine that sufficient power may be brought to bear that the client's right will be recognized, will prevail in the end. Lawyers have never much had to study or apply the problem-solving tools of human emotion, the bonds of relational loyalty, or the pressures of moral psychology. They had power instead. And yet few would deny the potential efficacy of those alternative tools for addressing human problems. Why, therefore, should

---

[2] J.L. Austin, HOW TO DO THINGS WITH WORDS 5 (2nd ed., 1976)

[3] Id.

lawyers leave those tools unexplored, even where lawyers continue to have possible access to state power? Can *some* problems be addressed better–more cheaply, more durably, without adverse side-effects--using these alternative, non-power tools? If lawyers had better skills with these tools, using them as helpful supplements to traditional lawyering skills, would lawyers be more effective, have stronger professional satisfaction, and enjoy a different social reputation?

In the approaches to lawyering raised by Part Two, Problem-Solving and Therapeutic Jurisprudence, I imagine and others actually describe how lawyers might approach their clients problems *without* such a heavy reliance on deliberative, imposed power. This conscious use of alternative means of resolving problems can affect the emotional and psychological well-being of lawyers, clients, and those in relationships with them.

The R/S/P paradigm is internally coherent–an image of detached, scientific investigation that then imposes a solution within a system of classified standards. So also is the emerging U/I/A paradigm consistent within itself. It is ecological, seeking to understand problems as embedded in broader environments, with solutions that try to harness the internal ordering of the system itself. By respecting the internal forces inherent in an environment, U/I/A solutions can work more like the crystalline structure of a snowflake. It possesses its own internal ordering capabilities. Through mutual accommodation of the molecules one to another, the crystal will adopt a virtually infinite variety of shapes without the need for outside manipulation. Sometimes, strong resolutions to problems (even if not fully predictable solutions) may be found by permitting or enabling systemic forces to operate. Once again, the analogy of the psychologist can be used. Often the best solution to a troubled relationship is to set up stronger, more honest communications among the parties. The particular arrangements reached is unpredictable, because it will turn on the outcome of the parties' conversations. And yet the psychologist has been effective in addressing the original problem.

At its most ambitious, the U/I/A paradigm may in some instances actually *transcend* the dilemma rather than fashion an acceptable trade-off between the competing needs. Later chapters explore some of the reasons for the emergence of the U/I/A paradigm and the skills that are needed by attorneys to work competently within it. For now, we should underscore what it represents: a new possibility for how our society might cope with the fundamental dilemma.

END OF PART ONE

PART TWO:
PROBLEM SOLVING AND
THERAPEUTIC JURISPRUDENCE

CHAPTER XIV
A REVIEW OF THE EMERGENCE OF THE U/I/A PARADIGM AND OVERVIEW OF PART TWO

Part One of this book described the traditional Western paradigm of legal method (Rationality/Separation/Power or "R/S/P") and contrasted the characteristics of emerging new approaches (Understanding/Integration/Accommodation or "U/I/A"). R/S/P thinking was identified as reductive, paring away the context or environment of human problems so as to apply legal rules more precisely and reliably. Preventive methods, in contrast, consciously expand those contexts or environments. Only when a risk is understood within a connected environment can the antecedents to problems be fully recognized, and the possible points of intervention identified. A variety of rewards accompany the use of these preventive approaches, primary among which are:

- problems may be averted that otherwise could have resulted in injury and loss;

- when they do arise, problems may be less virulent;

- in coping with these problems the attorney may have made significant proactive contributions toward achieving the client's ultimate objectives; and

- the attorney may forge a better, more satisfying relationship with clients and others.

In this Part Two, two additional U/I/A approaches to resolving legal problems are explored: Problem-Solving and Therapeutic Jurisprudence. Neither of these approaches is mutually exclusive with each other, nor with Preventive Law. Problem-Solving and Therapeutic Jurisprudence begin, in a sense, where preventive and proactive approaches conclude. If the risks and goals that are the subject of the preventive approach are not fully successful, then primary attention turns to Problem-Solving or Therapeutic Jurisprudence to deal with an erupted problem or injury.

Even in such cases, however, we should keep in mind that prevention is still relevant in two distinct ways. First, preventive thinking tries to ensure that any proposed problem resolution does not simply reflect "quick-fix" thinking and outcomes, but instead attempts to address the root causes of the problem. Otherwise, of course, the problem will simply recur in identical or disguised form. Second, Preventive Law remains significant by reminding us that every intervention or problem resolution has ripple effects. Lawyers should imagine the second-order consequences of their undertakings toward problem resolution, including impacts on the personal relationships of clients. Once those remote consequences of problem solving are contemplated, steps can be taken to ensure that any negative effects are ameliorated. For these reasons, the readings in Part Two will not leave behind the preventive approaches.

Roughly, we can think of Problem Solving and Therapeutic Jurisprudence as coming later than Preventive Law in the life-cycle of risks and problems. Before beginning our explanation of the Problem Solving and Therapeutic Jurisprudence approaches, however, we should ask why any new approaches may be needed. It certainly makes sense to attempt to avert a problem from arising. But if it does occur, why not simply entrust the problem to traditional R/S/P legal methods?

Several reasons may be advanced, first among which is that some *problems* presented for formal adjudication are simply not well resolved. These problems make demands on decisional procedures that the R/S/P methods cannot readily meet. Indeed, the proportion of these especially "problematic problems" within the legal system seem to be increasing. These problems have in common that for one reason or another they challenge one or more of the pre-conditions of the R/S/P methods:

- the *rationality* of the parties and judges;

- the ability to *separate* parties, analytically and adversarially; or

- the availability of de-personalized state *power* to effect a remedy by compelling or foreclosing particular human behavior or relationships.

In dealing with such problems, R/S/P methods are clumsy or ill-suited to the needs of the people seeking help. The U/I/A paradigm is emerging, in part, because of the invention of new procedures that better handle the sorts of problems that are resistant to R/S/P methods.

A. Problems with Rationality

Where people interacting with the legal system cannot comport themselves to the form of rationality demanded by R/S/P, the law's effectiveness in dealing with those persons' problems will be significantly undermined. The easiest examples include the chronic disruptiveness or criminal behaviors committed by people who are addicted to alcohol or drugs. Traditional legal solutions tend to be ineffective because they assume that people will respond rationally to the contingencies set up by legal solutions.

Notably, the legal problems of addicted persons are probably the most common impetus for creating specialized "problem-solving courts." Drug courts, for example, have sprung up over the past two decades, and are now widespread. In drug court proceedings, traditional legal procedures are discarded where they separate a defendant's behaviors from the broader aspects of the defendant's personality or compulsions. Instead, the drug court approach attempts to deal with the broader context of the repeated behavior, including the defendant's addiction.

Following entry of a guilty plea in a traditional court, the drug court judge works closely with the defendant, social services, and psychologists to get at the addiction that is causing the ongoing criminality. The proceedings are not compacted into a single trial. Instead, the defendant appears periodically before the judge so that the defendant's progress toward sobriety can be monitored. In these appearances the judge has a direct conversation with the defendant and social services representatives. Congratulatory ceremonies may be held within the courtroom, in which the judge celebrates milestones in a defendant's abstinence from alcohol or drugs. A more detailed look at the methods of a problem solving court (one dealing with domestic violence) will appear in a later Chapter.

Other problems similarly challenge the "rationality" precondition for the effectiveness of R/S/P methods. Examples include:

- **Defendants who suffer from mental illness:** It is often inappropriate for persons under a mental disability to be judged by traditional criteria of accountability. Even if legal responsibility can be fairly established, these defendants may be unable respond appropriately to traditional legal remedies. Problems surrounding mental illness were the original impetus for the creation of the Therapeutic Jurisprudence approach pioneered by Professors Wexler and Winick.

- **Matters in which the people involved are intensely emotional.** R/S/P methods tend to have limited effectiveness in addressing these issues. This is common where the parties to a problem are embedded in an intimate relationship, especially where that relationship is breaking up or dysfunctional.

- **Matters involving religion.** Where, by definition, people operate through faith or belief rather than through scientific rationality, they may be psychologically resistant to R/S/P inquiries, judgment, or remedies.

- **Matters involving politics.** Where ultimate values or visions of social goals differ, the disputes cannot easily be reduced to the particular rationality of R/S/P.

- **Matters involving indigenous peoples.** The traditions, history, identity, and loyalties of indigenous persons may conflict with R/S/P rationality, and also with its associated assumptions about human identity as based in geographically and socially mobile, rights-based individuals.

- **Matters involving aesthetics.** "Taste" cannot be determined objectively. The law's long struggle with violence and obscenity in the media is a case in point. What is repulsive or shocking to one person may be expansive or thoughtful to another. Once again, on a practical level the law's reach will be limited.

B. Problems with Separation

Issues surrounding indigenous people are especially tricky, because they can be discordant with the R/S/P paradigm on its "separation" dimension as well as its rationality dimension. Often the law assumes that problems are better dealt with by separating the persons involved in a dispute. Far more difficult for traditional legal methods, therefore, is to effect a remedy in which people must remain together in a peaceable, healthy relationship.

With Native Americans, for example, federal policy has historically oscillated between segregation and assimilation. Sometimes the approach has been to separate Native Americans physically, culturally, and even legally into reservations. At other times the law has largely ignored distinct identity or needs. Neither full separation nor full connection may be exactly appropriate for addressing a particular problem about indigenous integration and cultural preservation. Creating a legal framework for such an appropriate integration, and making judgments accordingly, is especially elusive for R/S/P methods.

Other social issues similarly challenge R/S/P methods along both the rationality and separation dimensions. In child custody cases, for example, high emotions accompany the basic questions about splitting parenting duties and opportunities. And as with issues involving indigenous persons, the premise that a problem can be better resolved by separating the parties does not work without substantial risks of undesirable spill-over effects. Simply ordering the child to be separated from one parent or the other may undermine the purpose behind bringing the problem to the law for resolution. The point is to find a set of relationships among the parents and child (and others significant to the child's social environment, like friends and teachers) that serves the best interests of the child. Flexibility and connection through cooperative joint custody better suits the problem.

The problem of illegal immigration provides another example. To claim that this problem should be dealt with simply by deportation is not to take the problem completely seriously. New immigrants will continue to arrive illegally. Separation could be part of the solution, but not fully. Separation may even exacerbate the problem, or at least lead to difficult spill-over effects as where the illegal immigrant has given birth to a child in the U.S. who then enjoys full citizenship. Separating the illegal immigrant through deportation can mean separating parent from child, raising its own long-term problems.

Other problems are also difficult along the separation dimension. Minority shareholders in companies, for example, need to be accorded a fair position *within* the ongoing operations of the business. It does not solve the problem of minority freeze-outs to assume the parties can be separated, because the minority shareholders continue to hold an economic interest in the enterprise. The challenge is in devising a productive relationship among all of the owners.

Or consider problems set within strong communities of loyalty, like cases of corruption or brutality within the ranks of the police. The "code of silence" among police officers impedes investigation and successful prosecution of illegal behavior by an individual officer, even where the other officers may recognize and disapprove of the individual's actions. Police solidarity interferes with the separationist (and in a sense the rationality) assumptions of bringing legal accountability to an individual.

C. Problems with Power

Many problems presented to the legal system for resolution raise difficulties along the "power" dimension of the R/S/P paradigm. Power problems occur for various reasons, some of which also challenge the rationality or separation dimensions.

First, the exercise of legal power may be difficult because the law cannot find an adequate point of leverage for imposing its solution. Regulation of Internet content or privacy comes to mind: a pressure point must be found through which the law can effectively impose its will. The sources of content or of information collection are too widely dispersed, across too many jurisdictions, for the law to be fully effective. Election financing reform offers another example. The problem is unregulated money flowing to influence particular public elections, but the variety of possible sources of those funds and the many different ways in which the funds can be hidden or spent have frustrated attempts to bring election finance under full control of the law.

Second, power may be an ineffective tool because it cannot be applied in the small, frequent doses that would fully reach the interface between individuals and their social environment. Examples would include virtually any issue in which problem-holders must routinely interact with others in multiple ways. Problems of sexual harassment or racial discrimination in the workplace often fit in this category. The problem is elusive because prejudice can simply move underground, out of the range of legal vision, retaining its offensive impact.[4] The law simply cannot oversee and regulate completely the nuances of human aggression or offensiveness.

Third, power to resolve a legal problem is difficult where issues arise about the legitimacy of using that power, as with international matters or other multi-jurisdictional issues. The fits and starts of the International Criminal Court may illustrate this, but so also do more mundane issues of international trade like illegal dumping of products at prices below cost of production. Where national governments subsidize production of the goods directly or indirectly, how should the dumping laws be enforced, and against whom? How may accounting practices that differ across international boundaries be held to a required standard?

Finally, the use of legal power is ineffective on a practical level wherever the cost of summoning official state power outstrips the amount in controversy. This limitation on traditional legal effectiveness is destined to become far more prevalent as transaction costs continue to fall and economic activities globalize. Transactions that historically were prohibitively expensive have become efficient with the Internet's dramatic lowering of information costs, and with continuing economies of scale in transporting goods. A typical American consumer, for example, may now find it easier and cheaper to order a $200 planter

---

[4] *See* B.F. Skinner, BEYOND FREEDOM AND DIGNITY 38 (1971) discussing the difficulty of resisting the lure of positive reinforcers that have deferred aversive consequences.

vase directly from Thailand via the Internet rather than shop for its substitute in a local gardening supply store. If something goes wrong with the transaction, however, is it realistic to imagine that the problem will be resolved through invoking the power of the law? Quite apart from the conflicts-of-law issues concerning what laws should apply to adjudicate the problem, the cost of summoning governmental authority through traditional means would almost immediately outstrip the value of the dispute.

So what are the courts to do when asked to resolve a problem for which their evolved R/S/P methods are ill-suited? The courts could simply refuse to hear a case, declaring the problem to be "non-justiciable."[5] That solution is rare, however, and bears high risks. The law and courts are sometimes institutions of last resort, when more traditional problem-solving is unavailable or has been unsuccessful. Turning away a problem may mean either the continuation of an injustice, or a resort to violence, or both. Before invoking the non-justiciable label on a problem, therefore, the courts will usually want to be satisfied that some alternative non-violent problem solving institution is available to address the problem.

Where the demands of a problem are **not** well matched with the structural capabilities of the procedure being employed to resolve the problem, I call the problem "dissonant" to the procedure. The problem and procedure are like a round peg trying to fit into a square hole. To avert self-help, however, courts will often agree to hear dissonant problems rather than turn them away. To cope, courts may *modify their procedures* so as to fit with the structural demands of the problem. They may attempt, in other words, to round out the square edges of procedural holes, so that the round peg will fit. Alternatively, judges may *modify the problem* so that it can fit within traditional procedures: Judges will try to square off the problem peg, so as to accommodate it within the square holes of the procedures.

These adaptive behaviors can be ingenious and sometimes account for the appearance of "legal fictions,"[6] but the modifications are make-shift: they do not necessarily result in an optimal solution to the problem. The inadequacies of cobbling together various coping measures spark the creation of new procedures and mentalities like those of the U/I/A paradigm: Preventive/Proactive Law, Problem Solving, and Therapeutic Jurisprudence.

D. *Fitting Problem Solving and Therapeutic Jurisprudence into the U/I/A Paradigm*

As we saw in Part One, Preventive Law stresses contextual *understanding* as a corrective to the narrow rationality of R/S/P. Problem Solving and Therapeutic Jurisprudence complete the U/I/A paradigm by employing *integration* and *accommodation,* respectively, as correctives to the R/S/P reliance on separation and power.

---

[5] *See generally* Thomas D. Barton, *Justiciability: A Theory of Judicial Problem Solving*, 24 Boston College Law Review 505 (1983).

[6] *See generally* Lon L. Fuller, LEGAL FICTIONS (1967).

R/S/P methods tend to treat all problems as structurally alike, applying the same legal thinking and procedures to any problem. One aspect of the Problem-Solving approach, in contrast, attempts to identify structural ways in which problems differ from one another--*apart from their substantive content*. By making such distinctions, the hope is that a particular sort of procedure can be matched efficaciously to a particular sort of problem. This is one aspect of the integration dimension of the U/I/A paradigm, together with the idea of integrating people and their needs to find a mutually beneficial solution, rather than teasing apart separate claims and then adjudicating the supremacy of one claim or interpretation over the other.

R/S/P also tends to treat people as universally alike–as formally equal–rather than inquiring into the diverging life histories, loyalties, and capabilities of individuals. Therapeutic Jurisprudence, in contrast, concerns itself with the psychological well-being of the particular individuals who present themselves to the legal system. In approaching those people and their legal problems, Therapeutic Jurisprudence attempts consciously to harness personal accountability, respect, kindness, and other emotions rather than the sheer power of the state. This is part of the accommodation quality of the U/I/A paradigm, together with the idea of structuring an environment that better facilitates psychological well-being.

In the Chapters that follow, these emerging U/I/A methods are addressed through three questions:

- First, **"what"** are the Problem Solving and Therapeutic approaches? What do they hope to accomplish?

- Second, **"why *now*"**? Why only now have we seen the dramatic increase in interest, innovation, and official acceptance within the legal profession of these alternative methods? Traditional R/S/P methods, i.e. rules, analysis, adversarial proceedings and judgment, have persisted for centuries in their readily recognizable forms. Why have the U/I/A methods so strongly expanded in just the past three decades, when their underlying principles of contextual understanding, strength through connection, and mutual adjustment by parties to a dispute have been available far longer?

- The third question is actually comprised of many distinct matters, but can be stated generally as **"how"** these approaches can best be used. How can one know when problems have been fully resolved? How can one guard against unforeseen consequences of attempted solutions? How can problems and procedures be best coordinated? How will use of these approaches affect a lawyer's personal identity and professional satisfaction? Finally, how have the U/I/A approaches been used effectively–by lawyers working alone or in collaboration with other professionals--in addressing various legal and social issues?

CHAPTER XV
THE "WHAT" OF PROBLEM-SOLVING: Purpose, Meaning, Values, and Goals

The following text is reprinted with permission of the California Western Law Review. It constitutes excerpts from my article entitled *Creative Problem Solving: Purpose, Meaning and Values* which first appeared at 34 CALIFORNIA WESTERN LAW REVIEW 273 (1998). Some of the formatting, footnote numbering, and language have been changed to conform to this book.

A. Introduction: The Nature of Problems

Problems are an unavoidable feature of human existence. This is trivially true in the sense that all people experience difficulties in life. Yet to think of problems as human also has a more profound meaning: "problems" do not exist in a purely natural realm. Whatever turbulence or destruction or deprivation may occur in nature is simply part of natural processes, inappropriate for the label "problem." This is so because only humans can construct their environments in alternative ways; and only humans can respond to their environments by significantly changing them.

A fire that burns in a wilderness will certainly alter the survival chances of the plants and creatures living within it, but without human intervention nothing can be done to change the odds. Nature will simply take its course. The fire and its implications are not strictly speaking "problems," because the very idea of a problem implies the capability of conscious adjustment to the physical, social, relational, or psychological environment in which the problem arises.

By making problems exclusively human and by tying that human quality to the ability to manipulate the environment, an encompassing definition of problems suggests itself: ***Problems are mismatches between environment and human purpose.*** [T]hree possible approaches to problem resolution will thus be at least dimly visible. One approach is instrumental: it seeks to bend the environment to human demands. The second approach is persuasive adaptation: it urges an adjustment of human purpose to fit within environmental constraints. Finally, for problems beyond human comprehension or control, resignation may offer the only possible "solution." One may simply acknowledge both the enormity and intractability of the problem, and understand it as a reminder of human limitation.

Legal solutions traditionally are instrumental, relying on both power and truth to fashion rules that attempt to conform a social environment to the purposes of a person or group. In part, the aim of Creative Problem-solving is to make law a more sensitive and respectful shaper of the social, physical and relational environment. Further, however, Creative Problem-solving seeks to give lawyers the understanding, skills, and attitudes needed to apply tools of persuasion and reconciliation where that may be more appropriate. ...

Before the search begins, however, one important point should be underscored. Creative Problem-solving does not disrespect the law. Far from it; the rule of law represents a dramatic advance of self-governance. In its consistency and assumptions of formal equality, the rule of law acknowledges the fundamental human dignity of every individual. Yet the search for better procedures for solving problems--legal or otherwise--should never be considered concluded. Legal procedures are liberating, yet they may also be isolating or destructive of spirit. To regard traditional legal procedures as beyond improvement is to deny the power of human imagination to propose something better. [T]he lawyer as creative problem-solver ... is an attempt to expand and refine the repertoire of procedures and skills for resolving legal problems, so that those problems will be resolved more efficaciously and respectfully of human relationships. Whatever skills may be identified, their application should proceed with values of inclusiveness, decentralized decision-making, and respect for both human differences and the bonds of non-coercive relationships.

In exploring legal problem solving, [this Chapter] begins at a general level by identifying the common fallacy of defining and classifying problems according to the procedures typically used to solve those problems. That misconception leads to inertia in problem-solving and a failure to imagine alternative procedures to solve a given problem. I then examine how procedures should be conceived as fitting with the demands of problems. Legal problems are distinguished from mechanical problems, marketplace exchange problems, and technical problems by two special demands made by legal problems: the subjectivity of the contexts in which they arise and the complex blend of power and truth required for their solution. ...

B. Problems Explain Procedures; Procedures Do Not Define Problems

Since problems are exclusive to humans, all problems in one sense are of human making. So also are the procedures conceived to solve those problems; [they are] devices ... invented to cope with chronic problems of particular sorts. The procedures exist merely to serve the problem; they neither create nor define the problems. In other words, problems preexist decisional procedures, and arise independently of procedures. This is self-evident: were it not the case, one could presumably eliminate all social problems by simply abandoning any procedures for solving them.

In common parlance, however, problems are often erroneously defined by the decisional procedures that traditionally attempt a solution of those problems. A "market exchange" problem is typically classified as one that plays out through exchange; a "technical" problem is one that an expert is attempting to fix. Yet thinking about problems through the characteristics of procedures is illogical. Notice how little sense it makes to say, "I have a random selection problem." The truth is that one has a problem, and it may make sense to resort to the procedural device of random selection in solving it.

The confusion arises because there is indeed a correlation between particular kinds of problems and particular procedures for their solution. The causal direction, however, is clear: problems have their own attributes and then migrate to particular resolving procedures. Typically, the migration occurs because the procedure employs techniques suitable to the demands of the problem. But sometimes by tradition or lack of imagination a problem is imprisoned within a decisional procedure that offers little prospect of solving the problem. Defining problems by procedures obscures the possibility that a given problem may be better solved within a different decisional context than the one in which it typically resides. The practice, therefore, of conceptualizing problems according to the procedures commonly used to solve them is not a harmlessly clumsy turn of phrase.

This [Chapter] compares three institutional procedures for solving problems--market exchange, experts, and the law. Doing so will permit an analysis of problem-solving that focuses on the attributes of the problems rather than the procedures for solving them. Each of the three institutions will be seen to respond best to problems with particular features. Once this central premise is established, a logical case will have been made for the central thesis of the Chapter: that better problem-solving by lawyers requires expanding the diversity of alternative procedures they may call upon for resolution. Problems present the solver with a choice of procedures. The greater the range of procedures available to be applied to a problem, the more likely it is that a procedure may be found with decisional features that conform to the demands of the problem.

C. Fitting Procedures to Problems

1. Why Law Needs Its Own Problem-solving Analysis

All problems make demands on the procedures invented to try to resolve them. The demands posed by various kinds of problems, however, are not necessarily alike. For that reason, concepts of problem-solving have been developed within many different disciplines--mathematics, cognitive psychology, management theory, for example--each with a slightly different focus that reflects the typical attributes of problems faced by professionals within that discipline.[1] Although the perspectives taken in the existing problem-solving literature may be useful to the lawyer, none addresses the particular difficulties of solving problems in a legal setting.

Legal problems typically make two special sorts of demands that make them more sensitive and complex than the logical and analytical problems commonly encountered as examples in traditional problem-solving books. First, legal problems tend to arise in subjective environments that, for both ethical and practical reasons, resist manipulation. Resolving legal problems thus often requires careful sensitivity to the various contexts of human relationships in which they are embedded. Second, legal problems often cannot rely for their resolution on a strong version of truth that is consistent with physical, mechanical, or biological properties. To compensate for this lack of empirical underpinning, legal solutions nearly always rely to some extent on power as well as truth.[2] Yet a too-heavy reliance on power risks disruption of the human relationships that accompany legal problems. Moreover, solutions based too strongly on power tend over time to unravel, leaving social disrespect or fear of the law.

These two features of legal problems--the broad variety of their relational settings and the special truth demands they make--require that legal problem-solving proceeds according to a unique set of meanings, purposes, and values. To set the stage for that inquiry, the demands posed by legal problems will be contrasted with the demands made by simple mechanical problems, by market exchange problems, and by expert or technical problems. Each sort of problem will be compared by two variables: the subjectivity or objectivity of the settings in which they arise, and the blend of power or truth typically required for their solution.

2. Mechanical Problems

Many mechanical problems make narrow demands on the appropriate tool for their solution. The settings of mechanical problems are strongly objective, and their resolutions rely heavily on empirically demonstrable

---

[1] Phyllis Marion, *Problem Solving: An Annotated Bibliography,* 34 CALIFORNIA WESTERN LAW REVIEW 537 (1998).

[2] I am indebted to Professor Arthur W. Campbell for suggesting the depth and frequency with which legal solutions depend on power.

principles. Suppose an object is fastened by a screw that has come loose. No subjective relationships are involved between object and its fastener: there are no feelings to be hurt, no deception, no power plays, no issues of love or loyalty. The problem demands employment of a simple problem-solving device (a screwdriver) to effect a fully containable and well understood environmental intervention (tightening the screw). This resolution may be carried out within the narrowest possible range of concern for error or for side-effects like relational disruption or social controversy. The solution has truth on its side, and the only attachments concerned are physical rather than emotional. This problem and its solution obviously fit neatly together because the mechanism and the tool were specifically designed for one another. Designing specific tools for specific problems, however, is largely a luxury enjoyed within objective realms where the properties of the problem environment are well known.

A different tool than a screwdriver could conceivably tighten the screw, but probably less effectively or with undesirable side effects. If, for instance, a hammer is used to force the screw back into place, then the immediate problem may be solved: the screw may be tightened in its hole, thus fastening the object more securely. Using the wrong tool, however, carries an obvious cost. The threads of the screw are likely stripped so that removing the screw for any later repair is made far more difficult. Use of the hammer ignores the mechanical principles demanded for efficacious solution. The hammer solves problems by pushing; the problem of the loose screw instead demands a solution that involves turning. Hammering as a problem-solving procedure is not well conformed to the contours of this particular problem.

Where a decisional procedure is not naturally compatible with the demands of the problem, the procedure must rely more on power than truth. The procedure forces the problem to conform to a relatively artificial shape that will succumb--however imperfectly--to the assumptions or attributes of the procedure. In the case of the hammer and screw, this is done by forcibly stripping away what was unique to the screw, namely its threads. As a consequence, the future functioning of the screw is compromised. Problem-solving is more effective, more sensitive to the contextual demands of problems, and less risky for producing side effects where the procedure conforms to the problem rather than where the procedure forces the problem to adopt a shape that is easy for the procedure.

The easy harmony between mechanical problem and manipulative solution contrasts starkly with issues that arise in the subjective social, political, and financial worlds. Such problems often seem to entail solutions that manipulate behaviors, attitudes, or environmental arrangements in ways regarded as threatening to human dignity and independence. Tools for solving human problems are thus ethically constrained by an underlying respect for individuals and their relationships. Problems arising in these settings are also less patterned and more idiosyncratic than those arising in the mechanical world, raising questions of human motivation and emotional needs that are not well understood. Tools for solving human problems must therefore be fairly general. Yet general tools lack precision and often risk side effects from their use. Paradoxically, therefore, human relational problems require tools that are less refined for specific tasks but which simultaneously must be used with much greater care than the tools of the mechanical world. Furthermore, the knowledge on which intervention is based is far thinner than the relatively simple principles governing the physical world. With that backdrop, the sections below consider institutional procedures for solving human problems: market exchange, experts, and the law.

3. "Market Exchange" Problems

What are typically labeled as "market exchange" problems could more accurately be labeled as "exit" or "substitution" problems. That is, market exchange problems are better conceptualized by their attributes of the feasibility of escaping a troubling or deprived environment and the subsequent embracing or acquisition of some substitute state.[3] For example, one may "fix" the problem of a wet basement by selling the house and finding one that is better constructed. One may "solve" the problem of an underperforming mutual fund by discarding it and acquiring a substitute investment.

Markets, in the form of the availability of alternative goods or environments, are responses to problems characterized by the human decision and power to abandon existing arrangements and substitute new ones. These attributes of market exchange solutions therefore attach to particular problems by conscious human choice. A demand for foodstuffs arises, and thus a market develops, when people seek to avoid an environment of food deprivation. A demand for, and hence a market for, exotic foods grow up when people who are bored with their existing diets have the power to acquire something different. A market exchange solution is simply an escape to alternative arrangements.[4]

---

[3] George P. Fletcher, LOYALTY: AN ESSAY ON THE MORALITY OF RELATIONSHIPS 4-6 (1993) describing the work of Albert O. Hirschman, EXIT, VOICE AND LOYALTY: RESPONSES TO DECLINE IN FIRMS, ORGANIZATIONS, AND STATES (1970).

[4] Fletcher, *supra* note 3, at 4.

Using an especially non-financial example may illustrate the attributes of a market exchange problem and thus reveal the mistaken practice of defining a problem according to the procedures by which it is typically resolved. Suppose a lovers' quarrel where both parties seek to split up and find new partners. Since this problem does not involve the medium of money or organized exchange, it is not usually conceptualized as a "market exchange" problem. But viewed from the perspective of what the people want to accomplish, the lovers' quarrel is indeed a market exchange problem. It is resolved by exiting and finding alternatives. The solution simply abandons the troublesome environment--in this case a troublesome relationship--in favor of a new one.

Locating market exchange problems along the two continua of objective/subjective and truth/power reveals their tremendous variability. First, market exchange problems may theoretically arise as easily in the subjective world of human relationship as in the more objective realm of physical deprivation or environmental annoyance. Of course a given problem may be easier or harder to escape, and substitutes may be more or less plentiful; but whether the irritants and substitutes are people or mechanical objects does not *in itself* affect the desire to exit and substitute. If the problem is a noisy neighbor, one could alternatively move to a different neighborhood, or pay the neighbor for silence, or invest in earplugs.[5] Sustaining human relationships may or may not be important to the holder of a market problem; that would depend on their preferences when choosing substitute arrangements.

The second notable aspect of market exchange problems is that the "truth" of the problem is, in most respects, irrelevant to the solution. Marketplace solutions do not require uncovering the etiology of the problem. If two lovers are quarreling, they may exit and find substitutes without any clear declaration of the cause of the relational breakdown and without attributing fault to either person. The feasibility of market exchange solutions expands not by refining an understanding of the irritation, but rather by increasing the power of the problem-holder to obtain more substitutes. Flexibility as well as efficacy in marketplace problem-solving comes through market power--i.e., control of resources--rather than through moral truth.

In a market exchange problem, the people wish to go beyond merely

---

[5] *See* Guido Calabresi and Douglas Melamed, *Property Rules, Liability Rules, and Inalienability: One View of the Cathedral,* 85 HARVARD LAW REVIEW 1089 (1972).

"lumping it,"[6] i.e., simply putting up with the physical or social environment which is raising perceptions of deprivation or annoyance. In a market exchange problem people consciously seek a substituting or restructuring so as to eliminate the cause of the annoyance. The problem-holder does this by employing the procedure of a market: abandoning and moving to a different position or somehow buying out the irritant in the preexisting environment.

The existence of a suitable market reflects an appropriate fit having been achieved between problem and procedure. Where no such market exists, however, the problem is still one of "market exchange." The problem will, however, not be resolved effectively using marketplace procedures. Perhaps frustratingly to the problem-holders, a different procedure will be required. Conversely, where marketplace procedures are applied to inappropriate problems--ones not given to environmental abandonment or ones in which moral values are especially salient--we apply especially scathing labels like "inhuman" or "monstrous." Market exchange solutions that contemplate the abandonment or purchase of children,[7] for example, are inappropriate. Similarly, if one person's problem is failing kidney functioning, our culture deems unacceptable the solution of that person purchasing someone else's kidney.[8]

4. Technical Problems and Expert Advice

A market exchange problem may be contrasted with a "technical" problem. Suppose the quarreling couple considered above had desired to preserve their relationship through better communication and understanding of one another's needs, rather than abandon their relationship. In such a case, the couple do not want exit and substitution; they are "not in the market" for new partners. Instead, lovers with this sort of problem may want counseling from a therapist to uncover and change the underlying dynamic that lead to their quarreling. Their problem is thus technical, in which the parties seek to understand or redesign an interaction or environment rather than to eliminate or escape it.

Technical problems frequently employ the procedure of expert advice

---

[6] *See* William L.F. Felstiner, *Influences of Social Organization on Dispute Processing,* 9 LAW & SOCIETY REVIEW 63 (1974).

[7] *See* Richard A. Posner, *The Ethics and Economics of Enforcing Contracts of Surrogate Motherhood,* 5 JOURNAL OF CONTEMPORARY HEALTH LAW & POLICY 21 (1989).

[8] *See* GUIDO CALABRESI AND PHILLIP BOBBITT, TRAGIC CHOICES 186-91 (1978).

for resolution. Experts recommend changes in environmental structure, social role or individual behavior that result from the insights the experts gain in investigating a problem. The procedure works where human knowledge is sufficient to diagnose the problem and apply a solution known to rectify the cause or the symptoms satisfactorily.

To illustrate again the mistake of defining the problem by the available procedures, consider the following. Suppose a hopelessly terminal cancer victim turns to a conjurer in a desperate attempt at finding a cure. The procedure of expert advice is here being applied inappropriately because the problem will not be improved from insight or understanding. The particular expert fails due to the limitations of human understanding. To such efforts in which the expert should have realized the limitation but proceeds anyway, we apply such labels as "incompetence" or "quackery." Even though the problem cannot be resolved by experts, even though the traditional procedures for solving a technical problem are inappropriate, the problem may nonetheless remain technical if the problem-holder seeks improvement of the environment through insight and understanding. The problem-holder may stagger through successive attempted fixes only to be frustrated, like the holder of a market exchange problem for which no market exists.

Alternatively, the holder of a technical problem for which no solution exists may simply become reconciled emotionally to the fact that the problem exceeds the current state of human technology to solve it. The terminal cancer patient, for example, may seek the advice of clergy or hospice director to cope better with the inevitable. Although the environment of the illness cannot be altered through medical treatment, the victim's mentality toward the illness may be reconciled through spiritual or psychological/philosophical counseling and understanding.

Regardless of whether a technical problem is resolved in a traditional sense by "fixing" the environment or rather by a reorientation of attitudes or emotional reaction, the solutions take far stronger positions toward truth than do market devices for problem-solving. The efficacy of technical solutions depends on accuracy of diagnosis and appropriateness of recommended solution. Reliance on power rather than truth is virtually antithetical to the idea of an "expert" or to the emotional reorientation through deeper understanding of the problem. However, like market exchange problems, technical problems may or may not be concerned with the preservation of human relationships. Such relationships may be central to the issue (as with the quarreling couple), or may be virtually nonexistent in solving the problem (as with the mechanic who diagnoses the loose screw). Frequently, relationships may accompany a more objective problem in some significant way (as with concerned relatives, co-workers, and friends of the cancer patient).

5. *Legal Problems*

Law is sometimes said to be a residual problem-solver, a device of last resort.[9] Translating that into attributes of the problem rather than the procedure, one may say that holders of legal problems often have nowhere else to turn. Legal problems may often be characterized as market exchange or technical problems whose resolution is frustrated. Exit may be impossible or undesirable, or substitutes unavailable. Where a problem shows up on the doorstep of the law, social arrangements are not easily abandoned. If the environment *could* easily be abandoned, it often would have been by the problem-holder, with another substituted in its place.

Similarly, legal problems are often characterized by the lack of a refined body of knowledge to treat the problem through applied knowledge or technology ,or even to promote reconciliation to the problem through understanding its intractability. If the source or treatment of the problem *were* completely within the realm of technical understanding or emotional reconciliation, the problem would likely have succumbed already to some fix or psychological resignation. Once again, the law's intervention would not have been needed.

In evaluating the historical performance of the law in solving problems, recognition should thus be given to the especially challenging nature of many legal problems. They are often set within a troubling but virtually inescapable subjective context and they present issues on which human understanding is limited. With such constrained malleability of social arrangements and incomplete comprehension about the propriety of possible intervention, the law depends on "voice:" the articulation of alternative positions that typically seek a normative rather than empirical restructuring of the environment.[10] In adopting one or the other normative alternatives, the best instincts of judges and legislators must substitute power[11] wherever truth leaves off.

---

[9] *Cf.* Sally Engel Merry, GETTING JUSTICE AND GETTING EVEN: LEGAL CONSCIOUSNESS AMONG WORKING-CLASS AMERICANS 172 (1990).

[10] HIRSCHMAN, *supra* note 3, at 30-31, *cited in* FLETCHER, *supra* note 3 at 4-5.

[11] *Cf.* Robert Cover, *Foreword: Nomos and Narrative* 97 HARVARD LAW REVIEW 4 (1983); Austin Sarat and Thomas R. Kearns, *A Journey Through Forgetting: Toward a Jurisprudence of Violence, in* THE FATE OF LAW 209 (Austin Sarat & Thomas R. Kearns eds., 1991).

Suppose, for example, our quarreling couple have decided to divorce. They must first secure a court decree dissolving their marriage. This in itself is simply a ministerial change in status. Thus far, the law is merely acting as adjunct to a marketplace solution in which the couple have decided to escape their relationship. The legal problems begin to arise in dividing the couple's property, and even then the problems are only *potentially* "legal." Although property allocation may be difficult, the couple could escape their problem by selling assets, splitting the proceeds, and finding substitutes. Where they cannot agree on the particulars or are unwilling to liquidate the assets, they must turn to the law instead of a possible marketplace solution.

The couple's dispute begins to present uniquely legal qualities where a disagreement emerges over custody or visitation of their children. For this problem, all of the parties--both biological parents and their children--are tied together in significant and inescapable ways. Exit and substitution will not resolve the problem where both parents want custody. Moreover, there is neither a technical fix available,[12] nor will either parent easily be emotionally reconciled to the absence of his or her child. Neither science nor therapy, in other words, will expertly resolve the issue.

The law must determine this issue by invoking social norms, under conditions in which the parties are likely frustrated with their lack of decisional options and where the "truth" of any proposed solution is elusive. The law may do its best to follow prevailing cultural wisdom, be that a presumption in favor of the father, the mother, joint custody, or the "best interests of the child." Yet in the end this problem, situated squarely in legal decision-making for lack of a better alternative, makes special demands owing to the inescapable human relationships and the limitations of human empirical or emotional understanding. In that sense it is quintessentially legal.[13]

Hence when others have written about problem-solving from mathematical or operations research or systems analysis or brain functioning approaches, their suggestions do not necessarily apply well to the lawyer's task. The crisp, clean-edged solutions of logic games may not be available to

---

[12] No doubt some people--though not I--would advocate the application of cloning technology to this problem.

[13] This conclusion agrees with Martha Fineman's reluctance to release child custody cases from the domain of the law in favor of social workers or psychologists, on the grounds that human truth has not advanced to the stage in which experts may be trusted on such matters. *See* Martha Fineman, *Dominant Discourse, Professional Language, and Legal Change in Child Custody Decisionmaking*, 101 HARVARD LAW REVIEW 727 (1988).

the law as it attempts to regulate the incidents of social relationships that are not wholly voluntary, and concerning aspects of life for which there are no simple empirical truths. At least a beginning may be made, however, in describing how law traditionally has attempted to solve problems, and how in the future it may do so with more creativity and sensitivity to the side-effects that using its imprecise tools may leave.

D. Describing Problem-Solving in a Legal Context

In starting to identify the meaning and values of Creative Problem-solving it is useful to begin with the prevailing mentality about the law. The demands of problems on the legal system were described above as special, owing to the troubled relationships in which they tend to be embedded and the frequent indeterminacy of their solutions. This Section evaluates how well the traditional processes of the common law meet these especially challenging attributes of legal problems. It concludes that the common law process supplies a tool of broad and enormously useful generality, but one that is insufficiently nuanced and flexible in its understanding of human motivation and the provisional, contingent ways in which human environments are structured.

The common law tends to approach human problems with a flattened vision of humanity. Applying traditional tools of legal problem-solving to such narrow human conceptions may be like using the hammer to tighten the screw. Finding no harmonious fit between legal rules and human circumstance, the law may rely too heavily on power to conform the problem forcibly to the requirements of the procedures designed to resolve disputes. The legal system does this by defining problems as exclusively involving adversarial contests of rights. Such conceptual constriction of problems reflects the needs of the legal procedures--rules supplemented by litigation. It risks, however, stripping away valuable attributes of problem environment (usually people and their relationships). *Conceiving lawyers as problem-solvers tries to do the opposite: it attempts to develop and use legal procedures according to the variable demands of legal problems, rather than force problems to conform to the needs of legal procedures.*

. . .

CHAPTER XVI
THE "WHAT" OF PROBLEM-SOLVING: The Fit and Misfit of Problems and Procedures

Traditional R/S/P legal methods pay relatively little attention to the nature or "structure" of problems, as distinct from their substantive content. Yet structural attributes of problems can be important no matter the particular content of the problem. The structure of problems is analogous to, say, the quality of "color" that every fruit possesses. Regardless of whether the color of any particular fruit happens to be red, green, or orange, every fruit possesses the structural quality of possessing a color. Further, the attribute of color can in itself be studied: it functions importantly in the evolution of plants and their suitability to various environments.

Admittedly, color is not what first comes to mind in thinking about fruit. The structure of problems–as distinct from their content--is similarly neglected. And yet, the idea of a problem's structure is significant in some of the same ways that the idea of color is important to fruit. The structure of a problem is important in understanding how the problem relates to and influences other aspects of the legal system, especially how our *procedures* evolve. In turn, that evolution is vital to whether problems are resolved in ways that are acceptable, efficient, and "accurate" in the sense of fulfilling whatever truth demands people expect when a problem of this sort is addressed.

As suggested in earlier Chapters, the structural demands of problems may be dissonant to the procedures that attempt to resolve those problems. In such a misfit, we may perceive that the problem is being handled clumsily. Even if we are not able to articulate exactly what is going wrong in the efforts to resolve the problem, we may sense that the procedure is not working along one or more dimensions of acceptability, efficiency, or accuracy. Uncomfortable with the possible consequences of an unfair or inaccurate outcome, the decision-makers may attempt to avoid the problem.

Alternatively, the decision-makers may attempt to adapt the fit of the problem with the procedure. The incompatibility may be resolved by re-defining the problem itself (perhaps by resorting to a fiction or other contrivance) so as to take on structural qualities that are more easily or effectively handled by the procedure. Alternatively, procedural methods may be revised so as to comport better with the demands of the problem. Either way, the fit is improved.

Because of the likely unfamiliarity of these ideas about the structures of problems and procedures, I offer an introduction below. Some of the text below is excerpted directly, or is edited and rearranged from an article I authored entitled *Justiciability: A Theory of Judicial Problem Solving*, 24 BOSTON COLLEGE LAW REVIEW 505 (1983).[1] Some of the citations

---

[1] Thomas D. Barton, *Justiciability: A Theory of Judicial Problem Solving*, 24 BOSTON COLLEGE LAW REVIEW 505, 513-536 (1983) (copyright held by author).

appearing in the original version are omitted here, and some formatting has been changed.

The discussion hearkens back to the first example offered in Part One of the proper fit between a problem and procedure for resolving the problem: the flip of a coin to begin an athletic event. We were able to understand *why* the coin toss procedure is so well suited to the problem. We considered the structure of the problem, and then matched it to the capabilities of the procedure. The problem calls for a choice between only two alternatives: "home team or visitor;" "server or receiver," etc. The procedure is crude, offering only two possible outcomes: heads or tails. ***Yet the simplicity of the procedure matches perfectly with the primitive structure of the problem.*** The procedure also satisfies the efficiency and fairness needs of the problem. Flipping a coin as a procedure is inexpensive, readily mastered even by children, and its randomness quality is viewed as unbiased. Obviously, however, few problems are as structurally simple as that of beginning an athletic event. Similarly, few are so easily matched up with a decisional procedure. The sections below introduce additional variables that ratchet up the complexity in fitting problems with procedures.

A. *The Problem Context of "Simplex" v. "Multiplex" Human Relationships: Can the Procedure Safely Ignore the Past or Future?*

The relationship between the two contending athletic teams is what a sociologist would describe as "simplex" rather than "multiplex."[2] That is, the sole nexus between the parties to this problem is this particular transaction, this athletic event. In finding and applying a procedure for resolving the issue of which team goes first, we therefore need not concern ourselves with any prior meetings between these two teams, nor with any future contests. We are concerned only with this one because it is a discrete transaction, rather than part of a larger relationship. The purpose to be served by the procedure is simply to get the competition started in a timely fashion that both teams will regard as even-handed. The coin toss does not take in evidence about the past, nor does it speculate about the future.

Most real-life problems, however, are not discrete transactions, completely divorced from relational qualities among the people involved. Even in our hypothetical athletic event, strikingly different procedures are adopted once the game has begun and the performances must be judged.

In judging figure skating or gymnastics, for example, a subjective quality is introduced into the procedures. The athletes begin to have a history or relationship with the audience and judges. The performances of an athlete on previous episodes in this competition (and perhaps in unrelated past competitions), will influence to some extent the scores on the later judgments in the tournament. A fall on one jump or landing will be less severely penalized for an athlete who

---

[2] Max Gluckman, THE JUDICIAL PROCESS AMONG THE BAROTSE OF NORTHERN RHODESIA 19, 20 (1955). The substance of Gluckman's distinction has been used by others, most notably in the important article of Ian MacNeil, *The Many Futures of Contract*, 47 SOUTHERN CALIFORNIA LAW REVIEW 691 (1974).

has performed brilliantly on previous efforts in the competition. Such influence may not be admitted by the judges, and mandatory penalties may be imposed to mitigate the halo effects of past performance. Nonetheless, the blurring of present with past no doubt affects at least some of the discretionary, subjective procedures that are used to judge the competition.

Some would argue that permitting historical performances to influence present judging is not unfair. The goal of the competition, so goes the argument, is to identify the best performer. Under this theory the truly better athlete, all things considered, is the one whose past performances are taken into account. Subjective judging allows the relationships the athlete has built within the sport to affect the outcome on any particular event.

Is this a more accurate or fair method for identifying the best performer? Perhaps that question is unanswerable. Perhaps discretionary judgments are inevitable and necessary until the sport has evolved a better procedure for making the required quality determinations about athletic performance. More will be said below about these relationships among the demands of the task, the sophistication of the procedures, and the deferring to non-reviewable human discretion. For the moment, we should recognize that vesting athletic officials with a scarcely questionable subjective authority may be a practical necessity for playing the game.

We may also note that other areas of life sometimes face problems that are similarly challenging: problems whose subtlety or complexity outstrips the sophistication of the procedures that are as-yet devised to cope with the problem. In political life as in athletics, for example, some procedures accord unquestionable judgment to a single umpire. Vesting such authority in an individual, however, may be called "tyranny."[3] The stakes are therefore high as we identify below some structural dimensions of fitting legal problems with R/S/P procedures, asking how well their structures fit or misfit.

B. An "Interactive" Problem: Can It Fit with R/S/P Procedures that Assume "Simple" Variables?

A given problem is easier to resolve to the extent it is composed of "simple" variables, and more difficult to the extent its variables are "interactive." These terms do not describe the content of a problem, but rather describe the relationship between or among the variables that comprise the problem.

Returning to our fruit analogy, describing an apple is relatively easy because it can be thought of as comprised of a series of simple, non-interactive variables. "Apple" could include color, and degrees of crispness, juiciness, and tartness. None of those variables affects any of the others (or at least not in my amateurish botanical understanding, and it is worth noting that it is just such inability to comprehend the interactional, systemic qualities of phenomena that distinguishes amateur from professional understanding). Each property could theoretically be

---

[3] Lon L. Fuller, *Irrigation and Tyranny*, 17 STANFORD LAW REVIEW 1021 (1967).

maximized until one reaches the Platonic apple.

An interactive problem, by contrast, is one where trade-offs exist among the variables that comprise the problem. For example, if the task were to decide how many apples to produce in any given season, the salient variables of costs of production, demand, revenue, market share, and profits cannot all be maximized; they can only be optimized. As costs go up, for example, profits are likely to go down. Each of the variables interacts in some way with all the others, and a proper solution to the problem considers the trade-offs among all the intricate connections. No variable can validly be considered in complete isolation from the others.

Analysis of a problem comprised of simple variables should be familiar to the legally trained reader, *because that is the underlying assumption of legal analysis.* A legal rule is broken down into distinct elements that then are separately examined, as though they are disconnected. Rarely, however, do problems really display such crisp, discrete separation of events and people. And yet that is a fundamental quality of R/S/P legal thinking. "Are the criteria of this element satisfied by the facts of the case?" This is a key admonition of law professor everywhere: the elements of legal rules are to be considered one by one. Legal rules are assumed to be comprised of simple variables. Several elements may be identified, and those elements may be difficult conceptually or in application, *but typically they do not interact with one another.*

Where legal rules cannot readily be reduced to discrete elements, a court may instead identify "factors" which a court should take into account in reaching a legal decision. Factors may be inconsistent with one another; and if so the weight of each should be balanced against one another. Sometimes, although not always, the factors describe variables that do actually affect one another–in which case the legal rule is being conceived as comprised of interactive variables, and its resolution is more therefore more difficult for the courts.

Professor Scott Ehrlich suggests an example of a multi-factored legal problem in which at least some of the factors interact–thus making the legal conclusion especially tricky.[4] He posits a private landowner, whose 10 acres are adjacent to a much larger municipally owned parcel on which a new airport is planned. To insure the safety of the runways, the city attempts to impose a zoning restriction on the private land, forbidding any structure or plants exceeding 14 inches in height. Will such a zoning attempt constitute a "taking" under the Fifth Amendment of the U.S. Constitution? If so, compensation must be made to the landowner. This legal issue eludes easy articulation and application of discrete elements. Instead, the U.S. Supreme Court has identified a series of interacting factors that should come into the analysis.[5]

---

[4] Scott B. Ehrlich, INTRODUCTION TO LEGAL SKILLS: ANALYSIS 37-38 (photocopied materials, 2008).

[5] *Penn Central Transportation Company, et. al., v City of New York, et. al.,* 438 U.S. 104 (1978), *cited in* Ehrlich, *id.,* at 38.

Some of the factors, however, interact. For example, the severe height restrictions mean that the government will not need to make any physical invasion onto the land in order to effect their purposes–a factor weighing *against* requiring government compensation to the landowner. And yet that same severity of the restriction increases the economic impact of the regulation, which weighs in *favor* of requiring compensation. If the landowner's preexisting use were, say, a heavy manufacturing plant that constituted a "noxious use" or nuisance, that factor argues *against* compensation; but the very scale of the operation that contributes to the nuisance quality also reflects higher "investment backed expectations" of the landowner at the time the regulation was enacted, which leans *toward* granting compensation. Such offsets among the variables that comprise the problem lead the Court to avoid strong legal rules, and instead to rely on ad-hoc factual balancing.

For the most part, however, legal rules and legal procedures using the R/S/P paradigm are assumed to be comprised of non-interactive, simple variables. *The underlying and misleading assumption, therefore, is that the problems to be resolved by the legal system are ALSO comprised of simple variables, or of variables that interact in ways that can be resolved through the rational, deliberative courtroom process.*

In the agrarian economies in which most common law rules evolved, the assumption that problems are comprised of simple variables may have had some empirical backing. But one important source of the increasing dissonance between R/S/P procedures and the problems being presented to them is that more modern problems are more often comprised of interacting, rather than simple, variables.

All problems exist somewhere on a continuum between consisting entirely of simple variables, and consisting entirely of interacting variables. No matter where on the continuum a problem is found, however, it can be solved by the application of some combination of rational principles and intuition. Problems comprised of a series of highly interactive variables were termed "polycentric" by philosopher Michael Polanyi.[6] Even among polycentric tasks, however, their difficulty and therefore their appropriate procedure for resolution will vary. For certain tasks, such as understanding the forces among girders of a steel bridge, the connections may be so well understood that all of the interactions can be mathematically described. For other tasks

---

[6] Michael Polanyi, THE LOGIC OF LIBERTY: REFLECTIONS AND REJOINDERS 170–200 (1951). Legal theorist Lon Fuller adopted this phrase describing multiple interactive variables into several of his writings. *See, e.g.,* Lon L. Fuller, *The Forms and Limits of Adjudication* 92 HARVARD LAW REVIEW 353, 394-404 (1978); *Adjudication and the Rule of Law,* 1960 PROCEEDINGS OF THE AMERICAN SOCIETY OF INTERNATIONAL LAW 1. Polycentricity, says Fuller, is distinct from complexity. A problem may contain numerous and difficulty variables, and yet the relationship among such variables may be simple. Second, polycentricity is not a matter merely of a multitude of affected parties: a polycentric problem can arise between two persons.

(including many economic issues[7]) the relationships between variables are susceptible only to a series of well-informed approximations.[8] For yet other problems, the interactions are essentially incomputable, perhaps apart from the realm of chaos theory.

These latter problems—the ones whose interactions are so intricate as to be incomputable or incomprehensible, simply cannot be solved "deliberatively"—i.e., through the imposition of external rationality or design. The interactions, and the repercussions of any such interaction, exceed human cognition. Rather, such extremely interactive problems can only be resolved intuitively, or "spontaneously," that is, by allowing any *internal* forces acting among the variables to play themselves out.[9] In other words, intensely complex interactions sometimes possess an internal dynamic by which the system *will structure itself.* An example would be the formation of snowflakes or ice crystals, each of which is unique. Snowflake production cannot be rationally designed. Instead, their formation will occur spontaneously in response to internal crystalline molecular forces.

Some polycentric problems, in contrast, *can* be rationally or "deliberatively" resolved, but optimizing the variables requires a tremendous amount of information about the variables and how they interact. Computers may be of great help in coping with such problems. The question is whether it is worthwhile to attempt a deliberative design or management of the variables, rather than to permit internal forces to create a spontaneous solution.

An example would be the allocation of seats on an airplane. On some airlines, the seats are allocated by a computer program using what I assume to be a complex optimization of variables including consumer preferences, number of persons traveling together, and the airline status level of the travelers. On other airlines, by contrast, it is essentially "first-come, first-served"—a spontaneous process. All those who enter the aircraft choose a seat which optimizes individual preferences among the choices that remain available.

In a sense, the spontaneous approach is more sophisticated, capable of responding to environmental factors that even a computer is unlikely to pick up. When the plane is half-full, for example, those who enter have a more limited choice of seats, but they *are* presented with a variable that was not available to those entered first, or to a computer selection. The late boarders may select or reject available seats after sizing up the passengers already occupying neighboring seats. They may prefer to share a row with someone reading the *Economist* magazine, for example, or instead with someone listening to an IPOD. No deliberative system could pick up all of those interactive subjective preferences.

---

[7] Polanyi, *supra* note 6, at 173-75.

[8] Fuller, *Adjudication and the Rule of Law, supra* note 6, at 4.

[9] Polanyi, *supra* note 6, at 154-57, 176

Increasingly, courts are often asked to resolve matters that involve high interactivity among multiple variables. Asking this of any deliberative procedure would be challenging. Asking it of a court–considering its constraints on evidence gathering and its typical need to pronounce a binary judgment–is especially unrealistic. Consider a couple of examples from the category of "regulatory" problems: highway siting and aesthetic zoning judgments. The proper routing of a highway is an optimization of many competing considerations about cost, terrain, soil conditions, preexisting uses, surrounding population density, the availability of nearby alternative routes, and the sociological impact on the neighborhood through which the highway is proposed to be built. And about aesthetic issues, one commentator wrote: "[T]he number of potential designs is infinite; the choice as to any single factor, say materials, has an impact of all other factors; and one cannot identify any non-aesthetic features that will even begin to consistently justify the application of any aesthetic concept."[10]

Both highway siting and aesthetic regulation are dissonant with R/S/P methods that assume problems to be comprised of simple variables. In coping with these two problems, the courts sometimes refuse to review the problem.[11] Alternatively, they may modify traditional judicial methods. Sometimes, for example, a court will adopt a substantive standard of judicial review that defers to the discretion of some planning board or other administrative agency.[12] Through according broad discretion to another decision-maker, the court is essentially acceding to that other procedure.

On other occasions, the courts indirectly adopt what amounts to a marketplace rather than legal solution. For example, in making aesthetic judgments the need for optimization arises because "objective rules" of aesthetics are elusive. Beauty cannot be fully analyzed in non-aesthetic terms like "square" or "circle;" ultimately, resort must be had to such terms as "unified, balanced, integrated, lifeless ... ."[13] If the variables all could be expressed according to a common denominator, however, their optimization could be accomplished simply by adding together all the various positive and negative values. The weighing of one variable against another would be inherent in the expression of each variable, using the common denominator.

When courts attempt to validate an aesthetic judgment about a property by referring to the market value effects of surrounding properties, the court is both finding such a common denominator and also aggregating the judgments of countless individuals as a surrogate for the

---

[10] Stephen F. Williams, *Subjectivity, Expression, and Privacy: Problems of Aesthetic Regulation,* 62 MINNESOTA LAW REVIEW 1, 18-19 (1977).

[11] *See, e.g.,* Nashville I-40 Steering Committee v. Ellington, 387 F.2d 179 (6th Cir. 1967), *cert. denied,* 390 U.S. 921 (1968).

[12] *See, e.g.,* State ex rel Stoyanoff v Berkeley, 458 S.W. 2d 305 (Mo. 1970).

[13] Williams, *supra* note 10, at 18 n. 52.

court's own judgment. The court is employing a mechanism that permits it to harness decentralized, multiple personal assessments of the money value of each relevant aesthetic variable. In the aggregate, market value can reflect whether a proposed house design is at least perceived as either grotesque or beautiful. In effect the court is referring the problem to the marketplace, which employs a far more spontaneous rather than deliberative method of problem solving. Such indirect relegation of a problem to a market solution is an attractive adaptation where courts are faced with highly interactive problems.

Alternative decisional mechanisms could be found for coping with interactive problems that, like the marketplace, are more spontaneous than R/S/P courtroom methods. Sending a problem to a democratic political process would be one example. The courts do this when they refuse to hear a matter by invoking the prudential doctrine that the problem constitutes a "political question." Returning a matter to the political process is in effect resorting to the decentralized, aggregated structure of individual voter assessments. In the end, the resolution reflects a spontaneous rather than deliberative process.

C. Problems for Which Decisional Criteria are Unknown or Disputed, Clashing with R/S/P Assumptions of Knowable Rules

Even among problems with simple rather than interactive variables, the problem is more easily resolved where the criteria for its solution are well established. In one rather crude sense, this point is self evident: solutions come easier where governed by precise, well-known rules. The point is also true, however, in a more subtle sense. Even where no rules specify a particular outcome, solutions come easier where two things are well established: (1) what considerations are relevant; and (2) what weight each relevant consideration is generally given in determining the overall solution.

The binary quality of the problem posed in beginning an athletic event represents the simplest version of this structural dimension. The decisional criteria for resolving the problem are truly undemanding. They are, essentially, "either one or the other, but not both, and it really does not matter which it is."

Problems seldom present so few procedural challenges. The actual judging of some athletic performances can come close, however, where the relevant considerations and their relative weights are well known. In most footraces and swimming events, for example, the decisional criteria for determining the winner are simply (1) the athlete reaching the finish line first; and (2) without having broken any rules of the game along the way. Applying the procedure of a stopwatch combined with one or more watchful umpires suffice. The important thing is to get right the sequence of finishers, and technology for better timing devises and cameras for photo-finishes can refine the efficacy (and fairness) of the procedure.

But contrast figure skating or gymnastic competitions. In events of that sort, the "best performer" cannot be so easily measured. Indeed, not all judges would agree even on all of the possible criteria. What should be included in the judgment before each judge records a score: Degree of difficulty? Poise? Gracefulness? Strength? Dexterity? Artistic interpretation of accompanying music? Ability to rouse a crowd? Even if agreement could be reached about the criteria, can we imagine that the judges concur on their respective weighting in making an overall assessment?

Where the relevant criteria for solving a problem are unclear, or the appropriate weight to be accorded each criterion is unknown, a problem necessarily becomes harder. Professor Melvin Eisenberg illustrates this point by discussing the selection of a college golf team.[14] Choosing such a team, Eisenberg is careful to point out, is not a polycentric problem because "golf is played on an individual basis and selection of the team therefore entails little or no interactions between choices."[15] Nevertheless the problem is difficult, for two reasons. First, because the relevant criteria are somewhat doubtful. Should one consider such factors as experience, desire, intelligence, and compatibility? Second, the problem is difficult because "even if all the relevant criteria could be listed, no criterion would be authoritative in the sense that it would trump other criteria, or even in the sense that it carried an objective weight in relation to others."[16]

This structural quality of problems is similar to, but distinct from, the manner in which a problem becomes more challenging as the number of its interactive variables increases. First, fuzzy criteria like those for judging a figure skating competition can be simple, rather than interactive (this is Eisenberg's point about selecting a golf team). Scoring well on one criterion does not degrade or otherwise affect the other criteria. Further, the dimension of "well-established versus unknown decisional criteria" can change greatly over time as a function of both the decisional history of the particular problem and the manner in which the problem is to be settled. Any instance of first impression in adjudication, for example, will be at the difficult end of this variable because the decisional criteria will, by definition, be unknown. As precedents build, however, the problem will gradually move to the easier end. The history of dealing with a problem can therefore change how the problem is described along this dimension of "unknown versus well-established decisional criteria." No such movement can occur along the dimension of "simplicity versus interactivity" of variables making up the problem. That quality remains constant for a problem, although the problem can become easier with experience, as the decision-makers come to understand better exactly how the variables interact.

A good illustration of how courts cope with problems bearing elusive decisional criteria is found in circumstances in which courts are asked to "judge the whole person," as in non-mandated criminal sentencing hearings or in PINS ("persons in need of supervision")

---

[14] Melvin A. Eisenberg, *Participation, Responsiveness, and the Consultative Process: An Essay for Lon Fuller,* 92 HARVARD LAW REVIEW 410, 425 (1978).

[15] Id.

[16] Id.

determinations in which courts are asked to judge whether an unruly child should be removed from the child's home and family. Because of the unusually broad scope of both of these problems, their decisional criteria clash with another assumption underpinning traditional R/S/P methods: the assumption that courts judge discrete behaviors rather than the moral worth or overall social contribution of the persons who exhibit the behaviors. This assumption of "judge actions, not people" is reflected, for example, in the common law procedural device of pleadings. Pleadings function in litigation to limit the inquiry of the court precisely on discrete events or behaviors, and thus *not* on the overall personality or social contribution of the people involved in the dispute.

Fighting traditional R/S/P methods, the broad personal inquiries required for deciding non-mandatory criminal sentencing and dealing with ungovernable children allow only limited appeal to rules or doctrine. As a result, court decisions accept a wide, fluid standard for what constitutes relevant evidence in the inquiry and risk being influenced unconsciously by inegalitarian assumptions that disfavor the poor or uneducated. This procedural adaptation means that the court uses a mirror image of traditional methods. As a result, two commentators concluded about PINS adjudications that the "legal supervision of [this] parent-child relationship cannot be undertaken consistent with the rule of law."[17] The conceived solution to ungovernability "extends official concern beyond discrete misbehavior to the condition of the whole child."[18] Similarly, in discretionary criminal sentencing judges receive information about the offender through the "pre-sentencing report" usually prepared by a probation officer. The scope of the report is broad, encompassing "[t]he subject's homelife, childhood, educational and employment history, political and religious attitudes, and sexual experiences ... ."[19]

D. Public versus Private Problems

Beginning the sporting event with a coin toss is easy for yet another reason: It can be resolved privately, as opposed to publically. We need not summon the power or expertise of the state in order to resolve this problem. Athletic events are private leisure activities. Procedures to deal with the problem of how it begins can also be private. The private flip of a coin is, therefore, again a good match to the demands of the problem.

"Transparency" is a distinct issue. In many athletic events, a referee will complete the toss in full view of the players. Even so, however, the procedure remains private: state power

---

[17] Al Katz & Lee Teitlebaum, *PINS Jurisdiction, the Vagueness Doctrine, and the Rule of Law,* in BEYOND CONTROL: STATUS OFFENDERS IN THE JUVENILE COURT 202 (L. Teitlebaum & A. Gough, eds. 1977).

[18] Id.

[19] John C. Coffee, Jr., *The Future of Sentencing Reform: Emerging Legal Issues in the Individualization of Justice,* 73 MICHIGAN LAW REVIEW 1361, 1370 (1975).

need never be summoned. In the event of some extraordinary confusion or claim of rigging the selection device for beginning a competition, an appeal would be made within the voluntary organization putting on the competition: the World Tennis Federation, perhaps, or the National Football League. It would not go to a state legal authority like a sitting judge. Private resolution is deemed adequate, and indeed socially desirable: few people would be pleased to have the outcome of athletic events made contingent on a courtroom review of replay tapes on any aspect of the game. Were we to use the courts, the final outcome of some football games played three years ago could still be uncertain.

But private resolution of disputes is not always desirable.[20] One must always inquire by what *means* such a private resolution would proceed. Sometimes a private resolution is effected by self-help, which can take forms that are highly unfair or disruptive. Sometimes private resolution is by physical violence, rights being determined by relative might. Even where private resolution is more consensual, it may be unacceptable, as where the parties are grossly disparate in sophistication or bargaining power. Under any of these circumstances, the undesirable prospects of private resolution may pressure a decisional institution to impose its own solutions.

Private resolution is especially undesirable where a problem involves a "tragic choice."[21] Choices are tragic where they involve social allocations that entail great suffering or death, like decisions about whom to send as soldiers in a war, or the level of resources to be devoted toward rescuing miners following a cave-in of the mine shaft.[22] When attention is riveted on such distributions they arouse emotions of compassion, outrage, and terror. Understandably, societies attempt to justify the allocation of suffering and death by referring to "humanistic values which prize life and well-being."[23] In reality, such allocations are made by the exigencies of cost and the caprice of nature. Yet to admit this risks social upheaval. Tragedy befalls the humanistic justification, which inexorably succumbs to fate and practicality.

One example of a tragic choice is the allocation of the use of a kidney dialysis machine,[24] an example also considered briefly in Chapter XV above. Suppose two persons require access to kidney machine in order to survive, but the machine has the capacity to treat only one person. Suppose private resolution of this problem is perfectly feasible: the patients are both in the waiting room and the hospital agrees to allow one party to buy out the other. A private resolution is clearly feasible, but manifestly undesirable. First, society is uncomfortable to learn what life,

---

[20] *See generally* Owen M. Fiss, *Against Settlement,* 93 YALE LAW JOURNAL 1073 (1984).

[21] Guido Calabresi and Phillip Bobbitt, TRAGIC CHOICES (1978).

[22] Id., at 18.

[23] Id.

[24] Id., at 186-91.

in this context, is worth in monetary terms. Second, society is uncomfortable in confronting the effects of the existing distribution of wealth. The poorer person presumably will lose this bidding; the question is at what point must he or she stop?[25] Ten thousand dollars? One thousand? One hundred?

Problems involving tragic choices therefore typically are referred to institutions for decision, rather than left to private resolution. Such problems, however, place extraordinary demands on the resilience and creativity of such institutions. The allocation must be made, yet it must be made in such a manner that will "preserve the moral foundations of social collaboration. If this is successfully done, the tragic choice is transformed into an allocation which does not appear to implicate moral contradictions. Morally debasing outcomes are averted."[26] Hence in the special case of a problem involving a tragic choice, not only is there special pressure on institutions to decide the issues because private resolution is undesirable, but great care must be taken in the form and articulated justification of the decision.

E. Whether Private Resolution of the Problem is Feasible or Infeasible

Whether the parties could or could not feasibly resolve their problem amongst themselves is important, not so much to decide *how* an institution might best approach the problem as to decide *whether* an institution should even attempt a solution. Most commonly the parties to a dispute have sufficient access to one another that they could, at least theoretically, resolve their differences privately. Occasionally, however, obstacles block such private resolutions.

Consider an example based on the well-known case of *Boomer v. Atlantic Cement Co.*[27] Imagine a factory that is emitting large amounts of ash and soot, most of which falls on the properties of 1,000 surrounding landowners. Theoretically, they could negotiate an agreement with the factory owners whereby the factory stops polluting in exchange for the payment of compensation. The first obstacle to this private resolution is organizational: How can the 1,000 homeowners coordinate their activities? The second obstacle is economic: How are the homeowners to share the cost of compensating the factory?

This problem is intensified by the "free rider effect." Invariably some of the 1,000 homeowners will refuse to contribute any money, claiming it is simply not important to them to have a yard free of soot and ash. Their real strategy may be to avoid contributing to the collective purchase of the factory's right to pollute. Obviously, if too many homeowners adopt this strategy, the cost to the remaining homeowners will be too high, and the purchase of the

---

[25] Guido Calabresi, *Another View of Torts,* lecture delivered at Cambridge University, 1980.

[26] Calabresi and Bobbitt, *supra* note 21, at 18.

[27] 26 N.Y. 2d 219 (1970).

entitlement will be frustrated.

Similar obstacles would prevent a private resolution where the factory wants to pollute (because pollution controls would be very expensive or impossible), but the law gives the homeowners (through nuisance law, for example) the right to be free of such ash and soot. The private resolution of this case would entail the factory buying up the individual rights of the 1,000 homeowners. Even if the practical obstacle of approaching 1,000 homeowners is overcome, the factory would face the economic phenomenon of the "hold-out." As soon as any single homeowner realizes that the factory is buying up the rights of her neighbors, and realizes further that the factory cannot emit the smoke unless it buys up *all* of the 1,000 "rights," the single homeowner may well hold out for an impossibly high price for her single right. Again, if too many homeowners behave in this way, the private resolution will be frustrated.

Practically speaking, private resolution is infeasible in these cases. To be solved, the dispute must be resolved by an outside person with sufficient power to compel payments by all the homeowners. Other practical problems of various sorts can also beset the practicality of using different private dispute resolution or market procedures. Cataloguing those inefficiencies and barriers to entry is not possible in these materials. Suffice it to say that where private resolution is infeasible for any reason, public decisional institutions like the law may feel a special urgency to hear the dispute. Conversely, where such private resolution is feasible, the public institution may erect barriers to entry to prevent strain on institutional resources.

F. "Predictive" and "Planning" Problems that Clash with R/S/P Assumptions of Judging Past Events

It seems self evident that it is easier to solve a problem where the decisional criteria look to past events rather than future events. No doubt every sort of datum upon which a decision is based is subject to some uncertainty. Yet as flawed and interpretative as historical investigation may be, historical conclusions are likely more accurate than those based on predictions. Notwithstanding their inherent difficulty, future-based problems can be successfully addressed. The procedures for doing so, however, should possess certain structural features.

More specifically, future-based problems–those for which solutions depend on predictions of the consequences of intervention[28]–raise issues about whether a given procedure to resolve the problem is "active" or "reactive." An active decisional system is one that can initiate internally the investigation and treatment of problems. A reactive procedure is one that depends on outside parties to identify the problem. Reactive procedures are generally limited to considering the sorts of problems that private parties perceive and pursue.[29] Certain problems,

---

[28] *See* Friedrich von Hayek, THE ROAD TO SERFDOM 34-87 (1944).

[29] *See* Austin Sarat & Joel B. Grossman, *Courts and Conflict Resolution: Problems in the Mobilization of Adjudication*, 69 AMERICAN POLITICAL SCIENCE REVIEW 1200 (1975).

however, are difficult for untrained persons to detect. Where a long hiatus exists between a harm-causing occurrence and the manifestation of injury, reactive procedures are certainly inefficient, and the passage of time may impair the accuracy of their outcomes.[30]

Attempts by the common law to deal with health problems caused by environmental pollution illustrate this point.[31] Often a plaintiff is exposed to the harmful agent years before the injury surfaces. Even where Statute of Limitations problems are overcome, evidentiary problems--particularly those related to causation--can frustrate recovery. Furthermore, even if recovery is obtained, it still is possible that other injuries that occurred during the hiatus might have been prevented by an earlier edict of some more active decisional system.

The overall effectiveness of reactive procedures is limited by the necessary dependence on private initiatives in pursuing claims. For example, the victims of incest or rape may not report the incident, and victims of child battering, being under the parents' control, are often incapable of complaint. On the other hand, an active system may well develop such rigid and restrictive internal policies of problem identification that it ultimately considers a lesser diversity of problems. Moreover, under some conditions reactive systems may be preferable because such procedures enhance opportunities for decisional participation by persons who suffer restricted access to the power structures of active systems. Minority groups or others with less than average participation and influence in active systems (as in legislatures, for example) will normally fare better in reactive systems like the courts.[32]

Traditional adjudication is reactive,[33] and thus well-suited to problems that arise out of past events. Problems requiring analysis of future events are better suited to active procedures. This conclusion follows from two premises: first, the dependence of reactive systems on the perceptions of untrained outsiders that a problem exists; and second, that future-based problems tend either to be of a "policy" nature, or else to be relatively subtle problems affecting large numbers or people. Untrained outsiders have difficulty perceiving the underlying social patterns which give rise to future-based problems. Hence reactive systems, which depend on such

---

[30] Sheldon Goldman and Austin Sarat, AMERICAN COURT SYSTEMS: READINGS IN JUDICIAL PROCESS AND BEHAVIOR 8 (1978).

[31] Harold P. Green, *The Role of Law and Lawyers in Technology Assessment*, in M. Cetron and B. Bactocha, TECHNOLOGY ASSESSMENT IN A DYNAMIC ENVIRONMENT 630-31 (1973); Marcia R. Gelpe & Dan Tarlock, *The Uses of Scientific Information in Environmental Decisionmaking,* 48 SOUTHERN CALIFORNIA LAW REVIEW 371 (1974).

[32] J. Woodford Howard, Jr., *Adjudication Considered as a Process of Conflict Resolution: A Variation on Separation of Powers,* 18 JOURNAL OF PUBLIC LAW 339, 346 (1969).

[33] Abram Chayes, *The Role of the Judge in Public Law Litigation*, 89 HARVARD LAW REVIEW 1281, 1283 (1976).

untrained persons for identification and articulation of problems, are not likely to cope well with future-based problems.

It is possible that a future-based problem would simply never be raised within a reactive system; or that the problem would be presented piecemeal or incoherently; or that the initiatives might come too late to be effective.[34] Effective, efficient dealing with future-based problem is enhanced in an active decisional system with its more systematic, inclusive approach, its better access to predictive information, and its greater ability to manipulate the environment according to some preconceived plan.

Conversely, accepting the Aristotelian notion that those who feel the pinch best know how its hurts[35] leads to the general conclusion that it is more accurate and acceptable for past-based problems to be presented by those persons who have been specifically injured--even if they are not trained within the decision system.[36] Such piecemeal problem-solving may be less efficient than the approach taken in an active system, but considerations of enhanced accuracy and acceptability nonetheless may prevail over concerns about inefficiency.

Future-based, and therefore more difficult, problems are of two sorts. The first are "predictive" problems that require an unalterable present action, the accuracy of which cannot be judged until the occurrence of one or more future events. The second type of future-based problems are "planning" problems that set a goal more or less extended into the future, and then attempt constantly to manipulate the environment in order that at the specified time the goal will have been met. Both sorts of problems are generally more difficult than problems which can be solved by bringing to bear historical information.

When judges hear "predictive" problems, they tend to resolve the dissonance by modifying the problem so as to treat it as past-based. When judges hear "planning" problems, they tend to resolve the dissonance by adapting their procedures to become more proactive than the traditional reactive posture of the courts.

1. Predictive Problems

Predictive problems most commonly are presented to the judiciary in the context of requests for "technology assessments," *i.e.,* disputes about the environment or health impact of

---

[34] Goldman and Sarat, *supra* note 30, at 8.

[35] Howard, *supra* note 32, at 343.

[36] Aristotle's assertion is not always true. For example, where the injury is not tangible, but rather legally defined (as in the case of persons being deprived of some welfare benefit to which they did not know they were entitled) the best initiator is clearly someone other than the person injured. David Fleming, personal communication.

some proposed ongoing activity. Such problems are future-based because a decision either to permit the activity, or to enjoin or regulate it, is necessarily grounded in determining not only current effects, but risks of future effects. The ultimate wisdom of many such decisions can be judged only by the hindsight of future generations. A reactive system of decision-making such as traditional adjudication lacks the informational resources to deal properly with predictive problems.

Moreover, the incremental decision-making of adjudication inhibits a comprehensive and coherent treatment of predictive problems. Judges normally have before them in a given case only limited aspects of a predictive problem. They are, therefore, similarly limited in their ability to dispose of the problem. When heard by judges, predictive problems tend to be converted into more familiar and less demanding past-based problems by both procedural and substantive means. Procedurally, judges manipulate the burden of proof standards; substantively, they artificially discount future costs.[37]

In establishing procedural devices for adjudicating predictive problems concerning the uncertain environmental and health effects of certain proposed activities, three alternative models are used: the "free market" model; the "regulation-market failure" model; and the "state of the art" model.[38] The models differ in which party bears the burdens of persuasion, and production of evidence.

In the "free market" model, a presumption exists in favor of allowing unregulated market forces to operate as a means of determining whether risks of harm are outweighed by the benefits of engaging in the activity. Heavy burdens of production and persuasion are placed on those who would regulate the activity.[39] Under this model, a lack of information can defeat the regulator. Even where information about potential injuries can be produced, the regulator will lose if the risk of injury is not probed by a "preponderance of the evidence."[40] This requirement is crucial because much information about *potential* injuries is inherently probabilistic, speculative, or unavailable.[41] By placing very high standards of production or persuasion on the regulator, what

---

[37] *See generally* William H. Rodgers, *Benefits, Costs, and Risks: Oversight of Health and Environmental Decision-making,* 4 HARVARD ENVIRONMENTAL LAW REVIEW 191 (1980); Yellin, *Judicial Review and Nuclear Power: Assessing the Risks of Environmental Catastrophe,* 45 GEORGE WASHINGTON LAW REVIEW 969 (1977); Laurence H. Tribe, CHANNELING TECHNOLOGY THROUGH LAW (1973).

[38] Rogers, *supra* note 37, at 219-25.

[39] Id.

[40] Id.

[41] *See* Gelpe & Tarlock, *supra* note 31, at 407–12.

in reality is a dispute about *risk* is transformed to an issue of whether the regulator can conclusively prove some future *injury*, almost necessarily by coming forward with proof about injuries that have occurred in the past.[42]

Under the "regulation-market failure" model, the burdens of proof are simply reversed.[43] The regulator's *prima facie* showing of a *risk* to human health is determinative unless the proposing actor can rebut the presumption with conclusive evidence of either the falsity of the risk, or of the gaining of overwhelming future benefits by allowing the activity.[44] Once again, given the inherent uncertainty of information in this sort of predictive problem, the operation of the burdens of production and persuasion serve to foreclose a balanced inquiry about future risks and benefits. Once again the case turns on evidence of existing effects drawn from past experience rather than on purely predictive evidence of future effects.

In the free market model, virtually conclusive weight is given to the present benefits of the activity, and the costs of regulating it. In the regulation-market failure model, virtually conclusive weight is accorded the present costs of the activity (in the form of provable risks). The two models taken together demonstrate the alternative problem modifications used by judges when faced with the inherent awkwardness of a predictive problem.

It is only on those rare occasions that courts use the "state of the art" model in which a balanced investigation of future costs and benefits is undertaken. This model embraces a "standard of proof [i.e. burden of persuasion] that tolerates uncertainty, and thus seeks pragmatically the best decision for the moment. It anticipates a decision with data already known, requiring only that agencies use the best available evidence in reaching judgments."[45] Under this model the burden of production of evidence is also assigned pragmatically, "with the party possessing information being the one expected to produce it."[46]

Even under a model free of debate-confining presumptions, pressure exists to discount future consequences in favor of consequences that might be proved by referring to past experience. Sometimes this takes the form of a court's reluctance to accord the status of "evidence" to proofs that are admittedly probabilistic. At other times, the discounting of the future is the indirect result of an oversimplified analysis of the notion of a future "risk." This tends to occur where the court faces a predictive problem, like the permitting or enjoining of a

---

[42] Id., at 412.

[43] Rogers, *supra* note 37, at 224, 225.

[44] Id.

[45] Id., at 222, 223.

[46] Id., at 223.

nuclear power plant, involving a very low probability of harm but where such harm would be catastrophic.[47] For such problems, courts tend to equate the notion of future "costs" or "risks" with the probability of harm occurring.

For example, "nuclear risk analyses have adopted the ... rule that probabilities are *determinative* of risk."[48] A more accurate appraisal, however, would be to apply the traditional negligence standard for determining risk, namely that risk is the product of probability multiplied by consequences.[49] It is not even unknown in the law to determine risk *solely* on the basis of consequences, with virtually no legal weight accorded to "the degree of precautionary care [or] the remoteness of the possibility of catastrophe."[50] Such a rule is applied in determining liability for "abnormally dangerous" or "ultra-hazardous" activities.[51]

Where a problem with a low probability of occurrence but with potentially drastic consequences is judged by risk standards that fail to consider consequences, the effect is to discount future costs unjustifiably in favor or present benefits. The risk rule that has been applied in such cases can be explained as a problem modification to relieve the dissonance of considering future-based problems. Probabilities of harm from the operation of nuclear power plants can be based largely on past safety records, and on descriptions of reactor safeguards. Hence, analysis proceeds according to such criteria, regardless of how unrepresentative that may be of the full extent of the problem.

In summary, the judicial reluctance to base adjudicative decisions on future-based evidence causes distortion in the articulation, and often the resolution, of a predictive problem. Courts avoid the necessity of actually making the prediction by casting the burdens of production and persuasion in such a manner that one party is precluded from establishing its version of the likely future. Where this is not possible, and courts actually undertake to make a decision based on a prediction of the future, courts are likely to avoid making a complete analysis by considering only the likelihood of a given event occurring in the future, and not its possible consequences. Each of these adaptations, by virtue of diminishing the predictive element, also serves to make the dispute resolution procedure more "reactive" than "active."

---

[47] *See generally* Yellin, *supra* note 37.

[48] Id., at 986.

[49] Id., at 982.

[50] Id., at 984.

[51] Id., at 983.

2. Planning Problems

Planning problems are entirely distinct from predictive problems, and they evoke a different judicial response. Whereas decisions about predictive problems are conditioned on uncontrollable future events, decisions on planning problems assume the future can be manipulated to comport with the decision. Planning decisions are interventionist and are instrumental in performing some task or achieving some goal. Planning is "laying down how the resources of society should be 'consciously directed' to serve particular ends in a definite way."[52] Such decisions, to be effective, cannot leave the future to chance. If the decision is indeed to be instrumental in reaching some goal or state of affairs, then necessarily the decision-maker must "foresee the incidence of its actions."[53] Hence, planning decisions are inescapably future-based.

Not all decisions that are instrumental toward meeting a goal, however, are truly future-based planning decisions in the sense here meant.[54] A true planning decision is one that is instrumental in achieving some goal which does *not* contemplate the optimally efficient allocation of resources.[55] A planning decision contemplates committing resources in a manner different from the allocation that would obtain "... if decisions were made about the use of resources on the basis of whether the marginal loss of preserving them exceeds the marginal amount people are willing to pay for their preservation."[56]

Suppose, for example, an agency is entrusted with supervision of airline flights between London and New York.[57] Suppose also there exists sufficient demand and airline capacity to support twenty flights daily. The agency faces both a first-order and a second-order determination.[58] The first-order decision is how many flights to allow, and the second-order decision is how to allocate the flying rights among contending airlines.

Imagine that in order to advance some goal like currency protection, income

---

[52] Hayek, *supra* note 28, at 35.

[53] Id., at 76.

[54] Tribe, *supra* note 37, at 53-56.

[55] Id.

[56] Id., at 57.

[57] This example is taken broadly from Charles Reich, *The Law of the Planned Society,* 75 YALE LAW JOURNAL 1227, 1232–34 (1966).

[58] For use of the terms "first-order" and "second order" determinations, *see* Calabresi and Bobbitt, *supra* note 21, at 19.

redistribution, or simply paternalism,[59] the agency decides to allow only ten flights per day. This is a true planning decision, a commitment of social resources on grounds that do not seek optimally efficient use of resources. Suppose in making the second-order allocation among the airlines the agency lets out the rights for competitive bidding, except that it prohibits two airlines from competing because of chronic past unreliability and flight cancellations. This agency decision is not a true planning decision; rather, the agency is attempting to correct an imperfection in the market method of seeking optimal allocation of resources. If instead the method of making the second-order determination is to grant an exclusive license to the national airline so as to protect its market, that *is* a true planning decision.

Legal decisions correcting market failures, as in the initial second-order determination considered above, are common and present no great dissonance with the procedure of traditional adjudication. Where judges are faced, however, with the need to make true planning decisions exemplified by the above first-order decision, they tend to adapt their procedures in various ways, especially towards making adjudication more active than reactive.

The traditional judiciary very rarely face planning problems, and hence this argument must be from analogy to administrative agencies. Planning problems commonly are assigned to such agencies, which often are required to deal with such problems in a more or less adjudicatory fashion. The awkwardness of solving planning problems with reactive procedures creates some procedural adaptations.[60] The deciding agency uses numerous criteria in making a decision.[61] The parties therefore present evidence on every conceivable issue, since they have no idea which issue may be dispositive of the decision.[62] For the same reason, the agency likely will admit any evidence offered, and the record of the proceedings therefore could be enormous.[63] "It is the limitless and unfenced range of the agency's probable basis of decision that lies at the root of the procedure problem."[64]

The problem, in other words, is that once efficiency is abandoned as the criterion for allocating resources to do some regulatory task, the decision-makers are left with a value choice in finding an alternative distributional criterion. Commonly, nothing in the pertinent statute

---

[59] Tribe, *supra* note 37, at 57-58.

[60] Reich, *supra* note 57, at 1241.

[61] Id.

[62] Id.

[63] Id.

[64] Id.

informs such a choice other than that it be in the "public interest."[65] This vagueness results in the formless trials described above, and in an institutionalized arbitrariness of decisions arguably inconsistent with the rule of law, since "the use of the government's coercive powers will no longer be limited and determined by preestablished rules."[66]

Furthermore, a decisional system assigned to achieve a certain goal cannot remain procedurally reactive, waiting for fortuitous cases to come its way. Bureaucratic pressures to implement particular results will result in either the convening of hearings regardless of whether a normal "case or controversy" presents itself for determination, or perhaps in a careful screening of cases for selective hearing. Preservation of traditional reactive methods of obtaining cases will be seen as inefficient, or stifling of change, or even dangerous.

Planning problems pressure courts to abandon traditional reactive procedures in favor of active procedures. Such a shift is so fundamental, however, that decisions on such matters usually are made by administrative agencies possessing loose standards of evidence and participation. As with predictive problems, planning problems starkly present value choices. For reasons of structure and therefore perhaps also of legitimacy, the judicial system avoids or closely manipulates such issues. When judges face problems that are dissonant because they are a future-based rather than in past-based, the judge either subtly modifies the problem so as to base his or her decision on historical information, or else the proceedings become policy-centered and lacking that procedural narrowness of purpose that normally characterizes adjudication.

---

[65] Id., at 1238-40.

[66] Hayek, *supra* note 28, at 82.

CHAPTER XVII
THE "WHAT" OF PROBLEM-SOLVING: Tools and Techniques of Problem Solving

In Chapter 3 of their fine book NEGOTIATION IN SOCIAL CONFLICT,[1] Dean G. Pruitt and Peter J. Carnevale discuss the tactics and tools of problem solving. Their inventory is especially helpful. Mutually beneficial ("win-win") resolutions of problems held between two persons, they say, can be advanced by the following conceptual tools: (A) expanding the pie; (B) exchanging concessions, or "logrolling;" C) resolving underlying concerns; and (D) "bridging."[2] Each of these the tools will be explained briefly below, and then applied to a hypothetical problem.

A. Expanding the Pie

"Expanding the pie" is a way to move parties to a dispute away from what may appear to them as a "zero sum game:" i.e., a problem which can be solved only by one person gaining *at the expense of another.* If the resources or advantages of a solution can be expanded sufficiently, then the resources can be divided between the parties and both can be made better off. A cooperative spirit is easier to maintain where the parties do not view themselves as fighting over limited resources. If the problem can therefore be re-directed toward a common enterprise of finding ways to increase the available resources for both parties, then the spirit and content of the conversation is likely to be much different than playing out a zero sum game.

But how might the pie be expanded? Sometimes, imagination can increase the resources effectively or subjectively available to a problem, even without what some might call an absolute or objective increase. For example, imagine a dispute in which a husband and wife are fighting over custody of a child, but the wife's parents (the grandparents of the child) also want custody. It may appear that the child is a single indivisible resource, and that custody is therefore a zero sum game. But the "child" as a resource can actually be effectively increased in various ways.

First, a joint custody arrangement can be found in which the child splits her time among the contending adults. This is familiar, and technically is cutting the pie rather than expanding it. But if the arrangement is done sensibly and sensitively among the parties, each contender may be able to be with the child during days of the week or hours in which the other party would be unavailable. Each of the three parties could *perceive* virtually full custody of the child, as measured by the time each of the parties would actually have available to interact with the child.

Second, a distinction can be made between physical and legal custody of the child. For some persons, physical custody–time to spend physically interacting with the child--is what matters most. For such persons, legal custody (*i.e.,* the ability to make decisions about the child's education, religious upbringing, health care, etc.) is of secondary concern. For other

---

[1] Dean G. Pruitt and Peter J. Carnevale, NEGOTIATION IN SOCIAL CONFLICT (1993).

[2] Id., at 36–41.

caregivers, however, the opposite may be true. Once again, therefore, the idea of "custody" can be experienced simultaneously by more than one party, and that creates the opportunity to find mutually beneficial outcomes.

Third, if the couple's marriage is being dissolved, conceivably the wife could move back into the house of her parents. Doing so could have many financial advantages to a single parent, and possibly have relational advantages to the child. Such a living arrangement effectively expands the resource of time with the child, because it shifts the mentality or framing of the problem from "allocating" the child herself, toward an image of the child and adults being in the same place together. Once custody is so re-framed, more than one adult can simultaneously experience having custody of the child. Altering the physical environment in this way could actually have the spill-over effect of improving the relationship of the grandparents with the grandchild, and possibly the relationship of the grandparents to their own daughter. Finally, having three people rather than just a mother involved in various aspects of the child's life may give greater flexibility in how the father's interests and schedule could be most fully accommodated.

B. Exchanging Concessions

Win-win agreements can also be found, say Pruitt and Carnevale, by each party trading off concessions on issues that are of low priority to themselves but of high priority to another.[3] This process can occur without each party necessarily knowing the priorities or goals of the other party, although it would be quite cumbersome to do so in a hit-or-miss fashion. Making concessions without knowing the actual priorities of each side risks making a hasty agreement that is sub-optimal, and that also cuts off communication early. A conclusion that is made with limited information preempts learning more about various other matters that could be important for both sides.

Effective trading of concessions thus requires the sharing of information about interests and priorities. Making such mutual disclosures is one of the hallmarks of the interest-based negotiation pioneered by Roger Fisher and William Ury.[4] Where the items traded are on a formal agenda, the process is termed "logrolling" by Pruitt and Carnevale.[5] If an issue is not on the agenda, discerning and respecting that undeclared interest of the other side is termed "non-specific compensation:" one party gets what it wants, and the other party is repaid on some

---

[3] Pruitt and Carnevale, *supra* note 1, at 37.

[4] *See, e.g.,* Roger Fisher & William Ury, GETTING TO YES: NEGOTIATION TO AGREEMENT WITHOUT GIVING IN (1981).

[5] Pruitt and Carnevale, *supra* note 1, at 37.

unrelated issue.[6] Non-specific compensation is possible, of course, only where the interests of the parties have been more deeply explored, beyond the formal agenda.

Exchanging information obviously involves trust that the information divulged will not be used exploitatively. Where trust is *not* high between parties, the problem-solving negotiator should proceed by asking many questions and giving away some information. Since negotiators tend to match the behaviors of the other party, unconditional disclosures are likely to increase cooperation. Also, the negotiator in an atmosphere initially lacking trust should ask for non-binding preferences among proposals, so as to gain insight about priorities. Where possible, trust can then be built by conceding on matters identified as a high preference.

C. "Cost-Cutting" and "Bridging"

Exchanging concessions is advanced by honestly communicating one's own interests to the other party. "Cost-cutting," by contrast, is advanced by empathizing with the risks and costs that one's proposals must pose for the other party, and trying to mitigate those concerns.[7] Where one's own capabilities toward satisfying the other party's reluctance are limited, Pruitt and Carnevale point out that sometimes the help of third parties may be enlisted, and at little cost. As Fisher and Ury famously point out, "getting to yes" is greatly helped by allaying concerns and thinking of ways to make it easy for the other side to agree.[8]

For example, where one party's reluctance stems from the unpredictability of future circumstances, cost-cutting may be achieved either by mandating good-faith renegotiations if particular events occur, or by pre-specifying adjustments in prices or quantities of goods because of unfolding circumstances. More generally, the parties could set up a standing neutral, as described in Part One by James Groton. Knowing that a neutral advisor is available for consultation and problem solving may be comforting in a variety of circumstances. As a last resort it could be helpful to permit termination of a contract upon notice or upon the occurrence of a condition subsequent.

"Bridging" is a tactic involving both parties' concerns, rather than just one person's. Bridging is finding a possibility, perhaps something completely new, that fully satisfies both party's interests.[9] As discussed above, differentiating physical from legal custody of a child is one example of bridging what otherwise could be a bitter dispute. Another example would be offering a long-term management job in a larger enterprise for the not-ready-to-retire

---

[6] Id.

[7] Id., at 38.

[8] Fisher and Ury, *supra* note 4, at 48-49 (re recognizing basic human needs); 76–79.

[9] Pruitt and Carnevale, *supra* note 1, at 38.

entrepreneur whose small business is being acquired. Yet another would be setting up an internship opportunity for students at the business of a fledgling concern whose owner-alumnus cannot afford to donate scholarship funds to her *alma mater*. Successful use of the bridging technique obviously requires imagination and experience.

D. *Using Promises Rather than Threats*

"Promises are the mirror image of threats; they commit one to reward the other for compliance to one's demands instead of punishing the other for noncompliance."[10] Promises "tend to build credit rather than resentment. Liking and respecting tend to go up, making the party using [promises] more influential in the future."[11] Promises also tend to be more successful in getting the other person to offer reciprocal concessions.[12]

With all of the advantages that Pruitt and Carnevale point out for the use of promises rather than threats, why, they ask, are threats used so much more often than promises?[13] First, threats may be effective in signaling limits below which one will not concede. But further, as the authors suggest, threats are cheaper (if they work) than are promises.[14] If a promise is successful in securing an agreement, then the promisor must carry out the promise, which of course means that the promisor must bear whatever costs are entailed by the promise.[15] A threat that is successful in intimidating another party, by contrast, costs nothing. Or at least not in the short run. Threats may be successful, but only at the cost of incurring immediate or latent resentment by the person who buckles under. When the opportunity presents itself, perhaps much later and in indirect ways, the person who has been subordinated may well find a way to retaliate.[16]

E. *Example: Facilitating a Solution to a Community Problem*

In considering how to apply some of these problem solving techniques, imagine the following hypothetical. Let us suppose that "Cabot Bay" is a small seaside community along the New England coast. Outsiders have proposed that casino gambling be authorized by the state

---

[10] Id., at 43.

[11] Id., at 44.

[12] Id.

[13] Id.

[14] Id.

[15] Id.

[16] *See generally* M.P. Baumgartner, *Social Control From Below*, Volume I, TOWARD A GENERAL THEORY OF SOCIAL CONTROL: FUNDAMENTALS (Donald Black, ed.) 303-339 (1984).

and brought to Cabot Bay. Although the day-to-day operations of the casino would be run by a private enterprise corporation like Bread and Circus, Inc., all net revenues would go to state government.

The state Governor supports this gambling proposal, because the state needs additional revenues and the Governor does not want to raise state taxes. The Governor faces a re-election campaign in two years, and thinks that this project would advance the Governor's political ambitions. As a selling point, the Governor has promised that all revenues derived from the casino would be specifically earmarked and spent only on education in the state.

Local and county officials oppose the measure, however, because they fear having to fund the requirements for the associated infrastructure of roads, traffic signals, municipal parking, police, and sewers. The Governor maintains that local property values would be enhanced by the presence of the casino, and thus local property taxes would rise fast enough to cover additional infrastructure needs of Cabot Bay.

Meanwhile, a sociologist teaching in a nearby college has written that a casino would change the charming, old fashioned character of Cabot Bay, undermining its quality of life with higher rates of crime, prostitution, suicide, and traffic. Some local citizens share these concerns about crime and congestion, and oppose the idea of bringing in the casino. Other local citizens, especially those owning restaurant and hotel businesses likely to prosper with the arrival of a casino, support the idea. Yet other citizens, local as well as state-wide, oppose casino gambling on religious and moral grounds.

Suppose that you have been approached by the head of a local council of religious leaders. The council wishes some sort of injunction to be brought to stop development of the casino idea in Cabot Bay. You have agreed to represent this group, after discussing the desirability of exploring a variety of options in which their interests could be met rather than filing immediately for the injunction.

You first should analyze the structure of the problem, using a Dauer Matrix and the variables discussed in these materials. The Cabot Bay problem is complex: We have various multiplex relationships among a number of stakeholder differently situated, and furthermore the problem calls for a public solution. You therefore decide to convene a public meeting in which representatives of the various stakeholders are present.

Your goals for this public meeting are to facilitate a conversation in which: (a) parties feel their respective interests are being heard; and (b) using problem solving tools as described by Pruitt and Carnevale and others, you spawn a variety of potentially bridging ideas. As I describe the meeting in the sections below, the interest-based negotiation philosophy used is taken from Fisher and Ury.[17] The techniques of the facilitation itself are taken from insights and experiences

---

[17] *See generally, supra* note 4.

described in a most useful book entitled MANAGING PUBLIC DISPUTES: A GUIDE FOR GOVERNMENT, BUSINESS, AND CITIZENS' GROUPS, by Susan L. Carpenter and W.J.D. Kennedy (2001).

1. Bringing Stakeholders to the Table

The first question might be: which specific parties should be invited to attend and participate in this public meeting? As Kennedy and Carpenter advise, "look for people who are knowledgeable about the substance of the issue, are respected members of their interest groups, and are able to get along with individuals from other parties. People who are technically competent but who tend to become abrasive or confrontational do not serve their own party's best interests in a negotiation, because hostile behavior offends other participants and makes them less willing to listen to legitimate concerns or agree to reasonable solutions."[18]

Certainly a representative of the Governor's office should be present; and a person knowledgeable about primary and secondary education (like an official of the state Parent-Teacher's Association); the mayor of Cabot Bay; the sociologist; a representative from the gaming industry, perhaps from Bread and Circuses, Inc.; a local business owner who would benefit from the casino, like a restauranteur; a local resident unlikely to be economically advantaged by the casino, and one in a position to talk with a diversity of residents–perhaps a local doctor or pharmacist; and your client, the head of the religious council.

In staging the facilitation, one should keep in mind some basic goals:

* strong listening and honest communicating;

* the understanding of the conflict through uncovering and understanding interests;

* collaborating and finding solutions of mutual gain through insight, creativity, and judgment; and

* designing the features of a possible solution so that regular communication will be channeled to people who will be able to use the information to foresee and prevent problems.

2. Listening and Communicating

Once the group is convened, you should introduce yourself and the client you are representing. Explain your role, and the ground rules for the process you are adopting. Make

---

[18]   Susan L. Carpenter and W.J.D. Kennedy, MANAGING PUBLIC DISPUTES: A GUIDE FOR GOVERNMENT, BUSINESS, AND CITIZENS' GROUPS 104 (2001) (hereafter "Carpenter and Kennedy").

this as clear and detailed as possible. Then invite questions, a sign of respect. Allow as much democracy as possible, assuring people of their opportunity to speak. Ask various persons to present his or her version of the problem, and of the issues. After each speaker, summarize back what each has said, and check with the person as to the accuracy of what you have said. After all have spoken, synthesize the nature of the problem and the issues that you see.[19]

3. *Understanding Conflict by Understanding Interests*

Try to determine the underlying interests of each stakeholder. Ask whatever direct questions of the person that you may need to accomplish that. As an example, it may be that the interests of the religious leader are in purity of behavior of every person in the community, creating an atmosphere of reverence or public spirit, and supporting a mentality of spirituality. It may be that the restaurant owner wants more customers, or a more sophisticated clientele. The doctor or pharmacist may want to preserve a small town feel, charm, or way of life; or may want to avoid new taxes, crime, traffic, etc. The PTA leader is likely to want better education, and will also know how financial resources can be put to best use. Articulate what you see as the underlying interests, and check those with each person individually. Attempt to get each party to *prioritize* his or her interests.[20]

4. *Collaborating and Finding Solutions of Mutual Gain*[21]

Consider some of the techniques for problem-solving: first, try to expand the pie. Brainstorming and re-framing may be required to get off the zero sum "casinos versus quality of life" mentality or the "better education versus lower taxes" mentalities. In doing this, imagine what items can be unbundled to create additional resources. Explore the possible exchange of concessions, and log-roll low priority items for high priority items. Try to uncover underlying concerns, and suggest ways possible cost-cutting measures. What risks and costs does a given proposal pose for other parties? How can those risks/costs be mitigated? Non-specific compensation: what are the other stakeholders' goals and values? What can be done to satisfy them? And look for bridging possibilities: can a new sort of solution be found that would satisfy all, or at least more, of the basic objectives?

---

[19] Id., at 159-60.

[20] *See* Pruitt and Carnevale, *supra* note 1, at 36–37, 41; Robert H. Mnookin, Scott R. Peppet, and Andrew S. Tulumello, BEYOND WINNING: NEGOTIATING TO CREATE VALUE IN DEALS AND DISPUTES 256-65 (2000) (hereafter "Mnookin").

[21] Pruitt and Carnevale, *supra* note 1, at 16-17; Fisher and Ury, *supra* note 4, at 56–80; Mnookin, *supra* note 20, at 12-17;

Try to look at the interests and possible solutions from different perspectives, or by clumping aspects of the problem in different ways. This will help elaborate the possible solutions. For example, perhaps the Cabot Bay problem can be unbundled into three distinct categories of activities: (1) those done by local people, versus those done by tourists; (2) activities done during the day-time, versus those at night-time; and (3) those necessarily done inside Cabot Bay, versus those that might be done outside of the town limits. Then imagine what a casino/town relationship would look like under different permutations of those variables being clumped together. Bridging opportunities might then present themselves.

- If the concern of the religious leader and others is about the corrupting influence of casino gambling on the local population, could a hotel be connected to the casino with gambling restricted to hotel guests? Could a chapel and gambling addiction counseling center be placed on the casino premises, perhaps at the expense of the casino operating company? Could some slot machines be designated so that all payoffs would benefit local charities, *i.e.,* those choosing to play those particular machines would know that their losses are actually charitable contributions? The potential corrupting influence on the local population would be minimized, and the chapel and counseling center could offer an opportunity to serve new populations.

- If the concern is about congestion and traffic on small town streets, could the casino be located some distance outside town? Or be put on a ship that would be anchored in the Bay, served by water taxi? Or could gambling and entertainment activities be restricted to the evening hours, so as to interfere less with everyday Cabot Bay life?

- If the concern is about crime and prostitution sparked by the presence of a casino, could the atmosphere be designed to encourage entire families of tourists? Could a child care center or activities for teenagers be a designated part of the larger casino complex? Could alcohol be limited in the casino?

- If the concern is about the casino siphoning restaurant business away from existing individually-owned Cabot Bay restaurants, could a food court be established inside the casino that would showcase local restaurant offerings? Or could some food concessions/restaurant operations be reserved to locals?

In planning a facility that is broadly integrated with the community, a consortium comprised of state officials, gaming industry representatives, local planners, and a cross section of the citizenry could be constituted that would be responsible for issues like site location, architecture, the size of facility or number of hotel rooms, associated services and concessions, security arrangements, transportation or shuttle buses, and hours of operation of the casino.

6. Shaping a Culture

Apart from the planning for the physical placement of the casino, setting the hours of operation, and arranging some of the transportation and security infrastructure, the consortium could also address the cultural dimension for ensuring the mutually beneficial coexistence of a casino and small town values. To instill values of safe, family-oriented entertainment within the casino operations, the consortium and casino together should consider the principles suggested by Ed Dauer for shaping a culture:

- promulgate codes of proper behavior;

- include employees in the development of those codes;

- communicate (train and educate) the principles effectively;

- illustrate the principles with consistent leadership from the top;

- establish visible accountability;

- enforce the codes fully and fairly;

- allow for enforcement and reporting by [various] employees;

- measure the results; and

- reward success.[22]

7. Designing Systems to Prevent Problems

Best efforts notwithstanding, some disputes inevitably will arise. In dealing with those disputes, the consortium should design and construct a systemic process by which the problems can be communicated and resolved in ways that are respectful, decentralized, and participatory. In their book GETTING DISPUTES RESOLVED,[23] William L. Ury, Jeanne M. Brett, and Stephen B. Goldberg have created a most helpful framework for creating such a system. Their approach attempts to find resolution by harnessing diverse interests, rather than by relying primarily on

---

[22] Edward A. Dauer, *The Role of Culture in Legal Risk Management,* 49 SCANDINAVIAN STUDIES IN LAW 93, 100-105 (2006)

[23] William L. Ury, Jeanne M. Brett, Stephen B. Goldberg, GETTING DISPUTES RESOLVED 41-64 (1988).

either power or legal rights. In designing a system, Ury, Brett, and Goldberg present six basic principles:[24]

1. Put the focus on interests;

2. Build in "loop-backs" to negotiation. In other words, from a contest that becomes mired in claims about rights, build in ways to provide enough information and clarity about the parties' respective rights to permit the parties to negotiate from a position of knowledge about their relative entitlements. In contrast, from a contest bogged down in a power-struggle, build in automatic triggers for "cool-off" periods, crisis negotiation procedures, and intervention by third parties.

3. Provide low-cost rights backups, like ready access to mediation, arbitration, or hybrid procedures.

4. Provide low-cost power backups (by this, the authors mean that the system should provide for devises like voting or "rules of prudence" in which the parties in advance agree to limit the tactics or tools they will employ in the event of a controversy);

5. Build in consultation before, and feedback after, resorting to dispute resolution procedures. This could include devices like mandated negotiation prior to invoking dispute resolution procedures, and providing post-dispute analysis forums.

6. Sequence procedures from low-to-high cost, by creating procedural steps that start with interests-based negotiation, then if necessary go to loop-back procedures, and then finally offer low-cost rights and power backups as discussed above. The sequence can be imagined as a series of rungs on a "dispute resolution ladder."[25]

---

[24] Id., at 42.

[25] Id., at 62.

CHAPTER XVIII
THE "WHAT" OF THERAPEUTIC JURISPRUDENCE: Introduction in the Context of Problem Solving

The following Chapter is comprised of excerpts from my essay entitled *Therapeutic Jurisprudence, Preventive Law, and Creative Problem Solving: An Essay on Harnessing Emotion and Human Connection* that first appeared in 5 PSYCHOLOGY, PUBLIC POLICY, AND LAW 921 (1999) (reprinted by permission). As with the *Creative Problem Solving* article above, some of the formatting, footnote numbering, and language has been changed slightly to be standardized with other chapters of this book.

Therapeutic Jurisprudence, Preventive Law, and Creative Problem Solving: An Essay on Harnessing Emotion and Human Connection

Creative Problem Solving is an approach that expands the repertoire of techniques by which lawyers and judges attempt to resolve interpersonal and social problems.[1] Therapeutic Jurisprudence explores the ways in which "[l]egal rules, legal procedures, and the roles of legal actors (such as lawyers and judges) ... produce therapeutic or anti-therapeutic consequences."[2] Preventive Law is a "proactive approach to lawyering" "emphasiz[ing] the lawyer's role as a planner" so as to "[avoid] the high costs of litigation and [ensure] desired outcomes and opportunities.[3] In this Essay I attempt to marry the values and principles of Creative Problem Solving with the insights and practices of Therapeutic Jurisprudence and Preventive Law.

Consistent with the mission of Creative Problem Solving, I argue that legal professionals can become better problem solvers by learning more about an alternative style of solving problems, a style typically employed by psychologists. I call this alternative approach to problem solving *accommodation*.[4] Accommodation may be contrasted with the "judging" style used often

---

[1] *See generally, Symposium: The Lawyer as Creative Problem Solver*, 34 CALIFORNIA WESTERN LAW REVIEW 267–565 (1998).

[2] Bruce J. Winick, *The Jurisprudence of Therapeutic Jurisprudence,* 3 PSYCHOLOGY, PUBLIC POLICY & LAW 184, 185 (1997).

[3] Dennis P. Stolle, David B. Wexler, Bruce J. Winick, & Edward A. Dauer, *Integrating Preventive Law and Therapeutic Jurisprudence: A Law and Psychology Based Approach to Lawyering,* 34 CALIFORNIA WESTERN LAW REVIEW 15, 16 (1998).

[4] "Accommodation" can connote fatalism, which in this context would mean passive resignation to a problematic environment. Emotional fatalism is not, however, the meaning of "accommodation" primarily intended in this Essay. I prefer a stronger meaning for accommodation, involving considerable resistance to a perceived problem: tactical adjustment, for example, or engaging another person cooperatively in achieving some goal.

in formal legal procedures, but also used informally when a legal professional assesses a legal problem and formulates strategies for its solution.[5]

[The judging problem solving style measures some behavior or activity against a norm, and then applies a sanction where a violation of the norm has been found. The accommodation style is virtually the converse of judging. With accommodation, the problem holder acknowledges the power of a surrounding environment, and adjusts physically or emotionally to its requirements. Although norms provide guidance toward appropriate problem resolutions, orderly predictability is a far less important criterion of success in the accommodation style than in judging. The use of power is limited in accommodation. Emotional well-being and strong, fulfilling human relationships are used both as measures of problem solving success, and as important instruments for achieving problem resolution.] Therapeutic Jurisprudence is an appropriate vehicle for opening the legal system to the accommodation style of problem solving.[6]

Bringing accommodation skills into legal problem solving would supplement the judging style, not displace it. Lawyers and others would simply be afforded greater flexibility in approaching problems. Greater availability of problem solving options offers a variety of possible benefits. At least *some* existing legal problems may be resolved better, more efficiently, and with fewer adverse side effects through using accommodation rather than judging. Some other, potential problems may be prevented. Individual client satisfaction with lawyers' services may improve, along with the clients' psychological well-being. Lawyers themselves may find more professional satisfaction. Social perceptions of lawyers as callous and insincere may be softened. More broadly, the legal system may offer American culture an alternative rhetoric to the discourse of power and rights that is becoming increasingly prevalent in day to day interaction.[7] Finally, and most ambitiously, bringing a measure of accommodation into the legal

---

[5] Lawyers, of course, often facilitate transactions and engage in settlement activities, both of which depart significantly from the "judging" style model of problem solving. Furthermore, judicial decision-making is neither so detached from real world consequences nor so objectively rooted in abstract norms as the formal model of legal process would suggest. For analytical clarity and ready comparison between law and psychology, I have simplified somewhat the image of both the legal system and judging.

[6] *See also* Dennis P. Stolle and David B. Wexler, *Therapeutic Jurisprudence and Preventive Law: A Combined Concentration to Invigorate the Everyday Practice of Law*, 39 ARIZONA LAW REVIEW 25, 28-30 (1997). Stolle and Wexler's article is consistent with the aims of this Essay. They describe ways in which lawyers may combine Therapeutic Jurisprudence and Preventive Law principles to serve clients beyond what would be suggested by the traditional model of lawyering.

[7] *See generally,* Mary Ann Glendon, RIGHTS TALK: THE IMPOVERISHMENT OF POLITICAL DISCOURSE (1991); David M. Trubek, *The Handmaiden's Revenge: On Reading and Using the New Sociology of Civil Procedure*, 51 LAW & CONTEMPORARY PROBLEMS 111, 123-125 (1988).

system acknowledges that a more humble, fallibilistic form of truth may sometimes be appropriate to the resolution of legal problems.[8]

Creative Problem Solving offers a conceptual framework for exploring the different styles by which law and psychology typically approach problems. By showing the way for legal professionals to engage in "accommodational dialogues" with problem holders, Therapeutic Jurisprudence and Preventive Law offer the prospect of enabling new problem-solving capabilities in the legal system.

. . .

Bringing the Accommodation Style to the Legal System

1. Caveats and Prospects for the Accommodation Style

Two caveats should begin the discussion of how to bring accommodational dialogue to legal system interactions. First, the accommodation style will not be suitable for every type of legal problem or every sort of client. All problem solving styles carry inherent limitations; that is an important principle of Creative Problem Solving. The Creative Problem Solving goal here is simply to make lawyers and judges more effective by revealing alternative new tools, and supporting sufficient understanding of those tools to enable intelligent flexibility in their use. The accommodation dialogue recommended in this Essay should be explored slowly and cautiously, building a fuller comprehension of the contexts in which it is most appropriate and effective.

Second, in suggesting that lawyers may usefully integrate the skills of the accommodation style into their practices, I am not saying that lawyers should become therapists. Not only would that be presumptuous, but lawyers who attempted to do therapy would likely violate professional ethics by overstepping their training and capabilities. When a lawyer engages in an accommodational dialogue with a client, the point is not to diagnose or formulate treatment for psychological impairment or distress. If the conversation with a client suggests significant psychological problems, the lawyer should refer the client to a mental health professional.

There is room for the accommodation style to become part of the everyday legal system because fully functioning, well adjusted, mentally healthy people can have problems that cause them to consult a lawyer. Although such persons do not need psychological therapy, nonetheless

---

[8] Or, stated conversely, that the law may appropriately attempt to treat problems centered in the most complex and subtle human relationships. *See* the dialogue between Judge Richard Posner and James B. White, in: Richard A. Posner, LAW AND LITERATURE: A MISUNDERSTOOD RELATION (1988); Richard A. Posner, *Law and Literature: A Relation Reargued*, 72 VIRGINIA LAW REVIEW 1351 (1986); and James Boyd White, *What Can A Lawyer Learn from Literature?* 102 HARVARD LAW REVIEW 2014 (1989).

their problems may be accompanied by strong emotions or relational complications. It is for such problem holders that an accommodational dialogue within the legal system is most appropriate.[9] It is for such problems that the accommodation style holds most promise for finding a result that the judging style alone could not easily reach.

I advance one ... central, argument for why I am hopefully not conveying a trite and irresponsible message about lawyers becoming psychologists. When legal professionals engage in accommodational dialogue, the content of the conversation is likely to be quite different from dialogues between psychologists and clients. In other words, even where legal personnel use the active listening skills and relational systems analysis commonly employed by psychologists to initiate an accommodational dialogue, the legal professionals will not become psychologists. They may, however, achieve something different. Owing to their differing training, lawyers are equipped to raise different ideas than psychologists, and are likely to interpret responses of clients differently than would psychologists. Yet this very difference in the likely content of the accommodation dialogue when used by lawyers and judges provides an important social reason why they should engage in the dialogue. Accommodational discussion by legal professional holds cultural promise for elaborating and disseminating certain concepts about personal responsibility and civic life that are relatively neglected not only in law, but also in psychology, politics, and even philosophy.

When psychologists use the accommodation style, they naturally pair it with the background concepts of their profession. Consequently, apart from their focus on better communication skills for their client, psychologists largely help clients work through debilitating emotions like rage, fear, despair, hatred, bereavement, shame, guilt, anxiety, envy, and self-doubt. Although lawyers could probably help ease such distress by lending an empathic ear to their clients, the more likely contribution to be made by lawyers using an accommodation style would be in addressing the moral, relational, and civic emotions (or, for purists, emotion-related concepts)[10] like trust, compassion, forgiveness, loyalty, respect, charity, and tolerance.

These moral and civic concepts are obviously raised daily in psychological therapy, especially trust, forgiveness, and respect. Owing to the nature of legal concepts, and the training

---

[9] Some legal system accommodation dialogues, such as that by a judge with a sex offender, ... do assume a certain level of pathology in the problem holder. The adjustment sought by the sex offender dialogue is toward acceptance in the offender of greater moral responsibility, and is therefore within the expertise of the legal professional.

[10] Susan Bandes, *Empathy, Narrative, and Victim Impact Statements* 63 UNIVERSITY OF CHICAGO LAW REVIEW 361, 365 (1996); Dan M. Kahan & Martha C. Nussbaum, *Two Conceptions of Emotion in Criminal Law*, 96 COLUMBIA LAW REVIEW 269, 275 (1996) (descriptions of contested elements of "emotion.")

of lawyers in history and political philosophy, lawyers are likely to process conversations these emotions in different (yet also valuable) ways than psychologists do.[11]

Unfortunately, moral and civic concepts currently fare poorly in legal practice. Law currently marginalizes these positive, pro-social emotions by relegating them to outside private or intimate institutions like charities and the family. Scarcely any mention is made, in either the substance or the procedures of law, of any of these communitarian or relation-building emotions.[12] Their invocation would be awkward in virtually any traditional legal analysis, and a lawyer who spoke long about any of them in open court would likely meet an embarrassed silence. Yet lawyers and judges are well equipped to explore these issues. Legal problems almost always spring from some human relationship, even if one that is less dense or intimate than those that are typically the subject of therapy. Lawyers have an ethical as well as an experiential sense about these limited relationships. Their advice about how moral or civic emotions pertain to those relationships could be helpful in securing accommodational solutions to problems that arise in those settings.

Adding back these emotions and relationships to the legal system would not dilute its basic purpose of ensuring social order and facilitating peaceful human transactions. Quite the contrary. Emotion is, after all, vital to being human.[13] Creating any social community, indeed virtually any personal relationship, depends on the willingness of individuals to display generosity, trust, loyalty, and forgiveness toward others.[14] Therapeutic Jurisprudence, with its emphasis on social and legal reform through stronger dialogue between clients and professionals,

---

[11] *See, e.g.,* GEORGE P. FLETCHER, LOYALTY: AN ESSAY ON THE MORALITY OF RELATIONSHIPS (1993); Carol M. Rose, *Trust in the Mirror of Betrayal,* 75 BOSTON UNIVERSITY LAW REVIEW 531 (1995).

[12] The blunting of "negative" emotions fares little better in the legal system than the advancement of pro-social, relational emotions. Feelings of rage, loss, despair, remorse and the need of redemption often accompany the injuries and behaviors that cause people to become enmeshed in the legal system. Legal rules and procedures ignore these emotions almost entirely, although a growing movement permitting victim testimony in the sentencing phase of criminal proceedings indulges their venting. *See generally* Bandes, *supra* note 10 (victim impact statements).

[13] *See generally* Robert H. Frank, PASSIONS WITHIN REASON: THE STRATEGIC ROLE OF THE EMOTIONS (1988); John Sabini and Maury Silver, EMOTION, CHARACTER, AND RESPONSIBILITY (1998).

[14] *See* Samuel H. Pillsbury, *Emotional Justice: Moralizing the Passions of Criminal Punishment* 74 CORNELL LAW REVIEW 655, 676-77 (1989); D. Don Welch, *Ruling With the Heart: Emotion-Based Public Policy,* 6 SOUTHERN CALIFORNIA INTERDISCIPLINARY LAW JOURNAL 55, 85-86 (1997).

may be the natural vehicle by which lawyers could initiate conversations concerning moral and civic emotions. Through such conversations, a richer conceptual framework could gradually emerge.

Social emotions have little relatively currency in the vocabulary of contemporary culture.[15] Greater articulation of such concepts in the discourse of law could also have positive spill-over effects in everyday life. Law could begin to reclaim the role of moral guide, or at least moral facilitator, that was largely abandoned after the rise of analytical positivism in legal theory.

2. Finding the Appropriate Access Point for Emotion and Relationship in the Legal System

Together, Creative Problem Solving and Therapeutic Jurisprudence reveal the problem-solving limitations of the legal system. Yet together they also suggest a way to overcome it: bringing into the legal system a stronger accommodational element of emotion and human connection, through active engagement with the feelings and personal relationships of those who come before the law. Finally, observing preventive law principles can help lawyers take accommodational initiatives at a time when they may be most effective.

Finding the appropriate access points for the accommodation style, however, is crucial for several reasons introduced above. First, incorporating emotions and relationships at the *wrong* stage in the legal process presents dangers to a liberal society. Second, bringing in emotions and relationships at the *right* stage of the legal process offers opportunities to strengthen civic life rather than threaten it.

The possible access points for bringing the accommodation style into the legal system are: (A) at the level of *constructing* legal norms, in which the basic rules themselves would be flexible to the emotional or relational contexts of people's behaviors; or (B) at the level of *application* of those norms, in which particular persons' behaviors are judged against the norms; or © at the level at which people facing a legal problem are interacting with their lawyers, or other legal professionals in roles not explicitly judging compliance with legal norms.

Incorporating the accommodation style into the legal system is problematic at both the level of constructing legal norms, and in their application to particular fact patterns. Although both of these access points are theoretical possibilities, each should be approached with much

---

[15] For a historical study linking emotion to social change, see the essays collected in EMOTION AND SOCIAL CHANGE: TOWARD A NEW PSYCHOHISTORY (Carol Z. Stearns & Peter N. Stearns eds., 1988). To trace change in discourse about emotion, see the excerpts of writings of philosophers and psychologists from Aristotle to modern writers collected in WHAT IS AN EMOTION? CLASSICAL READINGS IN PHILOSOPHICAL PSYCHOLOGY (Cheshire Calhoun & Robert C. Solomon eds., 1984).

caution.[16] The universality of legal norms and the neutrality of judicial procedures are important principles of the liberal society deserving of strong protection.

a. The Dispassion and Universality of Norms

Emotion and human relationships could be imported directly into the design of legal norms in at least two ways.[17] First, norms could be explicitly variable in application. That is, norms could vary in application or strength of penalty, depending on the emotions that motivated their violation. Second, norms could be particularized according to group identities, essentially varying according to the status of the person being judged.

The best example of the first sort of norm is found in the law of homicide. For centuries the common law has recognized that if a person is sufficiently provoked, that person may become so enraged that any ensuing homicide should be mitigated in its punishment.[18] Closely related is the law of self defense, in which a person experiencing "reasonable" fear of imminent death or serious bodily harm may use violent measures to prevent that injury.[19] Recently these emotion-based norms have shifted so that battered spouses and endangered females may use them more easily, a welcome trend toward particularizing norms according to systematic differences of the positions of people.[20] Such moves are nonetheless controversial.[21] In large part this is because they start to blend with the second sort of norm, in which differences in the law depend on group identity, which is a sort of permanent human connection or status among certain persons.

---

[16] Christopher Slobogin, *Therapeutic Jurisprudence: Five Dilemmas to Ponder*, 1 PSYCHOLOGY, PUBLIC POLICY & LAW 193, 210 (1995).

[17] A third way is ... rare. Norms may be made explicitly assessable by resort to emotion. *See* Neal R. Feigenson, *Sympathy and Legal Judgment: A Psychological Analysis*, 65 TENNESSEE LAW REVIEW 1, 18-19 (1997) (giving example of the "shocks the conscience" test to determine the constitutionality of a search and seizure).

[18] *See* Kahan & Nussbaum, *supra* note 10, at 301-323; Pillsbury, *supra* note 14, at 678-79; Alexander Reilly, *The Heart of the Matter: Emotion in Criminal Defenses* 29 OTTAWA LAW REVIEW 117, 131-40 (1997); *see generally* Victoria Nourse, *Passion's Progress: Modern Law Reform and the Provocation Defense,* 106 YALE LAW JOURNAL 1331 (1997).

[19] *See* Kahan & Nussbaum, *supra* note 10, at 327-32; Reilly, *supra* note 18, at 140-44.

[20] *See* Kahan & Nussbaum, *supra* note 10, at 332-33; Reilly, *supra* note 18, at 141-44.

[21] Kahan & Nussbaum, *supra* note 10, at 332-33; Reilly, *supra* note 18, at 143.

Status-based norms violate the general historical Western progression identified 150 years ago, from "status to contract."[22] In general, modern society pulls instinctively away from laws or practices that seem to offend formal equality. Modern law does make some such distinctions that are considered relatively innocuous. In commercial contract settings, for example, "merchants" are sometimes held to different standards than are consumers.[23] In tort law those with expert knowledge are treated differently from the general population.[24] Liberal values are strongly implicated, however, by any law that is applied differentially to various groups. Hence the construction of norms is a generally inadvisable access point at which to recommend the systematic incorporation of accommodational problem solving.

b. Objectivity in Judging

Putting emotion and consideration of relational ties into the application or judging of universal norms is also beset with dangers, for two reasons. First, decision-making under conditions of high emotionality is likely less reliable than under conditions of lesser emotion.[25] Recent scholarly literature contests both the historically sharp dichotomy drawn between reason and emotion, and claims that emotion degrades decision-making.[26] Nevertheless, most would

---

[22] *See generally* Grant Gilmore, THE DEATH OF CONTRACT 5-34 (1974); Henry Sumner Maine, ANCIENT LAW: ITS CONNECTION WITH THE EARLY HISTORY OF SOCIETY AND RELATION TO MODERN IDEAS (1927); Manfred Rehbinder, *Status, Contract, and the Welfare State*, 23 STANFORD LAW REVIEW 941 (1971).

[23] *See, e.g.,* Uniform Commercial Code §2-104, Official Comment 1: "This Article assumes that transactions between professional in a given field require special and clear rules which may not apply to a casual or inexperienced seller of buyer. It thus adopts a policy of expressly stating rules applicable "between merchants" and "against a merchant ... ."

[24] William L. Prosser, LAW OF TORTS § 32, at 161 (4th ed. 1971).

[25] *See* Feigenson, *supra* note 17, at 4, 15, 17, 40-64. Feigenson reviews the psychological literature and concludes that:

> sympathy need not lead decisionmakers any further from the ideal of reasoned deliberation than they already are when they try to decide without sympathy. Increasing the role of sympathy in legal judgment, however, is likely to make the process of decision-making more subjective and to bias decisions improperly.

Id., at 41. *See generally* George C. Christy, *Objectivity in the Law* 78 YALE LAW JOURNAL 1311 (1969).

[26] *See, e.g.,* Bandes, *supra* note 10, at 365-70; Kahan & Nussbaum, *supra* note 10; Martha L. Minow and Elizabeth V. Spelman, *Passion for Justice*, 10 CARDOZO LAW REVIEW 37 (1988); Pillsbury, *supra* note 14, at 674-84; Welch, *supra* note 14, at 58-59, 66-67.

agree at least that certain sorts of emotion, at certain levels, does make decision-making more subjective.

Even were that not true, however, social support for the legal invocation of state power does seem to depend on general perceptions that fair minded judges do their best to overcome their own immediate, emotional responses to facts presented to them. Hence any stage in legal proceedings at which an evaluation of the application of norms is being formally made is at least a dangerous access point for the accommodation style. This is not to say the accommodation style should never be used at those formal stages. It is, however, to caution against recommending its systematic inclusion at such points. As Samuel H. Pillsbury concludes,

> Bringing emotion into legal discourse has its risk. We must take care that decisionmakers' personal, nonmoral inclinations do not substitute for legal principles in the resolution of controversies. ... When we reach the limits of law, when we enter those areas where rules lose their power to direct us toward just results, however, recognition of and struggle with emotional influence becomes necessary. In those mysterious places we need to reconcile thoughts and feelings.[27]

c. Non-judgmental Interactions by Legal Personnel

Fortunately, less formal access points can be found that preserve the rationality of legal processes and the calm deliberateness of judges, even while the emotional and relational concerns of people governed by the legal system are taken more seriously. These access points are non-judgmental interactions between problem-holders and legal professionals. In such settings, an accommodation dialogue can be initiated with less risk to the assumptions of either formal equality or due process. Non-judgmental interactions are most commonplace where an attorney is speaking with a client. However, the accommodation style can also be incorporated, at least on a limited scale, into some interactions between judges and accused, and between police and citizens.

Therapeutic Jurisprudence scholarship has already reported instances of what is essentially the accommodational style being used by police, judges, and lawyers. This Essay applauds this scholarship, and encourages others to report similar models of the successful application of its principles. Some of those principles, together with examples of their use, are listed in the paragraphs that follow.

---

[27] Pillsbury, *supra* note 14, at 710.

d. Principles of Accommodation Style Derived from Therapeutic Jurisprudence Scholarship

i. Facilitate Understanding Through Giving Information

The most basic aspect of the accommodational dialogue would seem to be simple information given by legal system personnel to problem-holders. Information about legal rules or decisions can be given in a conclusory manner–the judging style–or it can instead be given in an accommodational or therapeutic way that facilitates as much understanding and participation as possible by the problem holder. The style of communication may sometimes affect legal outcomes. At the very least, the choice of style affects people's perceptions of themselves and of the legal system. "What judges and lawyers say to the consumers of law may have a significant impact on their appreciation of [legal] requirements and may help people to adapt to them in ways that have positive effects on their health and mental health."[28]

Professor Winick reports an example of this, regarding mental patients being transported to a hospital by police as part of an involuntary commitment proceeding.[29] Where the police understood the strongly fearful or confused emotions these patients must feel, explained to them something of the process of commitment, and assured them of an opportunity to talk with doctors and others, the patients felt less coerced.[30] Winick argues that patients treated in this way are more likely to respond better to their hospitalization.[31] Involuntary commitment proceedings thus are resolved with fewer adverse side effects where the police depart from their narrow role as implementers of a legal judgment or order, and instead engage in the most rudimentary of dialogues intended to aid the problem holder's adjustment to a difficult environment.

ii. Facilitating "Cognitive Restructuring"

Beyond facilitating understanding, the accommodational dialogue may serve "cognitive restructuring"[32] for a client or defendant. Professors Wexler and Winick describe an instance of

---

[28] Winick, *supra* note 2, at 201, 202.

[29] Id., at 202, *citing* the summary in Deborah L. Dennis & John Monahan, *Introduction, in* COERCION AND AGGRESSIVE COMMUNITY TREATMENT: A NEW FRONTIER IN MENTAL HEALTH LAW 3 (Deborah L. Dennis & John Monahan, eds., 1996).

[30] Id.

[31] Id., at 203.

[32] David B. Wexler and Bruce J. Winick, *Therapeutic Jurisprudence and Criminal Justice Mental Health Issues*, 16 MENTAL & PHYSICAL DISABILITY LAW REPORTER 225, 229 (1992).

this in the context of sex offender plea bargaining. Sex offenders often attempt to plead "no contest" to the crimes with which they are charged.[33] If judges were less willing to accept these "nolo" pleas, however, defense attorneys would be forced to engage in a blunt dialogue with their clients about the facts accumulated against the accused.[34] That in turn would force the accused to make an admission of guilt, thus avoiding the "denial and minimization" or "cognitive distortion" that characterizes their behavior.[35] In the long run, the dialogue between lawyer and client facilitates psychological adjustment. Toward the same purpose, judges also could "engag[e] in detailed questioning of the defendant about the factual basis of the [guilty] plea."[36] This judicial interaction, it is noteworthy, would be done outside the explicit role of judging the application of legal rules. The accused has already pleaded guilty to the charges.

iii. Give Clients Choice and Responsibility

Other principles suggested in previous Therapeutic Jurisprudence scholarship seem similarly transferable to accommodational dialogue. The dialogue should seek wherever possible to give clients a choice, or planning role, in solving their problems.[37] Professor Wexler offers some practical advice for accomplishing this. He recommends, by analogy, using the linguistic tips given by Donald Meichenbaum and Dennis Turk to health care providers who are attempting to implement an effective treatment regime for patients.[38]

First, whatever conversations occur must be particularized to the individual circumstances of the client, rather than abstract discussion of principles.[39] "The patient's active involvement in negotiating and designing the treatment program is of tremendous importance to adherence and favorable outcome."[40] "[D]irective terminology such as '[w]hat you are to do is

---

[33] Id.

[34] Id.

[35] Id.

[36] Id.

[37] David B. Wexler, *Therapeutic Jurisprudence and the Criminal Courts*, 35 WILLIAM & MARY LAW REVIEW 279, 292-293 (1993); *but see* Slobogin, *supra* note 16, at 194, 201 and sources cited therein.

[38] Wexler, *supra* note 37, *quoting* Donald Meichenbaum & Dennis C. Turk, FACILITATING TREATMENT ADHERENCE: A PRACTITIONER'S GUIDEBOOK (1987).

[39] Id., at 294, 296.

[40] Id., at 292.

...,' should be replaced by a softer, more bilateral statement, such as, '[s]o what you have agreed to try is ....'[41]

Talking directly with the patient about past failures in treatment compliance can also lead to better future compliance. Raising the obstacles and drawbacks while giving the patient the opportunity to describe how the patient will now approach the problem differently "foster[s] the patient's sense of control, commitment, and degree of hope."[42] Finally, involving in the discussion those persons with whom the client has significant personal relationship can encourage a favorable outcome.[43]

Conclusion

The principles of accommodation derived from Therapeutic Jurisprudence can be summarized as giving information to the client about the problem; encouraging the client to think in different ways about the problem; and empowering the client to make sound decisions about the problem. Creative Problem Solving further contributes the idea that neither the nature of the problem, nor the understanding of how it arose, nor the possibilities for its resolution need be approached exclusively by making judgments based in legal norms. A different, and sometimes better, solution to the problem may suggest itself where the lawyer and client work together to disentangle, understand, and engage the emotional and relational strains of the problem as well as its legal implications.

Initiating the accommodational dialogue that makes such collaboration possible requires that lawyers trust the capabilities of themselves, their clients, and their profession. *Lawyers trusting themselves* means having confidence that they can sensibly probe another person's feelings and relationships. That is, that they can uncover personal issues with accuracy and depth, that they will do no harm in the asking, and that they can offer advice that may be helpful to solving the client's problem. Gathering the information sensitively certainly requires skill, but not of a kind different than that already possessed by good interviewers: asking open-ended questions to promote narrative, plus following up with closed-ended questions for details; making reflecting statements about the client's verbal or non-verbal behavior to help identify the client's feelings; offering summaries of the client's statements and checking with the client to amplify or correct the summaries; and prompting the client to help identify alternative solutions and analyze the possible consequences of each alternative.[44]

---

[41] Id., at 293.

[42] Id.

[43] Id.

[44] *See* Leslie E. Borck and Stephen B. Fawcett, LEARNING COUNSELING AND PROBLEM0SOLVING SKILLS 11-47 (1982).

As to offering advice about emotions or personal attachments, legal professionals should appreciate the variety and extensiveness of their experience in observing how relationships and individual consciences are challenged by problems, and how they can be strengthened by the right sort of solution. As elaborated above, the lawyer's perspective will not be the same as the psychologist's, but legal training and practice nonetheless equips a person to make valuable observations.

Trusting clients means respecting that they are neither cynical nor morally debased, and that they are capable of reflecting on the broader implications of some course of action. Sometimes lawyers and clients seem to get caught in a feedback loop of mutual stereotyping that consigns conversation into purely instrumental discourse. The lawyer may assume that the client, by seeking legal help rather than counseling, has a self-serving goal. This may not be true. The client may approach a lawyer merely because the client assumes the problem to be "legal," is confused about the legal implications of some action, or is simply unskilled at accomplishing some end cooperatively. Yet if the lawyer assumes that the client has narrow parameters for problem resolution or for measuring the lawyer's effectiveness, the lawyer may tend too quickly to speak in a judging style, assessing the client's position against legal rules and making strategic assessments based on that position. Conversely, the client may not ask the lawyer about potential accommodative solutions, because the social image of law and lawyers does not suggest that such solutions will be pursued. The accommodative style may thus remain unexplored. Potential accommodative solutions may thus remain unexplored.

Breaking this cycle of expectations that channels dialogue into the judging style has long been the goal of preventive law. It begins by recognizing the potential of lawyer as well as client to talk in a different way. It also requires *trusting that the legal system itself* has room for solving problems accommodationally. The integrity of legal professionals is not jeopardized by simple efforts at empathic, personal conversations. Nor is the social order threatened by a lawyer's plain talk with a client about the need for that client to reconcile a torn relationship, or the need to be more respecting or charitable toward another person. Presuming to judge behavior in the absence of feeling or relational context inevitably weakens the expressive function of law–that force by which we come to understand our past and make statements about what we wish to become.

Positing a too-clear division between fact and value, says James B. White, reduces everything in the law to mere policy.[45] "[T]his in turn is to erase [the] arts of mind and life, and with them the whole system of distributional authority that is constitutional or legal culture."[46] Instead, law should be regarded as a humanistic discourse, "a way of creating and sustaining a

---

[45] White, *supra* note 8, at 2022.

[46] Id.

political and ethical community."[47] Law will always have its power. Its rationality is strongly protected by legal procedures. The legal system need not fear making attempts at deeper human understanding.

---

[47] Id., at 2047. *See also* Glendon, *supra* note 7, at 171.

CHAPTER XIX
"WHY NOW, and WHY LIKE THIS?"

Candidate explanations for "why *now*,"-- *i.e.,* why some tipping point was reached and the U/I/A paradigm is now rapidly being elaborated and adopted--and "why *like this*,"–*i.e.,* why certain methods and not some others--hearken back to our Part One description of the many elements that comprise the legal system. We should understand the legal system as not simply formal procedures, but a rich set of interactions among procedures, problems, skills, ethics, culture, and philosophical ideas about truth and the nature of human beings. Understanding the new methods of the U/I/A paradigm *and also where they come from and why they look as they do*, will broaden the understanding not only of the new methods, but of some of the shortcomings of the R/S/P methods.

As part of the expanded view of the legal system, we could identify all of the following (and no doubt more) as contributing to the explanations for "why now," and "why these methods" for the emergence of the U/I/A paradigm:

* growing pervasiveness of legal influence and thinking in everyday life;

* relatedly, a broadening of the sorts of human problems the law is being asked to resolve, and an increasing proportion of problems that are structurally different from those for which traditional legal procedures evolved;

* a change in ideas about the criteria for truth--from a theory that "truth is what corresponds to reality," toward a theory that "truth is what society constructs and accepts by consensus;"

* changing economic structure and methods, from the Industrial Age to the Information Age;

* growing cultural discomfort with the spill-overs of R/S/P methods;

* changing demographics among those entering the legal profession and judiciary, most strikingly the enormous growth in female representation within the legal profession;

* a decline in the preconditions for effective resolution of problems by application of governmental power;

* escalation of financial costs in resolving legal problems using R/S/P methods;

* and finally, a possible atrophying of non-legal, traditional institutions of authority.

The sections below expand upon, at least briefly, some of the above possible explanations. In doing so, they lend additional support for the integrated view of legal systems posited in Part One of this work.

A. *The Pervasiveness of the Law in Everyday Culture*

The explosion of interest in alternative methods for preventing and solving legal problems, and their accelerating implementation, is now evident in courts as well as in lawyers' private offices. Further, a spirit seems to have taken hold that embraces experimentation in the design of innovative legal processes and in potential collaborations with other professions. But why the past three decades of such active rethinking of fundamental assumptions about law and lawyering, after well more than two hundred years in which the basic structure of the adversarial system served society so steadfastly to ensure procedural regularity, trust in the rule of law, and individual civil liberties? Are the challenges to the traditional processes and mentalities of the legal system really new? If so, what changes in the intellectual environment are prompting their invention? If the ideas are not new, why for so long did they fall on deaf ears? What cultural movements or social conditions help account for the sudden expansiveness in legal thought?

1. *The Substantive Doctrines of the Law*

For a variety of reasons nicely described by Stanford legal historian Lawrence M. Friedman, "legal" problems are no longer as clearly differentiated as the once were from the non-legal difficulties of family, financial, or civic relationships.[1] Legal regulation is pervading virtually every aspect of human existence, at least in America, entering realms of life once clearly outside of or even formally immune from the law's reach: the air we breathe, the water we drink, most aspects of our schooling, workplaces, and healthcare, and even many aspects of our family lives. Further, law and everyday life once were more formally compartmentalized, with entry into many legal domains marked out by rituals that served to caution a person poised to engage in behavior that the law regarded as significant. Those legal rituals are now in steep decline. The result of this combination of expansion of legal regulation with shrinking of formal entry barriers to the law mean that law and everyday life are slowly melting together.

Said differently, the boundaries of the law are becoming more porous, and as they do so the content of the law expands into spaces not historically occupied. As a consequence, legal problems no longer arise exclusively in easily foreseen aspects of life as the result of a failure to obey some positive rule. Instead, legal problems are substantively far more like the frictions of everyday social life: they come from any person and any direction. More of our everyday activity must be "legal behavior" that consciously takes account of legal consequences and treats

---

[1] Lawrence M. Friedman, TOTAL JUSTICE (1985) (hereafter "TOTAL JUSTICE"); Lawrence M. Friedman, THE REPUBLIC OF CHOICE: LAW, AUTHORITY AND CULTURE (1990) (hereafter "REPUBLIC OF CHOICE").

others consistently with the dictates of legal rules.[2] On the other hand, this also means that more potential legal problems may be avoided through personal qualities: thoughtfulness, respect for others, and honest communication.

Finally, if everyday human behavior is affected by the melting away of legal barriers, so also is the substance of the legal system. It becomes more difficult for legal rules to remain at odds with prevailing cultural beliefs or trends. The law can no longer so easily maintain a distanced, abstracted, or incongruity with popular morality and sensibilities.

2. Procedures for Preventing and Addressing Legal Problems

As legal problems lose their substantive distinctiveness from other problems in our everyday lives, so also may we begin to question their ***procedural*** distinctiveness. In other words, we begin to assess the methods and criteria of legal problem solving by standards that we tend to use in non-legal problem solving. We come to expect that legal methods will express a higher concern for our individuality and personal histories; a greater respect for popular morality; and less appetite for examining the etiology of events we cannot reverse. We may also change our outlook on what constitutes appropriate legal solutions. Instead of looking backwards–seeking to establish personal blame, to vindicate legal rules, and to punish or redistribute resources by invoking authority and power–we may instead seek mutual accommodation, apology, or forgiveness.

Perhaps it is not surprising, then, that the alternative procedures now being devised for preventing and resolving legal problems attempt to harness the power of human relationships and aspiration rather than relying completely on state authority. Alternative approaches typically involve far greater personal participation by the dispute holders, in an attempt to facilitate their better communication and eventual mutual empathy.

These "new" tools for problem solving–the personal relationships in which problems are embedded and their need to continue, along with the sense of fallibility and shared responsibility that often comes from hearing the moral and emotional perspectives of both parties–are historically used by psychologists in resolving interpersonal problems. Psychologists never had the power of the state to back their efforts. They have always relied on the power of the parties themselves to accommodate a resolution. Lawyers are becoming more skilled in these tools as the new procedures with which they work give stronger voice to those human qualities and rely less on formal court authority. Lawyers have much to learn from psychologists in bringing insight and understanding to their clients, just as psychologists can usefully learn from lawyers about due process and civil liberties.

---

[2] Friedman, TOTAL JUSTICE, *supra* note 1, at 14.

3. The Trend: A Higher Proportion of Troublesome Problems

Pressure is growing for using the U/I/A to resolve at least some problems, because more and more problems being presented to the judiciary are dissonant with traditional R/S/P methods. The paragraphs below build on our earlier exploration of the common sources of dissonance between problems and procedures. Those sources of tension are becoming more commonplace in the legal system, for reasons explained below. Each of the paragraphs describes social trends that produce legal problems that bear structural qualities which are especially challenging for R/S/P methods.

The judiciary seem to be facing a variety of challenges, ironically, because of their success in being trusted and used as the default problem solver in our society. Problems are being sent to be resolved within the legal system that in a previous era would have been either shrugged off fatalistically, or else dealt with by traditional authorities: family elders, religious leaders, workplace bosses, teachers, ward politicians, physicians, or scientists.[3] The legal system is being asked to cope with a far broader range of human problems, and indeed all sorts of issues that a hundred years ago would not have been within the technological power of humans even to discern as possible questions, much less decide upon.[4]

Here are some dimensions along which more legal problems can be understood, causing difficulties:

a. Many more problems are **novel**, in the sense of lacking fixed legal rules to decide the problem, or even any social consensus about how the problem should be decided. As explored above, problems lacking well-established decisional criteria are necessarily more difficult than those for which clear rules are available for analysis. The increased proportion in the legal system of problems for which decisional criteria are lacking is a function of the accelerating rate of social change. It is not just that we do not have easy legal rules available to apply to these and similar matters; it is that the problems are so new that we also do not have inherited cultural norms about them.

b. A higher proportion of problems seem to be **intimate**, *i.e.,* embedded in long-standing, basic human relationships. The decline of the family harmony doctrine, higher divorce rates, the rise of far more complex standards for awarding child custody, and an increased willingness within our culture to address problems like sexual abuse, domestic violence, and elder abuse all contribute to this. These problems are more difficult on a number of dimensions. First, it is harder to take in appropriate evidence, because the witnesses may be incompetent or intimidated and because it is hard to draw appropriate lines about the relevance of

---

[3] TOTAL JUSTICE, *supra* note 1, at 80–93.

[4] REPUBLIC OF CHOICE, *supra* note 1, at 50–61.

much of the historical give and take and emotional episodes that tend to occur within intimate relationships.

Unlike judging criminal episodes or tortious interactions, healthy versus pathological relationships cannot easily be assessed by looking at a limited number of discrete episodes. Furthermore, the judicial task for these problems is often to create an environment for moving forward. Once again hearkening back to the structural fit and misfit of problems and procedures, judges are increasingly being asked to manage relationships for the future, entailing predictions that are far more within the normal realm of psychologists and social workers than with judges. Even if the evidence were really available for determining how best to design the future, how can the judiciary really enforce remedies that will ensure that future?

c. More **recurring** problems seem to be presented to the judiciary. Examples would be criminality and civil disorder problems stemming from drug or alcohol addiction, mental illness, gang membership, homelessness, or sexual predation. Behaviors are being performed that are directly illegal, and are the direct cause for the legal system to respond. But the people engaging in these illicit acts are doing so for reasons that are particularly resistant to power-based legal remedies. Therefore the courthouse and jailhouse become revolving doors for these folks to enter and leave repeatedly. Addressing the underlying causes of these problems effectively is a significant challenge to the legal system.

d. More problems stem from **initiatives of the modern regulatory state**. Examples would include issues like the siting of a new highway, or preservation of wetlands and open spaces, or the allocation of medical resources. As discussed above, these are often future-based predictive or planning decisions, and are comprised of many interacting variables. Where decisions traditionally relegated to decentralized decisional systems like the marketplace suddenly are sought to be made by a few persons, even presenting the issues becomes an enormous challenge. Beyond these issue-framing challenges, thousands of possible outcomes may require evaluation, and yet the empirical foundation is lacking for making valid assessments.

B. Changing Criteria of Truth

Both substantive and procedural reforms to the legal system are prompted by the gradual conflation of legal regulation with everyday behavior. Changes in what the legal system regards as truth, and how that truth is attained, reflects ongoing intellectual assaults on Enlightenment formal reasoning and scientific method. Enlightenment reasoning demands detached, objective consideration of facts that are parsed from confounding background or context. The purpose of experimental design is to isolate one matter for proper inquiry, just as historically legal pleadings played a similar role.

Once an issue is isolated, the testing itself must be done with precision and regularity so that the results are *reliable*–that is, that other persons testing or judging the same phenomenon would come to the same conclusions. The *validity* of the conclusion–whether the conclusion is correct or true–is distinct from the reliability of reaching the same decision by different judges. Validity is determined by the objective correspondence of the assessment or judgment against preestablished principles or laws. Some trials–scientific or legal–result in an elaboration of the rules themselves or even their rare overturning. In all Enlightenment trials, however, the integrity of the rules is crucial.

Over the past two centuries, however, the quality of truth obtained through these methodological assumptions has been questioned. Major movements challenging the objectivity or alleged completeness of Enlightenment truth include romanticism, relativism, and post-modernism. Each of these has contributed to a modern skepticism–ranging from mild to intense among commentators–about the claims of Enlightenment methods to uncover single right answers to issues, be they scientific or legal.

In the popular culture (as distinct from legal or scientific culture), decisional processes improve their legitimacy if:

- (1) they are open to personal insight through intimacy with the facts of the dispute or the problems holders (the romantic heritage);

- (2) they acknowledge that judges as well as the disputants are limited by the perspectives from which they observe the facts (relativism); and

- (3) the ethical values, political agendas, and sociological impacts implicit in the procedures themselves are held to account (post-modernism).

Each of these sources of skepticism about Enlightenment epistemology presents a distinct challenge to R/S/P legal methods. The popular culture often accords legitimacy to "truth" that is found through different methods than those of science or law.

Hence it should not be surprising that the nature of the alternative methods for preventing and resolving legal problems strongly involve the participants themselves in uncovering facts or emotional reactions, relatively unconstrained by evidentiary rules of relevance and materiality; are more future-oriented rather than solely concerned to uncover historical facts and allocate blame; aim toward consensus of the disputants around a proposed solution, rather than conformity to legal rules; and often even permit the parties considerable latitude in choosing third party settlement agents and the methods those persons may employ.

C. The Movement From an Industrial to Information Age Economy

In the paragraphs below I draw an extended analogy between the production and distribution of goods, and the production and distribution of legal regulation and legal problem solving. I posit that the basic methods and structures of economic activity will find corresponding shapes in the methods and structures of the legal system. An industrial economy, in other words, will be mirrored by an industrial legal system that exhibits similar qualities. If this is so, then as the Industrial Revolution gives way to the Information Age, the methods and structures of **both** economic activity and the legal system will change in parallel.

This analogy may seem especially fanciful, but it actually stems from the presumption explored in Part One about the legal system: that the legal system is not a self-contained, closed system of courts and civil procedure, but instead a far broader and well-integrated social and philosophical construct. Any change in one part of the system–like innovations in communication, transportation, or information retrieval–will cause reverberations and corresponding adjustments throughout the system. Some detail is offered below about industrial methods, all in an effort to show that R/S/P methods are bound up with particular historical trends. As the underlying social and cultural infrastructure that generated the R/S/P paradigm gives way, so also do I claim that we can understand why the U/I/A paradigm is gaining recognition. The new paradigm reflects emerging methods of economic exchange, transportation, and communication as well as changing ideas about truth and human nature.

1. Industrial Age Economics, Organization, and Distribution

From the time the Industrial Revolution began (its arrival was geographically varied, but we will deem it generally to begin in the late 18th Century), social institutions changed because of dramatic declines in the costs of communication, transportation, and information. Everyday tasks began to be mechanized as technological innovation tapped into the power of fossil fuels. This resulted in lower costs of producing and distributing goods and services, as compared with an agrarian society that depended on human labor as supplemented by animals.

Industrial methods of harnessing energy permitted the standardization of products, and their widespread geographic (and social) distribution from centers of production. The industrial era saw the following:

    a. Greater productivity and wealth;

    b. Growth of standardized, "branded" goods and services;

    c. Elaboration of highly specialized "niche" opportunities; and

    d. Refinement of assessment devices to fit particular goods and services with particular needs or interests.

I call these trends collectively "McDonald's efficiency." They are reflective of the economies of scale achieved during the industrial era through countless breakthroughs in the technologies of communication and transportation. New technologies gradually made feasible the routine shipping of goods and services across vast distances, while cheap international communications permitted control over employees and production standards. Larger-scale enterprises thrived because their costs of production were lower. By centralizing management and support services, and by standardizing the processes of production, the companies were able to gain a competitive advantage, and eventual market dominance.

McDonald's efficiency enabled growth through an accumulation of economic efficiencies: cheaper production and distribution, which was made possible by the projection of centralized authority and standardization of process, which in turn was made possible by better technologies in communication and transport.

McDonald's efficiency made goods and services cheaper, but did it make them more desirable? Unless people wanted the products, efficiency would obviously be useless. Only "commodities"—that is, goods or services that were mass produced and rigidly conforming—were suited to McDonald's efficiency methods. Fortunately for industrial-era enterprises, consumers did not resist standardized products. The commodities resulting from McDonald's efficiency were ultimately accepted for three reasons:

First, they were a good value. Their quality was predictable—and often quite good. Further, they were typically much cheaper than the competing goods that had traditionally been produced in small-scale, non-standardized cottage industries.

Second, companies made a virtue out of conformity, through "branding" or making the products synonymous with a particular producer or designer. Sometimes branding worked to add a cachet or social significance to its products. Even without that, however, branding was effective as a marker of that which was utterly familiar and predictable. At worst the branded goods seemed a safe choice, and at best they were icons of hip, modern culture.

Finally, the spread of standardized goods through industrial McDonald's efficiency was helped by social changes spawned, ironically, by the availability of the goods themselves. The existence in the market of these products led to social pressures for modernist reforms toward rationalizing social institutions and infrastructure that would in turn be able to take advantage of the relatively cheap, relatively high quality goods and services. In other words, the new products did not create their own demand as such, but they did make visible the changes that needed to be made for these products to be more practical to purchase and use. And people wanted that. Modernist culture spread over the next two hundred years, as did the demand for standardized products, as did the efficiencies, and the cycle intensified.

The social and economic forces that propelled McDonald's to crop up around the world built their success on: **sameness** (in the product); **homogenization** (in the preferences of the consumer); and **power** (in market share).

2. Industrial Era Legal Systems

Our inherited Industrial Age legal structures and tools are built on the same assumptions that underlie Industrial economics and political arrangements. The power to articulate rights and legal rules first was concentrated in a central source, and then emanated outward to an ever-expanding periphery. This could be done efficiently as transaction costs of communication and transportation fell, so long as what was sent out (laws/rights in the legal system, corresponding to products/market share in the commercial system) was commoditized. So long as enough power could be applied, progress could be made as measured by increasing standardization and penetration.

As discussed above, the law itself has obviously grown dramatically in the past century—in both sheer quantity of legal regulation and as a pervading influence in more and more aspects of our lives that once were considered intimate or otherwise immune from the reach of the law. This growth of the law—both its volume and the completeness with which it presumes to regulate—is a natural accompaniment of the same forces that led to McDonald's efficiency. Law has grown, in other words, because cheaper communication and transportation has intensified the volume of commercial interaction. Further, more of that interaction is among strangers—a function of increasing division of labor and projection of exchange across broader geographies. As that happens, more and more of life comes to rely on legal rights and rules rather than traditional sources of authority and conformity. The law grew during the industrial era in a way that mirrored McDonald's efficiency: through *power* exercised by centralized authorities (courts and legislatures); employing a largely *standardized* process by invoking laws that were sought to be made uniform; and seeking to treat all persons *equally*.

The gradual growth throughout the 20th Century of federal law, at the expense of local state standards, is a good example of the power of McDonald's efficiency. The current consolidation of law within the European Union is another example. Such standardization is not necessarily a bad thing, and it has not ended. We can expect that the pressures of globalization will increasingly standardize national legal systems. But just as McDonald's efficiency held out cultural opportunities to new markets and spawned social homogenization, so also will the arrival of Information Age efficiency create the potential for the design of social structures based on the alternative Information Age values of *connection, consent, and particularization* of both needs assessment and solution.

3. Information Age Economics, Organization, and Distribution

In the past twenty years, a new sort of efficiency has surfaced, based on the Internet and Information Age. Information Age efficiency is based not on standardization, but on *diversity* of procedures; not on homogenization of consumers and demand, but on their *differences*; not on market power and centralized authority, but on an appropriate *matching* of small scale supply with particularized needs.

Information Age efficiency is born of the dramatic decline in information costs as a result of computer technology and the Internet. These developments have so drastically reduced certain transaction costs that *it makes feasible the fairly frequent use of a social ordering that depends on very different tools* than the centralized authority, power, and conformity of industrialism and McDonald's efficiency. Put differently, decreases in information costs have enabled social goods to be delivered—including at least some law and lawyering services—in a way that rejects a "one size fits all" standardization.

Instead, information technology permits more social interactions on the basis of very particular responses, offered from among a broader palette of choices than previously available, to respond to particular needs. This is feasible because low information costs permit consumers or problem holders to communicate very broadly, even globally, about their needs. Reciprocally, those who would offer solutions or products can specialize dramatically in approach, because their potential clients, customers, or user base could be hundreds of millions of people. These efficiency gains of lower information costs permit dramatic increases in the division of labor and in niche product interests. That in turn permits a proliferation of variety in product or services. Which, finally, permits many more of life's needs to be resolved on the basis of mutual gain or at least consent–because greater diversity of choice means that more people can be served in ways that are not mutually exclusive or zero sum.

Ironically, as we become more and more splintered and separated in our individual knowledge and capabilities, we will also need better ways of organizing and connecting ourselves. If we cannot do that, then those potential productivity gains cannot be realized: we will have a world in which potential goes unused, for failure to find environments in which it can fully flourish. Differentiating ourselves offers the potential; connecting ourselves is required if we are to realize that potential. The Tower of Babel story comes to mind: We cannot expect to produce Renaissance people who can speak all the languages. So how best to connect all this disparate talent?

Tim Cummins, head of the International Association of Contracts and Commitment Managers (IACCM) speaks of three basic challenges/opportunities of the Information Age.[5] *First, connecting our labor-divided selves requires some organizational structure, and the Industrial models are not strong enough.* The Industrial era solution of a fully integrated firm that designs, produces and sells standardized goods and services seems unlikely to secure these new potentials. That is because the velocity and magnitude of change demands more flexibility than typically offered by the integrated firm, especially if it is strongly hierarchical. What once may have been efficient forms of organization–forms with centralized authority that projected standardized goods, services, or ideas outwards–may not be able to harness Information Age efficiency potential. What may work better are inter-firm networks: webs of relationships

---

[5] Address of Tim Cummins, IACCM Conference, Phoenix, Arizona, 2008. For further details of IACCM and its work, see http://www.iaccm.com.

among distinct contributors that can couple and decouple to suit particular projects. To accomplish this, businesses will need a collaborative mentality and inter-firm communication.

Second, building trust and strong relationships are crucial in these web relationships, again because of the need for speed, flexibility, and the ability to deal with high complexity. Many of these ventures would never begin, nor succeed if they did begin, were the parties to imagine they could dispense with trust and accommodation by setting out precise legal duties among the participants. Power and rules will decline as methods of organization, simply because in a ever-changing, decentralized, non-standardized world both rules and the leverage for applying power become elusive and inefficient. Cummins stresses that within these emerging weblike, transitory and flexible organizational patterns, we must *learn to respect relationships as much as legal rights.* I will add to his analysis that where rules and power decline in authority and efficacy, far different procedures must be developed to deal with problems.

Finally, new professional training will be needed, moving beyond the Industrial mentality. As Cummins says, "We must train to optimize, rather than to protect."[6] We must, in other words, foster a proactive mentality. Current legal training is instead largely toward protection, with the lawyer as circuit breaker. Law school focuses on legal rules, potential liability, and how to avoid or challenge that liability. Self-protection is deeply embedded in Western culture, as detailed in our Part One discussion about the privileging of self-protection over facilitating human interaction in coping with the fundamental dilemma of preserving social order. The need is to equip lawyers with both the mentality and the skills to become more proactive toward meeting their clients' goals, but Western culture as well as law school culture offers resistance.

We may elaborate this point by mentioning three influences that perpetuate a tendency to self-protect rather than optimize: (1) Our liberal political heritage; (2) our skeptical philosophical and scientific traditions; and (3) our adversarial legal system. All three contribute to an inertia in professional training, and an approach to problems that favors caution and skepticism instead of trust and collaboration toward goals.

First, our liberal political tradition trains us to distrust those who are in positions of power. It is not easy for Westerners to imagine themselves within harmonious, value-sharing groups. We imagine instead that permitting the free exercise of that power will result in tyranny. To prevent this, we build pluralistic structures of checks and balances in the exercise of power. We constrain people in multiple ways, buffering their discretion so as to protect ourselves from others' excesses.

What results, of course, is a slower, more stable environment. The difficulty is that the surrounding world is becoming faster and more dynamic. It may not wait for us. To thrive in the sort of economic turbulence of the Information Age we need trust, but instead we have social

---

[6] Id.

261

institutions built on distrust. We need collaboration focused on shared goals, but instead we have institutions built on pluralism.

Our institutions, in sum, are self-protective. How can we change that to achieve what may be needed in legal relationships as well as in modern business? Can we forge structures that prevent exploitative behaviors without resorting to a process that deliberately constrains initiatives? How, in other words, can we overcome distrust without sacrificing decisiveness and speed of decision-making? A Chapter below by Douglas Turner deals explicitly with the meaning of trust and how to enhance it.

Second, our skeptical philosophical/scientific tradition also contributes to a culture of protection. Scientific thinking advances largely through the efforts to falsify claims made by other people. When a hypothesis is made, efforts are undertaken to verify the hypothesis. Yet we are only confident about what is falsified rather than verified. It takes only one scientific trial to disprove a hypothesis, but endless trials to move toward confidence that the hypothesis is true. And hence our image of truth becomes an edifice that is constantly being questioned and torn down, until sufficient contradictions are revealed to enable a new paradigm to be offered up. Goals are viewed with suspicion. As any good empiricist will say, the data are the data. All the rest, according to Enlightenment philosopher Jeremy Bentham, is "nonsense on stilts."

Third, our adversarial legal tradition is arguably built upon both the liberal political tradition and our skepticism about truth. We test the legitimacy of legal propositions through setting parties against one another, to make the strongest possible arguments. Rights and duties are conceived as held by individuals, not groups. Relationships among people are conceived as limited by their informed consent. Loyalty has little meaning.[7] We need cooperation, but we have institutionalized feistiness and self-maximization.

It is not surprising, therefore, that Westerners–perhaps Americans and British especially, with their heritage of the adversarial legal process--may find it difficult to move toward a world of networked relationships built on qualities of trust, relationships, and active imaginations that articulate and achieve shared goals. Apart from our families and perhaps in religious life, these sorts of groupings are relatively unfamiliar. When we are placed in them, our instincts and skills may favor self-protection rather than optimization. The question is worth re-stating: how can professional training move toward better understanding and skills that will work better in these crucial new structures?

Another insight of Tim Cummins is that every major innovation in communication has been accompanied by a spike in trade, as people re-orient themselves to take advantage of the new opportunities. What is true about trade is also perhaps true of human relationships. People may be hard-wired to project their thoughts as widely as existing technologies will permit. And

---

[7] *See generally* GEORGE P. FLETCHER, LOYALTY: AN ESSAY ON THE MORALITY OF RELATIONSHIPS 4-6 (1993).

as communication penetrates among those who were strangers, new and stronger relationships and structures are created. Every major innovation in communication, in other words, redefines the potential for human relationships.

In the 1960's the popular social commentator Marshall McLuhan was famous for one slogan and an additional idea, both of which look increasingly prescient. The slogan was "the medium is the message," and the idea was the emergence of what he termed "the global village."[8] McLuhan's insights stem from his observation that cultures change with breakthroughs in methods of communication. Clearly that is happening with digital technology and the Internet.

This is the underlying message of media itself, as distinct from its particular content: how people orient themselves to what is possible. The global village is the emerging phenomenon of voluntary, relational groups that are horizontally arranged across a globe that has flattened.[9] Sometimes these villages will have a few individuals, sometimes millions. Any given individual will belong to a web of these relationships.

As voluntary groups these webs of relationship must be governed by something we think of as contract. But it is not "Contract Law" as we have known it over the past two centuries, with state-enforced rules. The transaction costs of articulating and enforcing legal contract rules across such a diverse physical geography climb higher and higher, even as the formation of the groups themselves cost less and less and it is efficient for the groups to engage in transactions that are smaller and smaller in economic value. As a society we must therefore invent new forms of governance–*forms that have costs that are low enough to make the governance device worth invoking.*

This is where trust, relationship, and reputation come in.[10] Governance of the global villages must be de-centralized, based largely on consent and avoidance rather than based in state power that is centrally administered through laws and legal institutions. Trust and reputation are highly particularized and self-enforcing. The bases on which they are created and breached are as individual as the purposes of the villagers. How can these qualities be best fostered where the people are not actually face-to-face? Have internet marketers perhaps created a model for how trust can be built, through cyber-reputations built up by customer feedback postings?

Where people are aware of the importance of trust and relationship, almost inevitably they will act preventively. Strong relationships are forged through exactly the same sort of

---

[8] Marshall McLuhan, UNDERSTANDING MEDIA: THE EXTENSIONS OF MAN (1964).

[9] *See generally* Thomas L. Friedman, THE WORLD IS FLAT: A BRIEF HISTORY OF THE TWENTY-FIRST CENTURY (2005).

[10] On the relationship of contract and trust, *see* Francis Fukayama, TRUST: THE SOCIAL VIRTUES AND THE CREATION OF PROSPERITY 151 (1995).

strong, empathic communication that will prevent misunderstandings and problems. Furthermore, those communication patterns will promote innovation, which will drive transaction costs yet lower, making formal legal rules and structures progressively less significant. A separate chapter below will amplify these thoughts about contracts and contract law.

4. *Information Age Legal Systems*

Information Age efficiency has significant implications for the future of the law and legal practice, as did McDonald's efficiency. As explained above, transactions and relationships of both persons and property that never before were feasible or efficient, suddenly are being discovered by millions of people who are easily capable of dealing with one another across continents. Should we expect that the ideas and methods of legal systems that are built on power and territoriality will work well to address relationships that are consensual and virtual? Does the movement toward the consensual resolution of legal problems, as practiced in the preventive approaches, represent a historically inevitable shift away from the feasibility as well as the desirability of invoking state power? Have we begun to find self-protection in the strength of our personal relationships as well as our individual rights? And if so, how are those connections best reinforced when they are called upon to resolve some tension? How might legal institutions and lawyers help strengthen those personal relationships?

Legal procedures of the future must respond to these questions. Failure to do so will risk the legal system being marginalized in cultural and economic importance.[11] We are as yet unsure, however, exactly how legal systems should change. As information costs have plummeted, the model of using power from central source in commoditized ways becomes less adequate and feasible. Businesses organized around mass commodities may plateau; politics organized through nation states may become less relevant; and legal systems that depend on lawyers summoning the power of the state will become grossly inefficient and probably ineffective for resolving certain problems.

Reflecting Cummins' larger economic and organizational analysis, the legal system also needs new structures that can transcend national boundaries; that rely less on power and more on consent, trust, and reputation; that more strongly respect underlying human relationships; and that focus more on prevention than on cure. As Grant Gilmore once wrote, "The better the society, the less law there will be. In Heaven there will be no law, and the lion will lie down with the lamb. ... The worse the society, the more law there will be. In Hell there will be nothing but law, and due process will be meticulously observed."[12]

---

[11] *See* Thomas D. Barton, *Troublesome Connections: The Law and Post-Enlightenment Culture,* 47 EMORY LAW JOURNAL 163 (1998).

[12] Grant Gilmore, THE AGES OF AMERICAN LAW 111 (1977).

D. The Cultural Importance of the U/I/A Paradigm

The law will almost certainly accelerate what has been happening over the past 20 years: the procedures available in the law and in the legal profession for resolving legal problems will proliferate yet further. We already see the birth of alternative, highly specialized problem-solving courts that will be examined in greater depth below: family courts, drug courts, homeless persons' courts, as well as new approaches by the judiciary like victim-offender reconciliation efforts. We also see a massive increase in the use of ADR methods, often formally sanctioned by the courts: arbitration, mediation, and various hybrids involving negotiated settlements. These alternative approaches are based less on power, and more on consent; less on treating people abstractly equally and more on acknowledging differences and trying to harness those differences; less on formal, uniform rights and more on the particulars of the ongoing relationships of the disputants.

Bringing stronger relationships into the law is certainly important for achieving the goal of preventing and resolving problems, but it may be just as important for broader cultural reasons. Without this movement, without an embracing of the parallel track of U/I/A methods, a possibly serious cultural problem could have intensified. In the paragraphs below, I elaborate the nature of this problem. Luckily, U/I/A innovation has at least partially addressed the problem. Facing the problem squarely, however, also serves the important function of suggesting limits beyond which U/I/A should *not* supplant the R/S/P paradigm.

1. Background and Overview

The problem is that R/S/P legal methods can have undesirable spillover effects on our broader culture. R/S/P legal methods, in other words, may be influencing our wider culture quite apart from their use as legal tools. It may be that R/S/P methods negatively affect the ability of people outside the legal system to build and manage their personal relationships. The power of the law and the simply clarity of its R/S/P methods *may be accelerating a decline in people's ability to resolve problems from within sustained human relationships.*

Resort to R/S/P legal methods may, in other words, potentially create a positive feedback loop. In this loop, the employment of traditional legal thinking and methods could *create additional demand for itself* by enfeebling the alternatives. The model of R/S/P may be so strong as to sap vitality from personal relationships and the development of interpersonal accommodational skills through which such relationships thrive. Where personal relationships are strong, law may not really be needed. But where personal relationships become troubled, R/S/P legal thinking may threaten to become an all-too-convenient substitute for stronger communication and personal understanding.

The story, however, is not clear-cut. The relationships between law and the traditional human ties of family, friendship, employment, ethnicity, or other sense of group belonging are complex and nuanced. Legal rights have cleared permitted social mobility. Where personal relationships are oppressive or malicious, or where initially good relationships turn destructive, the law and its R/S/P methods have often offered a crucial means of escape. For this reason, *R/S/P methods must never be fully supplanted: they are too crucial where public expression of values is required, and too crucial where individuals need to escape from oppressive or cruel personal relationships.*

And yet, if legal institutions somehow *contribute* to the decline of the social relationships or of the skills required to maintain them, then law inadvertently is building some of its strength at the expense of the alternatives. If that is so, then the solution is for the legal system itself to model the sort of communication and human regard that can *strengthen* human relationships.

As stated in Part One of this book, every interaction that people have with the legal system should be an opportunity for moral growth, self-awareness, and healthier personal relationships. That is the opportunity of U/I/A, and it seems to have been seized. That decision, made for all the reasons catalogued in this Chapter, is of enormous positive importance to Western culture. The paragraphs below identify not only the difficulty of the problem, but the reason why R/S/P methods must never be abandoned: R/S/P and U/I/A must work together.

2. *The Problem Defined*

The problem may have been most salient in the 1970's, just as the U/I/A methods began to flourish, but its implications remain sobering even if the problem has abated with the arrival of new methods in the legal system. Here, more formally stated, is the problem: "In theory, law makes trustworthiness unnecessary, even obsolete. When law is fully in command, morality itself loses relevance."[13] Is the law something fundamentally different from trust or morality? Does the law not need either? Worse yet, might the law actually *undermine* trust or morality?

As problems afflict us, we traverse the landscape looking for possible resolution. We stop at whatever way station seems comfortable or promising: at consolation or sacrifice; at inspiration or dogma; at bargain or discourse; at law or trust. Perhaps along this road the law has its own sign and attractions, minds its own business and remains respectable.

As explored in a previous chapter, however, more and more types of problems that once were serviced elsewhere seem to be stopping at the law station. Perhaps the station has grown

---

[13] Donald Black, SOCIOLOGICAL JUSTICE 85 (1989). Black's clear discussion of the social dependency and personal abdication of responsibility that can follow overuse of the legal system is especially valuable. *See also* Jerrold S. Auerbach, JUSTICE WITHOUT LAW (1983), which focuses on the differing public characters of legal and nonlegal processes and how law comes to capture nonlegal processes; and Carol J. Gilligan, IN A DIFFERENT VOICE: PSYCHOLOGICAL THEORY AND WOMEN'S DEVELOPMENT (1982) which reflects on rights, relationships, and responsibilities in ways that reveal the cultural construction of even our deepest concepts.

more robust, or perhaps its sign has simply become gaudier. Or perhaps the alternative stops, once elegant, are becoming threadbare or a bit desperate, scaring off those who fear commitment. But could there be a connection between the growing robustness of the law station, and diminishing occupancy at the lodgings of personal trust and relationships?

Practically and philosophically, conflict resolution within the traditional legal system differs markedly from that within sustained human relationships.[14] This divergence of legal and human relational problem-solving is not wholly undesirable, but the link between law and trust may be viewed through a more disturbing lens. Certainly legal institutions often stand ready, sometimes just ahead of personal violence, to supply a default resolution where traditional means of problem solving prove inadequate. At a deeper level, however, some find increasingly a tension between the regularity that seems fundamental to legal process[15] and the human qualities that both create and disturb personal relationships.[16] Could the muscularity of formal legal

---

[14] By "sustained human relationships" I refer to those of intimacy and deep friendship, the bonds of parent/child and other family attachments, and frequently the ties between employer/employee, lawyer/client, physician/patient, clergy/parishioner and teacher/student. In many instances these latter relationships lack the intensity or duration to qualify for the special concerns raised in this book. No mechanical test can be applied; the key is whether the relationship has developed self-healing mechanisms based on trust, personal regard, and expanded notions of truth.

[15] The regularity of legal processes that we often take for granted is probably only half true. The other half of legal procedure consists of parochialism, diversity, and particularity achieved through concepts of federalism, contract law, juries, locally elected judges, selected non-enforcement, *sub rosa* compromise, and corruption. Marc Galanter, *The Modernization of Law*, in MODERNIZATION 153, 163 (Myron Weiner, ed. 1966). *See also* Sally Falk Moore, LAW AS PROCESS 3 (1978) describing the inconsistency, discretion, and manipulation of rule application. The existence of this irregular side of law evidences, depending on one's point of view, demonstrates either the antagonistic tension between law and human relationships, or their practical partnership in which each strengthens the other.

[16] As explained by Lon L. Fuller in *The Forms and Limits of Adjudication*, 92 HARVARD LAW REVIEW 353, 371 (1978), adjudication may not be appropriate where "the effectiveness of human association would be destroyed if it were organized about formally defined 'rights' and 'wrongs'...." As examples, Fuller cited family life and other settings where successful interaction "depends upon spontaneous and informal collaboration, shifting its forms with the task at hand ...." Id. *See also* Lon L. Fuller, *Human Interaction and the Law*, 14 AMERICAN JOURNAL OF JURISPRUDENCE 1, 28 (1969). In *Mediation--Its Forms and Functions*, 44 SOUTHERN CALIFORNIA LAW REVIEW 305 (1971) Fuller described the purposes of mediation as helping the parties "to free themselves from the encumbrance of rules and accepting, instead, a relationship of mutual respect, trust, and understanding that will enable them to meet shared contingencies." Id., at 325. Such functions, said Fuller, are incompatible with the standard procedures of law,

solutions frustrate and enfeeble nonlegal relationships, which learn helplessness through their encounters with law?[17] If so, the law will increasingly find itself the forum for strangers and enemies.[18] American society could become gripped by a paradox in which the self-healing structures of our sustained relationships are impaired by the legal resolutions called upon when the self-healing flounders. As a consequence of its own interventions, therefore, the law may have to steel itself for yet more refugees from failed trust. The more law asserts itself, the more business it would attract.

Transcending this paradox, if indeed it exists, requires the path apparently taken through the development of the U/I/A paradigm: that the law offer methods and outcomes that are reinforcing rather than undermining of non-legal problem-solving mechanisms like trust and mutual regard. The U/I/A approaches bring more emotional and psychological regard into legal methods. Doing so softens the distinction between legal and non-legal problem solving in contexts of strong personal relationships. Doing so also strengthens and broadens the remedies available to the legal system in addressing those relationally-based problems. Finally, legal professionals can model empathic, candid communication methods that could improve the parties' skills and relationships once the legal problem is resolved.

As foreshadowed above, however, a cautionary tension must be identified and explored: no matter how well developed U/I/A methods may become, our society will always need to provide the means for people to escape oppressive people and relationships. The R/S/P methods

---

"for surely central to the very notion of law is the concept of *rules*." Id., at 327. Since rules are "impersonal" and "act-oriented," then human activities organized by different principles are not well directed by law or legal procedures. Id., at 330.

[17] As Donald Black concludes, "The intervention of lawyers may ... undermine the ability of the parties to an on-going relationship to resolve their conflict without recourse to law. Once lawyers become involved, a husband or wife may lose influence over a spouse and a supervisor may lose influence over a subordinate, ... and this too increases the likelihood of litigation." Black, *supra* note 13, at 14. Fuller sounded the same warning: that legalistic conceptions may undermine the mutual trust and confidence on which intimate human relationships are built. Fuller, 44 SOUTHERN CALIFORNIA LAW REVIEW 305, supra note 16, at 330.

[18] Law protects strangers, friends and enemies alike--and perhaps indifferently. As Shylock warns Antonio, "[S]ince I am a dog, beware my fangs: the duke shall grant me justice." William Shakespeare, THE MERCHANT OF VENICE, Act III, Scene III. *See also* Fuller, 14 AMERICAN JOURNAL OF JURISPRUDENCE 1, supra note 16, at 28-29 describing that for affective and operational reasons alike, contract law is ill-suited to govern either highly intimate relationships or extremely hostile situations; it rather is best used in the domain of "friendly strangers, between whom interactional expectancies remain largely open and unpatterned." Id., at 29.

may ensure escape better than U/I/A methods can offer.[19] And therefore we will always need a robust access to R/S/P legal methods for those in need of escape, or the sort of social mobility, that U/I/A methods may not secure. We will use the example of minority persons' needs and rights to examine this profound and fundamental difficulty.

3. The Tension of Preservation and Unfairness

A tension exists between fair treatment of individuals and the preservation of deeply embedded patterns of personal regard and authority. The tension is created because many traditional sustained relationships contain conflict resolution features that fight legal values of due process and formal equality. Instead, they rely on authority structures and role ascriptions that could not withstand a legal spotlight.[20] Neither preservation nor the assurance of fairness should be absolutely preferred as a value. Determining the proper balance between the two, however, can be painful.

Although the tension between preservation and fairness can surface from any resolution device that treats people capriciously or unfairly, the plight of disadvantaged people best illuminates the dilemma. Consider, for example, the implementation of the Indian Civil Rights Act.[21] On the one hand the due process and equal protection rights embodied in the Act are vital

---

[19] Lawrence M. Friedman's books TOTAL JUSTICE (*supra* note 1) and THE REPUBLIC OF CHOICE (*supra* note 1) brilliantly chronicle the shaking off of traditional authority patterns and the building of the modern self through law and other modernist developments.

[20] Often the power relationships of traditional authority structures reflect only "temporary inequality" rather than "permanent equality." As Carol Gilligan discusses, temporary inequality often accompanies human development, in such relationships as parent/child and student/teacher. A relationship built on permanent inequality does not, in contrast, seek its own ultimate dissolution, but rather seeks to perpetuate patterns of dominance and subordination. Gilligan, *supra* note 13, at 168. The distinction seems a helpful but not conclusive guide in resolving the tension between preservation and fairness.

Similarly, proper balancing of the two goals cannot be achieved solely from the dictates of the status quo, that is, on what are publicly recognized injustices. Such an approach would wrongly assume that cultural and personal consciousness toward permanent inequality cannot be raised. As Judith Shklar writes, the distinction between socially recognized offenses and our subjective responses to facts is one that is "no more secure, and no less political, than that between nature and culture or between the objective and the subjective view. It is a question of who has the power to define the meaning of actions." Judith N. Shklar, THE FACES OF INJUSTICE 7 (1990).

[21] The Indian Civil Rights Act of 1968 calls for the extension of Fourteenth Amendment rights to the tribes. However, owing to *Santa Clara Pueblo v. Martinez*, 436 U.S. 49 (1978) those rights are unevenly enforced among the tribes. *See* Christopher Wilkinson, AMERICAN

to our own society and arguably fundamental to human rights. On the other hand, Natives and non-Natives alike work to preserve Indian cultural practices precisely because they are different from European traditions and because the old ways are crucial to Native identity.[22] Suppose, however, that a particular tribal practice disempowers women. Can we in conscience "approve" this cultural feature, or should Native women be equipped with the legally enforceable rights that prevail in majority culture?

The American legal system is built on the values of the Enlightenment: individual freedom to escape confining social stereotypes, imposed roles,[23] and religious authority;[24] critical rationality based on beliefs in the power of the mind to detach from--and choose to overcome--environmental influences;[25] and the universality of norms and community-based judging, based on formal equality. Those values have both informed the development of individual liberties in

---

INDIANS, TIME, AND THE LAW 113-14 (1987); Ann Tweedy, personal communication, 2008.

[22] One dimension peculiar to the Native American example and not present in similar questions dealing with, say, the Amish community, is the history of colonial rule over Native Americans and the absence of their self-determination. Howard R. Berman, personal communication. Hence in judging between preservation and fairness in this case, preservation has a special appeal.

[23] *See* Shklar, *supra* note 20, at 35-36.

[24] As Shelley Burtt reflects on the modernist tendency to distinguish between critical rationality and religious thought, the importance of the quality of "detachment" to the definition of rationality is striking:

Current political theory puts a tremendous premium on developing the ability to 'distance [oneself] from prevailing desires and practices' or to engage in 'reconsideration of [ones] ends and commitments' as markers or personal autonomy and critical rationality. [citations omitted.] ... Because religious education ... does not encourage such radical skepticism, it is often characterized as hostile to critical reasoning more generally.

Shelley Burtt, *In Defense of Yoder: Parental Authority and the Public Schools, in* NOMOS 38 Political Order 416 (Ian Shapiro and Russell Hardin eds., 1996).

[25] *See* Leonard V. Kaplan, *Unhappy Pierre: Foucault's Parricide and Human Responsibility,* 83 NORTHWESTERN UNIVERSITY LAW REVIEW 321, 322 (1989). *See also* Sharon Lamb, THE TROUBLE WITH BLAME: VICTIMS, PERPETRATORS, AND RESPONSIBILITY 9, 10, 54 (1996); Samuel H. Pillsbury, *The Meaning of Deserved Punishment: An Essay on Choice, Character, and Responsibility,* 67 INDIANA LAW JOURNAL 719, 720 (1992).

270

the law, and have also empowered individual Americans to pry themselves loose of traditional authority and social, religious, and racial prejudice.[26]

Law has functioned powerfully, in other words, to allow people to separate from others *by invoking the concepts of self implied in those same Enlightenment values.* The social separation which American law has historically fostered was thus invoked as part of quest for a broader, *less particular* individual identity. The identity was abstracted from more highly elaborated, yet perhaps confining or oppressive, roles. No essential conflict emerged between the legal ideas used instrumentally to escape from hierarchical or discriminatory power authority, and the self-transformation that accompanied such an escape.[27] As developed below, the separation of self from its historical ties was liberating. The abstracted, disconnected self that resulted fit in well to the modernist Enlightenment law and its surrounding culture.

Notions of rights, equality, and due process simultaneously separated many people from oppressive or narrow-minded authority structures, and also contributed to a constructed identity

---

[26] *See generally* Patricia J. Williams, *Alchemical Notes: Reconstructing Ideals from Deconstructed Rights,* 22 HARVARD CIVIL RIGHTS -CIVIL LIBERTIES LAW REVIEW 401 (1987); TOTAL JUSTICE, *supra* note 1.

[27] Sociologist Sally Engle Merry insightfully explores the links between law, escape from community and relationship, and self-identity. *See generally* Sally Engle Merry, GETTING JUSTICE AND GETTING EVEN: LEGAL CONSCIOUSNESS AMONG WORKING-CLASS AMERICANS (1990). She writes:

As long as community is conceived according the romantic American folk vision of a warm, intimate, and supportive social group, it is hard to understand why anyone would give it up. But the very intimacy and totality of such a world make it miserable for the person who cannot or will not go along. ... For much of American history, the frontier provided, for people enmeshed in conflicts, opportunities to move away. ... Indeed, historian Robert Wiebe argues that it is a fundamental cultural logic in America to deal with difference by living apart. ... 'Society depended on segmentation.' ... [Americans] are continuing to move to suburbs, to choose privacy, separation, and, for social ordering, dependence on the law rather than the intimacy of community.

Id. at 173-74 (citation omitted). *Cf.* the discussion of the "constitutive perspective" of law in Austin Sarat and Thomas R. Kearns, *Beyond the Great Divide: Forms of Legal Scholarship and Everyday Life, in* LAW IN EVERYDAY LIFE 21, 27-32 (Austin Sarat & Thomas R. Kearns eds., 1993).

of detached autonomy.[28] Both the separation and the self-exploration afforded by law were real, although the journey was largely one of negation: a casting off of ethnic obligations, religious strictures, or racial stereotypes, and a taking on of a more abstract, disembodied identity defined by the very ideas of universality and freedom by which escape had been won. We began discussion of this topic in Part One; it deserves further exploration here.

For example, Patricia J. Williams powerfully describes how, for many African-Americans, the invoking of legal rights is both socially empowering and self-defining.[29] For a population seeking escape from the degrading stereotypes with which the majority often regard them, gaining greater facility with the world of law creates a welcome distancing or boundary that whites often take for granted, or even disdain.[30] She writes: "[T]o show that I can speak the language of lease is my way of enhancing trust of me ... . As a black, I have been given by this society a strong sense of myself as already too familiar, too personal, too subordinate to white people. ... For me, stranger-stranger relations are better than stranger-chattel."[31]

Williams's thoughts are mirrored in reports of the consciousness of working class women caught in relationships of violence.[32] Until they turn to the court for protection and learn some of the concepts of self-identity the law represents, they may regard "violence as inevitable."[33] They go to court seeking separation from abuse or alcoholism;[34] they may or may not fully achieve that end, but in the process they are offered new conceptions of themselves and family roles, ones that are more egalitarian and promotive of mutual respect.[35]

Historically, people have used the law to separate themselves from the domination of arbitrary authority in a variety of institutional settings: the workplace, schools, police stations,

---

[28] For a critique of the assumed connection between the exercise of choice and individual autonomy, see Robin West, *Authority, Autonomy, and Choice: The Role of Consent in the Moral and Political Visions of Franz Kafka and Richard Posner,* 99 HARVARD LAW REVIEW 384 (1985).

[29] *See generally* Williams, *supra* note 26.

[30] Id. at 407.

[31] Id.

[32] Merry, *supra* note 27, at 47-48, 73-74.

[33] Id., at 48.

[34] Id.

[35] Id. at 84; Merry, *supra* note 27, at 275.

the military, even hospitals.[36] The identities that had been ascribed to them by birth or social prejudice and operationalized in discriminatory or arbitrary treatment were also varied: racial, ethnic, sexual, religious, or age-based. In each setting and for each identity, escape using the law required individuals both to rethink their identities free of ascription and stereotype and to embrace instead an abstracted, universalized person to whom the concepts of rights and due process were addressed.[37] People still use the law to escape from abusive domestic relationships, or to keep away jilted boyfriends and girlfriends.[38] Neighbors still attempt to use the law to keep other neighbors away from their homes, or their children.[39] Even parents use the law against their children, mostly to control them but occasionally to force a separation from them.[40]

Regardless of whether escape is from institutional power or from a more personal relationship, people come to the instruments and identity construction of the law through the "cultural values of autonomy, self-reliance, individualism, and tolerance"[41] that its doctrines are intended to embody.[42] People come to the law seeking the tolerance and pluralism that law has trained them to value and expect, and that they have not found in local morality or their traditionally arranged institutions.[43]

Sometimes the self that is found, however, is too strongly defined, and therefore confined, by the reductive qualities of the law. Sometimes "the discourses of the courthouse continue to

---

[36] TOTAL JUSTICE, *supra* note 1, at 84-91.

[37] As Patricia Williams describes the process of simultaneous distancing and self-empowerment: "[T]he experience of rights-assertion has been one of both solidarity and freedom, or the empowerment of an internal and very personal sort; it has been a process of finding the self." Williams, *supra* note 26, at 414. *See also* Merry, *supra* note 27, at 178; Alan Wolfe, WHOSE KEEPER? SOCIAL SCIENCE AND MORAL OBLIGATION 1-5 (1991); Cf. TOTAL JUSTICE, *supra* note 1, at 89; Roberto M. Unger, KNOWLEDGE AND POLITICS 55-59 (1975); Mark V. Tushnet, *Following the Rules Laid Down: A Critique of Interpretivism and Neutral Principles,* 96 HARVARD LAW REVIEW 781, 783-86 (1983).

[38] Merry, *supra* note 27, at 52-54.

[39] Id. at 38-47.

[40] Id. at 54-59.

[41] Id. at 181.

[42] Id. at 172-182.

[43] Id. at 182.

constrain and restrict the way these problems are understood."[44] This tendency may be more pronounced where the liberated individual has challenged a particular hierarchy or rejected a particular cultural feature.[45] In such cases, the person seeks greater freedom, but does not necessarily want the Enlightenment-defined self that the law has on offer. In contrast are cases of discrimination, in which people invoke the law so as better to join the prevailing majority culture that has unfairly excluded them. In those cases, the law is being invoked because the individual seeks greater opportunity to thrive within the Enlightenment values and identities that are consistent with U/I/A legal methods. In either case, however, how can the law provide escape for a person from confining social relationships without jeopardizing ties that the person wishes to preserve? How can the law avoid burdening a litigant with unwanted cultural baggage? Does the law require a person to take on new personal qualities as the cost of invoking legal procedures? And should the law ever hesitate to permit individual escape, for fear of destabilizing a larger culture from which one litigant seeks rescue?

Some answers are easy. If the relational features that come before the law entail enslavement, physical harm or psychological damage, we should not fear cultural disruption. Where, for example, women are in abusive marital relationships without effective help from counseling services, other family members or the church, the law should provide an easy and effective means of protection or escape. Similarly, where discrimination in the workplace disadvantages members of minority groups, the law should not hesitate to intrude in the name of fairness.

Yet fairness should not prevail absolutely over preservation, at least not unless we are willing to accept the eventual prospect of a social life which is saturated with legal regulations. Preservation of sustained relationships, even those rooted in hierarchy or non-democratic authority, should have *some* hold on us for the sake of history or diversity or because the overall relationship comprises an aspect of humanity without which we would not be whole.

Most parents, for example, would not want to relinquish authority over their children, or want to accept structures of due process. Such resistance stems (normally) not from a love of power, but from a love for the child. Similarly, many physicians sincerely consider judicial control over medical/ethical issues to intrude not only into professional judgment, but to intrude also into the physician relationship with patients and their families. Neither does someone with responsibility within an organization easily embrace the formalizing of interactions with employees. Here the motives may certainly be mixed, but might well include that the employer would rather deal with workers on an individual, personal level.

---

[44] Id. at 181. *Accord*, Austin Sarat and Thomas R. Kearns, *Editorial Introduction, in* IDENTITIES, POLITICS, AND RIGHTS 1, 7-8 (Austin Sarat and Thomas R. Kearns, eds. 1995).

[45] *See* Merry, *supra* note 27, at 173.

Having stated the tension it may be somewhat relaxed. What we should value are not traditional structures for their own sake, but rather the bonds that people form and have always formed with those they love or respect. The goals of law should be expanded to enable these bonds rather than merely to protect alternative patterns of authority. The separation of legal from nonlegal relationships has insulated legal logic from the ravages of experience, but it has also cost law some influence over the human world. In other words, law has not influenced sustained relationships as it might have, had the law proceeded historically from a broader, more relational vision. Both law and relationships would benefit by a greater blending between the legal values of fairness and equality and the relational values of respect, love, tenderness, and personal concern.

Even where preservation is chosen, therefore, unfairness within the traditional structures of sustained relationships might gradually soften by encountering a less presumptuous and directive legal system. No blanket rules can be stated to guide the difficult choices of preservation versus fairness; but it should be recognized that in principle there is room in the law for deference to alternative institutions.

4. Opening Up Legal Truth

By expanding legal truth we can start to break any mutually self-destructive cycle that may be ongoing between legal and nonlegal institutions. By converging the mentalities of law and sustained relationships, the institutions of both may be strengthened. If law can no longer stand for the irrelevance of trustworthiness, then trust becomes indispensable to human relationships. If law can shape its outcomes to enhance rather than marginalize relational settings, then the self-healing of those relationships may flourish.

I offer three broad suggestions for making a start on these goals. First, the law should more strongly respect relational self-healing, within the boundaries of acceptable unfairness. Second, the law should listen openly to needs as well as rights. Finally, the law should consciously provide moral education by its processes and in its outcomes.

a. Respect the Self-healing Processes

The first conclusion was detailed above: The law should more strongly facilitate problem solving within the confines of sustained relationships. As concluded, we must understand the tension between preservation and unfairness and maintain the balance on a case by case basis. A broader law can never close its ears to unfairness, yet it must also continue to determine what human irrationalities are harmless, or have such vital cultural implications that they should not be intruded upon.

Legal self-limitation has another dimension, however, that comes into play even when the law has determined it must intrude into relational conflicts. If the law broadens its vision of truth, accepting more contextual narratives within legal processes, then traditional decision-making within the relationship will be less impaired. Personalistic conflict management, in other words, can be invigorated by an assurance that in applying its own more universal standard the law will nonetheless listen to the dispute with concern for traditional structures.

b. Listen to Needs as Well as Rights[46]

The protection of personal rights by the law has unquestionably contributed to a more open, tolerant, just and generally healthier society. For law to repudiate this role would be retrogressive.[47] Yet the law must not content itself with visions of formal equality; and the relative casualness of the law toward the genuine needs of the poor or the victims of our society is another consequence of the law's limited concept of relevance.[48] Having declared rights and made them universal, the law has felt justified in stopping short of empowering relationships by which the rights might become more genuinely integrated within our culture.

The vision of truth that separates needs and behaviors fails to see the obvious connection between the two: that behavior responds closely to needs and that addressing needs is not only morally responsible, but will lead to greater efficacy in the law. To transcend this separation the law must make itself available to language that is more concrete[49] and more purposeful.[50]

---

[46] For a fine treatment of the treatment of needs and rights in mediation, *see* Ellen Waldman, *Substituting Needs for Rights in Mediation: Therapeutic or Disabling?* 5 PSYCHOLOGY, PUBLIC POLICY, AND LAW 1103 (1999)

[47] Owen Fiss, *Against Settlement*, 93 YALE LAW JOURNAL 1073 (1984).

[48] Perception that sustained relationships may suffer in the hands of the law may also contribute to some feminists' concerns to avoid talking of women's differences in favor of asserting women's rights. In the hands of the judiciary, portrayal of gender differences may cast females into relational stereotypes as victims or domestics that could lead to a further deterioration of their standing. *See* Ann Scales, *The Emergence of Feminist Jurisprudence: An Essay*, 95 YALE LAW JOURNAL 1373, 1394 (1986); Patricia Williams, *Deconstructing Gender*, 87 MICHIGAN LAW REVIEW 797, 813-821 (1989). Quite apart from the plausible reality of these fears, even the perception of legal ham-fistedness does much damage. A historically disadvantaged population should not have to stifle expression of its needs or genuine differences, for fear that their articulation in the legal system will augment the suffering. To channel all advocacy into "rights" terminology may be the most effective strategy under the strictures of the current legal system. Nonetheless, a legal system open to broader dialogue could lead to a different, more successful, and more educational style of addressing the oppression.

[49] Marie Ashe, *Zig-Zag Stitching and the Seamless Webb: Thoughts on 'Reproduction' and the Law*, 13 NOVA LAW REVIEW 356 (1989); Scales, *supra* note 48, at 1388.

[50] *See* West, *supra* note 28, at 1501-02; Scales, *supra* note 48, at 1399-1403.

5. Provide Moral Leadership

Opening the law to a broader sense of humanity requires us to know what it means to be human, with full recognition that our responses, socially and legally, will affect those meanings. Perhaps this is what law fears: A humanity that provides inadequate protection against prejudice, evil, and irrationality. That is why, as Judith Shklar has argued, our sense of injustice must be awakened.[51] A more broadly relational law could be instrumental in that process. Justice has been regarded as narrowly as truth, being achieved wherever disturbances to the status quo are rectified.[52] When justice so defined is institutionalized by legal formality, our sense of injustice withers. We speak of the casualties of social existence as misfortunes rather than injustices, with resignation rather than anger.[53] The law should, says Shklar, provide moral education in the pronouncement of its outcomes, thus invigorating a public sense of injustice.[54]

Providing moral leadership equips law to integrate itself more fully in contemporary culture, by inspiring a renewed sense of responsibility. A moral law attracts our sense of obligation. A law that addresses forthrightly the problems of prejudice and evil not only engenders our respect, but helps us deal with evil more courageously, among ourselves.

E. Conclusion

Legal truth can be opened through better listening, more empathy, and a willingness to measure consistency by standards of social sensitivity as well as by doctrinal integrity. These traits reside within every judge and can be emphasized through our encouragement.

If these suggestions of this Chapter seem risky, we should ask what it is we fear. Is it a submergence of human rights to unreflective, ascribed authority? That fear is legitimate, and, as admitted above, leads to painful decisions that can be faced directly. If instead we fear a law on which we somehow lose our grasp, a law that comes to assert moral and cultural imperatives beyond our tinkering, then we must reexamine our need to dominate and control.

To fear a more human law is to perpetuate our social engineering, however unpredictable in its own consequences and however thin the reality of the democratic theory on which it rests. It is also to intensify the conflicts between our personal and public selves in which neither humanity nor citizenship are adequately defined or valued. By opening legal truth we unfold a more integrated culture, one in which our human and legal conflicts can speak in dialects that are

---

[51] *See generally* Shklar, *supra* note 20.

[52] Id., at 17-19.

[53] Id., at 1-14, 21, 83.

[54] *See* id., at 20-28, 88-89.

closer to one another. To work toward a broader vision of legal truth is to acknowledge how brief is the authority in which we have dressed and, sometimes, how oddly it fits.

CHAPTER XX (Janet Weinstein, Linda Morton, and Amy D. Ronner)
THE "HOW" OF U/I/A: Creativity, Insight, and Counseling

This Chapter is comprised of two parts that, in different ways, explore skills that are emphasized in the U/I/A approaches to law. In the first part, Janet Weinstein and Linda Morton examine the nature of creative thinking and how it may be developed among individuals and within legal education. Their work below is excerpted and adapted from an article entitled *Stuck in a Rut: The Role of Creative Thinking in Problem Solving and Legal Education*, 9 CLINICAL L. REV. 835 (2003). Professors Weinstein and Morton valuably describe a variety of methods for fostering creativity. These techniques enable problem solvers to examine and understand problems from multiple, diverse perspectives. The goal is to find insight and deeper understanding of the facts and their possible resolution.

The most important source in comprehending and addressing a problem is typically the problem holder or client. Sometimes, however, the client does not herself have full access to the facts–either literally or psychologically. In those cases the attorney must be able to prompt an awareness of what information is material, and help the client access that information. The techniques described by Weinstein and Morton can help with diagnosis of a problem (and related informational needs) as well as its possible solution.

Part Two of this Chapter is taken from presentations made by Amy Ronner at the International Academy of Law and Mental Health Conference in Padua Italy in 2007 and at the John Jay College of Criminal Justice: International Conference of Justice and Policing in Diverse Societies in San Juan, Puerto Rico, and based on her article *Dostoyevsky and The Therapeutic Jurisprudence Confession*, 40 JOHN MARSHALL LAW REVIEW 41 (2006).

Ronner gains insight into the protagonist of a classic work of literature, Rodion Roskolnikov in Dostoyevsky's CRIME AND PUNISHMENT. For decades literary scholars have puzzled over the motivations for this character's homicide and subsequent confession. By re-examining the facts in a free, "un-rutted" way, Ronner uses both creativity and psychological insight to advance a new hypothesis about Roskolnikov's action. Dostoyevsky's story and the character of Sonya, who hears Roskolnikov's confession, are offered as lessons in Therapeutic Jurisprudence: how criminal defense lawyers may deepen their understanding and help for clients.

CREATIVE THINKING IN LEGAL PROBLEM SOLVING[1]

Janet Weinstein[2] and Linda Morton[3]

Creative thinking is essential to problem-solving. And since problem solving is essential to lawyering, legal professionals should strive to develop more creative thinking. That raises questions, however: What exactly is creative thinking? Can people actually improve those capabilities, or are they instead consigned permanently to the level of creativity with which they were born? Thankfully, creative thinking is a skill that can be improved through practice and understanding.

1. Creative Thinking Defined

"Creative thinking is the generation of ideas (a) that are unusual, or original, and (b) that satisfy some standard of value."[4] It is an exploratory activity, distinct from notions like "artistry." As behavioral psychologist Robert Epstein explains, every individual gradually builds up patterns of behaviors to cope with problems or attain goals.[5] Novel behavior, or creativity, arises when those existing repertoires of behavior are in competition with one another.[6] Whenever we are forced to use our existing tools in a different way, or analyze which of two possible tools should be used for a new purpose, we are generating creativity.

Creativity helps us grow, and take more satisfaction from our social and professional lives. Exposure to problems outside of our comfort zone can force us to expand our behavioral

---

[1] This Chapter is an abridgment and adaptation of an earlier article entitled *Stuck in a Rut: The Role of Creative Thinking in Problem Solving and Legal Education*, 9 CLINICAL LAW REVIEW 835 (2003).

[2] Professor of Law, California Western School of Law.

[3] Professor of Law, California Western School of Law.

[4] Barry F. Anderson, THE COMPLETE THINKER 123 (1980). For example, to say that half of 8 is 4 satisfies our values, but is not unusual; half of 8 is 100 is unusual, but does not satisfy our values. However, to say that half of 8 is 0 (cut horizontally) or 3 (cut vertically) satisfies both standards of originality and value. Id.

[5] Robert Epstein, CREATIVITY GAMES FOR TRAINERS: A HANDBOOK OF GROUP ACTIVITIES FOR JUMPSTARTING WORKPLACE CREATIVITY 14 (1996)

[6] Id., at 15.

repertoire, leaving us with stronger flexibility and imagination as we next encounter new problems. Even reading interdisciplinary materials can be helpful, training us to maintain fluidity of perception and openness to multiple perspectives.[7] This re-framing may be termed "lateral,"[8] "divergent,"[9] or "whole-brain"[10] thinking. All seem to agree, however, that creative thinking is not limited by genetics, and can be developed over time. Creative thinking is a learned process by which we first understand, and then transcend, the familiar patterns of our cognition and behaviors. Creative thinking helps us climb out of the mental ruts in which we often find ourselves stuck.

2. Resources and Techniques for Creative Thinking

Social psychologists Robert J. Sternberg and Todd I. Lubart speak of six resources for creative thinking: Intelligence; knowledge; intellectual style; personality; motivation; and environment.[11] Intelligence permits us the flexibility to recognize problems in different ways–essentially, to re-define a problem.[12] Knowledge, similarly, is a prerequisite for creativity:[13] one must understand the materials or tools available. Intellectual style is the ability to use one's abilities in a particular manner.[14] This could be "executive," applying existing rules toward some goal, for example; or "evaluative," making judgments based on those rules. Creative thinking, however, tends to be progressive and "legislative," in which people invent their own rules or procedures.[15]

---

[7] Edward De Bono, SERIOUS CREATIVITY: USING THE POWER OF LATERAL THINKING TO CREATE NEW IDEAS 62 (1992).

[8] Id., at 15, 54-55.

[9] J.P. Guilford, *Creativity Research: Past, Present, and Future–Part One: The 1950 Presidential Address to the American Psychological Association,* in FRONTIERS OF CREATIVITY RESEARCH: BEYOND THE BASICS 41-44 (Scott Isaksen, ed. 1987)

[10] Stephen D. Eiffert, CROSS-TRAIN YOUR BRAIN 59-60 (1999).

[11] R. J. Sternberg and T. I. Lubart, *An Investment Theory of Creativity and Its Development,* 34 HUMAN DEVELOPMENT 1-31 (1991).

[12] Id., at 6-8.

[13] Id., at 9-10.

[14] Id., at 11-13.

[15] Id.

As to personality, creative thinkers tend to be tenacious, optimistic, principled, tolerant of ambiguity, and willing sometimes to fail.[16] They also are more internally motivated and innately curious, rather than dependent on external recognition.[17] Finally, the setting or environment can be either stifling or enabling of creative thought.[18] Homogeneity of culture, strong authority, and group norms can suppress creativity, while diversity, informality, and tolerance are stimulating.

Psychologist Abraham Maslow and others have suggested a two stage model of creativity.[19] The first stage involves unfettered, non-judgmental inspiration, permitting even random thoughts.[20] The second stage is disciplined and systematic implementation.[21] Legal training, unfortunately, tends to emphasize the second stage and ignore the free-roaming nature of the first stage of creativity.[22]

A variety of methods, however, can be employed to stimulate stronger "first-stage" processing, some of which are commonplace. "Insight," for example, is fostered when the creative thinker reexamines information that did not seem immediately relevant, or that has previously been ignored.[23] Analogies and metaphors also assist imagination, by mentally rearranging parts of problems and seeing them in different but similar forms.

Other methods seek Maslow's two stage process more consciously. "Brainstorming" is a group process that that fosters creativity. It combines several persons' thought to arrive at a solution by first asking the participants to generate multiple alternatives or dimensions to a problem *without evaluation.* Only after a complete set of possible ideas has been generated will the group apply discipline to the ideas by analyzing their relative merits.

---

[16] Id., at 13-14; Anderson, *supra* note 4, at 14.

[17] Sternberg and Lubart, *supra* note 11, at 14–16.

[18] Id., at 16-17.

[19] Described in David R. Culp, *Law School: A Mortuary for Poets and Moral Reason,* 16 CAMPBELL LAW REVIEW 61, 64-65 (1994).

[20] Id., at 65.

[21] Id.

[22] Id., at 66.

[23] Paul E. Plsek, CREATIVITY, INNOVATION, AND QUALITY 36 (1997).

Another technique is to change the emphasis of a problem, by looking at it from a different angle or perspective.[24] Or, one can consciously change the focus of one's attention. A clever way to achieve this is through random word association. In random word prompts, a word is considered that is not normally associated with the problem at hand.[25] One can choose a word at random from a dictionary, and then imagine any possible connections the random word could have to the actual problem. New aspects of the problem may suddenly become visible, or significant where they previously were not.

A variant on the random word association method is to associate the problem with various adjectives, which can aid in shifting the context in which the problem is viewed.[26] The brainstormers could choose adjectives to force thinking about the problem as "grand," "modest," "exciting," or "controversial."

"Word-clustering" or "mind-mapping" is related to random word association.[27] Using this method, the problem solvers create a variety of different directions for the problem as words come to mind. For example, if the problem were "child care," it would be written in the middle of a piece of paper. One word path might begin with "parent," and extend to "work hours," then "job site," then "day care," then "initiate on-site day care center job benefit." A different direction could be "non-parent," then "part- time," then "flexible," then "students," then "student child-minders."

"Visualization"[28] is yet another technique for strengthening Maslow's "first-stage" thinking. One can record an actual environment photographically, looking at it to spawn ideas of how the picture might be altered, or one can simply use one's imagination to examine a variety of alternative scenarios. An ideal, completed project could be visualized, or its opposite: the end game of current pathological trends. Or the exaggeration of one aspect of a problem can be played out mentally, all with the goal of seeing the problem from different perspectives, or repeatedly re-framing the problem. Visualization can also be prompted by surrounding an object representing the problem with a variety of other objects.[29] Different associations or environments may stimulate new connections and possible solutions.

---

[24] Id., at 59.

[25] Id., at 42, 247-267.

[26] Id., at 54.

[27] Eiffert, *supra* note 10, at 74.

[28] Plsek, *supra* note 23, discusses this idea using the terminology "cinematics" at 247-67.

[29] Epstein, *supra* note 5, at 51-60.

"Incubation/relaxation" is a technique described by Edward DeBono as "the creative pause."[30] Periodically one should disengage one's attention from a problem to do something different, so as to let the possible solutions incubate. The goal is to allow the ideas to "play" in order to permit space for new pathways to appear.[31] Stephen Eiffert's work on right/left brain hemispheres supports the usefulness of this technique. Playfulness, says Eiffert, helps to stimulate the right hemisphere, which is the site of pattern recognition.[32]

3. Conclusion

Creative thinking in a legal context requires understanding the complexity of many of the problems that clients bring to lawyers. Sadly, creative thinking is not encouraged by legal education. That is beginning to change, however. Law school courses that integrate skills, ethics and doctrine rearrange the traditional environment so as to stimulate the new pathways of thought that are necessary to creative thought. As important are the diverse intellectual styles that may be offered in these courses. Law school pedagogy traditionally focuses more on the executive (rule implementation) or judicial (evaluative) styles than the legislative, in which new procedures and perspectives are imagined. By paying more attention to the importance of creative thinking in lawyers, and how it may be developed, the legal system itself may eventually be reformed even as lawyers and their clients benefit from better problem solving.

---

[30] DeBono, *supra* note 7, at 86.

[31] Eiffert, *supra* note 10, at 70-74.

[32] Id., at 55-57.

B. Confession and Insight

DOSTOYEVSKY AND THE THERAPEUTIC JURISPRUDENCE CONFESSION

Amy D. Ronner[33]

Introduction

In Dostoyevsky's *Crime and Punishment*, Rodion Raskolnikov murders an old woman, a money lender:

> At that point, with all his might, he landed her another blow, and another, each time with the butt and each time on the crown of the head. The blood gushed out as from an upturned glass and her body collapsed backwards. He stepped back, allowed her to fall and all at once bent down over her face: she was dead. Her eyes were goggling out of her head as though she might burst from it, while her forehead and all the rest of her features were crumpled and distorted in a convulsive spasm.

When the victim's step-sister unexpectedly intrudes, Raskolnikov, again wielding his axe, makes it a double murder and absconds with valuables. About twelve days later, Raskolnikov turns himself in and confesses to the police. Raskolnikov is tried, convicted and sentenced to eight years of penal servitude in Siberia.

...

Therapeutic Jurisprudence can shed new light on the role of confessions. Let's face it. One thing indelibly ingrained in the minds of the more traditional criminal defense practitioners is that their main job is about keeping the client out of jail or at least doing reasonable damage control by obtaining the best possible sentence. And this is all fine. Of course, others who define themselves as defense lawyers with a broader calling also equate their mission with the protection of constitutional rights. Such goals are also valid and commendable. But my point is that this whole school of thought can tend to bring with it a certain mindset about client confessions.

---

[33] Professor of Law, St. Thomas University School of Law. J.D., 1985, University of Miami; Ph.D. (English Language and Literature), 1980, University of Michigan; M.A., 1976, University of Michigan; B.A., 1975, Beloit College. Before becoming a lawyer, Professor Ronner taught literature at the University of Michigan and the University of Miami.

The traditional criminal defense attorney has been trained to treat client confession as a Pandora's box that should remain hermetically sealed at all costs.[34] When it comes to confession, the client is hushed and good defense work means accomplishing such silencing as swiftly and efficiently as possible. Of course, there are reasons for this and my article deals with them at greater length. But, to put it succinctly, aside from the prosecution's use of confession, defense attorneys sometimes eschew the client's story becomes it hurls them into a whole rat's nest of issues involving ethics and professional responsibility. ...

Today I am going to suggest that what is quite commonplace - - namely, defense counsel's silencing of even the mere whisper of a confession - - oppugns some core tenets of therapeutic lawyering with its emphasis on voice, validation, and voluntary participation. In essence, what transpires in the traditional defense world is a lawyer despotically imposing choices on clients and blocking their voices and killing their stories. For some clients (AND I EMPHASIZE - - NOT ALL CLIENTS), the defense counsel confession-taboo can unwittingly ruin a human life by obstructing what can in certain circumstances be a rare and redemptive option.

Raskolnikov's Obsessive Need to Confess

Let us now return to Raskolnikov. I acknowledge that while *Crime and Punishment* entails a brutal murder of two women, the real focus of the novel is not on the crime itself. Rather, the focus is on the aftermath, on Raskolnikov's psychological anguish and on what eventually preempts all else - - the murderer's need, or rather obsessive compulsion, to confess. Raskolnikov probably could have escaped detection and gotten away with murder, but it is Raskolnikov himself who sabotages that possibility. There is just something that propels Raskolnikov to do himself in, to re-visit the crime scene, make incriminating insinuations to a police clerk in a bar, and bring himself to the attention of and even tease Porfiry Petrovich, who is the formidable examining magistrate assigned to the case.

Just about every commentator accepts what is seductively basic: namely, that Raskolnikov needs to confess because he has committed a crime. They have, however, put the cart before the horse. The real truth and I believe the kernel of Dostoyevsky's wisdom is that Raskolnikov commits the crime because he needs to confess. *But Raskolnikov's problem before the murder is that any confession he might make would be ethereally devoid of content. So, in essence, Raskolnikov murders to fill his confession with substance.* This is the reason why it is virtually impossible to find in CRIME AND PUNISHMENT a plausible motive for Raskolnikov's brutal act.

---

[34] For the discussion of the mindset of the traditional criminal defense attorney with respect to confession, I am indebted to an excellent article, Robert F. Cochran, *Crime, Confession, And the Counsel-At-Law: Lessons From Dostoyevsky*, 35 HOUSTON LAW REVIEW 327 (1998).

There are numerous articles in which scholars ask why Raskolnikov killed and have answered that question by simply grabbing one of Raskolnikov's own spurious rationalizations for his own crime. And there are essentially five theories here and I will briefly summarize them.

One, Raskolnikov murders Alyona for personal reasons: that is, he simply hates her. But if you read closely, Raskolnikov has no emotional investment in his victim whatsoever. She is more of a thing of neutral valence - - a non-person.

Two, it has been suggested that Raskolnikov kills Alyona because he equates her with all of the oppressive adversity in his life. But why does Raskolnikov decide to bludgeon *her* to death with an axe when there are all sorts of St. Peterburg specimens who are just as culpable and just as ripe for execution?

Three, there is a related theory, one in which the Freud folks seem quite smitten. They attribute the murder to Raskolnikov's tortured feelings towards his mother. And yes, undeniably Raskolnikov loves and abhors his mother. Yes, he unconsciously cordons his mother to that wicked facet of himself, but Alyona is not the only conceivable maternal surrogate. *Crime and Punishment* is chock full of mothers, like the landlady, the landlady's maid, Sonya, Raskolnikov's sister, Sonya's step mother and on and on. Why didn't Raskolnikov just go on a rampage and axe all of the mommies in the book?

Four, another putative motive assigned to impoverished Raskolnikov is monetary. In fact, Raskolnikov even tries to persuade himself that murder, along with robbery, is a logical economic escape hatch for himself and his family. But look at Raskolnikov's behavior throughout the entire novel. To say that Raskolnikov is not materialist is technically a litotes: one of the few consistent things we can say about the supposedly destitute scholar is that whenever he does get his hands on a few coins, he almost instantly gives them away to some needy subject or simply tosses them into the gutter. And after the murder, Raskolnikov has no interest in the spoils of the robbery. He hides the purse and valuables under a brick and never bothers to retrieve them. And, at his trial, it comes out that Raskolnikov can't even remember the details of the booty or what he actually stole.

Five, another supposed motive for the crime is one that Raskolnikov himself espoused in an article that kind of prefigures Nietzsche. Raskolnikov theorized that there are two kinds of people in the world: while the ordinary folk have to obey the laws, the superior caste has a perfect right to commit all sort of crimes. For the elite, the law simply does not apply. And Porfiry, the examining magistrate, playfully suggests to Raskolnikov that he committed a crime to prove that he was one of those superb, extraordinary Napoleonic men. But all of this is really hogwash. In the novel, Raskolnikov reveals on several occasions that he does not truly believe in his own thesis and he even concedes this to Sonya, the prostitute-angel that ultimately hears his confession.

Why does Raskolnikov kill? If you read the novel closely (and Dostoyevsky deserves that surely), you can detect that even before the crime, Raskolnikov desperately needs to come clean. He plans and commits a crime to secure content for a confession that will serve as a precursor to punishment and eventually to his own repentance. Raskolnikov's behavior after the crime is all directed toward getting caught, coming clean, and being reborn.

Dostoyevsky's Therapeutic Message

Throughout most of the novel, Raskolnikov and Porfiry, the examining magistrate, engage in a cat-and-mouse game. After Porfiry's final interview with Raskolnikov, he retreats, looking hunched and diminished. Although hopeful that Raskolnikov will turn himself in, "discharge the duty the justice requires, and ultimately let life begin anew," the examining magistrate sadly acquiesces in his own limitations. He knows that neither he nor any law enforcement agent can be the ones that can bring a true therapeutic triumph to fruition. He accepts that he, as the inquisitorial officer, will always be the adversary and that the completion of the real crowning accomplishment is properly delegated to someone else. In real life, that potential delegate is defense counsel. But in the world of CRIME AND PUNISHMENT, the healer, the one that hears the therapeutic confession, is Sonya. ... Sonya somehow has imbibed the wisdom that listening, along with empathy, acceptance, and encouragement can work miracles - - can raise a soul from the dead.

In therapeutic jurisprudence, the attorney is key. It is she or he who can help give clients that sense of voice, validation, and voluntary participation. In CRIME AND PUNISHMENT, Sonya, a non-lawyer, enacts the therapeutic role for Raskolnikov. Sonya uses reflective listening to give Raskolnikov voice and validation. It is Sonya who helps to effectuate Raskolnikov's participatory interests, encourages what he so desperately needs - - the voluntary act of confession - - and leads him to accept responsibility for his own actions. ...

Professor Wexler, analyzing the rehabilitative role of the criminal defense lawyer, explains that the therapeutic switch does not just shut off with a confession or a conviction or a sentence. For a client facing incarceration, the criminal lawyer should engage in dialogue about the future. As Professor Wexler suggests, the relationship between attorney and client is ongoing and even during and after incarceration, there are therapeutic opportunities, like the expected or hoped-for release or conditional release date or assisting the process of re-entry and readjustment.

Significantly, Sonya's service as therapeutic agent is ongoing and literally continues even after Raskolnikov is convicted and sent to Siberia. It is she that helps transform confession into a celebrated event and helps Raskolnikov make sense of his sentence. As both Porfiry, Sonya, and Dostoyevsky understand, confession is not just a prosecutorial tool for closing a crime file, but is and can be the very catalyst to healing and rehabilitation. As such, Raskolnikov's voluntary therapeutic confession instigates what Dostoyevsky calls a "new story of a man's gradual renewal, his gradual rebirth, his gradual transition from one world to another." Criminal defense attorneys can surely cultivate "Sonyaesque" skills, which can induce positive change and healing.

CHAPTER XXI (Michael J. Weaver and Robert G. Knaier)
THE "HOW" OF U/I/A: In-House Counsel

Keeping it In-House:
Guidance to General Counsel on Staying Out of Court[*]

Michael J. Weaver, Esq.[††]
Robert G. Knaier, Esq.[‡]
Latham & Watkins LLP

This article discusses ways for in-house counsel to avoid litigation. Although "[i]t is as impossible for a lawyer to wish men out of litigation as for a physician to wish them in health,"[1] no one should readily embrace loss of control of his or her own affairs by placing them in the hands of the courts. While disputes are common – often unavoidable – and lawsuits may otherwise be "a cost of doing business," careful planning and implementation of procedures can often mitigate if not eliminate the risk litigation offers to both plaintiffs and defendants. In truth, much of litigation avoidance consists simply in the dispassionate and consistent application of

---

[*] This article is excerpted from *Litigation Avoidance and Prevention*, in BUSINESS AND COMMERCIAL LITIGATION IN FEDERAL COURTS, Second Edition (Robert L. Haig, ed.) (Thomson West & ABA Section of Litigation 2005) and is reprinted with the permission of Thomson Reuters. Copyright © 2005. To order this publication, please visit http://www.west.thomson.com or call 1-800-344-5009. This article, as excerpted, first appeared in the Association of Corporate Counsel of America's ("ACCA") newsletter, *Focus on the San Diego Chapter*, on September 26, 2005. It is reprinted with ACCA's permission. This article expresses the opinions of the authors and should not be construed as legal advice.

[††] Mr. Weaver is a litigation partner in the San Diego office of Latham & Watkins LLP. In a professional career spanning more than 35 years, he has specialized in complex business litigation and trial practice. Mr. Weaver lectures frequently to various professional organizations. He is a Fellow in the American College of Trial Lawyers, a member of the Executive Committee and a Master of the Bench of the Inn, American Inns of Court, Louis M. Welsh Chapter, and was a founding member of the Board of Governors of the San Diego Association of Business Trial Lawyers.

[‡] Mr. Knaier is an associate with the San Diego office of Latham & Watkins LLP. He has significant experience in mass tort litigation, environmental litigation, commercial litigation, and appellate practice, and he is a member of several professional organizations, including the Association of Business Trial Lawyers and the Hon. William Enright American Inn of Court. He received his B.A. from the University of California, San Diego in 1999 (*summa cum laude*) and his J.D. from Cornell Law School in 2003 (*magna cum laude*). Prior to joining Latham & Watkins, Mr. Knaier clerked for the Honorable Richard C. Wesley of the United States Court of Appeals for the Second Circuit.

[1] Jeremy Bentham, English solicitor and social philosopher, 1748-1832.

common sense and sound business practices. Below, we briefly outline some of these practices; apply them to a few specific areas of concern, namely, disputes revolving around employment matters, potential claims under the Americans with Disabilities Act, and securities issues; and conclude with observations on the economics of settlement.

I. Common Sense and Sound Business Practices

Disputes often arise, and indeed result in litigation, for reasons that could have been prevented. For example, the way you manage your business conduct can affect your risk of becoming involved in a lawsuit. The following reminders should help avoid problems from the start:

- Conduct your business in a lawful *and* reasonable manner. It is not enough to conduct yourself within the literal bounds of the law. You must also abide by whatever norms apply to the industry with which you are involved.
- Know who you are dealing with. Discover what you can about the background, litigiousness, and ethics of individuals with whom you may have to interact.
- Address legal issues early, and look for early opportunities to resolve them. Make sure the lawyers involved have experience in the relevant subject-matter; seek the advice of outside-counsel if necessary. This will increase the likelihood that a matter can be resolved at the earliest stage possible.
- Communicate truthfully and effectively. Avoid the temptation to deal in half-truths, be prompt in responding to correspondence, and be on your best behavior even in "internal" communications. Purge writings of ambiguity and vagueness. If a dispute arises, be willing to discuss the matter.
- Have reasonable expectations. If you cannot, rely on someone who can; a dispassionate third party can prevent you from letting your emotions get the best of you and pursuing a dispute into litigation.

While conducting yourself in a lawful and reasonable manner can lessen the likelihood of becoming involved in litigation, it may be of little help if your business is in disarray. Proper business organization can better your chances of preventing or avoiding litigation. To this end:

- Keep adequate records and have a meaningful document retention policy. This will not only keep a business running smoothly, but also help it stay in compliance with the law. By maintaining both paper *and* electronic records, businesses can minimize the risk of liability in such arenas as discrimination and securities litigation.
- Maintain good attorney-client relations. Integrating yourself in your company's or client's goals and strategies can help you identify problems before they arise.
- See that managers and employees are well-trained. This will minimize the likelihood of litigation that accompanies a failing business as well as keep lines of communication open, thereby reducing the risk of workplace problems festering into lawsuits.

- Enforce sound internal policies and procedures. Having such policies, and ensuring that people are aware of them, can minimize the chances of a number of different kinds of lawsuits, including employee grievances, shareholder actions, and SEC proceedings.
- Let officers and directors do their jobs. Involving board members in a matter may provide a level of dispassionate professionalism needed to prevent a problem from becoming a lawsuit.

Finally, business and commercial litigation often revolves around one or more agreements entered into long before a dispute arises. Whether a lawsuit is brought on a theory of breach of contract, tortious interference with contractual relations, fraud, or some other ground, the outcome of such litigation can depend crucially on the language contained in agreements between the parties. The details of an agreement may provide not only the means to *resolve* a dispute, but also the means to *avoid* a dispute. Thus, to ensure that commercial agreements protect against resource-consuming litigation – rather than serve as the source of it – counsel should heed the following advice:

- Get it in writing. Put all agreements in writings that are clear and fully integrated – and then abide by them. Ensuring mutual understanding from the beginning can lower the probability of a later dispute.
- Include provisions designed to avoid or limit litigation. Alternative-dispute mechanisms, "force-majeure" clauses, "notice and opportunity to cure" language, limitations on liability, and cancellation provisions can all protect you against the dangers of litigation.
- Consider forum selection provisions. Carefully considering your preferred forum can be a valuable first step toward preempting an adverse outcome if litigation should arise.
- Consider attorneys' fees provisions. If your adversary is contractually bound to pay all fees and costs involved in bringing suit, he or she may hesitate to take that risk.

II. Specific Areas of Concern

Counsel should keep these basic considerations in mind when dealing with nearly every sort of potential commercial dispute. In the remainder of this article we demonstrate how common sense and sound business practices can minimize the risk of litigation in a few particular areas of concern.

A. Employment Disputes

Numerous avenues to litigation exist in the world of employment law. The following discussion offers practical guidance on how common sense and forethought can help prevent minor disputes from becoming costly lawsuits.

Knowing who you are dealing with, a topic noted above, is particularly important when the person with whom you are dealing is a potential employee. Accordingly, counsel should consider advising clients to screen unfit applicants through background checks. Remember that employees are people in whom your client or company places a tremendous amount of trust. They are intimately involved in the business. They may have access to sensitive and valuable information about your client. Your client may, for example, have a particular concern about guarding its intellectual property. If so, it would be well-advised to find out as much as it can about a prospective employee, rather than placing access to the lifeblood of the company in the hands of a stranger.[2]

When dealing with current employees, one way to help prevent minor disputes from becoming fodder for lawsuits is to deal with those disputes honestly and directly, as soon as they arise. But in a large business doing so will require that managers and supervisors – those closest to employees and issues that arise on a daily basis – be properly trained. Managers and supervisors should realize that they are a crucial link between a business owner and his or her employees, and that they need to not only take responsibility for addressing minor problems, but must also make you, as counsel, aware of more serious problems. To that end, you should advise your client to consider investing in an experienced human resources manager; such a person will know how to recruit and train people to be effective supervisors.

Dealing with disputes honestly and directly also involves prompt investigation of employee complaints. Whether a complaint implicates civil rights concerns, such as those arising under the Americans with Disabilities Act, or labor grievances under such provisions as the National Labor Relations Act, early investigation will help to ensure that you have an accurate understanding of the facts. Without such an understanding, you may not properly be able to address meritorious complaints – or prevent unmeritorious ones from becoming a thorn in your side. Either way, you risk the possibility that a problem which could have been easily remedied will find its way into a federal courtroom.

At a minimum clients should document all disputes with employees, whether those disputes are employee complaints or your client's own concerns about employee performance. Your client may ultimately find itself in the position of having to fire an employee with whom it has had disagreements. To prevent a misunderstanding, you should be able to demonstrate your client's reasoning through documentation. Indeed, under federal provisions designed to protect so-called "whistleblowers,"[3] the ability of a publicly-traded company to prevent litigation in a

---

[2] For a list of tools available to employers, see Linda L. Graff, BEYOND POLICE CHECKS: THE DEFINITIVE VOLUNTEER AND EMPLOYEE SCREENING GUIDEBOOK (1999). The internet has expanded the availability of inexpensive background checks, including use of the free search engine Google. *See* Jason Tuohey, *Who's Googling You*, P.C. WORLD, 12/3/04, *available at* http://www.pcworld.com/news/article/0,aid,118779,00.asp (citing a poll which shows that one quarter of respondents had used the free search engine to find information on co-workers, prospective employers, or prospective employees).

[3] *See* 18 U.S.C. § 1514A.

United States District Court may depend on the facts it can muster to demonstrate that it had good reason to discipline or terminate an employee.[4]

Finally, clear lines of communication and fair, consistent treatment of employees can help foster mutual understanding of employees' rights and obligations. If employment is "at will," take steps to ensure that employees understand what that means. When an employee knows to what he or she is and is not entitled *before* a dispute arises, that employee is less likely to misconstrue those entitlements later – and thus less likely to bring suit based on that misunderstanding. One way to ensure that employees have all the information they need is to draft clear policies regarding entitlements and obligations of both employer and employee, and to include these policies in offer letters to prospective employees and employment manuals distributed to current employees.

Once employees are hired, fair and consistent treatment can be key in preventing discontent that could ultimately result in litigation. Progressive discipline policies are one way to demonstrate that employees are being treated fairly. Imposing disciplinary measures proportional to the number and severity of a given employee's transgressions, and doing so in a way that is *consistent* with the treatment of similarly situated employees, can minimize the possibility that a disciplined employee will feel unfairly singled out for unreasonable discipline. Indeed, it can minimize the possibility that you will end up defending against a claim of *discrimination* in federal court.

B. Americans with Disabilities Act

The Americans with Disabilities Act ("ADA")[5] is a "Federal civil rights law that prohibits the exclusion of people with disabilities from everyday activities, such as buying an item at the store, watching a movie in a theater, enjoying a meal at a local restaurant, exercising at the local health club or having the car serviced at a local garage."[6] Thus, discrimination claims can arise in a variety of settings, including employment, public services, and "public accommodations."[7] To state a claim for discrimination, an individual must establish that she has a "disability," and that an employer, public service, or business discriminated against her with respect to that disability.[8]

---

[4] *See* 18 U.S.C. § 1514A(b); 49 U.S.C. § 42121(b)(B)(ii).

[5] 104 Stat. 353, 42 U.S.C. § 12181 et seq.

[6] ADA GUIDE FOR SMALL BUSINESSES, *at* http://www.usdoj.gov/crt/ada/smbustxt.htm.

[7] ADA GUIDE FOR SMALL BUSINESSES, *at* http://www.usdoj.gov/crt/ada/smbustxt.htm "Private businesses that provide goods or services to the public are called public accommodations in the ADA.").

[8] *See Spector v. Norwegian Cruise Line Ltd.*, 125 S. Ct. 2169, 2176 (2005) (describing extent of reasonable steps necessary to accommodate disabled customers).

Generally, lawsuits brought under the ADA revolve around claims that the defendant did not provide a "reasonable accommodation" to assist a disabled plaintiff with such things as the opportunity to work or access to either public facilities or certain private businesses. Accordingly, employers and business owners should make good faith efforts to accommodate disabled employees and customers. Doing so may not only help you avoid litigation, it may also make good business sense. Do not discount the possibility that providing accommodations can foster loyalty among employees and customers – whether disabled or not. In any event, the best way to avoid a lawsuit is to be proactive. If your client has a disabled employee, consider the possibilities of restructuring a job by reallocating or redistributing marginal job functions, establishing part-time or otherwise "flexible" work schedules, obtaining or modifying workplace equipment or devices, permitting the use of accrued leave for necessary treatment, and providing preferential parking.[9]

You should also consider accommodations particularly aimed at assisting the mentally disabled. For example, employee assistance programs can be quite helpful in this regard; providing or subsidizing programs through which employees can address problems at an early stage can reduce the likelihood of those problems becoming unmanageable, and may minimize the possibility that such employees will feel marginalized. As a corollary, when an employee reveals a mental disability, you may wish to consult with a mental health professional regarding the diagnosis and treatment of, and potential accommodations for, that disability.

For disabled customers, consider whether your client has provided reasonable access to its facility. This includes appropriate means of ingress and egress, as well as such things as access to and design of parking spaces, aisles, restrooms, signage, and seating areas.[10] While bringing a business into compliance might be costly, it may very well be less expensive than facing a federal lawsuit – and having to make the accommodations in any event.

Returning to the basic guidance outlined above, open lines of communication can be key to avoiding litigation. But this means more than communicating with those already determined to file suit. If employees or customers express the belief that you have not fulfilled your obligations under the law, listen to them. Engage them in dialogue. Do not be dismissive; the complaint may have merit. And again, if it does, you are better off addressing it early – before it becomes irretrievably drawn into the adversarial process.

Of course, a single person cannot be expected to be aware of and involved in every aspect of a business. Managers and employees must be able to identify and address potential areas of liability. Thus, be certain to train managers on at least the broad outlines of obligations under the

---

[9] The Equal Employment Opportunity Commission has provided easily accessible guidance to employers in order to comply with the ADA. *See* THE ADA: YOUR RESPONSIBILITIES AS AN EMPLOYER, *at* http://www.eeoc.gov/facts/ ada17.html.

[10] *See* U.S. Dep't of Justice, ADA STANDARDS FOR ACCESSIBLE DESIGN, *at* http://www.usdoj.gov/crt/ada/ stdspdf.htm.

ADA. For example, those involved in hiring employees should be cautioned against inquiring about mental or physical disabilities; doing so might raise an inference of discrimination.[11] But managers should also be trained to take proactive steps where appropriate, taking the lead in helping an employee who *requests* help or acting as a liaison between disabled employees and business owners. Similarly, employees should be trained to monitor existing accommodations to ensure they meet the needs of customers, and to listen to and faithfully relay customer concerns to management. The goal should be to create a team that not only takes responsibility at various levels, but also seamlessly communicates up and down the chain of command. Doing so can prevent lawsuits and, perhaps more importantly, foster a transparent and dynamic business atmosphere.

Finally, in litigation over alleged discrimination, what was or was not said or done, to whom it was said or done, who said it or did it, and what was done about it are all crucial facts. Did you ask an employee about his or her disability? Did your client ignore a customer's complaint about access to a restroom? Did your client offer to accommodate an employee's or customer's disability? If you cannot substantiate the answers to such questions, your client may be vulnerable. Thus, keep accurate, thorough records of interactions among management, employees, and customers – and the steps taken in response to those interactions. Indeed, you should encourage your client to adopt policies requiring as much. Document complaints and suggestions. Keep a record not only of whether your client offered to or actually did implement suggested accommodations, but also of those accommodations you deemed unreasonable. If a dispute arises, a careful review of these records may help to convince both sides that it need not or should not escalate to litigation.

C. Securities Issues

On February 14, 2005, NERA Economic Consulting provided its annual report on securities litigation in 2004.[12] Some of the more significant findings of the report include the following:

·   Over a five-year period, the average public corporation faces a **10% probability** that it will face at least one class action lawsuit.

---

[11] *See* THE ADA: YOUR RESPONSIBILITIES AS AN EMPLOYER, *at* http://www.eeoc.gov/facts/ada17.html ("It is unlawful to: ask an applicant whether she is disabled or about the nature or severity of a disability, or to require the applicant to take a medical examination before making a job offer. You can ask an applicant questions about ability to perform job-related functions, as long as the questions are not phrased in terms of a disability. You can also ask an applicant to describe or to demonstrate how, with or without reasonable accommodation, the applicant will perform job-related functions.").

[12] *See* Buckberg, et al., *Recent Trends in Shareholder Class Action Litigation: Bear Market Cases Bring Big Settlements*, NERA Economic Consulting, Feb. 14, 2005.

- Since the Reform Act was passed,[13] the annual likelihood of facing a shareholder class action suit has **increased** by 23%.
- The mean settlement value in 2004 was $27.1 million, 33% higher than 2003's $20.3 million. The increase reflects a subset of extremely high settlements in 2004: of the 119 settlements made last year, the top three (WorldCom, Raytheon and Bristol-Myers Squibb) totaled $3.3 billion (still only slightly higher than Cendant alone); nine were valued at $100 million or more; 16 settlements exceeded $50 million.
- The 2004 median settlement was $5.3 million, down 4% from $5.5 million in 2003, and 12% less than $6.0 million in 2002. Over 70% of settlements were valued at $10 million or less and over 44% of settlements fell under $5 million.
- Cases involving accounting issues, accounting irregularities, or restatements result in 20% higher settlement values on average.
- Larger companies make bigger settlements. For each 1.0% increase in a company's market capitalization on the day after the end of a class period, the typical settlement increases 0.1%. If an issuer is in bankruptcy or has a stock price less than $1 per share on the settlement date, the settlement will be approximately one third lower.[14]

These numbers should motivate anyone to strive to avoid being involved with a securities claim. The following discussion offers guidance on avoiding shareholder suits, and discusses problems specifically arising under the Sarbanes-Oxley Act.

A federal lawsuit brought by shareholders of a public company often includes allegations that the company violated the anti-fraud provision of the Securities and Exchange Act of 1934. The core of an action brought under Rule 10b-5 is an allegation that the company knowingly or recklessly misstated or omitted a material fact.[15] Shareholders often find evidence of scienter in the behavior of the company's officers and directors. In particular, where an officer or director of a public company sells shares of the company shortly before a downturn in the value of those shares, and such trading is uncharacteristic of the officer or director, courts are more likely to

---

[13] 2002 Sarbanes-Oxley Public Company Accounting Reform and Investor Protection Act, Pub. L. No. 107-204 § 804, 116 Stat. 745.

[14] Securities fraud settlements have been escalating for over a decade. *See* Joseph P. Monteleone, TIME IS RIGHT FOR CLAIM-MADE SETTLEMENTS IN SECURITIES FRAUD CLASS ACTIONS, published by National Underwriter Property & Casualty-Risk & Benefits Management (2001) (detailing a three-fold increase in average settlement value from 1995 to 1999). For an updated list of companies settling securities fraud cases, see http://www.lawyersandsettlements.com/search.html?keywords=securities+fraud. In 2005, for example, Citigroup settled a securities case for $208 million, TimeWarner for $510 million, and Morgan Stanley for $41.5 million. *Id.*

[15] *See* 17 C.F.R. § 240.10b-5; *see also Ferris, Baker Watts, Inc. v. Ernst & Young, LLP*, 395 F.3d 851, 854 (8th Cir. 2005) (noting that the "level of recklessness" required to hold defendants liable is that under which they "make statements that they know, or have access to information suggesting, are materially inaccurate").

find that shareholder-plaintiffs have presented evidence of scienter sufficient, at least, to survive a motion to dismiss.[16]

Common sources of alleged omissions and misstatements include press releases and public financial filings. For example, securities cases based on allegations of accounting fraud often are fueled by a public company's having "restated" its financials. The reason for this is that the company has already provided the shareholders with one element of the case: in restating its financials, the company tells the world that a prior statement of its financial condition was *false*. Shareholders suspecting wrongdoing thus have a head start in claiming that the company misstated a material fact.[17]

With these facts in mind, public companies are well-advised to follow a few basic practices that should help to minimize the likelihood that shareholders will bring suit. It should become clear that these practices are little more than concrete applications of the more general advice to establish and abide by internal policies and controls, maintain transparency, and properly train those within your organization.

Obviously, the best guidance on how to avoid incurring securities liability is to be *truthful and complete* in making public disclosures. But no matter how truthful one is, there exist numerous ways in which statements can appear contradictory, misleading, or outright false. So how can a large public company control the flow of information such as to avoid even the appearance of falsehood? One way is to minimize the number of persons within the organization charged with the responsibility of interacting with the public on matters pertaining to the organization's financial conditions and prospects. Having fewer sources of information fosters consistency, and consistency fosters trust. Thus, public companies should establish strict policies about exactly who is in charge of making public statements, and should take every step to abide by those policies.

Another way to minimize the possibility that shareholders will suspect fraudulent financial dealings is to establish mechanisms by which officers and directors trade in shares of the company on predetermined schedules or criteria. As mentioned above, suspicious trading activity can raise the eyebrows of both shareholders and courts. To avoid such suspicious activity, consider establishing and abiding by formal trading plans.[18]

---

[16] *See, e.g.*, Nursing Home Pension Fund, Local 144 v. Oracle Corp., 380 F.3d 1226, 1232 9th Cir. 2004) (reversing a district court's dismissal where the trading activity of Oracle's CEO was "highly inconsistent with his prior trading history").

[17] *See, e.g.*, *Gebhardt v. ConAgra Foods, Inc.*, 335 F.3d 824, 829 (8th Cir. 2003) reversing a district court's dismissal, and holding that although "restating earnings [does not make] the original misstatement material per se, especially in cases where the company is required to restate its earnings no matter how small the discrepancy . . ., those facts are part of the total mix of information available to investors and are deserving of some consideration").

[18] *See* 17 C.F.R. § 240.10b5-1.

In addition to the pitfalls of traditional securities fraud actions, counsel should be well-versed in the Sarbanes-Oxley Act, which has already begun to pose a special set of concerns for those who (sensibly) would rather not be involved in federal litigation. To note just a few, these concerns include requirements that have increased (1) the reasons that, and the rate at which, public companies restate their financials; (2) the duties and potential liability of officers and directors; and (3) the scrutiny placed on executive compensation. Here, staying abreast of legal developments and educating officers and directors on their responsibilities are of paramount importance.

Certain aspects of the Sarbanes-Oxley Act have "cross-fertilized" shareholder actions by increasing the rate at which public companies restate their financials. Section 404 of the Act requires annual reports of public companies to include "an 'internal control report', which shall state the responsibility of management for establishing and maintaining an adequate internal control structure and procedure for financial reporting."[19] The resulting increased scrutiny of accounting practices has caused a dramatic rise in the rate at which public companies restate their financials; from 2003 to 2004, restatements of annual and quarterly financials jumped 28%, to a record-high of 414.[20] Given the apparent tendency of restatements to foster shareholder litigation, public companies should be diligent in ferreting out accounting problems in a timely and thorough manner. While this may result in a restatement today, it should prevent further restatements tomorrow.

The Sarbanes-Oxley Act has also significantly increased the duties of corporate officers and directors, and, consequently, their potential exposure to liability. It is no longer merely a good idea to establish internal policies and procedures to ensure accurate and consistent public disclosures; Chief Executive Officers and Chief Financial Officers are now legally required to do so – and to "sign off" on public filings prior to disclosure.[21] As such, corporate officers are legally obligated to know what is going on in their organization, and thus cannot plausibly claim ignorance if a dispute arises. Thus, counsel for public companies should take steps to ensure that officers and directors are aware of their duties under this evolving area of law. Fulfilling these duties will not only help to minimize the possibility that the company will materially misrepresent its financial condition, but also avoid regulatory actions brought by the SEC.[22]

---

[19] 15 U.S.C. § 7262(a).

[20] *See* Huron Consulting Group, 2004 ANNUAL REVIEW OF FINANCIAL REPORTING MATTERS.

[21] *See* 15 U.S.C. § 7241.

[22] For a description of the role of in-house counsel under Sarbanes-Oxley, *see* Stephen M. Bainbridge & Christina J. Johnson, *Managerialism, Legal Ethics, and Sarbanes-Oxley Section 307*, 2004 MICHIGAN STATE LAW REVIEW 299 (2004). *See also* Scott Green, MANAGER'S GUIDE TO THE SARBANES-OXLEY ACT: IMPROVING INTERNAL CONTROLS TO PREVENT FRAUD (2004).

Finally, the Sarbanes-Oxley Act has given more power to the SEC to scrutinize executive compensation. Under Section 1103 of the Act, "whenever it shall appear to the Commission that it is likely that [an] issuer will make extraordinary payments" to an officer or director, the SEC may seek an order placing such payments in escrow for no more than 45 days while an investigation commences.[23] An en banc Ninth Circuit recently explained that "the determination of whether a payment is extraordinary will be a fact-based and flexible inquiry. Context specific factors such as the circumstances under which the payment is contemplated or made, the purpose of the payment, and the size of the payment may inform whether a payment is extraordinary."[24] Accordingly, publicly-held companies should be careful to document and explain decisions of executive compensation, noting with some particularity the rationale for those decisions.

III. Consider a Settlement

A dispute may persist despite adherence to the preventive measures discussed in this article. If it does, all is not lost; litigation is not inevitable. If and when you reach the stage at which compromise is an option, a monetary settlement may be the most sensible solution. Indeed, if adverse parties (1) had "perfect information" about such things as the facts of their disputes and how the controlling legal standards would be applied, and (2) were consistently capable of rationally acting on that information – a circumstance less common than it ought to be – then in principle *every* dispute that has any merit should settle. This is so because, in a given dispute, each side would be able to accurately value the claim and would realize that the costs of litigation would only reduce the plaintiff's recovery *and* increase the defendant's liability – with (outside) attorneys reaping the benefit. Where a plaintiff and defendant accurately agree on the value of a claim and settle accordingly, each can minimize the "transaction costs" involved in cumbersome litigation.[25] Indeed, the costs of litigation might be viewed as a "tax" on a party's miscalculation of the value of a claim – or perhaps on a party's emotional insistence on taking the claim to trial.

Of course, parties to a dispute often have less than perfect information about the value of a claim, and even more often have emotionally invested themselves in the dispute. Under these circumstances, a plaintiff may overvalue a claim while the defendant has undervalued the claim,

---

[23] *See* 15 U.S.C. § 78u-3(c)(3).

[24] *SEC v. Gemstar-TV Guide Intern., Inc.*, No. 03-56129, 2005 WL 647732, *11-12 (9th Cir. Mar. 22, 2005) (affirming a district court's finding that Gemstar's $37 million payment to two departing executives, an amount over five times the executives' base salary, was "extraordinary").

[25] *See, e.g.*, Kevin M. Clermont and Theodore Eisenberg, *Litigation Realities*, 88 CORNELL LAW REVIEW 119, 137 (2002) ("[D]isputes and cases that clearly favor either the plaintiff or the defendant tend to settle readily, because both sides can save costs by settling in light of their knowledge of the applicable law and all other aspects of the case. Difficult cases falling close to the applicable decisional criterion tend not to settle, because the parties are more likely to disagree substantially in their predicted outcomes.").

thus presenting an obstacle to settlement. A central goal of this article is to minimize the factors that can lead to this result. The business practices outlined throughout should help to maximize the quality of information available to all and minimize the extent to which emotion will cloud judgment. If consistently applied, settling a dispute can be a fair and reasonable experience – at least when compared to litigating that dispute.

CHAPTER XXII
THE "HOW" OF U/I/A: The Judiciary and Public Defenders

The Problem Solving approach stresses inclusion, consensual relationships, decentralized decision-making, and participation by problem-holders in the resolution of their own problems. Similarly, Therapeutic Jurisprudence seeks to promote psychological well-being for both the users and operators of the legal system by according as much choice as possible to those strongly affected by legal decisions, but ensuring that such choices are based on good information supplied within the system. Having exercised that autonomy, however, people must be accountable for those choices even while they are tangibly and psychologically supported in struggling to overcome obstacles to their self-determination based on addiction or mental illness.

A. *Judging*

How, though, can a judge advance those values of Problem Solving and Therapeutic Jurisprudence? These values (as well as those of Preventive Law toward proactively addressing risks and re-designing problematic environments) seem difficult to implement within the traditional role of an Anglo-American judge. Look at the constraints on judges in an adversarial system:

- The issues are framed and confined by the pleadings submitted by the attorneys;

- the attorneys construct a strategy for presenting the evidence so as to satisfy the elements of legal doctrine;

- the rules of evidence narrow the range within truth is defined;

- the judge does not investigate the etiology or root causes of problems;

- the depth in which problems are examined is left to the strategies of contending lawyers and the supportive evidence they muster;

- common law remedies are past-oriented, awarding compensation for proven damages; and finally,

- equitable remedies permit more latitude toward addressing future risks, but are said to be justified only where common law remedies are inadequate.

How would judges behave differently if they were to embrace the U/I/A paradigm? How would the structures of their courts and the procedures that summon them have to change? *Can judges take on such mentality and remain recognizable as judges? Would their authority be compromised?*

Professor Bruce Winick, a co-founder of Therapeutic Jurisprudence, summarizes the traditional role played by Anglo-American judges as he describes the rise of Problem Solving courts:

Courts traditionally have functioned as governmental mechanisms of dispute resolution, resolving disputes between private parties concerning property, contracts, and tort damages, or between the government and an individual concerning allegations of criminal wrongdoing or regulatory violations. In these cases, courts typically have functioned as neutral arbiters, resolving issues of historical facts or supervising juries engaged in the adjudicatory process.[1]

As explored in an earlier chapter, however, the effectiveness of that role has been questioned in the face of a higher proportion of problems being presented to the judiciary that involve recurring behaviors or novel issues, or those that for other reasons are highly resistant to the remedies traditionally available in the legal system. Winick agrees: "Recently, a range of new kinds of problems, many of which are social and psychological in nature, have appeared before the courts. These cases require the courts to not only resolve disputed issues of fact, but also to attempt to solve a variety of human problems that are responsible for bringing the case to court."[2]

The increased proportion of these problems has forced the creation of new speciality courts generally called "Problem Solving courts." These courts aim at "solving the individual defendant's personal problems that contribute to the recurring offenses, rather than addressing an aggregation of incidents."[3]

Specialty courts often "use a 'team approach' involving the judge, prosecutor, defense counsel, treatment or intervention provider, and probation or correctional personnel."[4] Typically a single judge works with a community team to develop a case plan, including appropriate treatment, for the defendant.[5] The same judge "monitors compliance and imposes criminal sanctions if the defendant fails to keep to the case plan."[6] Advocates for Problem Solving courts urge that outcomes may improve through increased "specialty knowledge critical to the case

---

[1] Bruce J. Winick, *Therapeutic Jurisprudence and Problem Solving Courts,* 30 FORDHAM URBAN LAW JOURNAL 1055, 1055 (2003) (citations omitted).

[2] Id.

[3] Rana Sampson, *Domestic Violence,* 45 COPS: PROBLEM-ORIENTED GUIDES FOR POLICE: PROBLEM-SPECIFIC GUIDES SERIES 37 (U.S. DEPARTMENT OF JUSTICE, 2007) available at www.cops.usdoj.gov. (hereafter Sampson, COPS: DOMESTIC VIOLENCE).

[4] Julia Weber, *Domestic Violence Courts: Components and Considerations*, 2 JOURNAL OF THE CENTER FOR FAMILIES, CHILDREN AND THE COURTS 23, 24 (2000).

[5] Sampson, COPS: DOMESTIC VIOLENCE, *supra* note 3, at 38.

[6] Id.

handling, ... timely attention to the case, and a concentration of appropriate resources that traditional courts do not have... ."[7]

Problem Solving courts are staffed by judges who tend to bring to them a new mentality and more proactive behaviors. As observed by Percy Luney, President of the National Judicial College:

> [Problem Solving] judges and courts are, in our minds, assuming a stronger managerial, administrative, protective and rehabilitative role toward those persons appearing before them. Some experts have coined the term 'therapeutic jurisprudence' to describe what is essentially a 'problem-solving, person-centered approach' to judicial decision making. This problem-solving approach stands in sharp contrast to the more traditional roles of judges as dispassionate decision-makers and of lawyers as providers of adversarial representation. Here, the judge in this model, sits passively while lawyers present their two contending visions of reality."[8]

A broad variety of these specialized Problem-solving courts have grown up, as described by Judge Susan Finlay, Director of Education of the Center for Problem Solving Courts.[9] What they have in common is that they "are all about collaborations ... partnerships, and ... disciplines working with each other."[10]

Problem solving courts are now established in eight or nine countries, reports Finlay, and include drug courts (separately for adults and juveniles); mental health courts; domestic violence courts; homeless courts; DUI courts; re-entry courts for those on probation; landlord-tenant or housing courts; and child support courts.[11] Finlay's description of this latter court highlights the contrast with traditional judicial treatment of a recurring problem:

> **Child support court.** This isn't your traditional come in and why haven't you paid child support, and if you don't we'll put you in jail, you have thirty days to get a job. These are problem-solving courts that assist people getting employment, that maybe they need to go to the career center, and maybe they need clean clothes for a job interview, maybe they need some vocational

---

[7] Id., at 37.

[8] CWSL Symposium, *Envisioning the New Lawyer,* 37 CALIFORNIA WESTERN LAW REVIEW 1, 11 (2000).

[9] Eleventh Annual Symposium on Contemporary Urban Challenges, *Alternative Approaches to Problem Solving,* FORDHAM URBAN LAW JOURNAL 1981, 1981 (2002).

[10] Id., at 1982.

[11] Id., at 1983–1986.

training, educational training. They are hooked up with what is necessary to get the job to pay the child support, and that's a problem-solving court.[12]

These judges, by working every day and with a different sense of responsibility about investigating the root causes of problems, seek *understanding* rather than mere rationality in their courtrooms. "Traditional courts limit their attention to the narrow dispute in controversy. These newer courts, however, attempt to understand and address the underlying problem that is responsible for the immediate dispute, and to help the individuals before the court to effectively deal with the problem in ways that will prevent recurring court involvement."[13]

They attempt to treat all aspects of the problem: *integration* rather than separation. "Judges must ... develop expertise in problem-solving and become more active in seeing that the services are provided to the persons appearing before them, rather than dealing only with the manifestations of the problems that fit within our traditional judicial task. This problem-solving approach may involve coordination with social service agencies or it may involve ongoing supervision of the service delivery."[14]

And finally, the Problem Solving court judges know that a social *accommodation* of some sort must be fashioned to deal adequately with these problems. Just pronouncing judgment and expecting success by employing the power of the state would not work: "all of a sudden the light came on when I understood addiction, and I realized that just telling a person, 'Don't do it again or I'm going to send you to jail,' was spitting in the wind. It didn't make a difference."[15]

Continues Professor Winick:

> All of these courts grew out of the recognition that traditional judicial approaches have failed, at least in the areas of substance abuse, domestic violence, certain kinds of criminality, child abuse and neglect, and mental illness. These are all recycling problems, the reoccurrence of which traditional interventions did not succeed in bringing to a halt. The traditional judicial model addressed the symptoms, but not the underlying problem. The result was that the problem reemerged, constantly necessitating repeated judicial intervention. All these areas involved specialized problems that judges of courts of general jurisdiction lacked expertise in. Moreover, they involved treatment or social service needs that traditional courts lacked the tools to deal with.

---

[12] Id., at 1986 (emphasis added).

[13] Id.

[14] CWSL Symposium, *supra* note 8, at 11.

[15] *Alternative Approaches to Problem Solving, supra* note 9, at 1983.

In response to these failures, courts decided that they needed new judicial approaches. These new approaches involve a collaborative, interdisciplinary approach to problem solving where the judge plays a leading role. Not only is the judge a leading actor in the therapeutic drama, but also the courtroom itself becomes a stage for the acting out of many crucial scenes. On this stage, the judge also assumes the role of director, coordinating the roles of many of the actors, providing a needed motivation for how they will play their parts, and inspiring them to play them well.[16]

Judges are being required to collect different sorts of information, and play new roles: raising the consciousness as well as understanding of the community about the problem being addressed in the court, and supervising the efforts of the treatment providers.[17]

In playing these new roles, says Winick, Therapeutic Jurisprudence can provide an important theoretical grounding to what began as practical experiments in finding a more effective approach.[18] Judges should seek to broaden their general knowledge of psychological principles, as well as their particular empathic insights.[19] Power will not solve many of these problems. Change must come from the problem-holders themselves. For this practical reason as well as the principle of according respect, dignity and choice to the defendant, Problem Solving judges should master the skill of *motivational interviewing*:

Five basic principles underlie this technique. First, the interviewer needs to express empathy. This involves understanding the individual's feelings and perspectives without judging, criticizing, or blaming. Second, the interviewer, in a non-confrontational way, should seek to develop discrepancies between the individual's present behavior and important personal goals. Applying this approach, the judge should attempt to elicit the individual's underlying goals and objectives. In addition, the judge should attempt to get the individual to recognize the existence of a problem through the use of interviewing techniques, such as open-ended questioning, reflective listening, providing frequent statements of affirmation and support, and eliciting self-motivational statements. For example, if the individual wishes to obtain or keep a particular job, the judge can ask questions designed to probe the relationship between her drinking or substance abuse and her poor performance in previous employment that may have resulted in dismissal. An interviewer will create motivation for change only when individuals perceive the discrepancy between how they are behaving and the achievement of their personal goals.

---

[16] Winick, *supra* note 1, at 1060.

[17] Id., at 1060-61.

[18] Id., at 1062.

[19] Id., at 1066, 1069.

Third, the interviewer should avoid arguing with the individual, which can be counter productive and create defensiveness. Fourth, when resistance is encountered, the interviewer should attempt to roll with the resistance, rather than becoming confrontational. This requires listening with empathy and providing feedback to what the individual is saying by introducing new information, which also allows the individual to remain in control, to make her own decisions, and to create solutions to her problems.

Fifth, it is important for the interviewer to foster self-efficacy in the individual. The individual will not attempt change unless she feels that she can reach the goal, overcome barriers and obstacles to its achievement, and succeed in effectuating change.[20]

B. Public Defenders

It is not only the judges who are applying the U/I/A to broaden the context in which problems are viewed, expand the methods to address those problems, and partnering with community social service agencies. Public defenders, traditionally perhaps the strongest embodiment of the lawyer-as-champion role, are embracing these principles as well. Cait Clark, a prominent public defender, offers these examples:

- A criminal case is closed, but the criminal defense team continues to help its client find an apartment, secure partial funding for college, and find a part-time job after he completes an in-patient drug treatment program.

- In 1989, a California public defender asks homeless veterans about their problems. He hears hundreds of veterans describe their fear of going to court to deal with old misdemeanor warrants. It is a vicious cycle. Outstanding warrants prevent the use of social services, which impedes access to employment and housing. An innovative defender convinces a judge and prosecutor to hold court at the homeless shelter, where they process several thousand cases annually with great success. Everyone wins - the homeless have a better chance at community reintegration by resolving their cases, and court administrators reduce backlogs. Today, the Homeless Court started by a public defender serves as a model for other jurisdictions interested in problem solving for the homeless.

- A public defender and staff members lobby alongside a victim's rights group seeking legislative support for alternatives to incarceration and

---

[20] Id., at 1080-81.

work release. These seemingly adverse parties both want more restitution and community-service programs to help victims, offenders, and communities.

- An experienced defense attorney observes that the behavior of many of her clients strikes her as odd, but she cannot identify what's really going on. She realizes that she has begun to see more mentally disturbed clients than in years past. The lawyer reaches out to a trained social worker in her office who conducts mental status exams and works to locate appropriate therapy and treatment alternatives. The social worker testifies in court hearings in order to prevent incarceration that could exacerbate mental illness and delay treatment. Judges depend increasingly on social workers' assessments. The defense lawyer sees the advantages of social worker input while preparing cases for trial, such as early collaboration to help in plea negotiations or at trial and sentencing, and begins to work regularly as a team member with forensic social workers and interns to address a myriad of client and family problems, helping clients successfully integrate back into the community.[21]

In a interesting example of how legal ethics also change as one element of a system undergoing shifts in problems, procedures, culture, and skills, Clark concludes: "In expanding traditional institutional arrangements for providing counsel to the poor, these public interest lawyers have not abandoned their role as lawyers able to engage in traditional adversarial or trial-centered representation. Rather, by building on their zealous advocacy skills, they build community connections by leveraging the 'crisis moment' of a pending criminal case and seizing the opportunity to work closely with social workers and key community members in order to resolve a client's underlying problems."[22]

How would this mentality of expanded initiative and framing of issues affect the judicial role and judicial ethics outside of specialty Problem Solving courts? Consider some of the following contexts in which traditional judges would face these dilemmas. In each instance, ask yourself how legitimate you would consider the behavior under traditional expectations of the judicial role.

Example 1: A judge is hearing the fifth instance of the same sort of tort claim, each brought by unrelated plaintiffs, but each brought against the same industrial defendant. In each case the plaintiff has lost, and the judge comes to believe it is because individual plaintiffs will

---

[21] Cait Clark, *Problem Solving Defenders in the Community: Expanding the Conceptual and Institutional Boundaries of Providing Counsel to the Poor,* 14 GEORGETOWN JOURNAL OF LEGAL ETHICS 401, 406–07 (2001).

[22] Id.

not be able to muster expert witnesses of the same caliber as those testifying on behalf of the defendant. Would it be appropriate for the judge to order the appointment of an independent neutral expert? Would it be appropriate for the judge to order an investigation of the terms and practices by which research money has been funneled by the defendant over the past three years into academic institutions whose employees are now testifying for the defendant?

Example 2: Suppose that a plaintiff has been pursuing a civil action for sexual discrimination by her medium sized business employer, on a disparate treatment theory. The jury awards damages to the plaintiff. In hearing the testimony, however, the judge believes that the work environment is hostile, even though that theory was never pursued by the plaintiff's attorney. Would it be appropriate for the judge, following entry of judgment for money damages in favor of the plaintiff, to further order that every employee of the defendant undergo gender sensitivity training, on the theory that the risk of future sexual discriminations should be prevented?

Example 3: Suppose that mediation of a dispute has been tried, and failed. The case is scheduled for trial. When the judge reads the papers and is sitting in a pre-trial settlement conference, the judge gets the strong impression that this is a grudge match. The parties are being both vindictive and self-destructive. It is not about needing a remedy, but about securing a pronouncement that the other person is wrong. Suppose, however, that the plaintiff's claim has some technical legal merit. Is it appropriate for the judge in that instance to declare, off the record in chambers, that either the parties come to some compromise, or the judge will dismiss the complaint?

Example 4: During a medical malpractice trial the judge comes to the suspicion that the physician defendant, who was never called to testify, was impaired due to drug abuse. Before the trial is concluded, a settlement is reached which the judge is asked to approve. The consequences of the settlement are that the physician will remain in practice. Would it be appropriate for the judge to order a physical or mental examination of the physician defendant to determine drug dependency?

Most of us will reach a point of discomfort in considering these examples. Judges have a vital role in the maintenance of the fundamental human dilemma–the problem of social order–that we explored in Part One of this book. In the examples above, we sense that the stakes are high. If judges generally begin to redefine their roles (and ethics), taking on characteristics more like the judges in Problem-solving courts, will the Rule of Law be compromised along with the softening of the R/S/P paradigm? To address this distinction, let us explore a bit more deeply the role and characteristics of the Rule of Law.

C. The Rule of Law

The Rule of Law is fearfully difficult to define. Basically, however, it means:

- impersonal rules;

- that are enforced;

- by socially designated individuals;

- who will not personally gain from any particular outcome.

Beyond those basics, other attributes are commonly ascribed to the Rule of Law:

- *Compulsory*: that is, the procedures are not fully voluntary.

- *Constraining:* on the decision-makers as well as on the disputants. Every person in the system--accused persons, lawmakers, judges, lawyers--are constrained by pre-existing standards.

- *Character-promoting*: the actors in a legal system tend to become loyal to the goals and rules of the institutionalized procedures, above their personal interests and beliefs.

- *Consistency:* the procedures achieve some measure of reliability of outcomes.

- *Constancy:* the procedures themselves achieve some stability of use; that is, the procedures resist change even while they evolve.

- *Credibility*: the procedures are respected by those who are governed under those procedures, and the outcomes or judgments of the system are enforceable.

- *Clarity:* the rules and principles by which the system operates are both transparent and comprehensible to those who use the system, and those who are governed by it.

- *Connection:* people who are governed by the system are able to participate in it, which helps to ensure both loyalty and trust toward the system.

The judges in Problem Solving courts remain independent and objective. Such courts may actually strengthen the Rule of Law attributes of character, credibility, and connection. Lessened, however, is first the quality of *constancy,* as legal procedures consciously and more frequently reform themselves as needed to enhance effectiveness in addressing problems.

Also perhaps lessened in Problem Solving courts is the quality of *consistency,* the idea that the actual result reached would be reliably the same from courtroom to courtroom, regardless of the particular judge involved. This is not a result of compromised objectivity among the judges, but rather the consequence that the judges are interacting more personally with the defendant. If consistency is lessened, that may stem from the greater participation and self-determination by the individuals in front of the judge. According that stronger participation by the defendant, and allowing the greater sensitivity by which it may be received by the judge, are exactly what may prompt the higher levels of loyalty and admiration for the court.

The real challenge to the Rule of Law in the post-Enlightenment West seems to come not from greater particularity and sensitivity among judges, but rather from the ever-increasing reach of the law. Are any human activities beyond its scope? As more and more aspects of everyday life come within the reach of the law, how can the Rule of Law be sufficiently sensitive to the particular context in which legal rules are said to operate? How can law become more personalized, more responsive to human differences? And finally, how can the law discharge its functions while also strengthening, rather than weakening, non-legal relationships?

The answer is not that rules should be designed less precisely, so as to increase discretion in their outcome. That strategy is self-destructive: it begins to undermine the basic qualities of the Rule of Law. The answer is also not to create rules that apply differently to different people. Having rules that are impersonal--or better yet "universal"--promotes a perception of fairness. Rather, the answer is to make legal procedures more democratic and participatory, more strongly communicative, and to embrace at least for some problems the U/I/A paradigm.

CHAPTER XXIII (Rana Sampson)
THE "HOW" OF U/I/A: The Example of Domestic Violence

A. *Problem-Solving Police Officers*

The police are another vital element of the legal system. They too have begun to approach problems in ways that reveal the influence of the U/I/A paradigm. This chapter offers a thoughtful analysis of domestic violence written for police departments by Rana Sampson, an expert on problem-solving policing. Sampson's work is entitled *Domestic Violence* and appears as part of a series of problem-specific guides for police made available through the U.S. Department of Justice Office of Community Oriented Policing Services ("COPS").[1] Nearly 80 of these problem-oriented policing guides ("POP Guides"), along with an innovative problem analysis module, are now available at the website of the Center for Problem-Oriented Policing (http://www.popcenter.org). POP Guides are an effort to provide those interested in preventing and reducing specific crime and safety problems guidance on how to do so or how to begin to approach the problem. The use of Sampson's guide here is by permission.

In the words of Herman Goldstein:[2]

> Problem-oriented policing is an approach to policing in which discrete pieces of police business (each consisting of a cluster of similar incidents, whether crime or acts of disorder, that the police are expected to handle) are subject to microscopic examination (drawing on the especially honed skills of crime analysts and the accumulated experience of operating field personnel) in hopes that what is freshly learned about each problem will lead to discovering a new and more effective strategy for dealing with it. Problem-oriented policing places a high value on new responses that are preventive in nature, that are not dependent on the use of the criminal justice system, and that engage other public agencies, the community and the private sector when their involvement has the potential for significantly contributing to the reduction of the problem. Problem-oriented policing carries a commitment to implementing the new strategy, rigorously evaluating its effectiveness, and, subsequently, reporting the results in ways that will benefit other police agencies and that will ultimately contribute to building a body of knowledge that supports the further professionalization of the police.

---

[1] Rana Sampson, *Domestic Violence,* 45 COPS: PROBLEM-ORIENTED GUIDES FOR POLICE: PROBLEM-SPECIFIC GUIDES SERIES 37 (U.S. DEPARTMENT OF JUSTICE, 2007) available at www.cops.usdoj.gov. (hereafter Sampson, COPS: DOMESTIC VIOLENCE).

[2] In these words taken from an unpublished manuscript, Goldstein is summarizing thoughts that are elaborated in Herman Goldstein, PROBLEM-ORIENTED POLICING (1990).

Sampson's work is especially valuable not solely for its substantive recommendations to police officers for dealing with domestic violence. Although her focus is how an individual officer might think about prevention and response, it further reveals a valuable step-by-step method for researching possible interventions through which a social problem might be addressed, especially where multiple agencies may collaborate. As such, the guide also helps upper echelon police department personnel reposition agency responses to be more effective in addressing the problem.

Sampson begins by stressing that the problem must be understood both systemically and locally. Doing so, she says, will help the police tailor a more effective response strategy. Stressing depth of understanding alongside local detail broadens the investigation, involves a variety of social service agencies beyond law enforcement, and yet continues to ground the problem in a practical way.[3]

First, she says, the various stakeholders must be identified, including persons and agencies with special expertise or information: "domestic abuse protection, counseling, and advocacy organizations; medical providers; public health agencies; employers; schools (if school-age children are affected); university faculty and research staff; [and] clergy."[4] Then, the problem-solving police officer must:

> [ask] the right questions ... [because] it is important for investigating officers to understand the context and history of domestic assaults to determine if the incident is part of a series of abuse the victim has sustained and if it's likely to recur or escalate to more serious violence. For instance, in assessing individual incidents it is important to find out how long the abuse has been occurring, the frequency of the abuse, if the abuse is escalating, specific threats (even threats of suicide), whether threats can be carried out or there is an indication that they will be carried out, and whether victimization also involves other criminal behavior (i.e., harassing phone calls, vandalism, theft, burglary)."[5]

Information about victims, offenders, locations, times, circumstances of calls, and patterns of abuse, arrest, and conviction in the community should be gathered.[6] This will inform officers of factual details that carry elevated risk levels, permitting the police to select more appropriately among responses that are graduated in intensity.

---

[3] Id., at 15.

[4] Id.

[5] Id., at 16.

[6] Id., at 17-20.

Then, the current responses of the police should be understood and evaluated. The questions posed by Sampson reveals how comprehensive the responses must be in order to be effective. It is as though a dense web of collaborating personnel in law enforcement, social service, education, and communications must radiate out from the domestic violence incident:

- "What do the police department and other local agencies do to encourage victims to report domestic violence to the police?

- "Are community support services adequate to address the counseling, housing, employment, childcare, substance abuse, emergency financial, and transportation needs of victims and child witnesses?

- "What percentage of domestic violence victims actually follow up with referral services?

- "What is the average nightly number of domestic violence victims that local women's shelters house? What percentage of the victims in the shelters called the police to report the physical abuse? What is the average length of stay? What follow-up do these shelters provide once a victim leaves the shelter? Are shelter beds sufficient in number for victims who exit abusive relationships?

- "What is the current police agency policy regarding domestic violence incidents?

- "What is the current prosecution policy regarding domestic violence incidents?

- "Is treatment available? If so, what kind of treatment is it, and has it been evaluated?"[7]

Then, says Sampson, the effectiveness of the current interventions must be evaluated. "Measurement allows you to determine to what degree your efforts have succeeded, and suggests how you might modify your responses if they are not producing the intended results. You should take measures of your problem *before* you implement responses, to determine how serious the problem is, and *after* you implement them, to determine whether they have been effective."[8]

---

[7] Id., at 20.

[8] Id., at 21.

"Impact measures" assess effectiveness of response, and would include looking at data like "reduced number of actual incidents of domestic violence [and] reduced number of domestic violence calls involving repeat victims ... [or] repeat offenders ... ."[9] "Process measures" chart the "extent to which you implemented your planned responses" and would include:

- "increased number of chronic or severe batterers incarcerated;

- "increased percentage of victims using referral services;

- "increased percentage of domestic violence calls to police made by victims, as opposed to other parties; ...

- "increased medical screening of women for domestic violence victimization; ...

- "reduced percentage of incidents where both parties are arrested; ...

- "increased partnering with researchers to design evaluation of efforts."[10]

In her analysis and recommended mix of measures recommended for police, Sampson's list resembles the categories of the Dauer Matrix and Preventive Law methods described in Part One. They touch the victim and offender (the problem-holders); the social environment in which the problem arises; and even ways that the non-social physical environment can be manipulated so as to reduce the risk of recurrence. She plots these into a useful matrix (overleaf):[11]

---

[9] Id.

[10] Id., at 22.

[11] Id., at 25.

Matrix of Responses to Domestic Violence				
Strategic Focus	**Strategic Times for Response**	**Goal**	**Police Role**	**Other Agencies, Organizations, Group**
At-risk population	Before incidents	Prevention; persuade those at risk that, if abused, call the police	Alert and educate at-risk victim population; educate/warn at-risk offending population	Public health organizations; domestic violence coalitions; schools and educators; medical professionals
Peers and neighbors of at-risk individuals	Ongoing	Getting peers and neighbors to call the police if they learn of domestic abuse	Educate these groups about the importance of calling the police to reduce the violence	Public health organizations; domestic violence coalitions; educators
Injured women and men	During medical care	Screen the injured for domestic violence; raise awareness of available services; provide medical care	Engage the medical profession and link medical professionals with appropriate referral organizations	Medical professionals
Individual incident	During	Violence cessation	Stop the violence; identify primary aggressor; accurately identify abuse history	Medical and public health professionals
Immediately after incident	After; ongoing	Prevent revictimization	Assist with victim safety; develop tailored strategies for victim and offender based on risk/physical violence history; increase focus on high-risk offenders; ensure victim is linked with needed resources; increase focus on high-risk victims; ongoing monitoring	Domestic violence victim advocates, victims' friends and family, shelters, victim services, criminal justice system, treatment services

As additional follow-ups, Sampson suggests that the police

"can include a variety of situational crime prevention opportunity blocking mechanisms, such as the following:

315

- "increased police surveillance of victims' homes;

- "greater coordination with other parts of the criminal justice system;

- "pendent alarms for at-risk victims;

- "cocoon watch over victims (*i.e.,* with a victim' permission, neighbors, friends, or all three are asked to look out for the victim and immediately call if the offender returns);

- "target hardening of victims' vulnerable properties;

- "police watch of offenders;

- "police opposition to bail;

- "electronic ankle bracelet monitoring of high-risk released offenders;

- "alarm-activated recording devices with two-way speech capability (allowing victims to speak directly to the police, and vice-versa)."[12]

Sampson underscores the breadth with which the problem must be understood, and the variety of interventions that must be made. "Law enforcement responses alone are seldom effective in reducing or solving the problem. Do not limit yourself to considering what police can do: carefully consider others in your community who share responsibility for the problem and can help police better respond to it."[13]

Police responses should include education measures, encouraging victims to call the police, providing emergency protection and services after an assault, threat assessment of repeat victimization, arrests, restraining orders, prosecution and publication of severe cases, and the possible establishment of domestic violence problem solving courts.[14] Finally, says Sampson, the police should "[encourage] other professionals to screen for domestic violence victimization and make appropriate referrals."[15]

---

[12] Id., at 27-28.

[13] Id., at 23.

[14] Id., at 28–37.

[15] Id.,at 30.

B. Family Lawyers

Private attorneys should logically be part of that group of professionals that help screen for instances of domestic violence, by raising the issue when client circumstances suggest a risk. In fact, however, lawyers are less proactive about domestic violence than they might be.[16] In speculating on why, Kathleen Waits first suggests that perhaps lawyers accept false but lingering social myths about domestic violence victims, and therefore do not ask their clients about possible ongoing violence. These social myths include:

- That battered women have visible bruises;

- that they could escape the violence if they really wanted to, especially wealthier women;

- that they refuse all intervention from outsiders; that middle and upper-class women are not battered;

- that battering occurs largely among racial minorities;

- that women who work in the "paid labor force" are not battered; and

- that affluent, respectable, professional men do not batter.[17]

Alternatively, says Waits, perhaps attorneys do not raise questions about domestic violence with their clients because they may not consider themselves competent to deal with the issue; or they may find the matters too personal or embarrassing to ask about; or because they fear false reports of abuse; or they may simply not want to become involved in these often emotionally taxing, difficult cases.[18]

Clearly, however, attorneys should seek a greater understanding of the problem and join in the network both inside and outside of the formal legal system that is addressing the issues. Many battered women are ready and even eager to reveal the abuse if only a sympathetic person would ask them about it. Furthermore, a family lawyer may be in a better position to help the victim self-identify than many other professionals. After all, by definition a battered woman has come to the family lawyer to make some changes in her life, whether it is divorce or custody. She has come to the lawyer because she is ready to take action, if not directly against the batterer, then

---

[16] Kathleen Waits, *Battered Women and Family Lawyers: The Need for an Identification Protocol*, 58 ALBANY LAW REVIEW 1027 (1995) (*passim*).

[17] Id., at 1033–35 (1995).

[18] Id., at 1037–1040.

at least to get away or to protect her children. Therefore, she may be ready to talk about and deal with the abuse."[19]

But how exactly should a screening for domestic violence be raised with a client? Waits cites checklists of questions taken from three alternative sources:[20] an American Medical Association pamphlet that advises physicians about how to screen patients for domestic abuse;[21] Susan Schecter's Guidelines for Mental Health Practitioners in Domestic Violence Cases;[22] and sample questions offered by the New York State Office for the Prevention of Domestic Violence.[23]

The AMA checklist includes the following questions, emphasizing that the answers should be received non-judgmentally:[24]

- "Are you in a relationship in which you have been physically hurt or threatened by your partner?

- "Are you in a relationship in which you felt you were treated badly? In what ways?

- "Has your partner ever destroyed things that you cared about?

- "Has your partner ever threatened or abused your children?

- "Has your partner ever forced you to have sex when you didn't want to? Does he ever force you to engage in sex that makes you feel uncomfortable?

- "We all fight at home. What happens when you and your partner fight or disagree?

- "Do you ever feel afraid of your partner?

---

[19] Id., at 1056.

[20] Id., at 1045-47.

[21] AMERICAN MEDICAL ASSOCIATION , DIAGNOSTIC AND TREATMENT GUIDELINES ON DOMESTIC VIOLENCE (1992) (hereafter AMA GUIDELINES).

[22] Susan Schechter, GUIDELINES FOR MENTAL HEALTH PRACTITIONERS IN DOMESTIC VIOLENCE CASES (1987).

[23] New York State Office for the Prevention of Domestic Violence, OPDV BULLETIN 6 (1994)

[24] Waits, *supra* note 15, at 1048.

- "Has your partner ever prevented you from leaving the house, seeing friends, getting a job, or continuing your education?

- "You mentioned that your partner uses drugs/alcohol. How does he act when he is drinking or on drugs? Is he ever physically or verbally abusive?

- "Do you have guns in your house? Has your partner ever threatened to use them when he was angry?"[25]

For a variety of reasons, the victim of abuse may not be readily forthcoming in responding to these questions. It is essential, says Waits, that the attorney convey clearly that the client will be taken seriously in reporting abuse.[26] "The family lawyer should [also] be sensitive," says Waits, "to certain behaviors that may indicate abuse, such as when: (1) a woman client seems afraid of her husband or partner, (2) a woman client moves suddenly and without adequate explanation, (3) the man has severely limited his partner's access to money, including money that she has earned, (4) there are repeated reconciliations followed by separations, and (5) the man is tenacious in his unwillingness to grant the woman a divorce even though she insists the relationship is over."[27]

Holding those conversations with a client may be uncomfortable–that again is one possible reason cited by Waits why the conversations are not more routine. As attorneys take on the more proactive and expansive role called for in the U/I/A paradigm, they will more often be faced with the prospect of initiating these conversations that are painful to clients who may experience shame about the events, or even fear the consequences of speaking openly.

In their fine book DIFFICULT CONVERSATIONS[28] that stems from the Harvard Negotiation Project, Douglas Stone, Bruce Patton, and Sheila Heen offer thoughtful advice toward becoming more competent at matters "you find it hard to talk about."[29] The domestic violence screening interview by lawyers would fit best in their framework as a "Feelings" conversation–one in which the situation is emotionally charged.[30]

---

[25] Id., at 1046, *quoting* AMA Guidelines, *supra* note 20, at 8.

[26] Id., at 1049 (citation omitted).

[27] Id., at 1057 (citations omitted).

[28] Douglas Stone, Bruce Patton, and Sheila Heen, DIFFICULT CONVERSATIONS: HOW TO DISCUSS WHAT MATTERS MOST (1999).

[29] Id., at xv.

[30] Id., at 19.

Keys to success at emotional conversations, say the authors, is first acknowledging that "feelings matter: they are often at the heart of difficult conversations."[31] Perhaps especially for lawyers, the tendency is to "fram[e] feelings out of the problem" as a way of coping with it.[32] Ironically, focusing too quickly and too instrumentally on a tangible or behavioral problem easily addressed can interfere with an effective conversation.[33] "It's tempting to jump over feelings. We want to get on with things, to address the problem, to make everything better."[34]

Dangerous behaviors certainly cannot be ignored, but often the abuse is psychological as well as physical. Just asking the questions conveys a deeper concern for the client. If a client expresses significant emotions, those emotions should be acknowledged.[35] Acknowledgment means "letting the other person know that what they have said has made an impression on you, that their feelings matter to you, and that you are working to understand them."[36] Receiving the feelings as well as the factual information in a respectful, empathic way will build trust and a stronger relationship between lawyer and client.

---

[31] Id., at 85.

[32] Id., at 87.

[33] Id.

[34] Id., at 106.

[35] Id.

[36] Id.

CHAPTER XXIV

THE "HOW" OF U/I/A: Contractual Relations

The following reflections on the contracting process and its functions are strongly indebted to several sources: the pioneering work of Ian MacNeil and Paul Gudel on relational contracts;[1] several articles by Steven Salbu;[2] the historical analysis of Ichiro Kobayashi,[3] and the Law and Economics thoughts of Donald Symthe.[4]

Private contracts could serve many functions:

- securing mutual benefits through exchange;

- reducing risks;

- increasing efficiency;

- building demand for products and services;

- aiding product development and quality control; and

- advancing internal company management and planning.

However, at least some of that functional potential remains unrealized, especially as one moves down the list. Although Contracts and contracting behaviors have advanced the security and profits of reciprocal exchange--even while reducing risks--more could be accomplished by everyday contracts along each of the six functional domains.

---

[1] Ian MacNeil and Paul Gudel, CONTRACTS: EXCHANGE TRANSACTIONS AND RELATIONS 3rd ed. 2003).

[2] Steven R. Salbu, *Evolving Contract as a Device for Flexible Coordination and Control*, 34 AMERICAN BUSINESS LAW JOURNAL 330 (1997) (hereafter *"Evolving Contract"*); *The Decline of Contract as a Relationship Management Form*, 47 RUTGERS LAW REVIEW 1271 (1995) hereafter *"Decline of Contract"*); and *Joint Venture Contracts as Strategic Tools*, 25 INDIANA LAW REVIEW 397 (1991) (hereafter *"Joint Venture Contracts"*).

[3] Ichiro Kobayashi, *The Interaction between Japanese Corporate Governance and Relational Contract Practice*, 2 NYU JOURNAL OF LAW & BUSINESS 269 (2005).

[4] Donald J. Symthe, *Bounded Rationality, The Doctrine of Impracticability, and the Governance of Relational Contracts*, 13 SOUTHERN CALIFORNIA INTERDISCIPLINARY LAW JOURNAL 227 (2004).

This raises two questions: First, why has contracting failed to realize its full potential? And second, how can contracts and contracting practices be constructed to serve these functions more comprehensively?

A. Why Has Contracting Failed to Realize its Full Potential?

In part the shortcomings of contracting may be due to the historically confining framework of contract law. Having evolved from within traditional agricultural economies which lacked sophisticated needs, contract rules may impede the development of structures and processes that are more institutionally advancing. The episodic, largely local transactions of an agrarian economy were amplified and extended geographically during the Industrial Revolution, but aside from the development of franchises and output/requirements contracts, the framework of contract continued to treat contracting as sporadic transactions rather than commercial relationships.

The industrial era did, however, face the increasingly common phenomenon of contracts being made between complete strangers. The elevation of moral hazard risks involved in such transactions prompted a new duty to be implied broadly in the performance and enforcement of contracts: the implied duty of "good faith."

This implied duty of good faith imposes several duties, but not necessarily under all circumstances. First, good faith prohibits one party from interfering with the performance of another party. This duty would be interpreted into virtually every contract. Second, good faith limits the possibility of one party exploiting another where contract language is unclear, or where a contract explicitly grants discretionary powers to one party. Third, but only occasionally, the duty of good faith will imply a responsibility to use one's "best efforts" in discharging contractual responsibilities or to share information with a contracting partner. Finally, *very* rarely will the duty of good faith include a requirement to cooperate affirmatively with another party to help achieve that other party's goals.

The good faith duty, in other words, is more of a negative duty to refrain from certain behaviors rather than a prompting toward proactive, cooperative communication and mutual understanding between the parties. Because of this robustness, the duty of good faith has only slightly shaken the prevalence of a competitive--even adversarial--mentality between contracting parties. This mentality may provide a second possible explanation for why contracting has failed to meet its full functional potential.

Once such a competitive mentality takes hold, it results in unrealistically sharp, mutually exclusive distinctions between the following ideas:

- winning versus losing;

- risk versus reward;

- duties versus freedom, or "obligations versus consent" using Salbu's language;[5]

- competitor versus customer;

- selfishness versus selflessness; and

- law versus business.

Such binary thinking tends to lock in a zero-sum, positional approach to contracts, both in their formation and in their enforcement.

The full functional potential of contracts may never be realized so long as contract remains rooted in these two traditions: contract rules with their limited assumptions about economic exchange and relationships; and the adversarial mentality of some who use that law, carrying with them a constrained vision of commercial and human advancement. The command and control style of traditional contracting–seeking to specify and assure as fully as possible the behaviors of the parties–reflects a simple, but inadequate attempt to replace the personal trust and flexibility of face-to-face dealings that increasingly lost from commercial transactions following the urbanization and expansion of trade in the Industrial Revolution. The implied duty of good faith that attempts to soften the command and control traditions is helpful, but insufficient, to unlock the full functional potential of contracting.

As the U/I/A paradigm advances, however, its influence is increasingly felt in the contracting process. Especially among multinational businesses, Information Age reductions of information costs are enabling more flexible commercial arrangements that begin to reveal more integrated, accommodative contracting. Rather than seek precision in contracts through a traditional command and control structure that resorts to adversarial behavior when trouble arises, U/I/A style contracts may:

1. create flexible "relational" bilateral contracts rather than rule-bound "discrete" transactional contracts;

2. facilitate the development of strategic networks or business alliances; and

3. Prompt accommodative, relationship-respecting behaviors when problems arise.

   1. Relational rather than Discrete Bilateral Contracts

In contrast to discrete contracts, relational contracts are characterized by:[6]

---

[5] Salbu, *Decline of Contract, supra* note 2, at 1278–1293.

[6] *See* Dori Kimel, *The Choice of Paradigm for Theory of Contract: Reflections on the Relational Model*, 27 OXFORD JOURNAL OF LEGAL STUDIES 233, 236-37 (2007); Nestor M.

- terms that are open-textured rather than specific and absolute;

- persistence through many transactions rather than confined by a single transaction;

- mutual understanding by the parties that terms and behaviors will evolve according to changing conditions; and

- a duty that parties will confer with one another throughout the life of the contract.

2. Strategic Alliances

Salbu describes strategic networks or alliances as characterized by the same web of strongly interconnected components or parties that we have visualized before to represent systems-thinking.[7] The vision is of a dense field of elements, each of which has links to every other element. These commercial alliances, says Salbu, have "mutual access and communicational connectivity;"[8] which deliver benefits of "strategic responsiveness, flexibility, and operational efficiency;"[9] and which differ widely in their "degree of integration or differentiation."[10] Rather than keeping with the integrated but insular firm model by which business was conducted throughout the Industrial Revolution, the flexibility, quick response times, and nimbleness required in the Information Age mean that firms are increasingly collaborating for specific projects, even among firms that for other projects are competitors rather than joint venturers. Any given large firm, therefore, may be integrated into dozens of differently composed groupings. The relationships, as suggested by Salbu, will be of differing durations and comprehensiveness. As economic activity becomes more complex and volatile, contracts must be able to draw in terms from outside their four corners, and also develop greater depth and creativity in the relationships and interactions of the parties to those contracts.

3. Accommodative Behaviors When Trouble Arises

When problems arise, good relational behavior can steer the parties to one or more of the substitutes to formal litigation, which include compromise and re-structuring the contract to prevent the problem from recurring. These positive relational behaviors flourish when the

---

Davidson, *Relational Contracts in the Privatization of Social Welfare: The Case of Housing*, 24 YALE LAW AND POLICY REVIEW 263, 280–83 (2006); Jay M. Feinman, *Relational Contract and Default Rules*, 3 SOUTHERN CALIFORNIA INTERDISCIPLINARY LAW JOURNAL 43, 56 (1993); *see generally* Ian MacNeil, *Values in Contract: Internal and External*, 78 NORTHWESTERN UNIVERSITY LAW REVIEW 340 (1983).

[7] Salbu, *Decline of Contract, supra* note 2, at 1304–32.

[8] Salbu, *Evolving Contract, supra* note 2, at n.7.

[9] Id., at n. 217.

[10] Id., at n. 7.

parties have exhibited mutual trust, respect, admiration, and gratitude for past generosity and understanding.[11] And yet the development of trust and other relation-respecting qualities can be difficult. The illustration below explains at least one historical circumstance prompting the emergence of these strong relational qualities.

B. Case Study: When is a Relational/Alliance Contract Advisable?

Ichiro Kobayashi, whom at the time of writing his article was the general counsel for the Mitsubishi company, engagingly explains the strong use in Post-World War II Japan of relational contracts and "keiretsu"–a collaborative form of strategic alliances involving banks, suppliers, assemblers, and distributors.[12] Kobayashi suggests that the uses of relational contracting and keiretsu were necessities under post-War conditions, as a response at least in part to prohibitively high drafting costs of contracts. [13]

Following World War II, Japanese law was generally weak, and business lawyers were few in number.[14] As the Japanese economy slowly resurrected itself, many firms simply could not find or afford the lawyering expertise to draft traditional discrete, transactional contracts.[15] They turned, therefore, to a more affordable alternative: open-textured relational contracts. These are much less precise, setting out goals rather than finely detailed specifications. Hence they could be drafted with far less legal expertise.

However, having saved money on one end–at the drafting or formation of the contract–Kobayashi says that firms faced higher costs in the event of trouble. This was because the relational contracts offers less clarity about the required duties of the parties. Still, however, the Japanese business community had to make do with very few resources. They could not afford to expend resources either on the making or enforcement of contracts. Rather than fight in the courts, Japanese corporate governance then took its characteristic shape (stressing stability of employees and long-term cooperation relationships with suppliers and banks) as a way of reducing contract enforcement costs.[16]

Essentially, instead of resorting to high-cost court judgments as a response to problems, Japanese companies substituted a strong form of trust and mutual alliances to preempt problems. Where relational contracts prevail in business practice, observes Kobayashi, the reputation of contracting companies is crucial. "Japanese corporate governance has ... functioned as a

---

[11] Salbu, *Decline of Contract, supra* note 2, at 1311–12.

[12] Kobayashi, *supra* note 3, at 272.

[13] Id., at 285–86.

[14] Id., at 282, 314.

[15] Id., at 284–86, 321.

[16] Id., at 286–93.

reputational signal ... ."[17] Companies built reputations for stability and loyalty, which in turn could lead to the sort of mutual trust and long-term predictability that works as a self-enforcer of contracts, rather than relying on courts.

Interestingly, Kobayashi maintains that as economic enterprises become more sophisticated, they build up transactional experience. This makes contract drafting costs go down, as firms more easily can add precision to their arrangements.[18] As that happens, he says, the reasons for adopting the relational approach fade in favor of discrete contracts: "Firms create relational contracts primarily because unknown contingencies, or the complexity of the required response to anticipated contingencies, prevent the specification of precise performance standards."[19] As firms accumulate transaction experience, however, they "may be able to write discrete contracts more cost-efficiently ... ."[20] Firms move toward discrete contracts "once they find that incomplete terms make legal enforcement too costly or that self-enforcement is more costly than legal enforcement."[21] As data accumulate, firms will continue to add more discrete performance standards rather than rely on relational contracts. Kobayashi concludes that "contract practice ultimately should converge into a discrete regime."[22]

It is certainly true that our economy is increasingly complex, and populated by more and more sophisticated players. But do unfolding conditions really favor discrete contracts over relational contracts? Greater experience can translate into the ability to incorporate more precise performance standards, but this happens most readily where firms continue to do the same sorts of transaction (and with the same contracting partners). That sort of continuity may be shrinking as the Information Age unfolds, a development that largely occurred subsequent to Kobayashi's article.

The Information Age is characterized by accelerating rates of change in various factors like consumer demand, capital costs and availability, just-in-time inventories, political change, technological innovation, and governmental regulation. That means that response times are shrinking, even while basic background conditions in business are becoming more volatile.

As a consequence, drafting costs may generally be going up rather than down. Unknown contingencies continue to multiply and become more pressing, even while sophistication and experience increase. Further, the opportunity costs of inflexibility are rising. Firms must remain nimble in their allocation of resources and in their ability to form new combinations with

---

[17] Id., at 322.

[18] Id., at 274–76.

[19] Id., at 274.

[20] Id.

[21] Id., at 281.

[22] Id., at 276.

strategic partners, as unpredictable events bring positive new prospects. Finally, legal enforcement costs (the primary form of enforcement for discrete contracts) continue to rise even while courts and contract rules attempt to supply contract law default rules and gap fillers.

All in all, the economic case for relational rather than discrete contracts is good. Especially is this so where, as Kobayashi suggests, the higher enforcement costs of relational contracts can be met through stronger inter-firm trust, mutual accommodation, and strong reputations for both honesty and reliability.

C. Relational Contract Provisions

A variety of contract clauses and devices have been proposed to strengthen relationships within contracting. Salbu first postulates a "neoclassical" contract that fits between the traditional discrete contract and a full relational contract. This compromise attempts to "enhance flexibility in long-term contractual relations while maintaining a significant degree of stability and commitment."[23] Among the devices recommended in a neoclassical contract are:

- incorporation of standards, i.e., extrinsic, objective criteria that are incorporated by reference,[24]

- avoidance of unwanted *silence* and *invisible terms* as discussed by Helena Haapio in Part One;[25]

- Where Haapio's *visible terms*–express contract clauses–fail to guide desired performance or to provide clarity as to how to proceed,[26] provide for third party determination of performance, i.e., figures like a contract referee or the standing neutral device discussed by James Groton, also in Part One;[27]

- "cost-plus" agreements calling for a fixed return above provable costs;[28]

- forced continued relations devices in the event of a dispute: mediation and other grievance procedures[29] like the "confer in good faith" clause that Kobayashi discusses.[30]

---

[23] Salbu, *Joint Venture Contracts*, *supra* note 2, at 401.

[24] Id., at 402.

[25] See Haapio, Chapter VIII of this book.

[26] Id.

[27] See Groton, Chapter VII of this book.

[28] Id., at 403.

[29] Id., at 401–05.

[30] Kobayashi, *supra* note 3, at 287, 309.

- Under conditions of high volatility, the parties may employ devices that are recognized as not legally binding, but that operate as important reputation markers. For example, Salbu discusses "agreements to agree" which are commitments to negotiate in good faith toward some end.[31] Kobayashi similarly advocates creating "letters of intent" or "memos of understanding" rather than binding agreements under conditions of high uncertainty.

- "Contingent sets of commitments:"[32] this is the liberal use of explicit conditions and options that work either to limit duties, or conversely to trigger the expansion of rights and duties. These conditions can be used in incremental layers to introduce flexibility that both reduce risks and can permit taking advantage of opportunities. Options can be held by either an obligor or an obligee.

- In probably his most bold set of suggestions, Salbu advocates constructing strategic networks in more circumstances–webs of companies with similar interests and capabilities that could band together to share information and reduce risks. These alliances would have some rough similarity to the keiretsu system in Japan. They would, however, face antitrust law obstacles that were not a difficulty in post-War Japan. Within the alliance the partners could agree to have broader powers to assign contract rights and delegate contract duties. Thus, when one firm encountered difficulties fulfilling a project, an alliance partner could assist.

  As a allied group, the coupling and uncoupling of firms for various projects would promote efficiency while reducing risks. To make the alliances work well, firms would be required to share information, thus avoiding "dysfunctional secrecy."[33] The alliance firms would have an incentive to move toward standardized contract provisions, which would make contract rights more easily transferable. In time, Salbu envisages a full-blown market emerging in contract rights.[34]

- Finally, in bilateral contract settings, why not require significant contracting partners to appoint permanent experts within each firm, whose job it is to learn as much as possible about the business goals and capabilities of the other contracting partner? Within any large firm ("A"), one or more persons ("Partner Specialists") would have the ongoing assignment of being the institutional reservoir of information and memories about all of the firm's significant trading partners ("B," "C," and "D"). Assigning these permanent persons would provide continuity across specific contracts and across minor changes in job descriptions.

---

[31] Salbu, *Joint Venture Contracts, supra* note 2, at 403.

[32] Id., at 405-07.

[33] Salbu, *Evolving Contract, supra* note 2, at 379–81.

[34] Id., at 381–83.

The tasks of these persons could be many. First, they could consult periodically with their counterparts, *i.e.,* those persons in firms B, C, and D who know about Firm A. This would advance understanding and trust. They could also be charged with brainstorming new contracting opportunities between the two firms. They could prompt honesty in dealing and the sharing of information at Firm A. This would put people together who are both well-informed and whose job it is to be forthcoming with contracting partner firms. In the event of a dispute about a particular contract, the firm specialists could be called upon to confer and attempt a quick solution.

CHAPTER XXV (Douglas N. Turner)

THE "HOW" OF U/I/A: The Meaning and Building of Trust

IT'S A MATTER OF TRUST

Douglas N. Turner[1]

A. What Is Trust?

Most people would agree that trust is an elusive concept. We tend to know it in the negative sense, that is, we know when we don't have trust and we can articulate that quite well. Our fears dictate our behaviour, the way we treat other people (personally and professionally), and how we react to given situations. If we think about it, we act in ways that belie our lack of trust dozens of times per day. Why do we lock our homes when we leave? Why do we put a locking bar on our car steering wheel? Why do we impose and enforce arbitrary rules of behaviour on our children, like "you can't go out on a date with someone older than you." Why do we say things like "you can't drive the new family car until you're more experienced"?

How does this lack of trust between people translate into the business world? We will see that even though we refer to "corporate reputation" and "business style" as being trusting or distrustful, we are actually dealing with people, human beings, all of the time. I have yet to see a business transaction of any size that was not done between at least two people with a pulse!

In the context of the business dealings between corporations, organizations like the International Association for Commercial and Contract Management (IACCM) have repeatedly conducted surveys to find out what features of business deals (contracts) consume the most time and effort in the negotiations. The answers have been the same for the past five years: the top 5 terms are those relating to Limitation of Liability, Indemnification, Intellectual Property, Payment, and Price Changes. These all deal, in various ways, with the consequences of failure. What happens if the other party doesn't do what they are supposed to do? How can I protect myself?

Consider the following extract from an actual contract, presented by a large corporation to another large corporation, both of which had never done business with each other before, to begin negotiations toward what was hoped would be a collaborative business relationship:

---

[1] Contracts Manager, British Columbia Institute of Technology

"This draft document and the discussions related thereto shall not create binding obligations between the parties and any definitive agreement shall be subject to the final written approval of each party, which approval may be retained [sic] at each party's sole discretion."

Hey, how do you like me so far?

We believe we have to protect ourselves. Note the word "protect." From what? It doesn't matter how likely or unlikely an imagined threat or risk is, we just need to protect ourselves from it, or make "the other guy" bear the risk or the consequences of failure. These all point to one thing. Lack of trust. Fear. Call it what you want, but trust is what's absent. And trust is important. "Researchers have known for years that most effective problem-solving requires a high level of trust."[2]

B. *Trust – Some Definitions*

So let's see how some others have tried to define this elusive concept:

* Confidence in a person or thing because of the qualities one perceives or seems to perceive in him or it.[3]

* "Reliance on the integrity, strength, ability, surety, etc., of a person or thing; confidence."[4]

* "Confident expectation of something; hope."[5]

* "To rely upon or place confidence in someone or something (usually fol. by in or to): to trust in another's honesty; trusting to luck."[6]

* "To permit to remain or go somewhere or to do something without fear of consequences: He does not trust his children out of his sight."[7]

---

[2] Carlton J. Snow, *Building Trust in the Workplace*, 14 HOFSTRA LABOR LAW JOURNAL 465, 520 (1997).

[3] *See* RANDOM HOUSE WEBSTER'S COLLEGE DICTIONARY 1401(1999).

[4] Http://www.thefreedictionary.com.trust

[5] http://dictionary.reference.com/browse/trust

[6] Id.

[7] Id.

As can be seen, trust means many things to many people depending on context, but the fact remains we know more about, or concentrate more on, lack of trust than we do abundance of trust.

C. What Happens When Trust is Present?

Stephen M. R. Covey in his book THE SPEED OF TRUST,[8] states that when trust is present, the speed of transactions increase dramatically and the cost decreases accordingly. When there is a lack of trust, transactions slow down and the cost goes up. He cites an example in which Warren Buffet acquired a business unit from Wal-Mart in a deal worth $23 billion and the transaction completed in 30 days with no legal due diligence.[9]

Warren Buffet said this was possible because everything Wal-Mart had ever said to him previously was true. There was an established relationship of trust. Imagine the impact on Warren Buffet's company, not only from a cost avoidance perspective, but from the fact they got an operating unit "up and running" much faster than they otherwise would have and presumably faster than their competition. The effects are stunning.

There are many other examples. Consider the airline industry pre- and post-911. Before the disaster, people flew without thinking about it very much. Safety and getting to their destination were taken for granted by travelers, and security screening of passengers and luggage was routine and relatively unobtrusive. Long line-ups were only due to peaks in traffic at particularly busy times or a weather phenomenon that temporarily closed the runways, and the like. Generally speaking, things ran smoothly with minimal delays. In the months and years since 911 we have seen phenomenal increases in security procedures, lists of restricted articles, longer check-in times, massive spending on sensors and personnel at airports, and of course long line-ups are now expected all of the time and the costs of operation have skyrocketed. What we have here is a dramatic shift in trust level. The passengers no longer trust the airlines to get them safely to their destination, so they fly less. Passenger volumes took years to recover. More importantly, the airlines don't trust their own customers. The speed of the transaction (getting a passenger on to an airplane) has decreased and the cost increased.[10]

Having a trusting relationship with your business partners and customers has a dramatic effect on success in the market place. In a recent case involving the sale of the NHL hockey team Vancouver Canucks, a three-party consortium had been unsuccessful, over a period of 18 months, in buying the team from its owner at the time. One party broke away from the

---

[8] Stephen M.R. Covey with Rebecca R. Merrill, THE SPEED OF TRUST: THE ONE THING THAT CHANGES EVERYTHING (2006).

[9] Id., at 15.

[10] *See* id., at 14.

consortium and approached the owner on its own. A deal was concluded in three weeks or so on terms that were not significantly different from what had been proposed before. Setting aside the issue of betrayal in the consortium (a judge ruled that nothing improper or unlawful happened), the important feature of this case for our purposes is that there was apparently a higher level of trust between the owner and the single party than there was between the owner and the three-party consortium, allowing the deal to proceed quickly.

D. What is Trust Made of?

There are two fundamental components of trust: character and competence.[11] Character is a combination of integrity and intent.[12] Competence is made up of capabilities and results.[13] Both character and competence have to be present in order for trust to happen.[14]

Consider the example of needing some electrical work to be done in your home. You may have a brother-in-law whom you like and know well and who has done some small electrical jobs in his spare time. You may also consider an established electrical contractor who advertises in the Yellow Pages and is appropriately certified that you have never dealt with before. Whom do you trust to do the important work in your house where the safety of your family is at stake? In the first case, your brother-in-law has the character but his competence is suspect. In the second, the contractor has the competence (as evidenced by certification) but you have no knowledge of how "honest" or "reputable" they are. You will of course do more homework before you decide, but the issues remain the same. Whom, ultimately, will you trust to do the work? Which one has the greater aggregate of character and competence?

E. The "Bank Account" of Trust[15]

As we have seen, trust is an elusive notion. We know when we have it and we know when we don't have it, but we are not very sure about what "it" is.[16] To help understand this,

---

[11] Character and competence comprise what Covey terms the tour "cores of trust." Id., at 30-31; 42; 54–57; 123-24.

[12] Id., at 55-57.

[13] Id., at 55-57.

[14] Id., at 30.

[15] Id., at 130-32.

[16] Nor do we know exactly how much of it we should have. "Behavior and attitudes that build trust–friendliness, openness, flexibility and generosity–do not come naturally to many

think of an imaginary bank account that contains all of the trust in a relationship between two people.[17] There is only one account and it is the reference for both people when they think of how they feel about the other person. Generally, but not always, each person will perceive the same "balance" in the account. That is, if you asked each person how much they trusted the other, you would generally get similar answers. This is not always true, and it is easy to think of situations where an imbalance in perception can lead to finger-pointing and blaming the other person for failure to succeed in the relationship.

Both people are responsible for building up the balance in the account. Every time you, for example, say you'll meet the other person at an appointed time and place, and you show up on time, you make a "deposit" to the account.[18] Similarly when you say you'll do something by a certain time, and you do it, you also make a deposit and increase the balance of trust. Repeated and consistent behavior like this over time gradually adds to the balance and makes a trusting relationship. In the Warren Buffet example, clearly there was a large balance of trust in the account between him and the Walton family.

Whenever something happens that is inconsistent, or surprising in the negative sense, or disappointing, a "withdrawal" is made from the account and it doesn't matter which person did it, the balance still goes down.[19] Getting caught in a lie, showing up late for an appointment, not calling home when you said you would, having someone show you how your actions don't match your words, gossiping about people who aren't present (more about that later) are all things that withdraw trust from the account.

The interesting thing about the transactions in this account is that deposits tend to be small and frequent and withdrawals tend to be large and infrequent.[20] Indeed, one withdrawal can wipe out the account altogether if the betrayal is bad enough, and it often is. The relationship may never recover from a single event if the actions so offend a person's values or beliefs that they no longer want to be associated with the offending person. Infidelity in a marriage, illegal use of money, embezzlement, and false statements in negotiations are all examples of potential relationship killers.

---

people, especially where there is already conflict and mistrust between the parties. ...[T]his is natural because trust entails making oneself vulnerable and hence is dangerous. Natural selection weeds out those who trust too much." George W. Dent, Jr. *Race, Trust, Altruism, and Reciprocity,* 39 UNIVERSITY OF RICHMOND LAW REVIEW 1001, 1010 (2005).

[17] *See* Covey, *supra* note 8, at 132.

[18] Id., at 146-47.

[19] *See* id., at 165-67.

[20] Id., at 131-32.

F. Integrity

Before we discuss what can be done to increase the trust balance, it is useful to talk about another vague idea, the idea of integrity and what it means. It generally has value judgment associated with it. That is, a person who has integrity is "a good person" but well see that this can be misleading. Think of a simple arithmetic addition:

$$MIND$$

$$+ MOUTH$$

$$+ HEART$$

$$+ FEET$$

$$\overline{}$$

$$= INTEGRITY$$

In this little construct, MIND represents what you are thinking. MOUTH represents what you say, how you speak. HEART represents what you are feeling and FEET represents what you do, your actions. If what you think is consistent with what you say, and if what you say is consistent or congruent with what you feel, and if what you feel is the same as what you do (your actions match your feelings), then we say that you are "living in integrity." With respect to value judgment mentioned above and the "goodness" of integrity, do you think it is possible for a convicted criminal to have integrity?

Clearly there is a strong link between integrity and trust. The head of an illegal gang is trusted by his members. Why? In the rest of this chapter we shall examine the personal behaviors that contribute to trust. If we consistently practice these behaviors we shall become more trusting and trustworthy people, with the resulting increase in ability to get things done through other people.

G. Accountability[21]

Next to integrity, personal accountability is probably the most powerful idea that underlies trust. If we are prepared to be accountable for everything that goes on around us, we

---

[21] *See generally,* Anita L. Allen, *Daniel J. Meador Lecture, Privacy Isn't Everything: Accountability as a Personal and Social Good,* 54 ALABAMA LAW REVIEW 1375 (2003).

don't play the blame game and others will notice that.[22] It is much easier to trust someone who you believe is unlikely to strike back at you if something goes wrong. "One thing that exceptional leaders, and people that others point to as models or successes in life, tend to have in common is the ability not only to reach a personal level of 'spiritual commitment,' but to forge a culture of trust, credibility, an 'us, not them' environment, and a bit of that same commitment in those who follow them and with whom they work."[23]

It important to distinguish here between "accountability", "responsibility" and "blame."[24] They are often used interchangeably. If you have been assigned a task, you are therefore "responsible" for its completion. If it doesn't get done, you can be accountable for the fact that it didn't get done, but it is NOT necessary to assign blame. Assigning blame actually accomplishes nothing constructive. There may have been circumstances you couldn't control, resources you couldn't get, other people who didn't do their part, and so on, and these would all be valid explanations of the reasons that the task didn't get done. If, in the face of this adversity, you remain accountable for the task even though you are not to "blame," people will notice. They will be more confident (trusting) that you will not pull the "blame trigger" when they fail to get something done, so long as they remain accountable. In other words, blame has no place in a relationship of trust, but accountability definitely does.

The well known CHICKEN SOUP author Jack Canfield, in his best-selling book THE SUCCESS PRINCIPLES (in which Accountability is Success Principle #1) applies this concept to the ultimate degree.[25] He says that, to be truly successful in your life you have to take 100% accountability for everything that happens in your life.[26] You have to give up all of your excuses and you can no longer blame anyone for things that don't happen the way you'd like them to. It is important to note that this does NOT mean you blame yourself. You don't blame anybody…not even yourself. Blame is not part of this picture at all. Accountability is, and this leads to greater self-trust, and less propensity to start finger-pointing. Again, people will notice this and the "trust machine" gets rolling.

What this all comes down to is holding yourself to a higher standard. Set the bar high, let everybody know that you will not be happy with yourself, or them, unless you all remain accountable for what is going on around you. The level of trust that results from this kind of a "no blame, high expectation" environment is amazing.

---

[22] *See Covey, supra* note 8, at 120-21.

[23] John J. Michalik, *It Might Just All Be About Attitude,* 25 No. 3 ALA NEWS 4 (2006).

[24] *See id.,* at 200-203.

[25] Jack Canfield (with Janet Switzer), THE SUCCESS PRINCIPLES: HOW TO GET FROM WHERE YOU ARE TO WHERE YOU WANT TO BE 3–18 (2005).

[26] Id., at 3.

H. Tell It Like It Is[27]

This is such a simple idea, but so often overlooked. When there is a difficult situation, many people succumb to the temptation of doing what is necessary to protect themselves, to serve their interests, rather than communicate honestly and clearly. But "trust is a critical factor in establishing organizational effectiveness,"[28] and is furthered by honesty, openness, visibility, and responsiveness to suggestions.[29]

What can we do? When we find ourselves in a situation that is difficult, go back to the elements of trust, namely intent and integrity. Ask yourself why you are not telling the truth and all of the right truth. What impression are you attempting to create? Is it the correct impression? Could the phrases "spinning", "baffle-gab", "double-talk", "putting make-up on the pig" and others like those, be applied to your communication? Check yourself. There is a powerful acronym that can be used here – W.A.I.T. This stands for Why Am I Talking? Think about it.

I. Treat Others As You Want To Be Treated

It is a universal tenet of all major religions in the world that you should treat other people with the level of respect that you would like to have afforded to you. Get in the habit of showing respect and dignity, showing that you genuinely care about others. Don't fake it. Do little things, especially for people who can't do anything for you. Speak to the night watchman or caretaker or cleaning lady whose name you don't know.[30] Ask her what her name is and then use it when you speak to her. Send a hand-written note to someone thanking them for doing something special for you. Send a card of condolence to an employee whose mother has just passed away. The unexpected touches are the most powerful.

The amazing thing about this behavior is that you get in the habit of doing little things and then big things happen, because people notice your behavior, are more likely to feel comfortable around you, and are more likely to do business with you. It just might be that competitive edge that makes the difference between winning the account and not, getting the promotion or not, being included in meetings or not, and so on.

---

[27] *See* id., at 136–143; Canfield, *supra,* note 25, at 336-41.

[28] Robert C. Bird, *Employment as a Relational Contract*, 8 UNIVERSITY OF PENNSYLVANIA JOURNAL OF LABOR AND EMPLOYMENT LAW 149, 189 (2005).

[29] Id.

[30] *See* Covey, *supra* note 8, at 146; Canfield, *supra* note 25, at 352–56.

J. Be Authentic[31]

This is sometimes referred to as being "transparent."[32] It is important not only to tell the truth, but to make statements that can be verified. People will check up on you. If they find inconsistencies or vagueness in what you say, their level of trust in the account will diminish. If, on the other hand they can independently verify something you said, the trust balance increases substantially. It is also important that people can rely on you to tell them all that is relevant about a given thing.

This is perhaps even more important at difficult times of transition in an organization. Citing Kerry A. Bunker & Michael Wakefield, LEADING WITH AUTHENTICITY IN TIMES OF TRANSITION (2005), five actions are listed in 06-3 Partner's Report 9, *Change Management* (2006) that increase trust during disruptive periods:

> 1. Be authentic. Maintaining trust is critical to any successful transition. In difficult times, leaders are often tempted to offer canned answers and to keep communication impersonal, resulting from their own stress and sense of responsibility to management. But these practices are two of the fastest ways to lose the trust of your employees. Cut to the chase with honest answers and real feelings.

> 2. Be empathetic and honest. Partners naturally feel the need to keep their people focused on the bottom line at any cost. But the cost is often the loss of trust from an excellent employee.

> 3. Give people time to digest change. It's a mistake to make longstanding judgments about members of your firm based on an initial response to change. People commonly need time to sort everything out. Once an employee has navigated the emotions connected with change, he or she may turn out to be your greatest asset.

> 4. Give yourself time to digest the change. When leaders show reservations or other emotions spurred by change, they compromise their ability to lead with authenticity and to help others cope. Take time to adjust.

---

[31] *See Canfield, supra* note 25, at 342–346.

[32] *See id.,* at 152–57.

5. Keep your doors open. Show members of your firm they can talk to you. Let them know you understand their concerns. With empathy comes trust.[33]

Always disclose more than you think is necessary, within the bounds of business ethics and confidentiality if there are legitimate restrictions that must be observed, but say so if there are. Making a statement to the effect that you can't disclose details because you are bound by a business arrangement is far more acceptable than just omitting the details and leaving people to wonder why, if they find out later.

We are all aware of the phrase "hidden agenda." If we look at the definition of integrity above, what pieces are out of alignment? In this case we are thinking "what she is saying is not what she is thinking", or "he doesn't walk the talk." Either one can be an example of hidden agendas, but clearly there is a violation of integrity either way.

K. When Things Go Wrong...Step up

Perhaps the best known case of a corporation "stepping up" in the face of a potentially crippling disaster is Covey's example of the Tylenol product contamination incident.[34] Through no fault of their own, people were getting sick and dying as a result of taking Tylenol capsules that had been injected with poison. The key factor here is that the president of Johnson and Johnson immediately took accountability (NOT blame, remember) and removed all Tylenol products from all stores, designed a new tamper-proof package, and replaced all packages with the new one. The public quickly trusted Tylenol again and there is considerable evidence that the product became an even bigger seller after the controversy. Further, Tylenol established an entirely new packaging protocol that is used by virtually all of the companies in that industry.

This can be applied on a personal level. If you make a mistake, admit it, and do whatever you can to make it right. Even if there is nothing you can do, admitting the mistake and being accountable goes a long way in the direction of greater trust. We all can smell a cover-up and the press particularly enjoys uncovering examples of where a public official tries to hide a mistake. Once found out, the political career of that person is often ended. The trust account is closed permanently. There is no greater sin than lying to the public to protect your pride.

---

[33] 06-3 Partner's Report 9, *Change Management* (2006) , *citing* Kerry A. Bunker & Michael Wakefield, LEADING WITH AUTHENTICITY IN TIMES OF TRANSITION (2005).

[34] Covey, *supra* note 8, at 120-21.

L. Loyalty[35]

People like to think that they can trust the people around them to be loyal to their friendship, that is, others will be supportive of them to others, when they themselves are not present. There will be no gossip. This is true in personal relationships and in business transactions. Nothing destroys a relationship faster than discovering that your friend or associate said things about you to someone else that were not consistent with what you thought they would say. In other words their behavior when you are present is different from their behavior when you are absent. This is a killer.

M. Do What You Say You'll Do[36]

There is no better way to generate trust than to deliver results when you say you will. This is a combination of demonstrating success, being accountable and keeping commitments. It is important to get the right things done and to accomplish what you are asked to do, whether it is a job, or a family commitment. (One could argue, as Covey does, that family commitments are the most important of all).[37] People will tend to trust people who are known to be competent, that is, they have consistently shown that they can they are successful and can deliver results. In corporate politics this is painfully clear sometimes. The boss will promote, and people will fall in line behind, the person who consistently produces the best sales figures, or whatever the key indicator of performance is. This is often the "default" characteristic that is used for success, and this is often the basis upon which people will trust a leader, whether their trust is well placed or not. (Remember, Character is the other piece!)

We mentioned that an important component of trust is integrity. This is clearly linked to keeping your word and doing what you'll say you'll do, i.e., Mouth and Feet are aligned.

It is apparent by now that these behaviors are not separate and distinct, but rather all linked together and consistent with each other. Who knows where Integrity stops and Accountability starts? Taking accountability for your results and the results of others, and not playing the blame game are obvious ways to engender trust in those around you. If you hold others accountable and communicate clearly that you will be doing exactly that, and then follow up with questions when the specified task is to be completed, people will get to know that your word means something and you expect people to do what they say they will do. And you'll check up on them. You won't let it just slip by. This is the key to strong team leadership. Clearly communicated high expectations!

---

[35] *See id.,* at 165–71. *See generally* George P. Fletcher, LOYALTY: AN ESSAY ON THE MORALITY OF RELATIONSHIPS (1993).

[36] *See* Canfield, *supra* note 25, at 359–63.

[37] Covey, *supra* note 8, at 220.

N. Listen[38]

It has been said that we have two ears and one mouth for a reason – so we can listen twice as much as we speak. Strong leaders have developed the ability to really listen, to hear what is being said and what is not being said. They listen with their ears, their eyes and their heart. They acknowledge what they hear without comment or judgement. The truly gifted listener can make you feel like you're the only person in the room, even when the room is crowded and noisy. Imagine how you'd feel if that happened to you. The trust account just got a HUGE deposit, right?

Pay attention to what you're thinking about when you are listening to some one in a conversation. Are you thinking about what you'll say next? If so you aren't really listening. This will show in your face, body language and in your words. Are you comfortable with occasional silences? Good listeners are. When you really listen to people they feel heard. People will trust a person who really listens, more readily than they'll trust someone who speaks eloquently and never listens.

O. Raise Your Bar[39]

It is important to always be improving. This is not to say that you can't be pleased with what you've accomplished, rather that you are always looking to the next level of competence, achievement, or service. The question is "how can I do this even better," no matter what "this" is. How can I be a better parent, brother, team leader, or friend? Can I learn even more about this field? In a world where things are changing very quickly it is critical to stay informed and current about the factors that influence your particular environment, whether it is a new technology or a new way of managing people in certain situations. Read what the experts say. Don't assume that what you learned in school 5 or 10 years ago is still relevant. When people see you or your organization always getting better, their confidence in your capability increases and this is one of the pillars of trust.

Even more important, from a trust perspective, is to ask people what they think of you. Get feedback and evaluation comments. If you act on that feedback you are showing respect for the people you asked, and also demonstrating accountability for yourself and your performance. Clearly this is another example of how various behaviors are linked together in the trust network. You can score a three-for-one just by showing that you genuinely care about what others think about you and that you care about yourself.

---

[38] Id., at 208–14.

[39] *See* id., at 180–81.

CHAPTER XXVI (Samantha Morton, Thomas D. Barton, and Jack Maypole)

COLLABORATION: A Reprise on Preventive Law in the Context of Preventive Medicine

Advancing the Integrated Practice of Preventive Law and Preventive Medicine[1]

Samantha Morton, JD – Deputy Director, Medical-Legal Partnership | Boston at Boston Medical Center[2]

Thomas D. Barton, JD, PhD – Louis and Hermione Brown Professor of Law, California Western School of Law; Coordinator, National Center for Preventive Law

Jack Maypole, MD – Director of Pediatrics, South End Community Health Center, Boston, MA; also affiliated with Boston Medical Center

I. INTRODUCTION

Legal and medical professionals occupy roles that are virtually unrivaled in their capacity to help individuals, communities, and society at-large. They confront complex problems and equally complex sets of potential responses, within strict ethical bounds. These two professional groups historically have exercised similar approaches: upon a client's or a patient's report of a problem, they identify and assess those problems against strongly ingrained frameworks of categories, rules, and concepts. Each then formulates and implements ameliorative strategies that focus directly on the problem as defined within their respective disciplines.

---

[1] The authors are indebted to Kate Marple, Medical-Legal Partnership | Boston's National Program Coordinator, for her significant editing contributions to this article; and to Marissa Wise, Medical-Legal Partnership | Boston Research Assistant, for her citation support. The citations use an editor-modified form similar to that commonly seen in scientific writing.

[2] Reference is made throughout this Chapter to the Medical-Legal Partnership | Boston (sometimes abbreviated in this Chapter as "M-L P | B"). As will be chronicled below, this organization was long known as the Medical-Legal Partnership for Children at Boston Medical Center. In January 2009, the organization bifurcated, creating (1) the National Center for Medical-Legal Partnership (NCMLP), and (2) the Medical-Legal Partnership | Boston, which carries the designation of MLP Network Founding Site.

Traditional legal practice casts a lawyer as a "fighter," who learns of a client's legal problems, and then applies well-honed oral, written, research, and strategic skills in zealously advocating for the client – and against opposing parties – before a formal tribunal. Adversarial advocacy and pursuit of litigation are the mainstays of this practice model; these characteristics emerged from the legal system's functions and structures, and correlate to the specific skills and mentality that are cultivated in lawyers and lawyers-in-training.[3]

Some problems unequivocally demand action by a "fighter"; for example, when a government agency effects and perpetuates discriminatory and unlawful conduct against a protected class, litigation may be the most appropriate response, as in that context "public pronouncements by the courts of binding rules and their clear enforcement by the state [may be] most valuable."[4] Analogously, certain medical situations absolutely require intervention by a surgeon, as opposed to by a primary care physician or nurse practitioner.

In the medical arena, whether a patient will need surgical intervention often depends on several critical variables, including the timing of the diagnosis, and the comprehensiveness of the diagnosis. These same variables are critical in the legal arena: whether a client will require an adversarial, litigation-oriented intervention often depends on when exactly the legal risk or legal problem was identified and addressed by a legal expert, and on how broadly the nature of the risk is understood. This recognition – that the highest standard of care in both the legal and medical professions seeks to do more than obtain immediate relief from distress symptoms – lies behind the practice of Preventive Medicine and Preventive Law, which aspire to identify medical and legal risks before they materialize as actual problems, and to do so with an awareness of the bundle of legal, biological, psychological, social, and economic challenges with which many people actually present when they seek professional assistance.

This paper urges the extension of the particular integration of Preventive Law and Preventive Medicine that is practiced by the Medical-Legal Partnership | Boston, which serves low-income, often medically vulnerable, patients at New England's largest safety net hospital. We envision the building of a "culture of advocacy" within the health care profession such that supporting patients in the satisfaction of basic needs is viewed as transcending the traditional boundaries of any one profession.

In the paragraphs below, the history and principles of Preventive Law are first described, followed by the analogous history of preventive efforts in health care settings. We then detail the history, mission, and outcomes of the Medical-Legal Partnership | Boston. Following an analysis of the advantages of the Preventive Law model, as well as the barriers to its widespread

---

[3] Thomas D. Barton, and James M. Cooper, *Preventive Law and Creative Problem-Solving: Multi-Dimensional Lawyering*, online at http://www.preventivelawyer.org/content/pdfs/Multi_Dimensional_Lawyer.pdf (accessed November 3, 2008).

[4] Id.

integration, we recommend measures to enhance the understanding of, respect for, and reach of, integrated preventive practices in law and medicine.

II. PREVENTIVE LAW AS A CONCEPT

A. A Brief History

Preventive Law is a mentality and set of skills first conceived and developed by Louis M. Brown, a California lawyer and educator during the second half of the twentieth century. Part of Brown's genius was in understanding, and seeking to transcend, a central assumption of lawyers when they counsel their clients. Brown realized that most lawyers communicate to clients, directly or indirectly, that the level of achievement of client goals is proportional to the legal risks the clients are willing to take. In this, the lawyers' advice is analogous to what a client might hear from a stockbroker. If you want to win more, the lawyers inform the clients, you must accept a higher risk.

Brown sought to develop methods that would reverse this traditional thinking. Brown wanted to help clients more powerfully, even while *lowering* their risks of landing in legal trouble. The approach that he pioneered will be familiar to public health advocates: learn as much as possible about the total environment in which a client's problems may arise. This will help to anticipate risks. Foreseeing and understanding risks will in turn enable the lawyer to suggest interventions that can disrupt pathways or environments that are potentially pathological. Through such preventive interventions, the client will remain healthy or become stronger.

To act in this preventive fashion requires regular communications between lawyer and client – "legal audits," in Brown's words – so as to treat incipient problems while they are still fluid and thus more easily re-directed. Over time, the lawyer and client will also build stronger trust. This will permit the lawyer to be more inventive and collaborative with the client in taking measures – both legal and non-legal – that will advance the client's larger interests.

One concrete example of these inventive, collaborative methods comes from Brown's practice. His client was a trucking company plagued by driving accidents that resulted in high litigation and compensation costs. By inquiring carefully about driving habits and the circumstances surrounding these accidents, Brown discovered that an abnormally high percentage of the collisions involved truckers making left-hand turns. Brown proposed, and the client accepted, the measure of instructing drivers not to make left-hand turns. Instead, wherever possible, they were to make three right hand turns. The frequency of collisions fell sharply, with the savings in legal costs strongly outweighing the extra time and fuel required to avoid trouble by simply going around the block. By understanding the nature of the legal risk *as it is embedded in the physical environment of traffic patterns and other drivers' behaviors,* Brown was able to suggest a practical, efficient, non-legal intervention that prevented future accidents. Brown simultaneously lowered the client's risks and furthered the client's goals.

B. The Elements and Methods of Preventive Law

As suggested above, three basic elements underpin the Preventive Law method of simultaneously advancing a client's goals and lessening legal risks. First, Preventive Law attempts to understand the root causes of problems that generate needs. Regardless of how effectively the immediate symptoms of a problem are addressed, to neglect the antecedents of those symptoms risks a recurrence of the problem in identical or disguised forms.

Second, Preventive Law attempts to uncover the broader contexts or connections in which needs arise. This element is less intuitive, but no less important. For any sort of recurring difficulty, lawyers should see the problem not just as a series of legal rules or principles, but as a series of human interactions embedded in a system comprised of various elements – social, biological, economic, or psychological, as well as legal. Often, the true extent of a problem can be seen only in that broader environment. Furthermore, understanding the problem as embedded in a multidimensional system may reveal a variety of alternate measures by which the pathological dynamic may be resolved.

Understanding the problematic system leads to the third element of Preventive Law. Lawyers should work proactively toward legal or non-legal interventions that disrupt pathological tendencies, or that strengthen resiliency, within the systems in which the client operates. Ideally, the interventions will not only preempt problems, but also contribute positively toward achieving the client's goals.

Taking the trucking example a bit further may help to distinguish traditional legal practice from the three elements of Preventive Law. Imagine that the trucking client were represented not by Louis Brown, but instead by traditional defense counsel. The conversations between lawyer and client would not be regularly scheduled "legal check-ups" but instead would be episodic, occasioned by the discrete collisions in which the trucking company had been involved. In each of those conversations, the lawyer would react to what on the surface would appear to be an incident disconnected from any other accident. Each collision would be separately analyzed as to potential legal liability, and the extent of damages. Settlement or even alternative dispute strategies could be devised.

Such episodic representation succumbs to what might be called "quick-fix" or "solutional" thinking. It fails to imagine and analyze how the accidents might be the end product of a recurring pathological dynamic. The lawyer is repeatedly responding to the immediate needs of the client. However responsible that may seem, the quick-fix approach inherently limits the depth with which the problem is understood. That in turn will limit the effectiveness with which the problem is addressed.

The lawyer should instead think systemically. By doing so, all three elements of Preventive Law will be revealed. Brown was not content to fight lawsuits again and again. Instead, he looked for patterns or correlations of facts that might suggest causes or at least identify chronically risky circumstances. Once left hand turns were discovered as problematic, Brown could imagine the ways in which physical, cognitive, and social aspects of the truck-turning environment interacted pathologically, resulting in accidents.

Brown's recommendation was ingenious. Once the total environment is identified and understood, however, even more alternative interventions suggest themselves. The interventions are not necessarily mutually exclusive. For example, larger, brighter, or specially colored lights could be affixed to the truck turn signals so as to better communicate the truckers' intentions to other drivers. Or the truck could emit a special sound when the left turn signal indicator is depressed, not unlike the beeping used in many trucks when they are put into reverse gear. The trucker could be given additional training to underscore the hazard of left turns, making the trucker a more defensive driver. More "left-turn only" arrows could be affixed to intersection stoplights where accidents have occurred. The point is that by considering these accidents within a system comprised of physical objects in a physical space controlled by human perceptions, cognition, customs and training, a variety of ameliorative interventions can be envisioned.

Systemic thinking also advances prevention by expanding the imagination of the professional in assessing the circumstances of *unrelated* clients. Once the trucking client's risks have been addressed preventively, the lawyer would be positioned to ask better questions of other clients who may also operate fleets of vehicles. Inquiring about their safety measures may push back yet further the time-line on identifying risks and preempting problems.

Even better, earlier communication may also improve the client's self-help abilities to avoid risks. At the very least the client will come to understand the more effective and efficient use that can be made of a lawyer's services through regular, broad consultation. Working toward a mentality of this stronger lawyer-client relationship, and the associated skills of more imaginative, proactive representation are the goals of the National Center for Preventive Law and the California Western School of Law, where the Center is housed.[5]

III.   ANTECEDENTS IN PREVENTIVE MEDICINE

The medical profession has been at the forefront of efforts to identify problems early on, place them in a larger context, and respond to them commensurately. Preventive Medicine encompasses oversight of the health of individuals, communities, and specific patient populations. Its objective is to protect, promote, and maintain health and wellness, while preventing or minimizing disease, disability, and death. In the second half of the twentieth century, preventive medicine formally became a mainstay of primary care physicians and

---

[5] Resources for applying preventive principles to various types of legal practice are suggested at the Center's website: http://preventivelawyer.org/main/default.asp?pid=aspects.htm (accessed December 1, 2008). To date, preventive law principles have been most notably integrated into estate planning and the in-house counsel practice for companies and organizations.

emerged as a recognized medical specialty in its own right.[6], [7] Practitioners of preventive medicine utilize a variety of scientific approaches in their work, including biostatistics, epidemiology, and research into causes of disease and injury in population groups. Separate from its emergence as an independent specialty, preventive medicine is often an integrated component of public health policies and practices that aim to address threats to community health.

The origins of preventive medicine date back to the beginnings of civilization. The ancient Romans and early Chinese recognized the health consequences of failing to properly and quickly dispose of human waste, and developed disposal in that context. Similar preventive practices and customs developed over time, including the quarantine of plague victims (actual or suspected) in the Middle Ages[8] and efforts to improve sanitation in the late medieval period in Europe.[9] Economic growth and population increases in Europe and the United States in the nineteenth century brought with them increases in population density, and concentrations of poverty and illness.[10], [11] These phenomena fostered the movement to apply a rational and scientific approach to disease surveillance and prevention, and ultimately, to government policy.

In 1850s London, physician John Snow used a spot map to illustrate how cases of cholera were concentrated around a contaminated water pump.[12] He also used statistics to illustrate the connection between the quality of the water source and the cholera cases. Snow's study is considered to be the founding of the field of epidemiology, and a milestone in public health and

---

[6] Steven H. Woolf and David Atkins, *The Evolving role of Prevention in Health Care: Contributions of the U.S. Preventive Services Task Force*, 20 AMERICAN JOURNAL OF PREVENTIVE MEDICINE 13 (2001).

[7] In 1954, the American College of Preventive Medicine (ACPM) was established as the professional society for physicians committed to health promotion and disease prevention. ACPM operates the AMERICAN JOURNAL OF PREVENTIVE MEDICINE, provides educational opportunities to its members and offers certification in preventive medicine. It engages in research and develops and advocates for public and practice policies consistent with Preventive Medicine by developing policy statements and position papers and by analyzing and responding to legislation, regulations and policy. See http://www.acpm.org (accessed December 1, 2008).

[8] Gian Franco Gensini, Magdi H. Yacouba, and Andrea A. Conti, *The Concept of Quarantine in History: From Plague to SARS*, 49 JOURNAL OF INFECTION 257 (2004).

[9] Dolly Jørgensen, *Cooperative sanitation: Managing Streets and Gutters in Late Medieval England and Scandinavia*, 49 TECHNOLOGY AND CULTURE 547 (2008).

[10] Simon Szreter, *Rapid Economic Growth and 'The Four Ds' of Disruption, Deprivation, Disease and Death: Public Health Lessons from Nineteenth-century Britain for Twenty-first-century China?* 4 TROPICAL MEDICINE AND INTERNATIONAL HEALTH 146 (2002).

[11] George Rosen, Elizabeth Fee, and Edward T. Morman, A HISTORY OF PUBLIC HEALTH 209–16 (1993).

[12] John Snow, ON THE MODE OF COMMUNICATION OF CHOLERA (1855).

preventive medicine.

With the appearance of antibiotics and vaccines in the early twentieth century, the focus of preventive medicine shifted from the control or elimination of infectious diseases to the prevention of chronic conditions. The increase in average life span that has been observed over the last one hundred years is widely credited to preventive medicine initiatives, such as anti-smoking campaigns, motor vehicle safety laws and practices, occupational health and safety efforts on behalf of workers, fluoridation of drinking water, and chronic disease-specific programs designed to decrease incidence of, for example, cancer, heart disease, and stroke.

In the United States, preventive medical and public health policies and guidelines are studied and coordinated nationally by the Centers for Disease Control and Prevention. Internationally, the World Health Organization plays a parallel role.

In the twenty-first century, preventive medicine has changed, as illustrated in the pediatrics context. In the past, pediatricians' efforts focused almost exclusively on the detection of health and developmental problems in children, and preventive action was largely limited to vaccinations and the like. Over the last few decades, however, the pediatrician's role has expanded to include preventing diseases beyond those addressed via vaccination programs, including chronic conditions such as obesity, asthma, and diabetes. These conditions are connected to a multiplicity of variables, many of them non-biologic, and their proper identification and treatment requires, fundamentally, that the practitioner affirmatively learn about the patient's total environment.[13]

One example of innovative preventive medicine is the Injury-Free Coalition for Kids ("the Coalition"),[14] whose national office is located at the Columbia University Mailman School of Public Health. This program was created in response to the observations of a pediatric emergency room physician at Harlem Hospital in New York City, who was treating thousands of children for serious trauma caused by preventable accidents. The Coalition works to, among other things, eliminate community hazards, such as dilapidated playgrounds, and to create safe play spaces. It also educates communities and patients about other key injury prevention issues, such as bicycle, fire, and window safety.

The most effective preventive medicine practitioners will interact with other systems and disciplines when serving patients – and those stakeholders will have much to learn from their medical colleagues, whose profession was an 'early adapter" to the importance of prevention.

---

[13] David Satcher, Jeffrey Kaczorowski, and David Topa, *The Expanding Role of the Pediatrician in Improving Child Health in the 21st Century*, 115 PEDIATRICS 1124 (2005).

[14] See http://www.injuryfree.org (accessed December 1, 2008).

IV. PREVENTIVE LAW AND LEGAL SERVICES DELIVERY TO LOW-INCOME CLIENTS

A. *Legal Services Delivery to the Poor Historically*

It goes without saying that Louis Brown's trucking company client, whose situation was described in Section II, presumably was a paying client who could afford Mr. Brown's legal fees. The ability of Preventive Law to take root in the current system of civil legal services delivery to the poor historically has been impacted by many variables, foremost among them the ongoing funding shortages that force legal services organizations to perpetually analyze maximal resource allocation and expenditure.

As outlined in the Center for Law and Social Policy's (CLASP's) most recent overview of the provision of civil legal services in this country,[15] the availability of legal services to those who cannot afford them has been in large part contingent on the availability of adequate funding streams to support legal services resources. Those funding streams initially were private, and in 1965 became largely federal – but in any event have never been even close to sufficient.

Currently, the largest single source of funding for civil legal aid programs is the Legal Services Corporation ("LSC"), a private, nonprofit corporation controlled by an independent, nonpartisan Board, appointed by the President and confirmed by the Senate. Those funds are accompanied by an extensive set of restrictions impacting both clients served and scope of service. In terms of adequacy, notably, the 2006 funding allocation ($326,577,984.00) was only 9% larger than the 1980 funding allocation ($300,000,000.00) – whereas a 2006 allocation tied to actual inflation increases would be $717,888,563.00.[16] Significantly, LSC reported in September 2005 that less than 20% of the legal needs of low-income Americans are being met.[17]

Against this backdrop, legal services organizations have had to, and continue to, make difficult decisions about resource allocation, or "legal triage."[18] Does the organization prioritize only those cases that are "emergencies"? Does the organization limit its practice to a few high-demand legal issues? Should service delivery be concentrated in litigation representation or pre-

---

[15] Alan W. Houseman and Linda E. Perle, *Securing Equal Justice for All: A Brief History of Civil Legal Assistance in the United States,* Center for Law and Social Policy, Washington, DC, revised January 2007. Online at http://www.clasp.org/publications/legal_aid_history_2007.pdf (accessed November 3, 2008).

[16] Id.

[17] *Documenting the Justice Gap in America: The Current Unmet Civil Legal Needs of Low-Income Americans,* Legal Services Corporation, Washington, DC, September 2005. Online at: http://www.lsc.gov/justicegap.pdf (accessed November 3, 2008).

[18] Paul R. Tremblay, *Acting "A Very Moral Type of God": Triage Among Poor Clients,* 67 *Fordham Law Review* 2475 (2007).

litigation advice and counsel? Should the organization prioritize reaching more clients with more limited legal assistance, or fewer clients with more comprehensive assistance?

This long-standing crisis has sparked a tremendous swath of research and thinking about ways to innovate legal services delivery to the poor, given the limited resources and growing demand. In 2002, the American Bar Association (ABA) Standing Committee on the Delivery of Legal Services Committee identified a number of emerging alternative service delivery models, including:[19]

- Collaborative lawyering

- Distance lawyering

- Holistic lawyering

- Micro-niched practices

- Networked practices

- Online case matching

- Outreach models

- Preventive law

- Subsidiary marketing

- Unbundled legal services

As defined by this ABA committee, several of these models – "holistic lawyering," "outreach models," and "preventive law" in particular overlap significantly in terms of serving the client on the client's terms, in frameworks that acknowledge the complexity of each client's situation and needs.

More recently, Preventive Law was explicitly invoked in a proposal to substantially restructure the system of delivering legal services to low- and moderate-income clients. In Jeanne Charn's and Richard Zorza's "Civil Legal Assistance for All Americans" (a report on a Bellow-Sacks Access to Civil Legal Services Project), the authors propose a complex, mixed-

---

[19] *The Delivery of Legal Services: Alternative and Emerging Models for the Practicing Lawyer,* ABA Standing Committee on the Delivery of Legal Services, American Bar Association, September 2002. Online at: http://www.abanet.org/legalservices/downloads/delivery/innovations.pdf (accessed November 3, 2008).

model delivery system encapsulated in a multi-layered "Service Pyramid," and embrace a preventive law model as part of the foundation of this model,[20] Significantly, the authors draw an analogy to Preventive Medicine principles in their argument:

> [A]n expanded delivery system should be consumer-driven, consumer-centered, and holistic. . . . Here we take these terms to mean . . . paying attention to a client's unique, real-world situation and recognizing that many clients will have multiple, inter-related needs which all require attention. While legal services alone can benefit a client, it is often the case that other services are crucial to remedy problems. Therefore . . . legal advocates should cooperate with other service providers when this benefits a client. . . .

> One dynamic is the benefit of early intervention or 'preventive law' approaches designed to reach clients when a problem is in a lower level of the pyramid – i.e., before a crisis develops that requires a high-level, costly response. For example, it is easier to aid a client with debt problems than to intervene when foreclosure on their home is imminent. Another dynamic involves transforming needs from high complexity/cost to lower complexity/cost matters by simplifying and clarifying legal procedures and communications to the greatest extent possible.

> One of the chief goals of a complex, mixed-model system is to increase the number of matters that are successfully resolved in the lower-cost areas of the service pyramid. This will require public education, outreach and marketing, similar to a public health model where costs of cure are reduced by extensive prevention, early diagnosis and prompt treatment.

This explication of application of the Preventive Law model in the legal aid context highlights two key advantages: (1) an enhanced likelihood of satisfying the full range of a client's unmet needs, through collaboration with other professional stakeholders; and (2) cost efficiencies for the delivery system and therefore society. Integrating this practice model into the existing legal services delivery structure will, without a doubt, involve challenges (see Section V, below). However, we believe that the experience of the Medical-Legal Partnership | Boston at Boston Medical Center offers a window into the model's wisdom and practicability.

B. Medical-Legal Partnership | Boston at Boston Medical Center:
Preventive Law and Preventive Medicine in Action

The Medical-Legal Partnership | Boston, sited within the Department of Pediatrics at Boston Medical Center (New England's largest safety-net hospital), is premised on the Preventive Law model. The Medical-Legal Partnership | Boston (hereafter "M-L P | B"),

---

[20] Jeanne Charn and Richard Zorza, *Civil Legal Assistance for All Americans*, Bellow-Sacks Access to Civil Legal Services Project, Boston, MA, 2005.

formerly known as the Medical-Legal Partnership for Children and as the Family Advocacy Program, was founded in 1993 by Dr. Barry Zuckerman, the hospital's Chief of Pediatrics.[21] After years of attempting to advocate on behalf of vulnerable pediatric patient-families with landlords and government agencies, Dr. Zuckerman concluded that, more often than not, the difficulties patients faced in securing their basic needs had solutions that required the involvement of a lawyer – the efforts of a doctor, nurse, or social worker, or the patient herself, would not be sufficient. He also realized that pediatricians occupy a special position in the lives of vulnerable families, allowing for early identification of social and environmental circumstances that negatively impact child health and family well-being. Against this backdrop, Dr. Zuckerman recruited a legal services lawyer to work full-time in Pediatrics, representing patient-families in legal matters impacting basic needs: food, housing, education, health care, and family stability and safety. Significantly, this lawyer was exclusively dedicated to advancing the legal interests of patients, not those of the hospital; close consultations with the hospital's office of General Counsel have been crucial to integrating this groundbreaking role.

Currently, 15 years after its inception, M-L P | B is now comprised of eight attorneys, three paralegals, and several administrative staff, as well as several part-time pediatrician and research and evaluation consultants. Its unique model of legal services delivery in the clinical setting gave birth to a National Center that now supports more than eighty partnerships in over 160 hospitals and health centers around the United States and Canada,[22] and formal evaluation of medical-legal partnership impact is underway.[23] Examining M-L P | B's core activities – training and education, direct legal assistance, systemic advocacy, research and evaluation, and replication and professional integration -- offers a window into the architecture of a successful Preventive Law practice that is premised on day-to-day integration in the health care setting.

C. Training and Education of Health Care Workers

One core tenet of M-L P | B's work is that enhancing and formalizing a culture of advocacy within the health care profession will improve the quality of health care for vulnerable patients. In other words, encouraging and empowering clinicians to view their patients in a broader socio-economic-environmental context (more holistically) will result in better patient care and medical outcomes.

---

[21] That same year Dr. Amos Deinard and attorney David Haynes spearheaded a partnership between Minneapolis-based law firm Leonard, Street & Deinard and the Community University Health Care Center (CUHCC), a health center serving primarily low-income, immigrant patients in the Phillips and surrounding neighborhoods of Minneapolis. The Leonard, Street & Deinard Legal Clinic is still in operation, and reflects the promising potential of *pro bono* lawyer involvement in medical-legal partnership. For more information, see http://www.leonard.com/pro_bono/legal_clinic.aspx (accessed December 1, 2008).

[22] See http://www.mlpforchildren.org/partnershipsites.aspx (accessed December 1, 2008).

[23] See http://www.mlpforchildren.org/evaluation.aspx (accessed December 1, 2008).

Low-income families often face obstacles when attempting to learn about or to assert their legal rights in a variety of high-stakes contexts – applications for government-sponsored benefits, landlord-tenant conflicts, immigration proceedings, special education cases, and family disputes involving custody, child support, and domestic violence, to name a few. Indeed, a low-income family seeking to meet its basic needs generally must navigate multiple government or community agencies, which are complicated in structure and often understaffed. The challenges for such a family are, of course, exacerbated when a household member is chronically or seriously ill.

Pediatricians occupy an unusual position relative to other professionals with whom low-income families come into contact. The frequency of medical appointments during childhood, and the fact that the pediatrician is charged exclusively with advancing the child's health and best interests, often produces a strong rapport and sense of trust between parents and doctor. Moreover, pediatricians by virtue of their training are clinically predisposed – more so than other doctors – to view their child patients as part of a "family system." M-L P | B believes that the convergence of these factors uniquely positions pediatricians to screen for non-medical barriers to child health and family well-being – which often take the form of legal issues.

In an effort to leverage the pediatric relationship with patient-families and to influence the ways that pediatricians think about their role, M-L P | B dedicates a significant amount of resources to the development and delivery of an advocacy training curriculum to medical faculty, residents, nurses, social workers, and students. M-L P | B utilizes teaching tools such as a poverty simulator from the Missouri Association for Community Action that introduces residents to the social factors affecting the low-income patients they treat;[24] advocacy code cards and advocacy clinical practice guidelines specifically targeting a clinical audience and addressing a number of distinct legal areas that impact basic needs, including: housing and utilities, immigration, public benefits, education, and family law; and an IHELLP mnemonic to assist residents and other frontline healthcare providers in remembering the social factors to address over the course of caring for a patient.[25] The goal is not to convert pediatricians into attorneys. Rather, the purpose is to:

- Help clinicians understand the connections between poverty and child health

- Acquaint clinicians with key terms and concepts that constitute legal "red flags" ("eviction," "deportation," "IEP," etc.)

---

[24] See http://communityaction.org/Poverty%20Simulation.htm (accessed December 1, 2008).

[25] "IHELLP" stands for income, housing and utilities, education, legal status (immigration), literacy, and personal stability/safety. Chen Kenyon, Megan Sandel, Michael Silverstein, Alefiya Shakir, and Barry Zuckerman, *Revisiting the Social History for Child Health* 120 PEDIATRICS e734 (2007).

- Encourage clinicians to appropriately screen for non-medical barriers to health

- Empower clinicians to refer families for legal assistance via M-L P | B

M-L P | B modifies its case-based training materials to suit the particular clinical audience and logistics involved, whether it be a one-hour Grand Rounds for a entire department, or a fifteen-minute meeting with five pediatrics residents during their lunch hour. Indeed, the program developed a three-hour Advocacy Boot Camp curriculum that provides in-depth exposure to multiple basic needs topics for clinical audiences. M-L P | B frequently integrates clinicians into its trainings as co-presenters, and utilizes clinician input to develop the trainings.

Arming health care providers with knowledge of the systems that patient-families must navigate helps to instill a culture of advocacy in the clinical setting, and helps healthcare providers move "from patients to policy."

D. Legal Assistance to Patients

Companion to promoting engagement with the social determinants of health in the medical profession is M-L P | B's vision regarding the structuring of service delivery in the legal profession (especially those lawyers serving low-income clients). Fundamentally, the idea is to bring the services to the client (as opposed to requiring the reverse) and to create a multidisciplinary advocacy team for each client that can respond to his or her varied needs. M-L P | B provides legal assistance to patient-families in the hospital and health center setting, and in partnership (subject to all relevant ethical and confidentiality constraints) with health care professionals. Some key aspects of M-L P | B's delivery model are very different from the traditional legal services model. For example:

- Lawyers have an on-site presence in the clinical setting; they conduct intake interviews with patient-families there

- The program only accepts case referrals from health care workers who have participated in the advocacy training described above

- The lawyers are constantly available to their clinical partners via pager for legal "case consults" (parallel to the practice of medical "curbside consults"), allowing for timely, finely-tuned triage of patient needs

These practices promote a number of Preventive Law-based efficiencies. First and foremost, lawyers practicing in this context are more likely to come into contact with a family when its legal concerns are in a preventive posture, thereby increasing the likelihood that those concerns can be resolved without engaging in stressful and time-consuming litigation. A typical scenario is as follows:

A low-income mother of an asthmatic child may express to her child's pediatrician that she's experiencing tension with the family's landlord because she is several months behind on the rent. The pediatrician, savvy to housing insecurity issues based on participation in M-L P | B's training, recognizes that this situation may be a precursor to eviction proceedings, and pages. M-L P | B conducts a brief consult with the provider, determines that an intake interview with the mother is appropriate, and conducts such an interview in person with the mother during which her rights and obligations with respect to housing are explained. M-L P | B then discovers, through additional conversations with the mother, that not only is she behind on the rent, but the family is at risk of losing utility service due to general financial insecurity. M-L P | B then advises the family of the appropriate requests to make of its pediatrician in order to secure the "shut-off protection" for which it is legally eligible. Finally, M-L P | B determines that the family is eligible for a number of income supports, and refers the family to a social worker for assistance in submitting those applications. Successfully securing these benefits will enable the family to pay the overdue rent and stay current with rent in the future, reducing the risk of eviction.

This scenario is representative of the types of legal interventions M-L P | B carries out in a variety of legal contexts; M-L P | B intentionally prioritizes interventions occurring in a preventive context, in the hope of mooting the likelihood of a future emergency.

Second, lawyers practicing in this context are better able to tap health care professionals for their expertise as needed over the course of the legal intervention, thereby enhancing service delivery to the client. As an initial matter, lawyers in a medical-legal partnership have an advantage in gaining access to crucial medical evidence, whether that be testimony for a Supplemental Security Income (SSI) appeal hearing, or an affidavit for a special education case or domestic violence-based immigration case. Indeed, the partnership is structured such that the referring provider is, as necessary and subject to all relevant confidentiality and ethics constraints, part of the advocacy team from the moment of referral to M-L P | B. This immediate relationship with the health care team further allows the lawyers to better evaluate the strength of a client's legal position at the time of referral: for instance, if a developmental pediatrician contacts M-L P | B to refer the family for help with a special education case, but indicates that she cannot attest to the medical circumstances the family wishes to assert, this helps to inform M-L P | B's allocation of resources and immediate advising of the patient-family. Separate from the enhanced availability of clinical evidence, lawyers working in this model additionally benefit from operating in a multidisciplinary context when a client's existing or emerging medical needs (often mental health-related) require a response. In the same way that the pediatricians can be assured that a legal professional is available to respond to a patient's legal needs, the lawyers can be assured that health care professionals are available to respond to a client's medical needs.

Third, the "one-stop shopping" dimension of medical-legal partnership provides another benefit to patient-families with legal questions or concerns – they are able to access legal services in the same location where their children receive medical care. By training pediatricians to think and act more holistically, and by engaging them as stakeholders in the referral process, the model not only promotes the early identification of legal issues, but also increases the likelihood that low-income families with legal needs – who often lack the time and the transportation resources to cross town to yet another agency for help – actually will be able to connect with legal assistance resources.

E. Systemic Advocacy

M-L P | B's work also converges with the third element of Preventive Law, referenced above - that is, working proactively toward legal or non-legal interventions within the systems the client is navigating. By actively collaborating with health care professionals, M-L P | B is poised to spot trends and synergies between specific legal issues and health, and to devise systemic responses that incorporate a focus on health impacts.

M-L P | B translates what it has learned about the connections between legal vulnerability and child health into best practices and recommendations for institutions and policymakers. These efforts seek to deploy the medical provider voice in policy arenas where that voice historically has not been heard. A few examples, reflecting an array of institutional stakeholders, include:

- Researching and documenting the connections between proposed policy changes and child health and well-being, resulting in the development and dissemination of Child Health Impact Assessments[26]

- Training and mentoring pediatric residents on basic policy advocacy strategies, including the offering of testimony before legislative committees considering legislation that bears on child health and well-being

- Generating policies and protocols for the host health care site (in collaboration with the office of General Counsel) that support provider engagement with safety net protections as to which they have unique capacity (for example, in Massachusetts, only physicians can certify that a family qualifies for protection from utility service shut-off due to medical reasons)

---

[26] Lauren A. Smith, et. al., *Affordable Housing and Child Health: A Child Health Impact Assessment of the Massachusetts Rental Voucher Program,* The Child Health Impact Assessment Working Group, Boston, MA, June 2005; and Lauren A. Smith, et. al., *Unhealthy Consequences: Energy Costs and Child Health – A Child Health Impact Assessment of Energy Costs and the Low Income Home Energy Assistance Program,* The Child Health Impact Assessment Working Group, Boston, MA, November 2006. Available at: http://www.mlpforchildren.org/chia.aspx (accessed December 1, 2008).

Ultimately, these policy efforts have been successful because clinical stakeholders were partnered with the lawyers in the advocacy process.

F. Research and Evaluation

Demonstrating that medical-legal partnership can help to disrupt the link between poverty and child health is critical. Having concluded a rigorous logic model and concept mapping process, M-L P | B (and other members of the national network) currently is engaged in a number of evaluation initiatives.[27]

G. Replication and Professional Integration

Since 1993, medical-legal partnerships have sprouted up in over eighty sites (serving more than 160 hospitals and health centers) around the U.S. and Canada, with a presence in thirty-seven states. This national laboratory, coordinated by M-L P | B's National Center,[28] has generated a vibrant array of medical-legal partnership models, featuring a variety of clinical and legal partners: urban academic hospitals and rural Federally Qualified Health Centers, legal aid offices, law schools and private law firms. M-L P | B's National Center provides substantial technical assistance to those emerging sites and cultivates the development of nationwide best practices through working groups, conferences and a national research agenda. While the model has its roots in pediatric practice, over the last seven years, partnerships have adapted M-L P | B's model to serve vulnerable adult populations in family medicine, internal medicine, oncology, and geriatrics.[29]

Significantly, professional medical and legal organizations are beginning to recognize the strength of medical-legal partnership and to encourage its use to improve health and well-being. In August 2007, the American Bar Association (ABA) passed a resolution in support of the proliferation of medical-legal partnerships.[30] The resolution built on existing ABA policy, which

---

[27] Recent M-L P | B evaluation activity is summarized in Ellen M. Lawton, *Medical-Legal partnerships: From surgery to prevention?* MANAGEMENT INFORMATION EXCHANGE JOURNAL, Spring 2007, available at: http://www.mlpforchildren.org/files/MIE%20Spring%202007%20Ellen%20Lawton.pdf (accessed December 1, 2008).

[28] In 2006, M-L P | B received major funding from the W.K. Kellogg and Robert Wood Johnson Foundations to develop a national center focused on replication of the medical-legal partnership model.

[29] In 2001, LegalHealth in New York City began integrating legal services in oncology and geriatric settings. Dozens of medical-legal partnerships now serve populations other than pediatrics.

[30] The resolution was proposed by the ABA Health Law Section and was co-sponsored by a number of other ABA branches. *See*

recognized connections between medicine and law in the areas of public health, HIV/AIDS, and cancer. It promotes the development of medical-legal partnerships to address health and legal issues that impact patient health and well-being.[31] The Health Law Section's accompanying report to the House of Delegates acknowledges the benefit of co-locating medical and legal services because of its ability to preserve scarce legal and health care resources.[32] The report also underlines medical-legal partnership's preventive law impact.

> Just as the medical profession advocates preventive health care, so too by entering into these partnerships with health care providers, the legal profession can advance a "preventive law" strategy for addressing clients' social and economic problems and thereby improve clients' health, and well-being, especially those from low-income and other under-served communities.[33]

In October 2008, the ABA signaled a further commitment to the medical-legal partnership strategy by developing a Medical-Legal Partnerships Pro Bono Support project. The project's goal is to further extend the reach of the model by engaging the private bar through an ABA-based national support center.[34]

Medical organizations have taken similar steps. In December 2007, the American Academy of Pediatrics adopted its own resolution, encouraging "closer and more frequent collaboration between legal service and medical professionals."[35] The resolution further acknowledged the connection between legal issues and the health and well-being of children.[36]

Medical-legal partnership is also becoming an integrated component in the training of medical and law students. Five pairs of medical and law schools around the country currently

---

http://www.mlpforchildren.org/files/ABA%20Resolution%20in%20Support%20of%20Medical-Legal%20Partnership–August%202007.pdf (accessed December 1, 2008).

[31] *See* id.

[32] *See* id.

[33] Id.

[34] The Medical-Legal Partnerships Pro Bono Support Project is a joint project of the ABA Standing Committee on Pro Bono and Public Service, the Health Law Section, the AIDS Coordinating Committee, and the ABA Center on Children and the Law, funded by the ABA Enterprise Fund. *See* http://www.abanet.org/legalservices/probono/nosearch/medicolegal.shtml (accessed December 1, 2008).

[35] http://www.mlpforchildren.org/files/American%20Academy%20of%20Pediatrics%20Resolution.pdf (accessed December 1, 2008).

[36] http://www.mlpforchildren.org/files/American%20Academy%20of%20Pediatrics%20Resolution.pdf (accessed December 1, 2008).

offer joint courses in medical-legal partnership.[37] These courses train future doctors and lawyers to conceptualize their work more holistically and to prepare them for future collaboration. The course at Roger Williams University of Law and Warren Alper School of Medicine at Brown University brings cross-disciplinary students together to discuss ethical concerns, practice interdisciplinary problem-solving, and learn about substantive issues that affect both professions' client populations.[38] Many medical-legal partnerships offer practical experience to students through internships, externships and clerkships. At Brown Medical School, students can participate in medical-legal partnership through the school's community health clerkship program. Medical students choose a specific project and work collaboratively with law students, an attorney and/or their supervising physician on the project.[39]

Formal integration of medical-legal partnership in medical school and law school curricula is a critical, but not exclusive, component of professional integration efforts. Because of the relatively sustained nature of physician training, there are several other venues in which physicians-in-training can be exposed to these principles and practices. For example, several times a year, M-L P I B legal staff serve as trainers during a two-week primary care block for pediatrics residents at Boston Medical Center and Boston University School of Medicine. There are a number of residency-based opportunities like this for medical-legal partnership integration.

V.   EXPANDING THE INTEGRATION OF PREVENTIVE LAW

As an idea, prevention is ancient. Our capabilities to develop and *use* the idea, however, have exploded over the past fifty years. Being effective at prevention requires gathering data, analyzing patterns, communicating results, and implementing systemic interventions. There will always be financial, social and technical limits to those activities. Clearly, however, those barriers are falling because of recent computer-based breakthroughs in the availability, processing, and communication of information. Technically and financially, the quality of information available has gone up just as dramatically as the costs of gathering it has gone down. Socially, the decentralization of information and authority accompanying liberal democracy has encouraged a spirit of skepticism, invention, and experimentation. As a result, our ability to perceive and analyze the broader contexts of problems has never been greater. Our heightened ability to forecast consequences of problems also increases our ability to generate alternative

---

[37] Medical-Legal Partnership Site Survey, Medical-Legal Partnership for Children. Boston: March 2008. Online at: http://www.mlpforchildren.org/files/2008%20MLP%20Site%20Survey%20Report.pdf (accessed on November 3, 2008).

[38] Elizabeth Tobin Tyler, *Allies not adversaries: Teaching collaboration to the next generation of doctors and lawyers to address social inequality*, 11 JOURNAL OF HEALTH CARE LAW AND POLICY 249 (2008). Online at: http://papers.ssrn.com/sol3/papers.cfm?abstract_id=1241648 (accessed November 3, 2008).

[39] *See* id.

ameliorative interventions. Both technically and historically, prevention is an idea whose time has come. The question is whether we will welcome its arrival, or keep it in the waiting room.

For economic and moral reasons as well as to advance community health and well-being, the concept of prevention should be embraced not only in law and pediatrics, but as a general orientation to social problems.[40] The advantages for physical and mental health illustrated by the success of the M-L P I B are legion. Imagine if even a fraction of the enormous social resources currently devoted to the *consequences* of legal problems – homelessness, illness, illiteracy, child abuse – were instead used to advance stability and prevention though supplying basic nutrition, prenatal care, housing, and job skills for all persons. Certainly our society in general would be economically healthier. We would spend less, even while benefitting enormously from the gains in human productivity and spirit that would be unleashed.

The economic advantages of the Preventive Law model, so strong at the social level, are just as compelling for particular individuals. If practiced effectively, very cheap adjustments to particular problematic environments often can be made that result in the complete preemption of substantial financial and psychological costs. Where problems do nonetheless arise, Preventive Law is highly pragmatic. As illustrated by the trucking example, Preventive Law is open to non-legal solutions, which can be far less expensive and time-consuming than litigation. Finally, as the incidence of problems decrease within a system, so also does the incentive to resort to expensive insurance systems that do not prevent problems, but merely buffer the effects of their sometimes catastrophic costs.

The barriers to wider adoption of the Preventive Law model are significant but not insurmountable. Among lawyers, Preventive Law is impeded by intellectual inertia, the limited scope of questions that legal rules may pose, and concomitant ethical concerns. In the medical-legal partnership context specifically, successful preventive law practice requires building trust between two professions which historically have not shared perceived values, vocabularies, or goals. The paragraphs below address these barriers – those applicable to Preventive Law generally, and those relevant to medical-legal partnership in particular.

As to intellectual inertia, part of the law's wisdom and effectiveness stems from its procedural regularity and from the body of rules and concepts through which lawyers understand human relationships. That essential stability, however, can also cause resistance where efforts are made within the legal community to reach beyond law's traditional boundaries. Preventive Law faces just such opposition. Lawyers are strongly trained to assess fact patterns by categorizing those patterns into the conceptual boxes of legal rules, rather than to attempt to unravel the history of how a problem developed. And legal rules are constructed to focus

---

[40] David I. Schulman, Ellen M. Lawton, Paul R. Tremblay, Randye Retkin, and Megan Sandel, *Public Health Legal Services: A New and Powerful Vision?* 15 GEORGETOWN JOURNAL ON POVERTY LAW & POLICY, (2008). Available at: http://papers.ssrn.com/sol3/papers.cfm?abstract_id=1112868 (Accessed on November 3, 2008).

attention on affixing possible liability for some real world event, rather than on explaining how the event came to be or might be prevented.

Crucial to Preventive Law thinking, by contrast, is an understanding of how diverse elements interact pathologically to produce trouble. Without that systemic comprehension, ameliorative interventions cannot be successfully devised. Issues of personal blame and liability are secondary. If anything, Preventive Lawyers may see those questions as potentially diverting. If people are satisfied that they have dealt adequately with a problem by finding someone to punish, the problem is likely to be only half-solved. Preventive lawyers must ask broader questions than those posed by legal rules, which requires a mentality and skills not typically addressed in legal education.

On occasion, lawyers also raise a related ethical concern about Preventive Law. If a lawyer's quest is not limited to finding vindication or compensation for a client, then is not the representation of that client somehow being diluted? Is a preventive lawyer somehow hedging his or her loyalty to a client by trying to understand the client's own contribution to the problem-producing pathology? Is the client being represented as zealously as professional responsibility requires? Under the modern Rules of Professional Conduct promulgated by the American Bar Association, lawyers may serve as advisors and evaluators as well as advocates (Preamble [2]). Rule 2.1 states explicitly that "[i]n rendering advice, a lawyer may refer not only to law but to other considerations such as moral, economic, social and political factors, that may be relevant to the client's situation." Indeed, a lawyer does a disservice to the client when not taking into account those factors and advising the client of their impact.

Some express a view that Preventive Law is not the "real" practice of law or is somehow more akin to "social work," for which lawyers are not trained and often harbor distaste. This perception seems to stem from the shifting of resources away from litigation and toward early advising, and the concomitant commitment to assessing the (often daunting) full scope of a client's needs. Admittedly, Preventive Law practice likely will not be fulfilling for lawyers who wish to be in the courtroom every day. But its successful practice requires, among other things, a capacity for wise and strategic legal advice and counsel (based on current legal research), effective negotiation, chain-of-command advocacy and other pre-litigation activity, and, if necessary, litigation skills. The "social work" concern strikes the authors as a knee-jerk reaction to the fact that the preventive law model asks lawyers to practice with new stakeholders, often on someone else's "turf," and this can trigger one's "discomfort zone."

In the medical-legal partnership context, mutual distrust between the legal and medical communities is a distinct issue. Even where the orientation of a lawyer is preventive, the successful integration of medical-legal partnership within clinical settings is hindered by the contrasting vocabularies used by doctors and lawyers to diagnose or suggest treatment for problems – separate and in addition to often negative perceptions of each other's professions.[41]

---

[41] Randye Retkin, Julie Brandfield, Ellen M. Lawton, Barry Zuckerman, and Deanne DeFrancesco, *Lawyers and Doctors Working Together: A Formidable Team*, 20 THE HEALTH

Often, however, these distinct articulations are only superficially different. The divergent vocabularies do not necessarily represent clashes in values or purposes. Furthermore, as illustrated in the sections above, patient needs are not neatly compartmentalized between the "legal" and the "medical." The exclusive use of *either* a legal or a medical vocabulary to address a patient's problems may be inadequate. Needs can often be addressed more efficiently and durably where lawyers and health care professionals work together, however different their professional languages (and based on a mutual understanding of what each professional can and cannot do in light of distinct confidentiality obligations). Arguably, the best way to address the historical misunderstandings between the professions is to work collaboratively toward the shared goal of serving client needs.

VI.   CONCLUDING RECOMMENDATIONS

The particular form of Preventive Law practiced by the M-L P I B and its national network offers a window into the tremendous potential of cross-disciplinary preventive law collaboration. The unmet basic needs of low-income individuals and families can best be served when medical and legal professionals work collaboratively (with each other and with other key professions, such as social work and public health). Aside from continued support for replication, research, and evaluation of the medical-legal partnership model, we recommend the following specific measures to enhance the understanding of, respect for, and utilization of integrated preventive practices in law and medicine

Training and Education, Professional Integration

- Disseminate an advocacy curriculum to more medical students and medical professionals and a preventive law curriculum to more law students and legal professionals. Currently, there are five courses taught jointly by American medical and law schools; more law schools and medical schools should develop joint courses to teach their students collaboratively.

- Integrate advocacy curricula into other stages of physician training, such as residency programs. Currently, this exists in only a handful of programs.

Direct Legal Assistance

- Legal aid programs, hospitals, and health centers should embrace the medical-legal partnership model. Medical-legal partnership promotes holistic health care by arming medical professionals with the tools they need to diagnose, triage, and refer unmet legal needs that are connected to health and well-being. The model also enhances low-income patients' access to legal assistance by making it available in the clinical setting, and increases the likelihood that patients' legal

LAWYER 33 (2007).

needs will be identified and resolved before they become legal and health emergencies.

- Legal aid priority-setting should be re-evaluated. In order for clients and society to reap the benefits of integrated preventive law and preventive medicine, legal aid priority-setting deliberations should be expanded to formally include front-line medical stakeholders; increased transparency between the professions ultimately will expose synergistic interests and benefit clients. Some legal resources should be allocated away from emergency response to prevention-oriented projects. Legal services agencies can incorporate medical-legal partnership projects as a new practice area.

- Medical-legal partnerships should maximize service capacity by incorporating *pro bono* service through the private bar and law schools. The ongoing imbalance between legal need and legal assistance resources means that medical-legal partnership programs are familiar with service capacity challenges, despite their preventive law orientation. Engaging law firms and law schools to perform *pro bono* work with medical-legal partnerships is essential strategy in both meeting client needs and helping to structurally re-orient service delivery. The creation of an ABA support center is a significant first step in this process.

Systemic Advocacy

- Medical and legal professionals should engage in systemic advocacy efforts jointly. Because of complementary nature of their skill sets, medical and legal professionals are uniquely qualified to work together to address systemic issues affecting health and well-being. Doctors are poised to assess proposed or existing policies' effects on patient health and health care delivery, while lawyers understand how to interpret, challenge, and change public policy. Pairing the clinical perspective with legal expertise on behalf of vulnerable clients can only enhance the prospects for meaningful reform.

While Preventive Law principles apply throughout legal practice areas and across client constituencies, medical-legal partnership highlights the particular advantages of deploying Preventive Law strategies in the context of legal service delivery to low-income clients. Adoption of the recommendations noted above will represent great strides in promoting the early and accurate diagnosis, triage, referral, and treatment of unmet legal needs through partnership with allied medical professionals.

Printed in the United States
221330BV00003B/1/P

9 781600 420764